KIERKEGAARD'S INFLUENCE ON THEOLOGY

TOME II: ANGLOPHONE AND SCANDINAVIAN PROTESTANT THEOLOGY

Kierkegaard Research: Sources, Reception and Resources
Volume 10, Tome II

Kierkegaard Research: Sources, Reception and Resources
is a publication of the Søren Kierkegaard Research Centre

Kierkegaard's
Influence on Theology
Tome II: Anglophone and Scandinavian
Protestant Theology

Edited by
JON STEWART

ASHGATE

Published by
Ashgate Publishing Limited
Wey Court East
Union Road
Farnham
Surrey, GU9 7PT
England

Ashgate Publishing Company
Suite 420
101 Cherry Street
Burlington
VT 05401-4405
USA

www.ashgate.com

British Library Cataloguing in Publication Data
Kierkegaard's Influence on Theology.
  Tome II, Anglophone and Scandinavian Protestant theology.
  – (Kierkegaard research ; v. 10)
  1. Kierkegaard, Søren, 1813–1855 – Influence. 2. Theology,
  Doctrinal – English-speaking countries. 3. Theology,
  Doctrinal – Scandinavia. 4. Protestant churches –
  English-speaking countries – Doctrines. 5. Protestant
  churches – Scandinavia – Doctrines.
  I. Series II. Stewart, Jon (Jon Bartley)
  198.9-dc23

Library of Congress Cataloging-in-Publication Data
Kierkegaard's influence on theology / [edited by] Jon Stewart.
    p. cm. — (Kierkegaard research v. 10)
  Includes indexes.
  ISBN 978-1-4094-4478-7 (tome I)—ISBN 978-1-4094-4479-4
(tome II)—ISBN 978-1-4094-4480-0 (tome III)
  1. Kierkegaard, Søren, 1813–1855—Influence. 2. Theology. I. Stewart, Jon
(Jon Bartley)
  BX4827.K5K55 2011
  198'.9—dc23

2011041730

Cover design by Katalin Nun

MIX
Paper from
responsible sources
FSC
www.fsc.org   FSC® C018575

Printed and bound in Great Britain by the
MPG Books Group, UK

Contents

List of Contributors

Mariana Alessandri, Philosophy Department, Pennsylvania State University, 240 Sparks Bldg., University Park, PA 16802, USA.

Sarah Pike Cabral, Portico Faculty, Fulton Hall 352A, Carroll School of Management, Boston College, Chestnut Hill, MA 02467, USA.

Svein Aage Christoffersen, Faculty of Theology, University of Oslo, Box 1023 Blindern, 0315 Oslo, Norway.

David J. Gouwens, Brite Divinity School, TCU Box 298130, 2800 S. University Drive, Fort Worth, TX 76129, USA.

Carl S. Hughes, Graduate Division of Religion, Emory University, 201 Dowman Drive, Atlanta, GA 30322, USA.

David R. Law, Department of Religions and Theology, School of Arts, Histories and Cultures, The University of Manchester, Oxford Road, Manchester M13 9PL, UK.

Paul Martens, Department of Religion, Baylor University, One Bear Place #97284, Waco, TX 76798-7284, USA.

Silas Morgan, Loyola University Chicago, Department of Theology, Crown Center, Room 300, 1032 W. Sheridan Road, Chicago, IL 60660, USA.

Kyle A. Roberts, Bethel Seminary, 3949 Bethel Drive, St. Paul, MN 55112, USA.

List of Abbreviations

BA   *The Book on Adler*, trans. by Howard V. Hong and Edna H. Hong, Princeton: Princeton University Press 1998.

C   *The Crisis and a Crisis in the Life of an Actress*, trans. by Howard V. Hong and Edna H. Hong, Princeton: Princeton University Press 1997.

CA   *The Concept of Anxiety*, trans. by Reidar Thomte in collaboration with Albert B. Anderson, Princeton: Princeton University Press 1980.

CD   *Christian Discourses*, trans. by Howard V. Hong and Edna H. Hong, Princeton: Princeton University Press 1997.

CI   *The Concept of Irony*, trans. by Howard V. Hong and Edna H. Hong, Princeton: Princeton University Press 1989.

CIC   *The Concept of Irony*, trans. with an Introduction and Notes by Lee M. Capel, London: Collins 1966.

COR   *The Corsair Affair; Articles Related to the Writings*, trans. by Howard V. Hong and Edna H. Hong, Princeton: Princeton University Press 1982.

CUP1   *Concluding Unscientific Postscript*, vol. 1, trans. by Howard V. Hong and Edna H. Hong, Princeton: Princeton University Press 1982.

CUP2   *Concluding Unscientific Postscript*, vol. 2, trans. by Howard V. Hong and Edna H. Hong, Princeton: Princeton University Press 1982.

CUPH   *Concluding Unscientific Postscript*, trans. by Alastair Hannay, Cambridge and New York: Cambridge University Press 2009.

EO1   *Either/Or*, Part I, trans. by Howard V. Hong and Edna H. Hong, Princeton: Princeton University Press 1987.

EO2   *Either/Or*, Part II, trans. by Howard V. Hong and Edna H. Hong, Princeton: Princeton University Press 1987.

EOP   *Either/Or*, trans. by Alastair Hannay, Harmondsworth: Penguin Books 1992.

EPW   *Early Polemical Writings*, among others: *From the Papers of One Still Living*; *Articles from Student Days*; *The Battle Between the Old and the New Soap-Cellars*, trans. by Julia Watkin, Princeton: Princeton University Press 1990.

EUD   *Eighteen Upbuilding Discourses*, trans. by Howard V. Hong and Edna H. Hong, Princeton: Princeton University Press 1990.

FSE   *For Self-Examination*, trans. by Howard V. Hong and Edna H. Hong, Princeton: Princeton University Press 1990.

FT   *Fear and Trembling*, trans. by Howard V. Hong and Edna H. Hong, Princeton: Princeton University Press 1983.

FTP   *Fear and Trembling*, trans. by Alastair Hannay, Harmondsworth: Penguin Books 1985.

JC   *Johannes Climacus, or De omnibus dubitandum est*, trans. by Howard V. Hong and Edna H. Hong, Princeton: Princeton University Press 1985.

JFY   *Judge for Yourself!*, trans. by Howard V. Hong and Edna H. Hong, Princeton: Princeton University Press 1990.

JP   *Søren Kierkegaard's Journals and Papers*, vols. 1–6, ed. and trans. by Howard V. Hong and Edna H. Hong, assisted by Gregor Malantschuk (vol. 7, Index and Composite Collation), Bloomington and London: Indiana University Press 1967–78.

KAC   *Kierkegaard's Attack upon "Christendom," 1854–1855*, trans. by Walter Lowrie, Princeton: Princeton University Press 1944.

KJN   *Kierkegaard's Journals and Notebooks*, vols. 1–11, ed. by Niels Jørgen Cappelørn, Alastair Hannay, David Kangas, Bruce H. Kirmmse, George Pattison, Vanessa Rumble, and K. Brian Söderquist, Princeton and Oxford: Princeton University Press 2007ff.

LD   *Letters and Documents*, trans. by Henrik Rosenmeier, Princeton: Princeton University Press 1978.

LR   *A Literary Review*, trans. by Alastair Hannay, Harmondsworth: Penguin Books 2001.

M   *The Moment and Late Writings*, trans. by Howard V. Hong and Edna H. Hong, Princeton: Princeton University Press 1998.

P   *Prefaces / Writing Sampler*, trans. by Todd W. Nichol, Princeton: Princeton University Press 1997.

PC   *Practice in Christianity*, trans. by Howard V. Hong and Edna H. Hong, Princeton: Princeton University Press 1991.

PF   *Philosophical Fragments*, trans. by Howard V. Hong and Edna H. Hong, Princeton: Princeton University Press 1985.

PJ   *Papers and Journals: A Selection*, trans. by Alastair Hannay, Harmonds-
          worth: Penguin Books 1996.

PLR   *Prefaces: Light Reading for Certain Classes as the Occasion May Require*,
          trans. by William McDonald, Tallahassee: Florida State University Press
          1989.

PLS   *Concluding Unscientific Postscript*, trans. by David F. Swenson and Walter
          Lowrie, Princeton: Princeton University Press 1941.

PV   *The Point of View* including *On My Work as an Author*, *The Point of View
          for My Work as an Author*, and *Armed Neutrality*, trans. by Howard V. Hong
          and Edna H. Hong, Princeton: Princeton University Press 1998.

PVL   *The Point of View for My Work as an Author* including *On My Work as an
          Author*, trans. by Walter Lowrie, New York and London: Oxford University
          Press 1939.

R   *Repetition*, trans. by Howard V. Hong and Edna H. Hong, Princeton:
          Princeton University Press 1983.

SBL   *Notes of Schelling's Berlin Lectures*, trans. by Howard V. Hong and Edna H.
          Hong, Princeton: Princeton University Press 1989.

SLW   *Stages on Life's Way*, trans. by Howard V. Hong and Edna H. Hong,
          Princeton: Princeton University Press 1988.

SUD   *The Sickness unto Death*, trans. by Howard V. Hong and Edna H. Hong,
          Princeton: Princeton University Press 1980.

SUDP   *The Sickness unto Death*, trans. by Alastair Hannay, London and New York:
          Penguin Books 1989.

TA   *Two Ages: The Age of Revolution and the Present Age. A Literary Review*,
          trans. by Howard V. Hong and Edna H. Hong, Princeton: Princeton
          University Press 1978.

TD   *Three Discourses on Imagined Occasions*, trans. by Howard V. Hong and
          Edna H. Hong, Princeton: Princeton University Press 1993.

UD   *Upbuilding Discourses in Various Spirits*, trans. by Howard V. Hong and
          Edna H. Hong, Princeton: Princeton University Press 1993.

WA   *Without Authority* including *The Lily in the Field and the Bird of the Air,
          Two Ethical-Religious Essays, Three Discourses at the Communion on
          Fridays, An Upbuilding Discourse, Two Discourses at the Communion on*

Fridays, trans. by Howard V. Hong and Edna H. Hong, Princeton: Princeton University Press 1997.

WL   *Works of Love*, trans. by Howard V. Hong and Edna H. Hong, Princeton: Princeton University Press 1995.

WS   *Writing Sampler*, trans. by Todd W. Nichol, Princeton: Princeton University Press 1997.

PART I

Anglophone Theology

Edward John Carnell:

A Skeptical Neo-Evangelical Reading

Silas Morgan

Edward John Carnell's academic life began and ended with the writings of Søren Kierkegaard. His Ph.D. dissertation in philosophy from Boston University was entitled *The Problem of Verification in Sören Kierkegaard*,[1] and its redacted version, *The Burden of Søren Kierkegaard*,[2] appeared in 1965 only a few years before his death. His reflection on numerous topics important to apologetics, theology, and philosophy of religion is embedded inside his indebtedness to, and his disagreement with, Kierkegaard's theology of existential faith, truth as subjectivity, and critique of Christian culture. He was rather convinced that Kierkegaard too easily jettisoned public evidences from the analysis of Christian theological claims in his embrace of paradox, subjectivity, and dialectics as markers of Christianity. For Carnell, God, as the proper object of Christian faith, is a verifiably historical fact that can be confirmed through the inner witness of the subject's heart. Kierkegaard disagrees: God is unknown and is not accessible via the conceited human attempts to rationally explain or account for God for the sake of their own intellectual prowess.[3] God is such that existence cannot be proven; faith, then, is paradox that offends the rational sensibility of the human person, calling the subject into a place of restless dread and painful risk.[4] Clearly, these theologians differ.

---

[1]   Edward John Carnell, *The Problem of Verification in Sören Kierkegaard*, Ph.D. Thesis, Boston University 1949.

[2]   Edward John Carnell, *The Burden of Søren Kierkegaard*, Grand Rapids, Michigan: Eerdmans 1965.

[3]   *SKS* 7, 222ff. / *CUP1*, 243ff. Any postulation of a "direct" relation to God is "pagan" to Kierkegaard, on account of the fact that it must ignore the central Christian truth, namely that God is infinitely invisible. Cf. *SKS* 7, 224 / *CUP1*, 246: "Nature, the totality of creation, is God's work and yet God is not there, but within the individual human being there is a possibility (he is spirit according to his possibility) that in inwardness is awakened to a God-relationship."

[4]   *SKS* 7, 297 / *CUP1*, 326: "the true of object of faith is not propositionally grounded doctrine, but rather the "actuality of another person; its relation is an infinite interestedness… in the answer to the question about a fact: Do you accept as fact that he actually existed?"

I. Biographical Summary

Edward John Carnell (1919–67) was one of the great American neo-evangelical theologians of the mid twentieth century. A fundamentalist early in his academic career, Carnell gradually distanced himself, staking claim to a new confession for conservative theology, but without the rhetoric and harsh attitudes of fundamentalism that Carnell found distasteful. He served in various professorial roles at several institutions, but made his mark as a faculty member and then president of Fuller Theological Seminary in Pasadena, California, during its most formative early years. A scholar of the highest level, his efforts were primarily in the area of apologetics, the philosophical defense of the Christian faith. He published nine books, most of which were innovative and creative attempts to reform the Christian apologetic account in light of developments in American neo-evangelicalism. He was also a frequent contributor to influential Christian publications like the *Christian Century* and *Christianity Today*, both of which were born during the rise of the neo-evangelical movement in the mid-twentieth century.

After studying philosophy with Gordon Clark (1902–85) at Wheaton College, Carnell attended Westminster Theological Seminary and was mentored by professors John Murray (1898–1975) and Cornelius Van Til (1895–1987). Participating in the fundamentalist interest to engage broader religious and cultural discourse, in 1948 Carnell received a Th.D. from Harvard Divinity School in philosophy of religion and history, after writing his dissertation on the theology of Reinhold Niebuhr (1892–1971), a volume eventually published as *The Theology of Reinhold Niebuhr* (1950).[5] He also managed to earn a Ph.D. in philosophy from Boston University the same year, writing a dissertation on Kierkegaard's religious epistemology under the instruction of Edgar S. Brightman (1884–1953). He shortly thereafter joined the young and adventurous faculty at Fuller Seminary, where he would eventually serve as president and remain as professor of ethics and philosophy of religion until 1967, the time of his untimely and strange death at the age of 47.[6]

His 1948 publication, *Introduction to Christian Apologetics*,[7] was the first of many books and won a prestigious award, catapulting him to the forefront of the progressive evangelical movement. His subsequent work on apologetics included *A Philosophy of the Christian Religion* (1952),[8] *Christian Commitment* (1957),[9] *The*

---

[5]   Edward John Carnell, *The Theology of Reinhold Niebuhr*, Grand Rapids, Michigan: Eerdmans 1950.
[6]   Rudolph Nelson, *The Making and Unmaking of an Evangelical Mind*, New York: Cambridge University Press 1987, pp. 177–221; John Sims, *Missionaries to the Skeptics: Christian Apologists of the Twentieth Century*, Macon, Georgia: Mercer University Press 1995, p. 104.
[7]   Edward John Carnell, *An Introduction to Christian Apologetics*, Grand Rapids, Michigan: Eerdmans 1948.
[8]   Edward John Carnell, *A Philosophy of Christian Religion*, Grand Rapids, Michigan: Eerdmans 1952.
[9]   Edward John Carnell, *Christian Commitment: An Apologetic*, New York: Macmillan 1957.

Case for Orthodox Theology (1960),[10] and *The Kingdom of Love and the Pride of Life* (1960).[11]

His rising status made him an excellent selection to lead the newly formed ascendant Fuller Theological Seminary. Carnell appreciated the opportunity but longed for the ease of the academic life of teaching and scholarship.[12] During his administration, Carnell established himself as a forceful advocate for progressive reform of fundamentalism in order to end the cultic practices and attitudes infused in their negative theology of legalism. His courageous offensive against fundamentalism can not only be found in his speeches but is the foundation of all of his published work.[13] He sought to create space for a conservative theological voice that championed orthodoxy without the ideological thinking, totalitarian spirit of conceptual control, and obsessive fear of heresy among creative and innovative theologies.

II. The Reception of Kierkegaard in the Work of Edward John Carnell

A. An Introduction to Christian Apologetics *(1948)*

Carnell's earliest publication, *An Introduction to Christian Apologetics* (1948), was a significant catalyst for his ascendance into the ranks of evangelical scholarship. Demonstrating his early interest in making the claims of Christianity respectable to outside forms of discourse, Carnell employed a philosophical strategy instead of a religious defense. Writing that "the aim of this volume is to discharge the obligation… by showing how Christianity is able to answer the fundamental questions of life as adequately as, if not more adequately than, any other world-view,"[14] Carnell argues for a coherence epistemology in order systematically to offer a philosophical response to the basic problems of apologetics: the nature of truth, the definition of faith, and the nature of proof. In the interest of constructing and defending "the Christian world-view," Carnell laid out a vision for the theological and philosophical defense of the Christian faith against other religious and philosophical world-views that seek to answer the same questions. But, it is also important to Carnell to claim that conservative Christianity is able to make sense of the world and the human experience of it, as diverse and complex as that may be, better than any other system of belief. Addressing questions like science, miracles, natural law, evil, and immorality, Carnell was eager to contend that Christianity is able to give reasonable explanations that are both deeply philosophical and practical. This book demonstrates Carnell's

---

[10]   Edward John Carnell, *The Case for Orthodox Theology*, Grand Rapids, Michigan: Eerdmans 1960.
[11]   Edward John Carnell, *The Kingdom of Love and the Pride of Life*, Grand Rapids, Michigan: Eerdmans 1960.
[12]   Nelson, *The Making and Unmaking of an Evangelical Mind*, p. 88; p. 94.
[13]   Sims, *Missionaries to the Skeptics*, pp. 114ff.; Nelson, *The Making and Unmaking of an Evangelical Mind*, p. 96.
[14]   Carnell, *An Introduction to Christian Apologetics*, p. 7.

early interest in matters similar to Kierkegaard; it also documents his indebtedness to Kierkegaard, despite his early dissatisfaction with his positions on key issues.[15]

Kierkegaard's particularly existential interest in questions of truth and faith clearly intrigued Carnell given his dissertation on the topic. And yet the reasons for his dissatisfaction with Kierkegaard's treatment become clear. The well-being of humanity is based on three principles one of which is the knowledge of truth, whereby normativity can be tested and established. Carnell defines truth as "a judgment, which corresponds to things as they actually are."[16] Theologically applied, this formulation means that "truth is a property of that judgment which coincides with the mind of God....Truth for the Christian, then is defined as correspondence with the mind of God."[17] This truth must be tested. Carnell employed the principle of systematic consistency; this is basically the argument for coherence. "A judgment is true and may be trusted when it sticks together with all the facts of our experience, while a judgment is false when it cannot."[18] Based on the law of non-contradiction, something is true only after the law has been systematically applied and both the formal and material facts cohere to meaningful reality as established by the mind of God. The centrality of the law of contradiction looms large for Carnell's reading of Kierkegaard's use of paradox and dialectic in his epistemology.[19] Carnell's resistance to Kierkegaard's ideas can be traced to his insistence on the primacy of this logical principle. "Without consistency," Carnell argued, "we have absolutely no way of telling the voice of the fool from the voice of the expert. The first element in any system of truth, therefore, is consistency."[20]

Convinced that "the division between faith and the apprehension of truth is false,"[21] Carnell avoided strong fideism by arguing instead for a strong rational defense of faith on the basis that it must be grounded in knowledge or else it ought to be considered meaningless and superstition. Carnell intentionally offered a philosophical defense of the Christian faith that can be respected by the outside world. He was concerned that the fundamentalists have unnecessarily distanced themselves from respectability on the basis of their ever-defensive, overly fideistic claims. Faith, then, is a trust in the truth of God's self-authenticating Word.[22] Clearly, the ability to ascertain the reliability of this Word as true is necessary for the believer. This comes through both an internal and external test, whereby the individual's faith in God is validated via the opened heart, "the truth which God has revealed through nature in general revelation."[23] Again the test of systematic consistency gets applied:

[15]   Sims, *Missionaries to the Skeptics*, p. 123.
[16]   Carnell, *An Introduction to Christian Apologetics*, p. 46.
[17]   Ibid., p. 47.
[18]   Ibid., p. 56.
[19]   Sims, *Missionaries to the Skeptics*, p. 131; Joe E. Barnhart, *The Religious Epistemology and Theodicy of Edward John Carnell and Edgar Sheffield Brightman: A Study of Contrasts*, Ph.D. Thesis, Boston University 1964, p. 93; p. 360.
[20]   Carnell, *An Introduction to Christian Apologetics*, p. 58.
[21]   Ibid., p. 65.
[22]   Ibid., p. 66.
[23]   Ibid., p. 69.

"If what is being believed makes peace with the law of contradiction and the facts of the experience, it is a faith which is prompted by the Spirit of God."[24]

Carnell's early concern about Kierkegaard revolved around the question of the "criteria of verification."[25] He identified this as the basic problem of religion: the ability to prove its propositional claims. Its importance cannot be understated, given that the philosophic defense he puts forth is grounded on the reliability of the law of contradiction to adjudicate between well-justified beliefs. Lauding demonstrative proof for its formal use of the law of contradiction and inductive proof for its reliance on historical probability,[26] Carnell offered, via systematic consistency, a proof by coherence that measures how well our propositional claims correspond to reality: "The better our propositions stick together, the more truth we have; the more truth we have, the more coherence we have. It is in this framework that the Christ offers proof for his system: it sticks together. It can solve the problems of personal happiness, represent a rational view of the universe and give a basis for truth."[27]

Christianity must adhere to basic rules of formal logic, the most important of which is the law of contradiction. "If one refuses to construe his propositions according to the axiom of contradiction, all one can do is to check him off his calling list. There is no longer anything to talk about."[28] He counted Kierkegaard among these who, "peacock their deficiency in objective truth,"[29] by rejecting the idea that God-talk makes sense and embracing the idea that claims about God are an offense to our ways of making sense of the world.[30] When a reason-governed person submits the claims of Christianity to a rigorous, scientific test against the objective facts of history and the subjective experiences of human life, one can expect to discover a near complete coherence with both narratives.[31]

God is the proper object of the Christian faith and, as such, is readily and universally accessible via both reason and spiritual experience, and it is natural and entirely plausible for the Christian self to have faith in their veracity. Carnell's epistemology, governed by the principle of systematic consistency, allowed for truth to be ontological fact that coheres not only with the content and teachings of the biblical witness, but also with the natural world. Truth is located inside the

---

[24]   Ibid., p. 70.

[25]   Carnell's original dissertation on Kierkegaard critically approached this question, eventually concluding that while Kierkegaard's ideal of restoring individuality is impeccable, these criteria do not sufficiently make sense of Christian life and practice, in that they reject reason as a proper criteria for verification. Cf. Carnell, *The Problem of Verification in Sören Kierkegaard*, pp. 289–90.

[26]   Carnell, *An Introduction to Christian Apologetics*, p. 106.

[27]   Ibid., p. 107.

[28]   Ibid., p. 108.

[29]   Ibid.

[30]   Ibid., p. 109.

[31]   Ibid., p. 111. Carnell does allow for some disparagement between the dates that Christianity, via the biblical genealogies, gives for the historical appearance of humanity and the dates provided by natural science, but refuses to suggest that this is a major problem for Christianity and finds no reason why one should doubt the veracity either of science or of Christianity on the basis of this disagreement.

claims of faith; in the opposite direction, the believing subject can verify the truth of her faith claims, not only by her experience of this confirmation via spirit,[32] but more foundationally in the universally accessible world of reasonable and logical systems, to which Carnell attributes the creative hand of God, the object of faith and the source of all truth. While he seemed momentarily open to faith as subjective immediacy, this view is ultimately rejected for its problems with verification, proof, and confirmation of truth.

B. Philosophy of the Christian Religion *(1952)*

Always a passionate voice in defense of the veracity of Christian faith in the face of modern challenges, Carnell provided in *Philosophy of the Christian Religion* a less dogmatic approach than that offered in his previous book on apologetics. Turning this attention to the role that value plays in religious conviction, Carnell spoke to the condition of modern humanity and addresses topics of importance to all believing subjects immersed in the difficulty of human life. Suggesting that the stages in the religious life may be compared to the rocks on which small boys hop when crossing a stream, moving from values for the "lower immediacies" of pleasure and self-interest to the "higher immediacies" to ultimately faith in the person of Jesus Christ, *Philosophy of the Christian Religion* was devoted to charting this path to the truth that can be found in the heart of the believer because "Christianity places a premium upon the third locus of truth—truth in the heart—because man is related to God personally; and in all personal affairs fellow rests upon trust."[33]

Kierkegaard played a larger role in this book than in *An Introduction to Christian Apologetics*. Carnell charged Kierkegaard with leading the charge against "a rationally necessary world-view."[34] Carnell rightly notes that Kierkegaard's primary problem with Hegel's "tortured, logical dialectic" was the inability "to accommodate the free individual himself."[35] Carnell recounted Kierkegaard's ironic polemic against Hegel, which suggested that Hegel, despite his own desire for erudition and his frenzied concern to get his manuscript into the hands of real people, cashes in his professorial wages, which were all earned in vain. Despite the vast totalizing force of the Hegelian system, it completely omits any room for the single individual.[36] Quoting at length from the *Concluding Unscientific Postscript*, Carnell used Kierkegaard's concerns about the Hegelian's *sub specie aeterni* to make a point that humans make choices when they truly live in this world—the either/or. It is becoming oneself—the ethical art of choosing oneself, says Carnell via Kierkegaard—that makes a person truly real, opening oneself up to God in authentic, world-actualizing relations. When Carnell noted that Kierkegaard "perceived that the ethical exists only when the individual mediates the terms of ethical decision in his own volitional life,"[37] he

---

32   Ibid., p. 74.
33   Carnell, *Philosophy of the Christian Religion*, p. 452.
34   Ibid., p. 202.
35   Ibid.
36   Ibid., p. 203.
37   Ibid., p. 259.

pointed to the critical Kierkegaardian conviction that the truth is only made to be so when embedded inside the ethically existing subject.[38]

Surely Carnell read Kierkegaard correctly here—but did Carnell agree? Reading Niebuhr's skepticism about the human's ability to act rightly even with the good in front of herself against Kierkegaard here, Carnell sided with the former in suggesting that the ethical life understood as act fails, for the self will never be able to perceive of the good rightly outside its own purview.[39] (This is Kierkegaard's point precisely!) Unable to accept that all the moral agent has is the act itself, Carnell went looking for a law of life that guides ethical reflection, but rightly asks along the way, "does the ethical come into existence only when one actually mediates through righteous living the law that defines the right?"[40] Turning to Kierkegaard again, Carnell settled on the idea that "the act is the thing itself. Therefore, the law of our being defines a condition, which may be met only when one *is* truth in his own person; not when he [gives] rational asset to its terms."[41] At the end, Carnell disagreed with Kierkegaard about the nature of the ethical assignment. Kierkegaard's use of irony in the life of the ethicist is only a "smoke screen" for what Carnell thinks is the primary objective of the ethically acting person—to fulfill the duty of the good heart to live under certain conditions.[42] The good heart is always governed by reality, mediated to the person as such only insofar as the person is, at her core, religious. Carnell thought Kierkegaard agreed:

> A man is religious whenever he gives a concerned response to reality over against him, for religion is simply the binding of man to reality....To respond wholly is—in the words of Kierkegaard—to respond existentially, i.e., as an existing person concerned over the responsibility of what it means to be an individual.[43]

Carnell seems willing, at this point, to concur with Kierkegaard's view of the ethical self as a dynamically existing single individual in relation.[44]

As an apologetic theologian, Carnell was very concerned with locating and defining truth. Defending forms of objective authority as that "which define rational evidence itself,"[45] he comes out against Kierkegaard by suggesting "in no instance do the Scriptures encourage the penitent to believe that by a subjective 'leap of faith' he may atone for a deficiency in objective authority. On the contrary, cordial trust in Jesus Christ is always grounded in reasonable evidences."[46] The distance between Carnell and Kierkegaard could not be clearer. And yet, moving beyond what he calls the "philosophical locus of truth," he argues for "truth in the heart" that acknowledges that the human individual is related to God in personal ways, including trust, that

---

38   *SKS* 7, 256 / *CUP1*, 281.
39   Carnell, *Philosophy of the Christian Religion*, p. 259.
40   Ibid., p. 265.
41   Ibid.
42   Ibid., p. 266.
43   Ibid., p. 346.
44   *SKS* 7, 325–6 / *CUP1*, 356–7. *SKS* 11, 229 / *SUD*, 117.
45   Carnell, *Philosophy of the Christian Religion*, p. 449.
46   Ibid.

forms the devotional relation of faith towards God. A person, who has faith in God, trusts God in her heart to be good of character—this is fellowship itself.[47]

In the final chapter of *Philosophy of the Christian Religion*, "The Loci of Truth," Carnell made his disagreements with Kierkegaard clear. Overall, his concerns were with Kierkegaard's epistemological choices regarding truth as subjectivity and the marginalization of objective evidences and reason in his account of faith. Reading almost exclusively from the *Concluding Unscientific Postscript*, Carnell first established Kierkegaard as the "fountainhead" of existentialism before outlining his basic project. Arguing that Kierkegaard's primary objective is to unsettle the single individual, making it difficult for the subject to easily embrace Christianity as her own, Carnell suggested that Kierkegaard's phenomenological emphasis on the human person's subjective inwardness led him to elevate the spirit as essential to the core of the human person's living activity in the world.[48] Truth, said Carnell, exists at the moment of synthesis when the human person successfully mediates dialectical relation between time and eternity. In fact, the human person is this synthesis and comes into being at the moment of the passionate, inward decision.[49]

The human person lives in a dialectical relation, brought together only by the ethical choice that makes the person a subject. This is how Carnell understood Kierkegaard's view of Christianity as Religiousness B as the process whereby an ethically existing subject is formed before God through the temporal moment of passionate, inward decision that is the very core of authentic Christian existence. Kierkegaard locates truth in the individual itself as an ethically existing subject:

> The truth becomes paradox. The eternal truth has come into existence in time. That is the paradox....now the eternal, essential truth is not behind him but has come in front of him by existing itself or by having existed, so that if the individual existing, does not lay hold of the truth in existence, he will never have it.[50]

Carnell thought Kierkegaard's axiom, *truth as subjectivity*, meant primarily "the subjective state of ethical decision," where "subjectivity is infinite passionate concern; it is the being of becoming, the attaining of the existential assignment."[51] Truth is not a substance or a categorization of propositional reality, but rather a lived dimension that measures the subjective relation between humanity and authentic embrace of paradox. This requires ultimate freedom, of course, and the radical contradiction of subjectivity (the dialectical synthesis of time and eternity via spirit, that is, consciousness) ensures that sin as untruth will always remain a problem and an obstacle to the single individual becoming an authentic subject, that is, a Christian—this is Kierkegaard's goal. He desires, much to Carnell's disappointment, to make both Christianity and the process of becoming a Christian, offensive and problematic. "Christianity has itself proclaimed itself to be the eternal, essential truth that has come into existence in time; it has proclaimed itself as the

---

47   Ibid., p. 453.
48   *SKS* 11, 225 / *SUD*, 113–4.
49   Carnell, *Philosophy of the Christian Religion*, p. 458.
50   *SKS* 7, 148 / *CUP1*, 159. *SKS* 7, 192 / *CUP1*, 209.
51   Carnell, *Philosophy of the Christian Religion*, p. 463.

paradox and has required the inwardness of faith with regard to what is an offense to the Jews, foolishness to the Greeks—and an absurdity to the understanding."[52] The embrace of the absurd then measures the validity of faith: "It is by way of the objective repulsion that the absurd is the dynamometer of faith in inwardness."[53] Carnell was concerned with this emphasis on inwardness that can only be measured from the perspective of the subject. Inwardness is created in the dialectical space of eternity/time, infinity/finitude, and necessity/contingency of the lived world; this, for Carnell, is a philosophically irresponsible explanation for truth because of the way it marginalizes and problematizes both reason and objective evidences as warrants.

Kierkegaard's break with reason as the ground of faith deeply bothered Carnell. Instead of arguing that Christian faith is grounded in reason, Kierkegaard suggested, true to his existential form, that faith is only possible when it is embedded inside the infinite passion generated by the uncertain and indeterminate claims in objectivity.[54] Basically, Kierkegaard does not think the authentically existing subject lives in a world of objectivity, constructed as usually described by formal logical descriptions of reality that are accessible via the rational uses of the mind. The mind does not live at the center of the human person for Kierkegaard, Carnell conceded, but rather the spirit, which proceeds to the higher understanding of faith. To be is not to know, but rather to be is to become through the impossible tying together of time and eternity that is future. This is not something the logical or formal categories of reason can accomplish, says Carnell's Kierkegaard, because the person always lives in the impossible space of synthesis between time and eternity.

Kierkegaard, while also suggesting that faith opposes what is determined reasonable, jettisons objective evidence as criteria for valid beliefs.[55] Offending the most basic of classical epistemological principles, Carnell's Kierkegaard renders proofs for God (and truth) as futile and preposterous. Kierkegaard wants to make Christianity offensive, and any attempt to prove the truth of Christianity renders its content, namely, the absolutely paradoxical claim of the incarnation of Jesus Christ, innocuous. The objective claims of proof actually stand in the way of faith (by virtue of the absurd) because it is the proofs of reason that faith opposes. Whatever it is that reason proves cannot be truly Christian! Reason will never prove the paradoxical juxtaposition of time and eternity that is existence, much less the absolutely absurd paradox of immanence and transcendence, that is, God and God-becoming-human nonsense, that is, the incarnation of Jesus Christ.[56]

But Carnell thought there is something more fundamental to Kierkegaard's rejection of reason, and it has to do with Kierkegaard's theological articulation of the role of paradox in the faith of the Christian person. Since truth for the subject is located squarely inside the personal striving in suffering towards impossibility, faith always believes against the reasonable, since the reasonable will always be the easier and more logical, or so said Carnell: "Christianity is the final religion

52   *SKS* 7, 195 / *CUP1*, 213.
53   *SKS* 7, 193 / *CUP1*, 210.
54   *SKS* 7, 178 / *CUP1*, 194.
55   *SKS* 7, 280–1 / *CUP1*, 307–8.
56   Carnell, *Philosophy of the Christian Religion*, pp. 471ff.

because it is based on the most thinkable offensive paradox....In the instance of the incarnation of Christ, however, the eternal God became an individual....When judged by the cannon of contradiction (declares Kierkegaard), the incarnation is complete nonsense."[57]

In the end, for Carnell, Kierkegaard was wrong to defend truth as subjectivity by rejecting objective evidence as a warrant for faith. Kierkegaard thought that the very nature of God, the proper object of faith resists warrants altogether; Carnell thought this only leads to atheism. Arguing that Kierkegaard forgot that Jesus Christ gave the human person a rational capacity, Carnell thought that it is a contradiction that human reason would not be able to apprehend Christian truth. Carnell said we cannot avoid using reason and understanding in making ordinary decisions in our daily life and that to "act passionately in defiance of the report of reason"[58] is to behave strangely. "The native person—the one unaffected by corrupting philosophic presuppositions—is at his best and is most ideally a man of faith, when he obeys, rather than defies, the report of a critically developed understanding."[59] Among these presuppositions is the idea that faith is obligated to reject what reason offers the single individual in favor of the passionate commitment to the absurdity of truth.[60]

Carnell is unable to reconcile this vision with his own commitment to rational evidence for verification of truth. For what reasons, outside of madness, would a person embrace something if it is as offensive to reason as Kierkegaard suggests?[61] Carnell eventually decided there were none, charging Kierkegaard with starting down the slippery slope towards skepticism and nihilism, where not only is subjective faith "empowered with authority to create its own objective of devotion,"[62] but "when taken to its full logical conclusion, Biblical Christianity itself vanishes"[63] into an irrational, incoherent but inwardly philosophical atheism.[64] Kierkegaard argues for a sliding scale of faith, it seems to Carnell: "As objective repulsiveness increases, the intensity of the existential commitment increases; as incoherence diminishes, faith diminishes."[65] This articulation directly offended Carnell's own interest in arguing for a philosophy of Christian truth based on its ability to make sense of the world and life inside it in the most coherent way available to the modern person. Kierkegaard wanted to protect the radical absurdity of Christianity's primary claim, namely, the Incarnation. The idea that God becomes human offends reason and resists every attempt to give an account of it through objective evidence; to be a Christian means that the single individual must be willing to jettison the reasoning ways of the world and take into herself the madness that is Jesus Christ. Carnell was willing to characterize the Incarnation as a mysterious phenomenon, but rejects the idea that it is an absurd paradox, given the idea that "it is most absurd to believe in the

---

[57]   Ibid., p. 469.
[58]   Ibid., p. 474.
[59]   Ibid., p. 475.
[60]   Ibid., p. 482.
[61]   Ibid., p. 471.
[62]   Ibid.
[63]   Ibid., p. 485.
[64]   Ibid., p. 496.
[65]   Ibid., p. 484.

whole God becoming an earthworm."[66] Carnell ultimately charged Kierkegaard with offering an existential rendering of Christianity that only slips into an irrational and incoherent madness where reason is betrayed for the sake of the absurd, leaving it impossible to determine what is true and what is erroneous—this cannot be faithful to the Christian Scriptures.[67]

C. Christian Commitment: An Apologetic *(1957)*

"Without the stimulation of the Danish gadfly, I probably would never have learned how to ask questions from the perspective of inwardness. It is my pleasure to acknowledge my indebtedness to Kierkegaard."[68] Thus began what appears to be a short excursus from the argument of the text to address the role of Kierkegaard in Carnell's own theological matrix. As we have already seen, Kierkegaard's general project to "interpret reality from the perspective of the free, ethical individual"[69] loomed large for Carnell; despite his disagreements, Carnell could not dismiss Kierkegaard's critique of detached philosophy, nor his passionate interest to make sense of the human person as expressed through ethical decision. Carnell defined in *Christian Commitment* a new method of knowing called *truth as personal rectitude*, whereby both existence and essence are united by spirit in the subject at the moment of right moral decision. This Kierkegaardian description attempts to articulate the synthesis that provides humanity with its properly moral character. With ontological and philosophical descriptions of truth offering only propositional content, Carnell offers Kierkegaard's critique of these visions of truth as an example of the insufficiency of these accounts for the sake of the "imperative essence," the product of the ethical harmony in the moment of the upright ethical decision.[70]

Carnell offered a rather Kierkegaardian definition of the human person as "freedom expressed through moral self-consciousness."[71] This moment of subjective awareness of one's ethical relation disclosed the very existence of God. Rather, the knowledge of one's relation to God comes to the subject through the freedom of the person's spirit that results in the spiritual transformation of an ethically existing self. "Whenever individuals rely on objective certainty as an escape from moral decision, they jeopardize their own individuality...[which] consists in ethical decision, for the real man is the moral man."[72] Carnell again gestured to Kierkegaard here by wondering aloud whether or not that is what Kierkegaard meant when he suggested "freedom is the truly wonderful lamp and that when a man rubs it with ethical passion God comes into being for him."[73] The confidence in the constitutive

---

[66]   Ibid., p. 486.
[67]   Ibid., p. 495.
[68]   Carnell, *Christian Commitment*, p. 73.
[69]   Ibid., p. 73.
[70]   Ibid., pp. 14–15.
[71]   Ibid., p. 139.
[72]   Ibid., p. 141.
[73]   Ibid., p. 109.

nature of God's existence for the human person comes from his willingness to say, alongside Kierkegaard, that God's existence is fundamentally necessary.[74]

Nonetheless, Carnell still pointed to what he considered a "serious structural flaw" from the perspective of "a consistent world-view."[75] In short, Carnell boldly charged Kierkegaard with failing to meet the requirements of logical consistency in his stout defense of the polarity between objective certainty and subjective faith. Carnell read in Kierkegaard a claim that "faith must choose in defiance of the intellect, for without risk, there is no faith."[76] This is rather unsavory to Carnell, who thought that this results in a zealous abdication of common sense where subjective faith is governed by a lack of regard for the obvious reality before the person.[77] Carnell repeated his prior affirmation that faith and reason must work together in order to provide warrants for Christian convictions. A person is warranted to hold Christian beliefs because of the objective evidence that fulfills the common-sense requirement for rational satisfaction. Kierkegaard's overactive "penchant for paradox" leads him only to set the rational self against the moral self needlessly.[78]

D. The Kingdom of Love and the Pride of Life *(1960)*

Carnell moved in a rhetorically different direction with the release of *The Kingdom of Love and the Pride of Life* (1960). Having established himself as an erudite writer, heavily skilled in the philosophical and ethical issues of apologetics, and perhaps reflecting personal challenges with depression and experiences with psychotherapy, Carnell examined the law of love. Interested in love as the point of contact between gospel and culture, Carnell desired to recapture the natural openness that children have towards God and others, exhibited in unconditional love.[79] Taking seriously Jesus' admonition that the children will inherit the Kingdom of God, Carnell set out to undermine problematic patterns of pride, greed and other vices in Christian ethics through a passionate exploration of the doctrine of life for Christian ethics and apologetics.[80]

Kierkegaard is not present in this text, and yet the most consistent affirmative way Carnell receives Kierkegaard is his interest in the centrality of love for the Christian life. It is truly hard for this reader to think that *The Kingdom of Love and the Pride of Life* is not representative, at least indirectly, of an indirect reception of this insight from Kierkegaard. Glancing at *Philosophy of the Christian Religion*, Carnell looks away for a moment from his usual exegesis of the *Concluding Unscientific Postscript* and *Philosophical Fragments* and examines the way that love functions in the decision of the ethically existing subject. Love places such rigorous demands on the self that one finds oneself completely unable to acknowledge love in its truest

---

[74]   Ibid., p. 130, note.
[75]   Ibid., p. 74.
[76]   Ibid., p. 75.
[77]   Ibid., p. 76.
[78]   Ibid., p. 78.
[79]   Carnell, *The Kingdom of Love and the Pride of Life*, p. 23.
[80]   Ibid., p. 160.

form as the mediatory link between time and eternity. Filled with dread, the subject turns to God in the face of the endless obligation to love the neighbor, but is unable to escape the necessity with which the duty impresses itself upon the self. "Love makes inwardness absolutely strenuous by joining an infinite possibility with an infinite necessity....The chain of dialectical tension is endless."[81]

Carnell's most positive evaluation of Kierkegaard comes when addressing *Works of Love*, the profundity of which the Christian community has yet to penetrate.[82] Love is the space where thinking about action is jettisoned for an ethical demand to do one's duty by loving the neighbor rightly before God. Against what Carnell called "formalist ethics," Kierkegaard's interest in love rests in his commitment to respond existentially; in other words, to actualize the authenticity of the self rightly before God by her willing works of love, despite the sheer impossibility of faithfully fulfilling the demands of loving each neighbor without particularity.[83]

E. The Burden of Søren Kierkegaard *(1965)*

Søren Kierkegaard served as a professional bookend for Carnell; he began and completed his academic career with treatments of Kierkegaard's work. His Ph.D. dissertation remained an unpublished manuscript until it was released in 1965. Originally titled, *The Problem of Verification in Sören Kierkegaard*, its redacted form was offered as *The Burden of Søren Kierkegaard*. As we have seen, it is hardly the first time that Carnell offers his opinions about Kierkegaard, but it is by far the most in-depth treatment. Carnell is primarily interested in letting Kierkegaard speak for himself on a number of issues, and he employs a strategy that involves long quotations with little or no commentary or critical analysis. He admits that in *The Burden of Søren Kierkegaard* he intends to be "affirmative rather than negative" and desires that "the reader might have the opportunity to evaluate the primary material for himself."[84] For Carnell, Kierkegaard's burden is to offer the existential defense of the individual as the ethically existing subject.[85] This is coupled with the mission to make it difficult to become a Christian by emphasizing the dreadfully restless risk of faith over against the ease by which many of his Danish Lutheran contemporaries claimed what they thought was the objective system of Christianity.[86]

Carnell understands there to be two major moments in Kierkegaard's theology; first, what Carnell called the "dialectic of inwardness," namely, Kierkegaard's commitment to the paradoxical nature of the human person as it is interfaced with the analogous nature of Christian claims about God and Jesus Christ;[87] second, his negative rejection of "speculation," "Hegelianism," and "objectivity" where

---

81 Carnell, *Philosophy of the Christian Religion*, p. 465.
82 Carnell, *Christian Commitment*, p. 74.
83 Carnell, *Philosophy of the Christian Religion*, p. 346.
84 Carnell, *The Burden of Søren Kierkegaard*, p. 7.
85 Ibid., p. 49.
86 Ibid., p. 38.
87 Ibid., pp. 84ff.

Kierkegaard's theory of truth as subjectivity is fleshed out in a decisive polemical step from which Carnell will eventually distance himself.[88]

This book offers very little in terms of new reception of Kierkegaard on Carnell's part. His strategy leaves much to be desired; there is too much documentation and not enough exposition by Carnell. What *The Burden of Søren Kierkegaard* amounts to is not so much a critical appraisal but rather an introduction to Kierkegaard's thought that does not so much offer a unique reading. *The Burden of Søren Kierkegaard* represents more or less a repetition of previous engagements in the *Philosophy of the Christian Religion* and the *Christian Commitment*, both his positive and negative receptions of Kierkegaard can easily be found in the texts we have already reviewed.

Carnell rightly located the existential rendering of the human person as central to understanding Kierkegaard's theology. True subjectivity is a movement from reflection (aesthetic), to moral decision (ethical), to passionate action (religion). Carnell rightly notes that Kierkegaard's objection to reflection lies in his mistrust of philosophical attempts to subvert faith's passionate striving in paradox.[89] The ideality of the actual is what the ethically existing subject struggles for, and this mode of existence is necessarily impossible for the subject to achieve; it demands stringent personal involvement that supersedes any appeal to the objective or universal for verification.[90] The subject, in order to find truth inside itself, must be continually in a state of ethical decision in order to actualize the mediation of time and eternity.

Carnell appreciated the way that Kierkegaard emphasized the necessity of suffering in the authentic experience of the Christian self. Dread, says Carnell, is the sign of the self, inching closer to the absolute paradox. Truth as subjectivity means that the self as subject must face the paradoxical nature of freedom and spirit, and grasping the burden of truth, namely the impossible mediation of the dialectic, turns to God in fear and trembling, fully aware of the strenuous demands of pure existence.[91] Kierkegaard wants to make it hard to be a Christian; his existential rendering of truth succeeds in making Christianity and its claims offensive. Carnell considers this "a strange goal."[92]

Kierkegaard jettisons objective reason on account of its inability to recognize the paradoxically dialectic that he considers central to the Christian confession about the incarnation of Jesus Christ, the absolute paradox.[93] Truth as subjectivity relies on restlessness; the indeterminate nature of one's claims to truth demand a willingness to live in impossibility and to suspend certainty for the sake of believing passionately in the absurdity. This makes all objective, logical, or rational attempts to make sense of the Christian faith pointless.[94] The very nature of the Christian confession is subjective, illogical, and irrational![95] Only the subjective inward decision by the

---

[88]   Ibid., pp. 114ff.
[89]   Ibid., p. 62.
[90]   Ibid., p. 68.
[91]   Ibid., pp. 74ff.
[92]   Ibid., p. 81.
[93]   Ibid., p. 97; see also *SKS* 7, 186 / *CUP1*, 204.
[94]   Ibid., p. 98.
[95]   Ibid., pp. 132ff.

single individual who is becoming a self before God, and who is willing to live in dreadful indeterminacy and face the paradoxical nature of everyday life is able to confront the absolute paradox of Jesus Christ as truth. Carnell rightly noted that, for Kierkegaard, "the very fact of the incarnation is an absolute paradox, that is quite offensive to the canon of reason,"[96] and in light of this insight, "truth faith, as it has been stressed, does not rest on rationally probable evidences."[97] Carnell proposed that, for Kierkegaard, "all apologetic zeal to prove God's existence must be terminated. A human being must live either for or against God, giving up the various attempts to settle the question of God's existence by rational disputation."[98]

It is not that Carnell read Kierkegaard incorrectly here. Carnell was simply unwilling to concede the dialectic of "either/or" and maintained, as we have seen him do repeatedly before, that a "both/and" strategy is the most faithful way to articulate Christian theological claims to the modern world. Carnell protected the regulative function of reason and objective evidence for the metaphysical justification for Christian claims; to do otherwise, in his view, is to ignore common-sense realities of objective certainty available to the human person through the rational process.

In my final words, I offer a summary of Carnell's primary points of positive and then negative reception. He summarized his own thoughts on Kierkegaard in this way: "Kierkegaard blended some very brilliant insights with some insights which (in our opinion at least) are not so brilliant."[99] First, Carnell deeply appreciated Kierkegaard's critique of the church.[100] He found an ally in his challenge to the church's attitude about its place in society and its function as a community of mission.[101] Carnell discovered helpful parallels for his own polemic against fundamentalism in Kierkegaard's critique of Danish Christianity as "cult," whose devotions to doctrinal creeds superseded their mission to be radical representations of Jesus Christ to the world.[102]

As I argued above, the primary point of Carnell's positive reception of Kierkegaard concerned his expositions of the Christian doctrine of love. Carnell read the thesis of truth as subjectivity as "another way of stating the Christian conviction that truth is love and that the ethical manners of the living person give reality to the substance of law."[103] Carnell saw love as the location of the binding together of time and eternity in the existing subject: the stuff that makes subjectivity. Since Jesus Christ alone loved perfectly, he alone was a complete individual, for in Carnell's reading of Kierkegaard, "Since God is love in his very essence, it is only when we conceive of God as the active agent in loving relations that we may pass from love on earth to heaven itself. Love is the true point of identity between time and eternity."[104] It is Kierkegaard's attention to the duty of love as the most central

---

[96]   Ibid., p. 116.
[97]   Ibid.
[98]   Ibid., p. 117.
[99]   Ibid., p. 165.
[100]   Ibid., p. 168.
[101]   Ibid., p. 122.
[102]   Ibid., p. 123.
[103]   Ibid., p. 153.
[104]   Ibid., p. 160.

of biblical themes which wins Carnell's most ardent affection. Carnell agreed with Kierkegaard that "the real man is the ethical man"[105] for it is only through love that the fulfillment of the law is even possible. Ethics is impossible unless it performs works of love; Kierkegaard's insistence on action over refection speaks volumes to Carnell in terms of Kierkegaard's interest in the fusion of love and the existential nature of the human person.[106]

Carnell's most enduring reception springs from Kierkegaard's strong insistence on dialectical relations between objective evidence as warrant for Christian faith versus the paradoxical demand for Christian faith as a mad embrace of the absurd. Christianity is subjectivity, Kierkegaard says, and thus any appeal to objective certainty, proofs for the veracity of Christian beliefs, or assent to propositional data is a mistake. Christianity involves a passionate decision to embrace the absolutely paradoxical nature of the absurdity of the Incarnation, not an intellectual assent of philosophical claims about external reality.[107] Carnell disagrees with Kierkegaard that appeals to proof (that is, objectivity and the universal) only result in the sort of complacency, reflection, and philosophical ease that preclude the suffering which the self must undergo in its faithful striving after God. Convinced that Kierkegaard's penchant for risk forces him to drive a decisive wedge between faith and reason, Carnell argues that this move dislodges Kierkegaard's epistemology from what is actually real. "Apart from a state of certainty, we have no right to claims that we are in possession of truth....When all is said and done, therefore, passion and certainty are friends and not foes."[108] Just because the self passionately believes something to be true does not make it so, says Carnell. "Unless the Christian religion is responsibly related to evidences which are both public and sufficient, it is simply not worth talking about."[109]

Carnell's charge that Kierkegaard's "very inadequate relation between Christian religion and public evidences"[110] results in a subjectively insufficient criterion for adequacy that is too broad to actually work in everyday human experience: "any religious position could be defended, providing a person held the position with sufficient subjective passion."[111] Carnell is very concerned with Kierkegaard's rhetorical claim that it is more favorable for an idol worshiper to pray to a false God with passionate subjective commitment than it is for one who calls herself a Christian to pray to God with a false spirit of complacency and ambivalent reflection,[112] though he appreciates Kierkegaard's willingness to be internally consistent since he agrees that this is the properly logical conclusion. That Kierkegaard resists attempts to characterize God as anything other than the unknown purely indeterminate

---

[105]   Ibid., p. 127.
[106]   Ibid., p. 167.
[107]   Ibid., p. 115: "In reacting against dead orthodoxy, there is little doubt that Kierkegaard went too far. But his general goal had many excellent elements in it, even though he did not always reach his goal."
[108]   Ibid., p. 169.
[109]   Ibid., p. 170.
[110]   Ibid., p. 169.
[111]   Ibid.
[112]   *SKS* 7, 184 / *CUP1*, 201.

paradox further demonstrates to Carnell what is ultimately unacceptable about his theology: Kierkegaard cannot and does not speak properly of the Christian God, nor does he articulate faithfully the content of Christian belief. He only obfuscates in his vain attempt to problematize what it means to become a Christian. Ultimately, Carnell appreciates Kierkegaard's intuitions but sharply distances himself from Kierkegaard's conclusions. In his early dissertation, Carnell passionately contends "there is no compelling arguments in the literature to gainsay the conclusion that a God-man myth in a pagan religion can elicit the same inwardness and Christ."[113]

III. An Evaluation of Carnell's Reception of Kierkegaard

There is no doubt that Carnell read Kierkegaard closely and took his work very seriously. His interest spans his entire academic career. His published works are full of his remarks on Kierkegaard about various topics of interest and concern. Carnell reads Kierkegaard at an interesting historical period in the American Kierkegaard reception, immediately after the final publication of the Lowrie translations, before the Hong volumes were in production. He offers a rather blunt reading that focuses primarily on the pseudonymous writings in the first authorship, but lacks sophistication or nuance concerning the relation between that authorship and the historical Kierkegaard. There is some knowledge of Kierkegaard's papers or journals to found in Carnell,[114] and most of the citations that Carnell provides come from the *Concluding Unscientific Postscript* and *Philosophical Fragments*. He does read and occasionally cites the later more religious works, *Works of Love* and *The Sickness unto Death*, but fails to acknowledge how they ought to be read any differently than de silentio or Climacus. Certainly, we cannot fault Carnell for this; the discourses on these hermeneutical issues had hardly begun, and the journals and papers were not yet available in English.

My constructive remarks on Carnell's reception will be limited to two primary points. First, that Carnell, as limited as his reading is, was not a poor reader of Kierkegaard and, in fact, interpreted him rather fairly and insightfully. Second, one can imagine that Kierkegaard would have appreciated how Carnell received his work, for it is precisely on the most salient points that Carnell and Kierkegaard part ways. It is these points that, for Carnell and Kierkegaard, address the nature and character of subjectivity, truth, faith, and radical action. One cannot say that Carnell misreads or misunderstands Kierkegaard; Carnell disagrees with how Kierkegaard articulates a vision of Christianity as that of paradox, dialectic, contradiction, and suffering, and draws a line in the sand at the point where Kierkegaard argues for the truth of Christianity as paradoxical absurdity, void of certainty and resistant to the closure of objectivity.

Carnell is careful to read Kierkegaard charitably when he can. If anything, his most sustained engagement, *The Burden of Søren Kierkegaard*, can be faulted for

---

[113]   Carnell, *The Problem of Verification in Sören Kierkegaard*, pp. 289–90.
[114]   Carnell makes a point in *The Burden of Søren Kierkegaard*, p. 15, note 3, to praise *The Journals of Søren Kierkegaard*, trans. and ed. by Alexander Dru, London: Oxford University Press 1938, over the Harper Torchbooks edition.

lacking critical commentary in the midst of its encyclopedic efforts to chronicle Kierkegaard's remarks on various subjects. His citations and summaries of Kierkegaard are taken seriously and read with admirable sincerity in the interest of scholarly veracity. Carnell's understanding of Kierkegaard's anthropology, the thesis of truth is subjectivity, and the nature of faith in paradox stand in line with standard contemporary accounts, and certainly reflect Carnell's erudition.

And yet, at the end, Carnell maintains "whatever guidance we may glean from Kierkegaard, we must draw the line at that point where reason is betrayed."[115] Carnell echoes sentiments uttered in the early text of *Philosophy of the Christian Religion*: "the native person—one who has never read Kierkegaard—is at his best...when the ethical life follows, rather than passionately defies, the verdict of a critically disciplined understanding."[116] Carnell, as a mid-twentieth-century neo-evangelical Protestant apologetic theologian, is simply unwilling to go beyond the task of demonstrating the truth of the Christian faith on the basis of reason and objective evidences. For Kierkegaard, both right reason and any objective evidences that seek to offer external warrants overlook the essential paradox in any claim to Christian truth, which is that the truth can only be "located" in the spirit of the passionately committed subject as it attempts to overcome the dialectic of time and eternity. Since philosophical and theological proofs for God try to eliminate the paradox, it follows, says Kierkegaard, that the connection between offense and Christianity is threatened.[117] Carnell reminds his readers at this point:

> Let us note the inner disgust, which Kierkegaard felt when he contemplated the way philosophers and theologians formulated rational "proofs" of God's existence. This kind of logical exercise brought no inner suffering; rather it brought a conceited sense of intellectual triumph and this conceit was further evidence that both philosophers and theologians tended to fear the want of prestige more than they feared the person of God.[118]

Carnell was committed to the idea that in order for Christianity to be "true," it had to be able to be defended on the basis of rationality and objective certainty through observation and demonstration. "Kierkegaard seemed to have missed this elementary philosophic insight, and as a result he made some judgments about faith which are dreadfully weak."[119] In the early dissertation, Carnell claimed that "Kierkegaard, by breaking with the ubiquity of coherence, left the criteria epistemologically and metaphysically unfortified. By encouraging men to become Christians in defiance of reason Kierkegaard corrupted the uniqueness of commitment to Christ."[120] This is exactly what Kierkegaard would have wanted. Carnell was unwilling to leave behind certainty and rationality to passionately embrace paradox, to risk absurdity for the sake of *Existenz*. The idea that Kierkegaard suggested this offended Carnell

---

115   Carnell, *Philosophy of the Christian Religion*, p. 489.
116   Carnell, *Christian Commitment*, p. 78.
117   Carnell, *The Burden of Søren Kierkegaard*, p. 73.
118   Ibid., pp. 72–3.
119   Ibid., p. 170.
120   Carnell, *The Problem of Verification in Sören Kierkegaard*, p. 289.

and rightly so, says Kierkegaard! The dialectical claim that inwardness makes on a subject is terrifying and disturbing, and yet this is what it means to be a Christian for Kierkegaard. Carnell simply rejects this vision and goes his separate way, writing volume after volume breathlessly arguing that no, in fact, the Christian must passionately pursue certainty, because it is only by demonstrating that the theological claims of faith are grounded and warranted that we can embrace them. The differences between Carnell and Kierkegaard cannot be clearer.

And yet, Carnell's final published words reveal a scholar who has spent a professional lifetime wrestling and struggling with Kierkegaard and is left with a special appreciation and deep respect. I, too, will close with them:

> Kierkegaard was a genius in his ability to bring man closer to God and God closer to man. His guiding rule was that an absolute devotion should be given to an absolute telos, and a relative devotion to a relative telos. With the help of this rule, Kierkegaard succeeded in defining an existential approach to the existing individual. This approach is exciting, to say the least.[121]

---

[121]   Carnell, *The Burden of Søren Kierkegaard*, p. 172.

Bibliography

I. References to or Uses of Kierkegaard in Carnell's Corpus

An Introduction to Christian Apologetics, Grand Rapids, Michigan: Eerdmans 1948, pp. 106–11.
The Problem of Verification in Sören Kierkegaard, Ph.D. Thesis, Boston University 1949.
A Philosophy of Christian Religion, Grand Rapids, Michigan: Eerdmans 1952, p. 202; pp. 259–66; p. 346; p. 449; p. 458; pp. 463–75; pp. 481–6; p. 489; p. 496.
Christian Commitment: An Apologetic, New York: Macmillan 1957, pp. 14ff.; pp. 73–8; p. 130; pp. 139ff.
The Burden of Søren Kierkegaard, Grand Rapids, Michigan: Eerdmans 1965.

II. Sources of Edward John Carnell's Knowledge of Kierkegaard

Allen, E.L., *Kierkegaard: His Life and Thought*, London: Stanley Nott 1935.
Clowney, Edward P., "A Critical Estimate of Søren Kierkegaard's Notion of the Individual," *Westminister Theological Review*, vol. 5, 1942, pp. 29–61.
Haecker, Theodor, *Søren Kierkegaard*, trans. by Alexander Dru, London: Oxford University Press 1937.
Kierkegaard, Søren, *Philosophical Fragments*, trans. by David F. Swenson, Princeton: Princeton University Press 1936.
— *Journals of Søren Kierkegaard*, trans. by Alexander Dru, London: Oxford University Press 1938.
— *The Point of View for My Work as an Author*, trans. by Walter Lowrie, London: Oxford University Press 1939.
— *Christian Discourses*, trans. by Walter Lowrie, London: Oxford University Press 1940.
— *The Present Age*, trans. by Alexander Dru and Walter Lowrie, London: Oxford University Press 1940.
— *Stages on Life's Way*, trans. by Walter Lowrie, Princeton: Princeton University Press 1940.
— *Concluding Unscientific Postscript to the "Philosophical Fragments,"* trans. by David F. Swenson, Princeton: Princeton University Press and American-Scandinavian Foundation 1941.
— *Fear and Trembling*, trans. by Walter Lowrie, Princeton: Princeton University Press 1941.
— *Repetition*, trans. by Walter Lowrie, Princeton: Princeton University Press 1941.

— *The Sickness unto Death*, trans. by Walter Lowrie, Princeton: Princeton University Press 1941.

— *Either/Or: A Fragment of Life*, vols. 1–2, trans. by David F. Swenson and Lillian Marvin Swenson, Princeton: Princeton University Press 1944.

— *The Concept of Dread*, trans. by Walter Lowrie, Princeton: Princeton University Press 1944.

— *For Self Examination and Judge for Yourselves!*, trans. by Walter Lowrie. Princeton: Princeton University Press 1944.

— *Kierkegaard's Attack upon "Christendom,"* trans. by Walter Lowrie, Princeton: Princeton University Press 1944.

— *Training in Christianity*, trans. by Walter Lowrie, Princeton: Princeton University Press 1944.

— *Works of Love*, trans. by Lillian Marvin Swenson, Princeton: Princeton University Press 1946.

Lowrie, Walter, *Kierkegaard*, London: Oxford University Press 1938.

— *A Short Life of Kierkegaard*, Princeton, New Jersey: Princeton University Press 1946.

Patrick, Denzil G.M., *Pascal and Kierkegaard: A Study in the Strategy of Evangelism*, vols. 1–2, London: Lutterworth 1947.

Safier, Fred Jacob, *The Philosophy of Søren Kierkegaard*, Ph.D. Thesis, Harvard University, Cambridge, Massachusetts 1934.

Swenson, David F., *Something about Kierkegaard*, Minneapolis: Augsburg 1941.

Thomte, Reidar, *Kierkegaard's Philosophy of Religion*, Princeton, New Jersey: Princeton University Press 1948.

Wild, John, "Kierkegaard and Classic Philosophy" *The Philosophy Review*, vol. 49, no. 5, 1940, pp. 536–51.

III. Secondary Literature of Carnell's Relation to Kierkegaard

Hein, Steven Arthur, *The Nature and Existence of Man in the Apologetic Mission of Edward John Carnell*, Ph.D. Thesis, Saint Louis University 1987, p. 2; pp. 52ff.; p. 56; p. 59, note 3; pp. 62ff.; p. 88; p. 205; pp. 209–10; p. 212; pp. 218–27; p. 233; p. 255; pp. 242ff.; p. 246; p. 252.

Nelson, Rudolph, *The Making and Unmaking of an Evangelical Mind*, New York: Cambridge University Press 1987, p. 5; p. 75; p. 84; p. 118; p. 127; pp. 151ff.; p. 161; p. 215; p. 221; p. 236, note 2.

Sims, John, *Missionaries to the Skeptics: Christian Apologists for the Twentieth Century*, Macon, Georgia: Mercer University Press 1995, pp. 143ff.

Harvey Gallagher Cox, Jr.:

An Uncomfortable Theologian Wary of Kierkegaard

Silas Morgan

The name Søren Kierkegaard is not often mentioned in the works of Harvey Gallagher Cox, Jr. (b. 1929). Nor is he cited, referenced or used frequently in his speeches, articles, or literature reviews. In fact, one is left wondering, even after a close review of his work, both early and mature, whether Cox has even read Kierkegaard closely. As such, no scholarly examination of Cox's reception of Kierkegaard existed prior to the publication of this article. Cox and Kierkegaard were interested in different things, fixated on solving different problems, and lived in different times. And yet, Kierkegaard is there, albeit at the margins, gestured to at critical moments. It is how and when Cox uses Kierkegaard that lends us some clues to what Cox knows of Kierkegaard and from where he might have learned of him. It is the task of this article to investigate that question.

I. Short Overview of Harvey G. Cox's Life and Work

Harvey Gallagher Cox, Jr. currently serves as the Hollis Professor of Divinity at Harvard Divinity School. Ordained as an American Baptist, Dr. Cox has served both in both academic and clerical roles as the Protestant chaplain at Temple University, a director of religious activities at Oberlin College, and an ecumenical fraternal worker in Berlin.

Early in his career, Cox published his landmark theological contribution in 1965: *The Secular City: Secularization and Urbanization in Theological Perspective.*[1] This book was an immense success, selling over one million copies and subsequently forming the theological conversation in America for decades. *The Secular City* seeks to reorient the critical study of religion in light of twin movements: secularization and urbanization. Celebrating the "collapse of traditional relation" as a positive movement for Christianity, Cox argues that the "present age" demands a radically new shape and style of Christianity, one that is freed from the tribal chains of "religion" and is freed to shape the church, not as an institution, but as a people of faith and social action. Following Bonhoeffer and Marx, this secular city (and the

---

[1]   Harvey Gallagher Cox, *The Secular City: Secularization and Urbanization in Theological Perspective*, New York: Macmillan 1965.

church's prophetic role inside it) demands the "exorcism" of religion as construed by modernity in favor of a dual commitment to revolutionary social change and a "secular way of speaking about God."[2]

While there was a time when *The Secular City* enjoyed great popularity, it has been often criticized in recent years for its earnest optimism reminiscent of the early 1960s and the American political pragmatism of the Kennedy era. Cox writes, "the *Secular City* was itself too sweeping, too global, too universalizing in its language."[3] In order to correct this, Cox moved in a more "spiritual direction" in his later work, eager to cull the theology and practices of base communities in Central and South America. Cox appreciates these traditions for the way they reflect the folk piety of American Protestantism; he enunciates the elements of liberation theology that he still values from his days as a fraternal worker in post-war Germany as well as his love for Bonhoeffer's eagerness to jettison religion altogether in the modern/ postmodern milieu.

Cox remains committed to the cause of a secular re-calibration of "religious" Christendom, whether by the use of comedy (*Feast of Fools*, 1969)[4] or a fresh examination of spiritual experience and global religious confession (*Seduction of the Spirit*, 1973;[5] *Turning East*, 1977).[6] In 1984 he published *Religion in the Secular City*,[7] signaling a major shift in his own theology towards an interest in Pentecostalism and liberation theology. Noticing the failure of modern theology, Cox welcomes the turn toward postmodern theology by examining two major theological options in the global scene: American Protestant fundamentalism and Latin American Catholic liberation theology. In search for a theology that comes up from the bottom and the edge, one that makes sense of the dissonance in the postmodern world, Cox determines that while fundamentalism offers little of use in the development of a postmodern theology, liberation theology proves to be a powerful resource for thinking through the critical issues that concern a global community in the postmodern milieu.

Cox's interest in the shape of global religion led to the publication of *Many Mansions* (1988),[8] an exploration into religious pluralism from a Bonhoefferian perspective, and *Fire from Heaven* (1994),[9] an attempt to make sense of

---

[2]   Ibid., pp. 241–2.

[3]   Harvey Gallagher Cox, "Response to Commentators," *Sociological Analysis*, vol. 45, no. 2, 1984, p. 109.

[4]   Harvey Gallagher Cox, *The Feast of Fools: A Theological Essay on Festivity and Fantasy*, Cambridge, Massachusetts: Harvard University Press 1969.

[5]   Harvey Gallagher Cox, *The Seduction of the Spirit: The Use and Misuse of People's Religion*, New York: Simon and Schuster 1973.

[6]   Harvey Gallagher Cox, *Turning East: The Promise and Peril of the New Orientalism*, New York: Simon and Schuster 1977.

[7]   Harvey Gallagher Cox, *Religion in the Secular City: Toward a Postmodern Theology*, New York: Simon and Schuster 1984.

[8]   Harvey Gallagher Cox, *Many Mansions: A Christian's Encounter with Other Faiths*, Boston: Beacon Press 1988.

[9]   Harvey Gallagher Cox, *The Rise of Pentecostal Spirituality and the Reshaping of Religion in the Twenty-First Century*, Reading, Massachusetts: Addison-Wesley 1994.

pneumatological spirituality in Latin America and its potential influence on a global characterization of religious confession and experience. Shortly after the release of a *Festschrift, Religion in a Secular City* (2001),[10] Cox published *When Jesus Came to Harvard: Making Moral Choices Today* (2004),[11] a result of decades of teaching a very popular undergraduate course on ethics at Harvard Divinity School.

Cox emerges into the twenty-first century as a major figure in American liberal theology. Never entirely comfortable with that label himself, he embraces what he calls a "radical" theology—an attempt to articulate religion, not as a set of closed world-views, but rather as a confessional commitment, and understands the church as the *avant-garde* of God's kingdom that offers hope for the future of all peoples—a hope that is both political and theological, both eschatological and immediate.

II. Kierkegaard in Cox's The Secular City (1965)

Analyzing the use of Kierkegaard in the work of Harvey Cox is particularly complicated, frankly, because Cox does not appropriate Kierkegaard in any clear ways. His references to Kierkegaard tend to be quite scattered and superficial. At no point does Cox offer a detailed reading of Kierkegaard, nor does he frequently provide a citation to point his readers to a particular place in Kierkegaard's work that he has in mind. Yet, what we do find in Cox is a certain characterization of Kierkegaard that proves salient, not only in better understanding Cox's own theology, but also Kierkegaard's place inside it.

Cox's *The Secular City* offers a sociological reading of Bonhoeffer's desire to speak of God in a secular fashion and find a non-religious interpretation of biblical concepts. Identifying the twin movements of urbanization and secularization as helpful, if not uniquely central, to biblical Christianity, Cox firmly argues that the religious and the secular are not disparate spheres, but rather dialectical ways of being. They do not exist in mutual exclusion—but in the case of the secular individual, for example—operate in paradoxical harmony.[12] Clearly, this concern has direct links to Kierkegaard's interest in articulating the single individual as both a religious and secular category that must be held in paradoxical tension. Cox's interest in holding the secular and "religious" together in the life of the human person is seemingly inspired by Kierkegaard's refusal to allow the secular to be isolated from the religious and vice versa. Just as Cox is not interested in abandoning Christianity for secularism,[13] but only the religious form of Christianity, Kierkegaard speaks against Christendom, belonging to the lower stages of existence—aesthetic and ethical—in favor of preserving biblical Christianity.

---

[10]   *Religion in a Secular City: Essays in Honor of Harvey Cox*, ed. by Arvind Sharma, Harrisburg, Pennsylvania: Trinity Press 2001.

[11]   Harvey Gallagher Cox, *When Jesus Came to Harvard: Making Moral Choices Today*, Boston: Houghton Mifflin 2004.

[12]   Brayton Polka, "Who Is the Single Individual? On the Religious and Secular in Kierkegaard," *Philosophy & Theology*, vol. 17, nos. 1–2, 2007, p. 162.

[13]   Cox, *The Secular City*, p. 20.

While much of *The Secular City* is of a sociological nature, Cox's most sustained theological concern (which seems to be sustained through his entire body of work, but most clearly in his early work) is to further and complete Bonhoeffer's search for a way to "speak in a secular fashion of God."[14] He cites Bonhoeffer extensively on this point, suggesting that Bonhoeffer's point is the natural one to consider, given that biblical Christianity ought to welcome secularization. Furthermore, in Cox's view, theology has never tried to speak about God at all, but rather only to attempt to make sense of the human experience of God as "that which we have named 'God.' "[15] It is because of the linguistic character of this naming that Cox articulates Bonhoeffer's question as a partially sociological one.

Cox and Bonhoeffer join together in working from the Kierkegaardian conviction that the language people use to speak about things is usually not their own, but given to them by others—namely, religious authorities and clergy; this is particularly problematic for Cox because it is only bound to result in mass confusion. Citing Kierkegaard's parable of the clowns and the circus fire as an example of the slippage between the communication of assigned meaning and the role of the communicator in the exchange, Cox challenged the "meaning-world" currently offered by the clergy, suggesting instead that the secular city serves to alter the social context in which "God" is named, addressing specifically the metaphysical system employed by most academics—very far from the experiences of ordinary people who are trying rightly to understand God for themselves.[16] This frustration echoes Kierkegaard's own sensibilities; he looked to free the Lutheran Church from pastoral hegemony and the deification of the social order.

The "secular city" of Cox's design is formed by sociological observations of urbanization and celebrates many features of the city previously opposed in Western intellectual and cultural tradition. For example, in regards to "anonymity" in the shape of the secular city, Cox tries to work against an established fear about loss of selfhood and identity in the mass amalgamation that is the modern city. Cox cities Kierkegaard as one who "fulminated brilliantly against certain elements of mass society and urban life in *The Present Age* (1846)."[17] He cites many other authors as

---

[14]   Ibid., pp. 241–3.
[15]   The indebtedness of Bonhoeffer to Kierkegaard on several counts is well documented. It will be come clear that just as there has been much discussion regarding how sophisticated Bonhoeffer's knowledge of the Kierkegaardian authorship was, the same concern is valid concerning the relationship between Cox and Kierkegaard. Cf. Stephen Plant, *Bonhoeffer*, London: Continuum 2004, pp. 46–9. Here Plant argues that while there appears to be considered conceptual parallels between Kierkegaard and Bonhoeffer, the fact that Bonhoeffer rarely discusses Kierkegaard directly, makes an attempt to give concrete articulations of their relationship, quite problematic. See also Andreas Pangritz, *Karl Barth in the Theology of Dietrich Bonhoeffer*, Grand Rapids, Michigan: Eerdmans 2000, pp. 53–6, for a clear treatment of Bonhoeffer's early interest in Kierkegaardian inwardness and individuality. A parallel should be drawn between the way that Kierkegaard functions in both the work of Cox and Bonhoeffer; it demonstrates the same general knowledge, but lacks the detailed textual knowledge of key Kierkegaardian texts.
[16]   Cox, *The Secular City*, pp. 246–7.
[17]   Ibid., p. 39.

fellow contributors to the intellectual resistance to urbanization, but suggests that their consternation is misdirected and misguided. Instead, he argues that urbanization provides "the possibility of freedom" in addition to assistance in the preservation of privacy.[18] For Kierkegaard, the "present age" of Christianity in Denmark was "a sensible, reflecting age, devoid of passion, flaring up in superficial, short-lived enthusiasm and prudentially relaxing in indolence."[19] These opening words to *A Literary Review* summarize what was, to Kierkegaard, the greatest threat to the health of the Christian faith in Denmark. The modernizing influences had led to a disappearance of the individual as center of value in favor of the modern democratic liberal ideal of equality: "The individual does not belong to God, to himself, to the beloved, to his art, to his scholarship; no as just a serf belongs to an estate, so the individual realizes that in every respect he belongs to an abstraction in which reflection subordinates him."[20] This has only succeeded in destroying the concrete historical community that forms the basis for biblical Christianity. Cox rightly notes that for Kierkegaard, democratic liberalism, the heart of Danish modernization and the foundation for "the secular city," leads to a negative unity that spuriously replaces the social and historical traditions for a new "leveled" definition of human nature, eradicating the ethical-religious form of life.[21] While Cox valorizes the way that urbanization leads to anonymity, Kierkegaard castigates his contemporaries for this very thing—the leveling of individuality into a corporate identity that erases the particularity of the single person in favor of an abstraction "that forms no personal, intimate relation to any particular individual, but only the relation of abstraction, which is the same for all."[22] For Kierkegaard, this sort of intimate relation is the very foundation of love and also faithful religion. The "leveling" of the society only contributes to a religiousness where the self can be never alone before God, but always faces God alongside others, an idea that Cox and Kierkegaard evaluate quite differently. "The environment, the contemporary age, has neither events nor integrated passion, but in a negative unity creates a reflective opposition that toys for a moment with the unreal prospect and then resorts to the brilliant equivocation that the smartest thing has been done, after all, by doing nothing."[23]

On one hand, Cox valorized the "shape" of the secular city for the way that "it denotes the disappearance of religious determination of the symbols of cultural integration."[24] This disenchantment leads to the anonymity[25] and mobility[26] that represents the secular city's deliverance for religious mandates, creating the space for radical social change. Cox clearly disagrees with Kierkegaard on the score that

18   Ibid., p. 40.
19   *SKS* 8, 64 / *TA*, 68.
20   *SKS* 8, 79 / *TA*, 85.
21   *SKS* 8, 71 / *TA*, 74. *SKS* 8, 83 / *TA*, 86.
22   *SKS* 8, 85 / *TA*, 88. It is precisely the abstract grouping in "the age of reflection" that prevents the sort of "revolutionary" relationship with the real world, constructed through action, from which, according to Kierkegaard, the authentic life of subjectivity arises.
23   *SKS* 8, 68 / *TA*, 69.
24   Cox, *The Secular City*, p. 20.
25   Ibid., p. 39.
26   Ibid., p. 49.

these characteristics of the city bring freedom, and yet for Kierkegaard, this freedom is a negative production of the aesthetic life,[27] where the primary concern is pleasure, not the good or religious life motivated by values and passionate action.[28]

Discussing the cross-cultural dimensions of the Gospel in the secular city, he cites Kierkegaard's pessimism concerning how faithful a Christian can be in a "religious" environment that has "religious values" that are cultural products: "Kierkegaard asked how it was even possible to be a 'Christian in Christendom.' He wondered how a man could say 'yes' to the Gospel when its message was so obfuscated by its compromised involvement with European culture and bourgeois values."[29] Cox certainly sees Kierkegaard as a church reformer. In an early 1969 article in *Cross Currents*, Cox refers to Kierkegaard as an example of the established "tradition of radical criticism of Christian beliefs by Christians," and cites (ever so briefly) his *Attack on the Church* as evidence of his participation in this tradition.[30]

Kierkegaard's denunciation of the State Church comes from his concern with its willingness to cooperate with the "Babylonian captivity" of nationalism, by forgetting that to be Christ-like is to live in imitation of the absolute paradox—Jesus Christ himself. The use of the Christian faith to advance any political agenda,[31] let alone one that sanctions abdicating the obligation to obey God, explicitly ignores the task of the Christian faith: to acknowledge the need for grace through an inward search of subjectivity for knowledge, not only of God, but to come to one's own self-knowledge through action.[32] The values of the Christian confession demand a certain criticalness that presupposes struggle and resistance[33] to the values of external European culture—anything else simply masquerades as "Sunday Christianity" and hypocrisy of bloodguilt.[34] Kierkegaard infamously castigates Denmark Lutheranism as "Christendom"[35] for its acquiescence to external forms of life and cultural discourse;[36] for him, absurdity of Christian confession refuses to be shaped by its

---

[27]   Ibid., p. 47.

[28]   Ibid., p. 40.

[29]   Ibid., p. 91.

[30]   Harvey Gallagher Cox, "Non-Theistic Commitments," *Cross Currents*, vol. 9, no. 4, 1969, p. 401.

[31]   *Pap.* XI–2 A 410 / *JP* 4, 4504.

[32]   *SV1* XII, 401 / *JFY*, 121–2. Kierkegaard is anxious to convince his reader that self-knowledge comes after the moment of action. It is in acting towards truth that one comes to know, rightfully, what is true, and thus avoiding the travesty that is self-denial, ironically missing out on what it means to be "sober." See also *SKS* 20, 57–8, NB:69 / *JP* 3, 2807. *SKS* 23, 27, NB15:33 / *JP* 3, 2821.

[33]   *SKS* 26, 14, NB31:13 / *JP* 4, 4709: "The characteristically Christian suffering is to suffer at the hands of men. This is consistent with the Christian view that to love God is to hate the world...."

[34]   *SKS* 13, 178–9 / *M*, 134–6.

[35]   For Kierkegaard, "Christendom" is not simply a derogatory identification of Christianity as the State Church in a Constantinian way. "Is not 'Christendom' the greatest possible attempt to worship God by 'building and adorning the graves of the righteous'?" *SKS* 13, 177 / *M*, 133.

[36]   *SKS* 24, 38–9, NB21:50 / *JP* 4, 4660.

relation to other cultural forms of life and discourse: "to be a Christian is, to speak merely humanly, sheer agony, an agony compared with which all other human sufferings are almost childish pranks. What Christ is speaking about—he makes no secret of it—is about crucifying the flesh, hating oneself, suffering for the doctrine, about weeping and wailing while the world rejoices."[37]

Cox disagrees and argues instead that the rapidly increasing secularization of Europe ameliorates Kierkegaard's concerns about living Christianly in a worldly cultural space. In some ways, secularization can be friendly to radical Christian living since culture sheds religious logic in its own self-description.[38] With the separation of society and religion, it has helped Christianity become more "religionless," which harkens back to the way that Cox understands Bonhoeffer's understanding of Christianity as "religionless." Focusing on the way that Christianity is, by nature, not a religion, but rather a confession of faith, strikes this reader as centered on Kierkegaard's original concern about faith, namely that faith is subjectivity and subjectivity is truth. In his journals, Kierkegaard muses: "The thing is to find a truth which is true for me, to find the idea for which I can live and die…what use would it be to be able to propound the meaning of Christianity, to explain many different facts, if it had *no* deeper meaning *for me* and *my life*…."[39]

Addressing the profane qualities of the secular person, Cox addresses Barth's appropriation of Kierkegaard's insistence on the "infinite qualitative distinction" between time and eternity as an example of how Barth is concerned about the human person's ability to bridge the gap between itself and God.[40] God extends God's self toward the human person, on the basis of God's own initiative, not as a response to any movement or inclination of the human person. The chasm is bridged by Jesus Christ alone; it is Barth's insistence that "God…doesn't need man; therefore He can let man live," that prompts Cox to say, following Kierkegaard, that "as the last stages of myth and ontology disappear…man's freedom to master and shape, to create and explore now reaches out to the ends of the earth and beyond."[41] This "freedom" can be recognized by the discriminating reader in Kierkegaardian parlance as, "truth as subjectivity," the acknowledgement that since truth cannot be located in natural objects, it must be located in the relation between two or more subjects; it is the intersubjectivity of truth to which Cox gestures here, albeit, ever so slightly. Perhaps Cox's implicit distrust of philosophy springs forth from Kierkegaard's principle of subjectivity, outlined in (among other places*)* Johannes Climacus' *Concluding Unscientific Postscript*. In noting that "to become subjective should be the highest task assigned to every human being, just as the highest reward, an eternal happiness, exists only for the subjective person or correctly comes into existence for the one who becomes subjective,"[42] this process of *becoming* subjective is thoroughly inward and involves the abdication of any striving towards the object. "To subjective

---

[37]   *SKS* 13, 239 / *M*, 189.
[38]   Cox, *The Secular City*, p. 92.
[39]   *SKS* 17, 24, AA:12 / *KJN* 1, 19.
[40]   Cox, *The Secular City*, p. 82.
[41]   Ibid.
[42]   *SKS* 7, 151 / *CUP1*, 163.

32 Silas Morgan

reflection, truth becomes appropriation, inwardness, subjectivity, and the point is to immerse oneself existing in subjectivity."[43] Cox follows Kierkegaard in the frequent insistence that religion is a way of life, a matter for the single individual. This subjective pursuit in passionate devotion is the only way for authentic faith to emerge—"only momentarily can a particular individual, existing, be in a unity of the infinite and the finite that transcends existing."[44] Philosophy fails because it pursues systems of fact that do not include the particularity of the individual person. Cox seems to take his cue from Kierkegaard in their joint contention that religion must be a personal choice, an intentional way of life, and a determined policy of action. "At its highest, inwardness in an existing subject is passion; truth as a paradox corresponds to passion and that truth becomes a paradox is grounded precisely in its relation to an existing subject."[45]

For Cox (and in many ways, Kierkegaard), theology is always political. Following the liberal political conceptions of the 1960s, this meant that theology in the secular city is fundamentally about encouraging and instituting radical social change—the backbone of Cox's secular city. This is tied intently to biblical eschatological notions of the realized future that opens itself up to humanity only to draw back its hand at the last moment, yet touching us ever so slightly. These experiences with the "emerging realities of history" open us up to new political possibilities, which require a vulnerability to progress. It is this generous, existential posture towards evolutionary history and progression that Cox reads in Kierkegaard. Citing him as saying "we are always becoming Christians,"[46] this process of becoming is precisely the evolutionary conversion demanded if we are to experience a true, "permanent revolution." Again, unfortunately, Cox simply mentions Kierkegaard here without offering us an idea of what text or passage he is considering. Yet, it is clear that Cox is conceptually housed inside Kierkegaard's notion of the single individual's inwardness in order to suggest the kind of political process demanded by this "secularization" of religion— namely, the renewal of subjectivity by way of inwardness and passionate action. This process of "becoming a self before God" is imbedded inside Kierkegaard's demand of the single individual: *choose or be offended!* For it is in *choosing* oneself that the single individual elects to live inside the paradoxical tension between the religious and secular, rather than be offended by the absurdity of the object of faith, namely God. For Kierkegaard, "faith is the contradiction between the infinite passion of inwardness and the objective uncertainty. If I am able to apprehend God objectively, I do not have faith. If I want to keep myself in faith, I must continually see to it that I hold fast the objective uncertainty."[47] While Cox more clearly has Marx in mind as he argues for a "permanent revolution" where the "human effort to come to terms with the new historical reality" is realized in the "phenomenon of conversion,"[48] he utilizes Kierkegaard's willingness to embrace the unpredictably emergent character

---

[43] *SKS* 7, 208 / *CUP1*, 192.
[44] *SKS* 7, 213 / *CUP1*, 197.
[45] *SKS* 7, 216 / *CUP1*, 199.
[46] Cox, *The Secular City*, p. 122.
[47] *SKS* 7, 221 / *CUP1*, 204.
[48] Cox, *The Secular City*, p. 122.

of truth in history—namely, that as the nature of subjectivities change, the reality of history demands our willingness to change with it.

Furthering his argument that the process of urbanization is not foreign to the Christian faith, but rather quite friendly to its themes, Cox ties the Christian tradition to themes of mobility and "wandering," suggesting that the mobile shape of the secular city reverberates from the core of early Christian reflections on its own identity as a traveling community. Cox suggests that the notion that the Christian life is a journey is reflected in "Kierkegaard," a somewhat oblique and general reference to Kierkegaard's works as a whole.[49] This rather oblique reference to Kierkegaard provides few clues as to exactly what text or sources from Kierkegaard Cox has in mind, but also represents the way that Cox often uses Kierkegaard. He does not provide detailed explorations, but often simply includes him as a noted interlocutor, leaving it up to the reader to ascertain what it all means.

III. Kierkegaard in Cox's Later Works

As Cox seeks to articulate the shaped contours of a postmodern theology, he is convinced that it must not completely reject the modern theological project, but must go through it, acknowledging its failures, but refusing to disparage it because of its liberalism or its intellectualism.[50] With regard to this, Cox follows Kierkegaard in his concerns. The project, namely, to make the precepts and claims of Christianity credible to the modern mind of progress, reason, and science, appealed primarily to the intellectual elite who, skeptical of religious confession, required considerable persuasion about the applicability of the Christian faith to the modern *logos*, and thus modern theologians worked tirelessly to redefine the purpose and, to some extent, the content of theology in order to service this "evangelical purpose." Surely, this echoes Kierkegaard's primary concern about the church's theology in his age, and Cox is apt enough to acknowledge this. While acknowledging that Kierkegaard can "often sound modern despite (himself), preoccupied as (he was) with the new age and the mistakes (he) believed (his) contemporaries were making in dealing with it,"[51] Cox questions how helpful Kierkegaard can be in working out of the modern paradigm, given how embedded his work is in the conversation of Enlightenment modernity. Cox's evaluation of Kierkegaard on this score provides perhaps the clearest clue to his overall reception of Kierkegaard. Wary of Kierkegaard's finer points, Cox still finds him conceptually helpful in making sense of some broad theological strokes.

Continuing in his quest to make better sense of the way religion functions culturally, particularly in North American, in *Feast of Fools* Cox offers a theology of play and comedy. In addressing the possible concern that a theology of comedic play might not be appropriate for a historical and political age dominated by war, violence, and poverty, Cox dismisses the objection on the grounds that it misunderstands comedy and forgets its subversive nature. "The comic sensibility can laugh at those who ferment wars and perpetuate hunger, at the same time it struggles to dethrone

---

49   Ibid., p. 57.
50   Cox, *Religion in the Secular City*, p. 68.
51   Ibid., p. 180.

them. It foresees their downfall even when their power seems secure."[52] This sort of "ironic" comedy inspires creative solutions to perennial problems by encouraging imaginative patterns for innovation that are lost on purely academic theorizing—according to Cox. This becomes problematic when thinking about the religious concern for Cox, because as he notes, there is a sustained philosophical problem with gaining an "external perspective" on a person's own religious confession and/or expression. Or as Cox suggests, "can we 'step back' from the symbols of our religion" or "does doing so require a sort of 'undoing' of sorts that leaves the symbols or language of our religion behind?"[53] Cox gestures towards Kierkegaard in a characteristically general mention by suggesting that he represents an argument that this external perspective, sought by Cox, on a subject's own religion is impossible. While Cox notes that "Kierkegaard was the first theological thinker in the modern period to say much about the comic, in his work on irony,"[54] he is skeptical of his position on the subject: "For Kierkegaard one always has to be "inside" some order of existence. Though a person can have a sense of comic distance about someone else's ultimate symbols, he cannot have such a perspective on his own. Otherwise he would not be existing at all."[55] Cox offers a *via media*, a theory of juxtaposition of the multiple and disparate spheres of life in which the modern person lives each day. This intentional life in tense spaces creates the comedic situations that open up innovative and critical spaces for reflection and interpretation. Kierkegaard calls this "the composition of oneself poetically."[56]

In the appendix of *Feast of Fools*, Cox lets us in on his own positions on the contemporary theological conversations at the time of authorship, the fourth of which was phenomenological method of Edmund Husserl, which he understands as an explanation and exploration of human consciousness, apart from rational or logical analysis, in order to make sense of the structure of human experience. This opens space for the phenomenological theologian to pay attention to things previously considered by philosophy as unhelpful or uninteresting. Cox mentions Kierkegaard as a suggested correlate figure to Husserl in that "some of his books" seem to reflect the sort of philosophizing suggested by Husserl's phenomenology.[57] Perhaps this is why Cox finds it helpful to identify Kierkegaard as a friendly resource for his examinations of folk religious experience; by reading Kierkegaard as a phenomenologist, Cox is able to locate, however superficially, Kierkegaard's own interest in the structure of relations as constitutive not only for "religious" experience, but even more fundamentally—the life of being itself.

For Cox, it is religion that threatens the actual world; comedy and irony help human persons get beyond the imposing specter of religious claims on the actual world. If the comedic is to be understood theologically as a subversive rejection of the status quo, Cox is right to distinguish his position for Kierkegaard's. From the perspective of the

---

52   Cox, *Feast of Fools*, p. 153.
53   Ibid., p. 196.
54   Ibid., p. 194.
55   Ibid., p. 154.
56   *SKS* 1, 316 / *CI*, 280–1.
57   Cox, *Feast of Fools*, p. 169.

latter, Cox's theology of ironic play is the attempt of the human person to become something of her own design—namely "to compose oneself poetically" outside the demands of the actual world. For Kierkegaard, we are not our own; we are, instead, called to become something in particular—individual selves before God.

Kierkegaard's early interest in irony forms an exegetical paradigm for his authorship, particularly his later pseudonymous writings. His earliest substantial published work, *The Concept of Irony*, establishes his articulation of pure irony as "infinite absolute negativity."[58] Kierkegaard articulates "irony" as the critical disengagement from ordered human society fueled by a detached stance and socio-political posture against "actuality."[59] Ironists are those individuals who desire to be freed from the particularity and normativity of the established social order and civil society (Hegel's *Sittlichkeit*). Motivated by a desire for negative freedom, those who live in irony—the "romantic ironists"—see gaps between what is and what ought to be (or more critically, what they wish it was),[60] and in pursuit of a creation of that ideal world, create an intentionally critical distance from what is "crooked" or disordered in this world in favor of the possibility of a beginning.[61] This beginning, in Kierkegaard's view, requires a suspension of the requirements of actuality and, as such, is a negative freedom—the creation of space to do nothing.[62] This freedom, passionately desired by the ironist is, in truth, a false and destructive abdication of the gift and task of the actual. For Kierkegaard, ironists relate mistakenly to irony, and as such they fail to grasp the point of living, the object of "poetry." In their attempt to compose themselves poetically, the ironists ignore the social and relational identity of the human person in favor of a destructive selfishness.[63]

Cox fundamentally believes that theology is peculiarly "political." In Cox's early work, *God's Revolution and Man's Responsibility* (1965),[64] he argued that the development of theology happens uniquely inside of and connected to particularly political moments. Christianity has a history of acquiescing to political power, mostly for the purpose of self-protection. Existing as passive participants in public spheres, this sort of ecclesial posturing leads to an essential "merging of faith and docility,"[65] a merging to which Kierkegaard, Marx, and Nietzsche would angrily object. Cox notes this:

> Each was condemned by the church, but each was right in his own way. Kierkegaard taught that the only real sin was "the despairing refusal to be oneself.".…For Kierkegaard and for those contemporary existentialists who are most influenced by him, the

---

[58]   *SKS* 1, 297 / *CI*, 259. *SKS* 1, 299 / *CI*, 261.

[59]   *SKS* 1, 286 / *CI*, 247. *SKS* 1, 292 / *CI*, 253.

[60]   *SKS* 1, 294–5 / *CI*, 255–6.

[61]   *SKS* 1, 295 / *CI*, 256.

[62]   *SKS* 1, 285 / *CI*, 258.

[63]   *SKS* 1, 306 / *CI*, 269–70.

[64]   Harvey Gallagher Cox, *God's Revolution and Man's Responsibility*, Valley Forge, Pennsylvania: Judson Press 1965.

[65]   Ibid., p. 46.

individual must choose his own identity and not allow himself to be named by images and expectations others inflict upon him.[66]

The choice facing the single individual before God, as Cox sees it in Kierkegaard (and rightly so), is namely this—choose yourself or be offended![67] "As Kierkegaard, Marx, and Nietzsche saw, to be a man involved personal, social, and cultural initiative and responsibility. It means to accept the terrifying duty of deciding who I will be rather than merely injecting stereotypes that others assign to me."[68] Cox receives from Kierkegaard the core mandate of the single individual when faced with the choice of faith in the midst of cultural demands. For Kierkegaard, this was the Christian moment, "the expectancy," by which one leaps from religiousness to the absurdity of faithfulness. M. Jamie Ferreira rightly calls this "the qualitative transition" into faith, not of faith, as if the faith is the energy behind the leaping, since for Kierkegaard, this leap is a volitional springing into the absurdity of what is claimed by the Christian.[69] The concept of the leap or transition starts in Johannes Climacus' *Concluding Unscientific Postscript*, where he links the religious transformation of the faithful leap as a sort of "letting go"[70] while reminding us that though Climacus is skeptical at best about the possibility of such a transformation, if one were to be possible, it would have to involve "an act of freedom, an expression of will" for there to be a decisive qualitative leap,[71] thus resisting the Hegelian preference for a category of transition that is either automatic or cumulative.[72] It could be said that it is precisely Kierkegaard's emphasis on decisive action and volitional engagement that Cox finds helpful in articulating why the political is so central to understanding the properly Christian participation in politics and religion in the modern world.

Brad Frazier argues that Kierkegaard's core object, as a religious author, is to examine the structure of consciousness as spirit.[73] Concerned not to give up the elastic creativity of the Hegelian dialectic of subjectivity, Kierkegaard understands consciousness as the particular irony that overcomes the opposition of what is real and what is ideal. Frazier right notes that this is not accomplished by resolution, but (ironically) through the contradictory tension that Kierkegaard calls "the first pain of becoming," that, while resisting domination by authoritative voices, becomes relativized in favor of the uncertainty of passion and of faith in order to become oneself, rightly before God."[74] Frazier is concerned to interpret Kierkegaard's interest in the inward process of becoming as oppositional to the ironic development of the

---

[66]   Ibid.

[67]   Ibid

[68]   Ibid., p. 47.

[69]   M. Jamie Ferreira, *Transforming Vision: Imagination and Will in Kierkegaardian Faith*, Oxford: Clarendon Press 1991, p. 207.

[70]   Ibid., p. 210. See also *SKS* 7, 48 / *CUP1*, 43.

[71]   *SKS* 7, 83 / *CUP1*, 83. *SKS* 7, 374 / *CUP1*, 381.

[72]   *SKS* 24, 429, NB24:165 / *JP* 1, 110.

[73]   Brad Frazier, "Kierkegaard on the Problems of Pure Irony," *Journal of Religious Ethics*, vol. 32, no. 3, 2004, pp. 417–47.

[74]   Frazier, "Kierkegaard on the Problems of Pure Irony," p. 441.

person as "living poetically."[75] Frazier cites Kierkegaard, "the poet does not live poetically by creating a poetic work…but he lives poetically only when he himself is oriented and thus integrated in the age in which he lives, is positively free in the actuality to which he belongs."[76] Frazier rightly notes "that Kierkegaard here equates living poetically with becoming positively free….For Kierkegaard, a person becomes positively free when she relates properly to her actuality, when she recognizes it as a gift and task and lives responsibly within it."[77] It is in locating the human person rightly inside the concrete world of actuality that Cox is concerned with in *God's Revolution*. While Cox and Kierkegaard are both interested in examining how the single individual might faithfully live, worship, and serve, embedded as she is in this complexly bound and textured space, it would be overreaching to suggest that Cox receives this emphasis from Kierkegaard, and overstating the way that Cox reads Kierkegaard as he later will disagree with Kierkegaard's particular concern with the individual in favor of a more interpersonal approach to the community's relation to God and world.

Examining the topic of testimony or giving witness and its lack of presence in theology in *Seduction of the Spirit*, Cox bemoans the lack of interiority by theologians and religious authors.[78] He notes of course that Kierkegaard (and other historical figures in theology) left us their journals in order to help make sense of the autobiographical dimensions of their work. Cox argues for "a reinstatement of the personal dimension among the others. It might combat the massive demotion of interiority that curses our age and correct the false impression that theology is written by sophisticated data processors."[79] This interest in more disclosure of a theologian's interiority is based on what is rather obvious—theology does not develop in or through a vacuum of real life or real people and that consciousness, theologically understood, must require reflection on topics previously deemed peripheral.

In *Common Prayers*,[80] Cox's exploration of the relationship between Christian and Jewish spirituality, he finds Kierkegaard's retelling and interpretation of the biblical narrative of Abraham and Isaac in *Fear and Trembling* to be as "extraordinary" as it is unpleasant. There is something about the nature and character of God that troubles us, something that we had rather believe to be untrue. Cox finds in Kierkegaard's narration of the story the undeniable and yet disturbing fact that God's ways are "arbitrary and inscrutable, even terrifying."[81] Cox finds Kierkegaard's emphasis helpful and appropriate, though it does not make him feel better about what the story reveals about God and the humanity. "The main point Kierkegaard sees in the Abraham & Isaac story is that obedience to God can require us to turn away from the cultural codes and expectations of our era….God gives and takes away without

---

[75]   Sylvia Walsh, *Living Poetically: Kierkegaard's Existential Aesthetics*, University Park, Pennsylvania: Pennsylvania State University Press 1994, p. 57.

[76]   *SKS* 7, 297 / *CUP1*, 326.

[77]   Frazier, "Kierkegaard on the Problems of Pure Irony," p. 443.

[78]   Cox, *The Seduction of the Spirit*, p. 98.

[79]   Ibid., p. 99.

[80]   Harvey Gallagher Cox, *Common Prayers: Faith, Family, and a Christian's Journey Through the Jewish Year*, Boston: Houghton Mifflin 2001.

[81]   Cox, *Common Prayers*, p. 22.

giving any reason."[82] While God's motive is not present in the story, Cox agrees with Kierkegaard that this is not important. What is crucial to Cox here is the way in which Kierkegaard battles against the culturalization of Christianity, resisting the idea that the Christian life is one of ease, complacency or simple observance, but instead argues in favor of a vision of faith that brings on "fear and trembling."

Searching after the inner meaning of the binding of Isaac in *Fear and Trembling*, Kierkegaard "sensed that what his comfortable bourgeois neighbors called Christianity was bogus."[83] One was not born a Christian, says Kierkegaard, and on this point, Cox heartily agrees. Cox finds in Kierkegaard a like mind: Kierkegaard, too, was after a return to New Testament Christianity that requires one to fight against the main currents of society. "This story resonates with my moral sensibility: my final obligation is not to the national ethos, established moral codes, or even to the teachings of the church. It is to the other, and in the Abraham and Isaac story, I believe God represents the claim on me of the 'Other.' "[84] But Cox is right to admit what Kierkegaard is after is broader and more expansive: "He never wanted to organize a sectarian movement to oppose what he considered bogus Christianity"— his writings were to the individual.

This is where Cox finds a division between a Jewish and Christian reading of the story. "In heeding God's command, Abraham seems to cut himself off from the rest of the world where we normally make our moral decisions, this was an example of faith transcending ethics, it demonstrated the fundamental conflict between the individual and the crowd, Abraham refused to submit to the ethos of the tribe or herd."[85] Whereas Jews tend to focus on the way in which corporate identity shapes religious and ethical decision-making, Kierkegaard's Abraham is a celebration of the individualization of moral choices—thus Kierkegaard makes Abraham a sort of Lutheran Protestant.

As Cox has said on a couple of occasions, he is bothered by the Lutheran tendency to stress an individual's relation to God at the cost of communal dimensions of religious experience, for example, that make up the Jewish spiritual imagination. "I immediately suspect that it makes sense because although I disagree with Kierkegaard more often than I agree with him, he and I do share, in some respects a common Protestant tradition. For this reason, I hesitate to push his interpretation ahead of others."[86] Finally, Cox notes that Kierkegaard helps him realize that some decisions require leaving behind "church and state and culture, and even established ethical norms,"[87] in order to properly address the broken, fragmented state of our sinful world.

Along with this realignment of values in ethics, Cox finds Kierkegaard to be particularly helpful in diagnosing what is wrong with our world with a healthy notion of the Fall.[88] Along with Paul Tillich and Reinhold Niebuhr, Kierkegaard defends the

---

82   Ibid., p. 33.
83   Ibid.
84   Ibid., p. 35.
85   Ibid., p. 34.
86   Ibid.
87   Ibid., p. 36.
88   Ibid., p. 51.

validity of the Fall and uses sin as a metaphor for our flawed and precarious human condition that stands opposite faith. Cox cites *The Sickness unto Death* in noting that when "contemplating human existence, [Kierkegaard] noticed the sense of vertigo and anxiety that arises when we become aware of our finitude and how expert we are at deceiving ourselves about it."[89] Cox appreciates this honest evaluation in light of the way that liberal theology has attempted to wrap sin inside narratives of human progress, dismissing the emphasis on sin in the theological tradition as reflective of historical concerns during the Reformation, not as a constructive reality of contemporary reflection.

Cox's work has always demonstrated a sustained interest in sociological dimensions in the critical study of religion. His early work focused on the phenomena of urbanization and secularization. However, in *Religion in the Secular City*, Cox demonstrates a major shift in his own theological project when he turns his theological gaze south, examining religious culture and folk piety in base communities in Latin and Central America. Attempting to make sense of the way that theology changed at the twilight of modernity, he examines two different resources currently present in global Christianity (fundamentalism and liberation theology) before finally settling on the latter as having the most promise to help form a postmodern theology that helps make sense of the life from the "bottom" and the "edge."[90]

In articulating a major conceptual claim of American fundamentalism, Cox contends that fundamentalist beliefs about the way "faith" functions preclude people from taking the Kierkegaardian leap of faith. They would be quick to frown upon an assumption that, given the content and expectation of Christian faith, the sort of confessional belief Christianity demands is "absurd." The attempt to relate positively to the modern world through the embrace of reason and science has led fundamentalists to articulate the Christian faith in overly positivistic ways that rely too heavily on modern assumptions. Cox contends that, for fundamentalists, this means that Christian truth (or rather the rationality of the truth of the Christian faith) is hardwired into the DNA of how the world works. "Fundamentalists could never accept Kierkegaard's idea of the 'leap of faith,' " Cox writes. "They hold that faith is a perfectly reasonable step, not a leap."[91] Cox does not particularly appreciate this decidedly "premodern" response to modern liberalism, and he mentions Kierkegaard in order to explain why. For Cox, following Kierkegaard, the nature of faith is embedded inside deeply relational language of openness to the "other" and the risky embrace of restlessness. Faith is not reasonable assent to propositional facts, but rather a single individual reflecting in form about the only proper object of faith in God.

Cox is resistant to Kierkegaard's particularly Lutheran stance regarding the individual's singular relation to God. This is demonstrated in his 2001 article in *The Christian Century* about his experience of celebrating Yom Kippur, where the liturgy involves corporate prayer that confesses the sins of others. Suggesting that the piety offered by Kierkegaard—where the individual comes singularly before God—limits the way that the community can help mediate encounters with God, Cox sides

89   Ibid., p. 55.
90   Cox, *Religion in the Secular City*, p. 21.
91   Ibid., p. 55.

with Martin Buber, deciding that "we come to God *through* the human ties within which we have been set. We are bound together with bonds that go deeper than skin."[92] So, while Cox may appreciate Kierkegaard's willingness to acknowledge the way inwardness postures the self before God, he remains uncomfortable with Kierkegaard's modern emphasis on individuality.

When it comes to Kierkegaard's disdain for academic scholarship, and professional theologians in particular, Cox is quite receptive. He understands the growth and popularization of "folk piety" as a reinterpretation of the significance of Christ in the daily "religious" life of ordinary people, as a paradigmatic challenge to the intellectualized rationality of modern religion. Kierkegaard's interest in the life and teachings of Jesus rests on his use of the significance of a personal relation to Jesus as a resistance to an empty, blank, and official religion that requires no inwardness, no choice, and in Kierkegaardian nomenclature, no existential subjectivity. Yet, Cox notices that in the instance of fundamentalism, this personal way of relation to God through Jesus Christ, which Cox sees in Kierkegaard, has been cultivated into an official way of making sense of public life in a privatized manner. "A perverted form of Kierkegaard's existential inwardness has become the predominant public theology, a support to the status quo and a pious bulwark against the wrenching changes in public life that God's kingdom would require."[93] Ironically, it is precisely "a public theology," "status quo," and "pious bulwark" that Kierkegaard finds so problematic in the church in Denmark that prompts him to articulate the religious vision of subversion, restlessness, and subjectivity that Cox seems to valorize, but from afar.

IV. Cox's Reception of Kierkegaard (or Lack Thereof)

Roger Poole opens his chapter on the reception of Søren Kierkegaard in the twentieth century by acknowledging that any attempt to systematize Kierkegaard ultimately fails, because that is the way Kierkegaard wanted it.[94] It is for and about the individual that Kierkegaard tirelessly worked; his project was, among other things, aimed at restoring the place of the single individual in intellectual and religious discourse. Only the single individual could rightly read his books, as Poole notes, for it was the individual for whom Kierkegaard wrote. He was primarily concerned with how one reader in her singularity would approach his writings; this embrace of hermeneutical subjectivity has ultimately resulted in the interpretative cacophony of both historical and contemporary Kierkegaardian studies and reception. It is this idiosyncrasy among many others that primarily contributes to the confusion about Kierkegaard's authorship that continually results in misunderstanding and interpretation.

[92]   Harvey Gallagher Cox, "Hunger Pains: A Christian Observes Yom Kippur," *Christian Century*, vol. 118, no. 25, September 12, 2001, p. 33.
[93]   Cox, *Religion in the Secular City*, p. 236.
[94]   Roger Poole, "The Unknown Kierkegaard: Twentieth-Century Receptions," in *The Cambridge Companion to Kierkegaard*, ed. by Alastair Hannay and Gordon D. Marino, Cambridge: Cambridge University Press 1998, p. 48.

Cue Dr. Harvey Gallagher Cox, Jr. He, too, is a theologian easily misunderstood. Writing at a critical time in the history of American political, religious, and intellectual life, Cox writes not for the individual, but for the city, the world, and for the poor. But, like Kierkegaard, Cox's work is easily made sense of by using schemes or systems, and often disappoints readers as much as he surprises them. While Kierkegaard and Cox share this problematic and complicated relationship with their readers, examination beyond cursory glances reveals a relationship between these figures that is not easily parsed.

While it is clear that Kierkegaard lives in the mind and work of Harvey Cox, it is not fair to speak of him as a major influence or a primary interlocutor. While it would be inaccurate to claim that Kierkegaard served as a primary, or even major, influence for Cox, I have attempted to demonstrate the way in which Kierkegaard's interest in the structure of human experience for critical study of religion shaped Cox's own particular manner of reorienting the meaning of religion in order to reflect complex and polyphonic individual experiences.[95] It seems that Cox's sources of knowledge about Kierkegaard are quite indirect and general; the idea that what Cox knows about Kierkegaard, he finds in Dietrich Bonhoeffer, the theologian whose legacy Cox readily inherits, comes from the fact that Cox uses Kierkegaard in a similar way as Bonhoeffer did: rather generally, with elusive references and rarely with a textual reference.

When Cox does mention Kierkegaard, it is hardly more than a mention, rarely a citation, and never an in-depth analysis or reading. Cox never actually cites a text when mentioning Kierkegaard except on one occasion when he references the review of *Two Ages*, leading me to postulate that much of Cox's knowledge of Kierkegaard is non-specific to the actual *corpus*, and thus—perhaps—Cox's source of knowledge of Kierkegaard comes by way of reading Bonhoeffer, for whom Kierkegaard served as a significant interlocutor.[96] The indebtedness, regardless of how implicit that may be, of Bonhoeffer to Kierkegaard is well documented, and it stands to reason that much of what Cox knows about Kierkegaard comes from Bonhoeffer's own reading of his Lutheran forerunner.[97]

---

[95]   Harvey Gallagher Cox, "Using and Misusing Bonhoeffer," *Christianity and Crisis*, vol. 24, 1964, pp. 199–201.

[96]   While the literature is somewhat conflicted on this score, the general consensus is that there exists a strong relationship between *The Cost of Discipleship* and Kierkegaard's emphasis on individuality, the concern about the synthesis of Christ and church, and the centrality of the courageous personal decision for an authentic existence and identity as a faithful Christian. Regarding Bonhoeffer's reception of Kierkegaard, see Wenzel Lohff, "Rechtfertigung und Ethik," *Lutherische Monatshefte*, vol. 5, no. 2, 1963, pp. 311–18 and Heinrich Traugott Vogel, *Christus als Vorbild und Versöhner. Eine kritische Studie zum Problem des Verhältnisses von Gesetz und Evangelium im Werke Sören Kierkegaards* (Ph.D. Thesis, Humboldt University, Berlin 1968). In recent years, how well Bonhoeffer actually read Kierkegaard has been disputed. Cf. *International Bonhoeffer Society Newsletter*, no. 44, May, 1990 and no. 45, October, 1990.

[97]   I say this with considerable caution, as there is no textual evidence of the nature of this relationship, but comes only from the examination of the above literature. Cf. Lee C. Barrett, "The USA: From Neo-Orthodoxy to Plurality," in *Kierkegaard's International Reception*,

While Cox is often wary of Kierkegaard's more "modern" positions on individualism, the state, and faith, he also appreciates Kierkegaard's concerns about religion, the public life of the Christian, and truth as subjectivity. While it is hard to surmise how sophisticated Cox's knowledge is of the aforementioned subjects in Kierkegaard's *corpus*, Cox, particularly his early work, seems to agree with Kierkegaard as often as he disagrees, and in a rare moment of transparency, says as much in *Common Prayers*. It is particularly challenging to pinpoint areas of "reception" since Cox's treatment is very general; there is little way to describe in detail exactly what kind of reading of Kierkegaard Cox offers his readers.

Major themes of Kierkegaard's theology are absent in Cox's work. Clearly influenced by his later, named authorship, most pseudonymous sources in Kierkegaard's *corpus* are missed in Cox. The nature of Cox's diverse theological and intellectual interests do, in many ways, stand in strong contrast to Kierkegaard's own. Yet, Cox and Kierkegaard join forces in their suspicion of politics, power, and secularism in favor of a renewal of "true" faith, freed from the bondages of religion, culture, and tradition. They share a concern for the individual, but differ on how the individual relates to God and the world. While Cox understands Kierkegaard as a radical, a friend to an effort to rid Christianity of religion in order properly to attend to the human responsibility to act in revolutionary ways to change the world, he appears ambivalent about much of what he finds in Kierkegaard's theology. Yet, he does not fail to recognize the powerful challenge and critique Kierkegaard posed to his world and ours.

Yet, in the history of the American reception of Kierkegaard, it has been the centrality of personal inwardness and authentic communication that has been the most powerfully appropriated. Cox does not deviate from this pattern, though, quite indirectly. Roger Poole considers this a trend in Kierkegaardian reception: "This is how a reading of Kierkegaard usually goes: a sudden self-identification with the thought of the man, which has a compelling existential significance and which causes a reformulation of all existing personal thought-structures."[98] He goes on to suggest that even though "every thinker who falls under Kierkegaard's way does so for his own reasons," the attraction to Kierkegaard is particularly salient to "theologians trying to make sense of the literal and historical claims of Christianity in a modern skeptical world."[99] As I have argued above, despite the lack of explicit acknowledgement on his part, we should consider Harvey Cox among those thinkers who find a friend in Kierkegaard's prophetic appreciation for the complex absurdity of God, the subjective restlessness of faith, the centrality of relation, and the power of spirit as they try to undo modernity's grip on theology.

Tome III, *The Near East, Asia, Australia and the Americas*, ed. by Jon Stewart, Aldershot: Ashgate 2009 (*Kierkegaard Research: Sources, Reception and Resources*, vol. 8), p. 234.

[98]   Poole, "The Unknown Kierkegaard: Twentieth-Century Receptions," p. 50.

[99]   Ibid., p. 53.

Bibliography

I. References to or Uses of Kierkegaard in Cox's Corpus

God's Revolution and Man's Responsibility, Valley Forge, Pennsylvania: Judson Press 1965, pp. 46ff.

The Secular City: Secularization and Urbanization in Theological Perspective, New York: Macmillan 1965, p. 36; p. 45; p. 57; p. 82; p. 91; p. 122.

"Non-Theistic Commitments," *Cross Currents*, vol. 9, no. 4, 1969, pp. 399–408.

The Feast of Fools: A Theological Essay on Festivity and Fantasy, Cambridge, Massachusetts: Harvard University Press 1969, p. 154; p. 169; p. 194.

The Seduction of the Spirit: The Use and Misuse of People's Religion, New York: Simon and Schuster 1973, pp. 98ff.

Religion in the Secular City: Toward a Postmodern Theology, New York: Simon and Schuster 1984, p. 55; p. 108; p. 236.

Common Prayers: Faith, Family, and a Christian's Journey Through the Jewish Year, Boston: Houghton Mifflin 2001, pp. 33ff.; p. 55.

II. Sources of Harvey Cox's Knowledge of Kierkegaard

Bonhoeffer, Dietrich, *Prisoner for God: Letters and Papers from Prison*, trans. by Eberhard Bethge, New York: Macmillan 1953, p. 72; p. 125; p. 143; pp. 231ff.

— *The Cost of Discipleship*, trans. by Reginald Horace Fuller, New York: Macmillan 1959, p. 43.

— *Dietrich Bonhoeffer Works*, vol. 6, *Ethics*, ed. by Ilse Tödt, Eduard Tödt, Ernst Feil, and Clifford Green, trans. by Reinhard Krauss, Charles C. West. and Douglas W. Scott, Minneapolis: Fortress Press 2005, p. 82; p. 127; p. 152; p. 168; p. 350; p. 416.

III. Secondary Literature on Cox's Relation to Kierkegaard

Barrett, Lee C., "The USA: From Neo-Orthodoxy to Plurality," *Kierkegaard's International Reception*, Tome 3, *The Near East, Asia, Australia and the Americas*, ed. by Jon Stewart, Aldershot: Ashgate 2009 (*Kierkegaard Research: Sources, Reception and Resources*, vol. 8), p. 234.

Blum, Fred H., "Harvey Cox on the Secular City," *Ethics*, vol. 78, no. 1, 1967, pp. 43–61.

Bouma, Gary, "Book Review: The Seduction of the Spirit: The Use and Misuse of People's Religion by Harvey Cox," *Journal for the Scientific Study of Religion*, vol. 13, no. 2, 1974, pp. 233–5.

Stanley J. Grenz:

An Unfinished Engagement with Kierkegaard

Paul Martens

When Stanley J. Grenz (1950–2005) died suddenly on March 12, 2005, he left many things unfinished. The seemingly tireless theologian had already published 25 books and hundreds of articles. His work kept getting more ambitious as time passed, and it is clear that Grenz was not finished with everything that he had started. In the big picture, his work towards rethinking and reforming evangelical theology was still ongoing.[1] This grand project was, of course, made up of many smaller engagements with postmodernity, foundationalism, Baptist polity, pastoral and ecclesial concerns, anthropology, and ontology, to name some of the more significant. In all of these, Grenz sought to rescue North American evangelicalism from both modernity and fundamentalism. As his good friend and co-author Roger Olson said, "Stan was a centrist theologian within the evangelical movement who strove to discover, strengthen, and renew an evangelical *via media* between unfettered theological experimentation cut loose from tradition and neo-fundamentalism that seeks to monopolize evangelical thought."[2] It should come as no surprise that nearly all of Grenz's academic and pastoral writings are shaped by this quest to revise evangelical theology.

As a centrist evangelical theologian, what use could Grenz have had for the thought of Søren Kierkegaard? And, perhaps just as interesting is the question of how Grenz understood Kierkegaard. The purpose of this brief article is to provide an answer to this latter question in order to suggest an answer to the former. The structure of this article is rooted in a chronological account of Grenz's engagement with Kierkegaard. Yet it is necessary to note that there are distinct links between chronology and thematic shifts that indicate a fluid and open-ended engagement determined by other forces at work in Grenz's *corpus*. To begin, we must attend to one of the anti-modernist formative influences on Stan Grenz while he was a young seminary student.

---

[1]   Perhaps Stanley J. Grenz, *Revisioning Evangelical Theology: A Fresh Agenda for the 21st Century*, Downers Grove, Illinois: InterVarsity Press 1993, is the most succinct expression of this trajectory.

[2]   Roger E. Olson, "Stanley J. Grenz's Contribution to Evangelical Theology," *Princeton Theological Review*, vol. 12, no. 1, 2006, p. 27.

I. In Honor of Vernon Grounds: Grenz's Early, Anti-Modern Kierkegaard

Vernon C. Grounds (1914–2010) was a long-time professor, dean, president, and eventually president emeritus at the Conservative Baptist Theological Seminary in Denver, Colorado. Grounds earned his doctorate from Drew University with a dissertation entitled *The Concept of Love in the Psychology of Sigmund Freud.* While writing this dissertation, he became acquainted with the writings of Kierkegaard, most notably *Works of Love* from which he "came to realize overwhelmingly the centrality and multidimensionality of love in biblical faith."[3]

In the face of derision from conservative evangelical colleagues and critics, Grounds extolled the positive possibilities offered by Kierkegaard. It is in a *Festschrift* for Grounds, published in 1986, that Grenz honored his mentor's unshaken attachment to Kierkegaard.[4] The chapter Grenz authored was titled "The Flight from God: Kierkegaard's *Fear and Trembling* and Universal Ethical Systems," and it was later published in *Perspectives in Religious Studies* as well.[5] Thematically, there is some unity in the *Festschrift* in that nearly all of the chapters address the theme of "Christian freedom." Grenz's chapter is no exception. In fact, Grenz ends his argument with a direct return to this theme: "The life of faith is not easy, but it is the way to true freedom. This is the message of Søren Kierkegaard."[6]

To make sense of this conclusion requires some work, if for no other reason than this is the first and only time "true freedom"—or any kind of freedom—makes an appearance in the chapter.[7] Further, this conclusion also seems a bit at odds with Grenz's introduction, which claims that "Søren Kierkegaard, the melancholy Dane of the nineteenth century, however, insightfully points out the folly of this universal human tendency," the tendency "to seek to mitigate [one's] immediacy

---

[3]   See Gordon R. Lewis, "Vernon C. Grounds: A Gifted Man for Others," in *Christian Freedom: Essays in Honor of Vernon C. Grounds*, ed. by Kenneth W.M. Wozniak and Stanley J. Grenz, Lanham, Maryland: University Press of America 1986, p. 19. Here, Lewis is also citing from Vernon C. Grounds, "Books that Helped Shape My Life, *Eternity*, vol. 23, no. 3, 1972, p. 45.

[4]   Grounds' influence on Grenz was significant, as noted by former teachers and himself. See Miller's comment that "the most important influence in seminary was that of Dr. Vernon Grounds, Dr. Gordon Lewis, and Dr. Bruce Demarest," in Ed L. Miller, "How I Took Barth's Chair, and How Grenz almost Took It from Me," *Princeton Theological Review*, vol. 12, no. 1, 2006, p. 4, and his own co-authored comment—"Yet we offer [the contents of this book] with humble gratitude, cherishing the honor of having been touched by his life"—prefacing *Christian Freedom*, ed. by Wozniak and Grenz, p. xiv.

[5]   Stanley J. Grenz, "The Flight From God: Kierkegaard's *Fear and Trembling* and Universal Ethical Systems," in *Christian Freedom*, ed. by Wozniak and Grenz, pp. 69–85; and *Perspectives in Religious Studies*, vol. 14, no. 2, 1987, pp. 147–59. Subsequent references to this article will include page numbers from both publications, beginning with the pages from *Christian Freedom*.

[6]   Grenz, "Flight from God," in *Christian Freedom*, ed. by Wozniak and Grenz, p. 83. (*Perspectives in Religious Studies*, vol. 14, no. 2, 1987, p. 158.)

[7]   Perhaps it might be fair to suspect that Grenz as co-editor overruled Grenz as author in this matter, as the introduction of freedom at the conclusion may add to the unity of the book's chapters at the cost of some disjunction within this particular chapter.

before God."[8] As indicated by the subtitle, the flight from immediacy before God is frequently accomplished through "universal ethical systems." In identifying the connection between the eclipse of one's God-relationship and the appearance of universal ethics through *Fear and Trembling*, Grenz is standing in both familiar and unfamiliar territory.[9]

On the one hand, Grenz's interpretation is very familiar in that it plays on the traditional anti-Kantian and anti-Hegelian themes associated with Kierkegaard for the majority of the twentieth century. Grenz first provides a brief summary of the ethics of Kant and Hegel for the purpose of demonstrating how their systems become "tempting façades, behind which the individual hides in the attempt to mitigate direct responsibility before God."[10] Against these misguided construals of morality, he appeals to interpreters of Kierkegaard most readily available in North America in the mid-1960s and early 1970s—Gregor Malantschuk, Walter Lowrie, Ronald Grimsley, James Collins, and Thomas Croxall—to provide an account of *Fear and Trembling* that prioritized faith, a faith that did not generate a system of ethics, an existential system, or any ethical "norm."[11] According to Grenz, *Fear and Trembling* prioritized a faith that brought an individual before God "as one responsible directly to the Creator."[12] As an interpretive summary of *Fear and Trembling*, Grenz's account is not exceptional: it addresses the question of each "Problem" or "Problema" in order; it stays within the limits of the text itself; it does not draw on any of the other texts in Kierkegaard's *corpus*; it critiques "the purely ethical way of life";[13] and it calls

---

[8]   Grenz, "Flight from God," in *Christian Freedom*, ed. by Wozniak and Grenz, p. 70. (*Perspectives in Religious Studies*, vol. 14, no. 2, 1987, p. 148.)

[9]   *Fear and Trembling* is the only text of Kierkegaard's referenced in this article, and Grenz worked from the Walter Lowrie translation, Princeton: Princeton University Press 1954.

[10]   Grenz, "Flight from God," in *Christian Freedom*, ed. by Wozniak and Grenz, p. 71. (*Perspectives in Religious Studies*, vol. 14, no. 2, 1987, p. 149.) In summarizing the positions of Kant and Hegel, Grenz references Kant's *Fundamental Principles of the Metaphysics of Morals* and *Critique of Practical Reason* along with Hegel's *Philosophy of Right*. In general, Grenz seems to be dependent on secondary sources here as he notes, "For a succinct summary of Hegel's book, see Thomas Henry Croxall, *Kierkegaard Commentary*." See Ibid.

[11]   The particular texts appealed to are noted in the bibliography that follows. It is also important to note that this is the first and last time these secondary texts are mentioned in Grenz's *corpus*. Of the excerpts that Grenz singles out from the secondary sources, perhaps the most important for his argument is drawn from Ronald Grimsley, *Kierkegaard: A Biographical Introduction*, New York: Charles Scribner's Sons 1973, p. 47: "A sacrifice like Abraham's raises in a very acute form the question of putting aside the fulfillment of moral obligations for the sake of some higher ideal. With religious faith of this kind we move from the safe ground of universal values to the paradox and uncertainty of individual faith…the 'knight of faith'…cannot relate his situation to the realm of universal values." ("Flight from God," in *Christian Freedom*, ed. by Wozniak and Grenz, p. 73. (*Perspectives in Religious Studies*, vol. 14, no. 2, 1987, p. 151.))

[12]   Grenz, "Flight from God," in *Christian Freedom*, ed. by Wozniak and Grenz, p. 78. (*Perspectives in Religious Studies*, vol. 14, no. 2, 1987, p. 154.)

[13]   Grenz, "Flight from God," in *Christian Freedom*, ed. by Wozniak and Grenz, p. 74. (*Perspectives in Religious Studies*, vol. 14, no. 2, 1987, p. 151.)

for the realization that "one may be called to suspend universal morality for the sake of God."[14]

On the other hand, Grenz's interpretation is somewhat unfamiliar because of the direction he takes in articulating the "twentieth-century echo" of Kierkegaard's position. As indicated earlier, Grenz was primarily concerned with North American evangelicalism and his early appropriation of *Fear and Trembling* reflects this preoccupation as well. Rather than turning to the Kierkegaardian echoes in Nietzsche, Sartre, or some other twentieth-century continental philosopher, Grenz turns to Joseph Fletcher (1905–91), natural empiricism, and most extensively, to Norman Geisler (b. 1932), a leading evangelical apologist who has served as president for both the Evangelical Philosophical Society and the Evangelical Theological Society. In short, according to Grenz, the "meaning" of *Fear and Trembling* that echoes forward is that Kierkegaard "resists any attempt to limit God within the sphere of any ethical system."[15] Unsurprisingly, neither a neo-Kantian non-conflicting absolutism nor Fletcher's situational application of the universal of love escapes Grenz's use of Kierkegaard's challenge. His harshest criticisms, however, are reserved for Geisler's hierarchicalism, a "system" that is allegedly rooted both in "a general intuitive basis" *and* "on the revelation of the Christian Scriptures."[16]

The key to Grenz's disagreement with Geisler lies in Geisler's description of one's relationship with God, and Grenz points to the following passage to summarize Geisler's position:

> Ethical hierarchicalism, on the contrary, takes issue with Kierkegaard's analysis, claiming that there was a higher ethical purpose or principle in view of which Abraham was ethically justified in his decision. The higher principle was his duty to obey God which always transcends one's duty to another man.[17]

On this basis, Geisler claims to agree with Abraham, but disagrees with Kierkegaard's description of Abraham's action because, in Geisler's view, Abraham was not irrational but was simply following a higher principle, a higher ethical norm.[18]

Initially, Grenz's critique is directed at Geisler's description. Geisler, first, seems to agree with Kierkegaard that ethical norms can be suspended for a higher *telos* while, second, self-consciously distancing himself from Kierkegaard in maintaining

---

[14]   Grenz, "Flight from God," in *Christian Freedom*, ed. by Wozniak and Grenz, p. 77. (*Perspectives in Religious Studies*, vol. 14, no. 2, 1987, p. 154.) Grenz understands Kierkegaard as a corrective who allows the Kantian and Hegelian systems to remain as long as individuals do not hide behind them. See "Flight from God," in *Christian Freedom*, ed. by Wozniak and Grenz, p. 74. (*Perspectives in Religious Studies*, vol. 14, no. 2, 1987, p. 151.)

[15]   Grenz, "Flight from God," in *Christian Freedom*, ed. by Wozniak and Grenz, p. 79. (*Perspectives in Religious Studies*, vol. 14, no. 2, 1987, p. 156.)

[16]   Norman L. Geisler, *Ethics: Alternatives and Issues*, Grand Rapids, Michigan: Zondervan 1971, p. 137.

[17]   Geisler, *Ethics*, p. 121.

[18]   One ought to note that, for Geisler, Kierkegaard is the forerunner of antinomianism, or to use Geisler's expression, "Kierkegaard's teaching is the soil for incipient antinomianism" (*Ethics*, p. 32). This is why Geisler refuses to identify himself with Kierkegaard despite their many similarities.

that Abraham's duty to not kill Isaac remains a universally valid ethical norm. Observing this, Grenz states that "in this non-traditional way Geisler appears to be playing a semantic game in which universals are not universally applicable and absolutes are relative."[19] Grenz continues: "Herein lies a glaring weakness of hierarchicalism. It claims to include a plurality of universal norms. But in actuality it contains only one norm, that which stands at the top of the hierarchy, for only that law must always be obeyed."[20]

At the end of the day, however, Grenz's issue is not with the number of universals, but with the idea of a universal norm itself. And, in this way, he obliquely introduces the possibility—and necessity—of Christian freedom. Rejecting Geisler's suggestion that one's higher duty to God is an ethical duty, Grenz pointedly and personally sums up his position: "No norm (not even Norm Geisler) will ever be able to mediate one's position before God. The life of the individual must always be directed toward God alone, who may on occasion ask one to act in a seemingly unethical manner."[21] Understood this way, the Christian faith exemplified in *Fear and Trembling* cannot be described or circumscribed in any ethical system. Any attempt to do so would, necessarily, entail a flight from God, a rejection of risk, and a refusal to act in humility, repentance, and fear and trembling. And, understood this way, one can see how Grenz's pronounced Pietist leanings align very well with his early, anti-modern, anti-universal Kierkegaard that requires an unmitigated and unmediated personal relationship with God.[22]

II. The Narratives of Twentieth-Century Theology: A Tale of Two Kierkegaards

In the 1990s, Kierkegaard reappeared as a significant figure in Grenz's *corpus*. By this time, Grenz had completed his doctorate at Munich under the tutelage of Wolfhart Pannenberg (b. 1928).[23] And, always seeking to acknowledge his mentors, Grenz began the decade with a book dedicated to introducing the systematic theology of Pannenberg appropriately titled: *Reason for Hope: The Systematic Theology of Wolfhart Pannenberg*.[24] This beginning marked a turn toward a broadening of

---

[19] Grenz, "Flight from God," in *Christian Freedom*, ed. by Wozniak and Grenz, p. 82. (*Perspectives in Religious Studies*, vol. 14, no. 2, 1987, p. 157.)
[20] Grenz, "Flight from God," in *Christian Freedom*, ed. by Wozniak and Grenz, p. 82. (*Perspectives in Religious Studies*, vol. 14, no. 2, 1987, p. 158.)
[21] Grenz, "Flight from God," in *Christian Freedom*, ed. by Wozniak and Grenz, p. 83. (*Perspectives in Religious Studies*, vol. 14, no. 2, 1987, p. 158.)
[22] According to Roger Olson, Grenz liked to describe himself as a "pietist with a Ph.D.," and this early article certainly does not refute this claim. See Olson, "Stanley J. Grenz's Contribution," p. 27.
[23] Grenz's dissertation was later published as *Isaac Backus, Puritan and Baptist: His Place in History, His Thought and Their Implication for Modern Baptist Theology*, Macon, Georgia: Mercer University Press 1983.
[24] Stanley J. Grenz, *Reason for Hope: The Systematic Theology of Wolfhart Pannenberg*, Oxford: Oxford University Press 1990.

Grenz's theological interest, particularly his interest in the theology of the late twentieth century.

In *Reason for Hope*, Kierkegaard appears in the background three times. In the most substantive of these, Grenz wrote:

> [Pannenberg] rejects the well-known thesis of Kierkegaard that dread is the starting point of the rise of sin, the holding fast to finitude. In contrast to the melancholy Dane, Pannenberg maintains that dread already includes sin, because it consists in the placing of the "I" in the middle of one's own interests. Despite this difference, he sees Kierkegaard as important for connecting the rise of sin to the modern problem of the relationship to the self.[25]

Further, Grenz later refers to Kierkegaard's "existential" account of the doctrine of human destiny without further explanation[26] and Kierkegaard's question "as to how a historical reality can be the sufficient ground of faith," again, without reference or further explanation.[27]

In all of the references to Pannenberg's use of Kierkegaard, Grenz's comments are succinct and suggestive, but hardly substantive. In his *Anthropology in Theological Perspective*,[28] Pannenberg provides an extensive interpretation of Kierkegaard's concepts of dread and despair, spanning eight pages and specifically naming *The Concept of Anxiety*, Kierkegaard's journals and papers, *The Sickness unto Death*, *Philosophical Fragments*, and several specialized secondary texts. These eight pages serve as the center to the many other references to Kierkegaard in *Anthropology*, yet all that Grenz notes in this connection are the comments provided above. His conclusion concerning Pannenberg's relation to Kierkegaard may be generally correct, but it also clearly indicates that Kierkegaard is not important for his own interpretation of Pannenberg.

When Grenz turns to twentieth-century theology, Kierkegaard takes a much more central role, a role essentially related to Karl Barth but also linked to several of the subsequent contributors, especially Emil Brunner (1889–1966), Rudolph Bultmann (1884–1976), Reinhold Niebuhr (1892–1971), and Paul Tillich (1886–1965). There are, however, two stories of twentieth-century theology told for two different purposes on two different axes. In the first story, Kierkegaard is a positive contributor, an instigator, one of the good guys; in the second story, Kierkegaard is a negative contributor, a hindrance, and one of the voices that probably ought to be jettisoned.

In 1992, two years after the publication of *Reason for Hope*, Grenz published his first summary of twentieth-century theology—*20th-Century Theology: God and the World in a Transitional Age*—with Roger Olson and the second—*Fortress Introduction to Contemporary Theologies*—written with Ed Miller, followed

---

[25]   Ibid., p. 126.
[26]   Ibid., p. 129.
[27]   Ibid., p. 218.
[28]   Wolfhart Pannenberg, *Anthropology in Theological Perspective*, Philadelphia: Westminster Press 1985.

in 1998.[29] The first begins with the legacy of the Enlightenment and ends with a revaluation of evangelical theology; the second confines itself to the twentieth century as it begins with Barth and ends with George Lindbeck's postliberalism. The first is thematically oriented around the contest between transcendence and immanence in the twentieth century; the second is oriented around individual authors who represent significant theological movements representing the general theological drift toward the articulation of socially and culturally situated theologies. In these narratives, Kierkegaard plays differing roles in relation to the same characters.

In *20ᵗʰ-Century Theology*, Grenz and Olson begin with a narration of a fall, a fall from the "classical balance" between transcendence and immanence that was forged by Augustine and "honed and tuned in the Middle Ages, only to be reformulated in the Reformation and by the Protestant scholasticism that followed."[30] The primary cause for this destruction is the Enlightenment, which "permanently and radically disrupted" this classical balance.[31] The outcome of the Enlightenment was that God became firmly bound with nature and reason to the extent that God's transcendence became dissolved in the divine immanence within nature and reason.[32] In the wake of the Enlightenment, Immanuel Kant, G.W.F. Hegel, and Friedrich Schleiermacher all further deepened the drift toward the immanence of God, culminating in various forms of Albrecht Ritschl's (1822–89) immanence of God in ethical culture.[33] The narrative of decline abruptly halts as the third chapter begins: "The guns of August 1914 sounded the death knell of the nineteenth-century intellectual ethos."[34]

Grenz and Olson follow conventional thinking in claiming that, theologically, Karl Barth's *Der Römerbrief* signaled the end of nineteenth-century optimism and the beginning of neo-orthodoxy. As they narrate the recovery of transcendence, Grenz and Olson argue that neo-orthodoxy sought to reassert forgotten themes to a world that needed to hear God speak from "beyond."[35] They continue: "In the quest to reassert themes such as human sin, divine grace and personal decision, twentieth-century neo-orthodoxy drew inspiration from a hitherto unheeded nineteenth-century voice who had spoken out against the dominant thinking of his day. That voice was the 'melancholy Dane,' Søren Kierkegaard."[36]

At this point, Grenz and Olson begin a brief digression to introduce Kierkegaard before moving on to address Barth's theology in greater detail. They begin biographically, highlighting Kierkegaard's unhappy childhood, education, and

---

[29]   See Stanley J. Grenz and Roger E. Olson, *20ᵗʰ-Century Theology: God and the World in a Transitional Age*, Downers Grove, Illinois: InterVarsity Press 1992; and Ed L. Miller and Stanley J. Grenz, *Fortress Introduction to Contemporary Theologies*, Minneapolis: Fortress Press 1998.

[30]   Grenz and Olson, *20ᵗʰ-Century Theology*, p. 16.

[31]   Ibid., p. 16.

[32]   Ibid., p. 23.

[33]   Grenz and Olson also suggest that the theologies of Adolf Harnack and Walter Rauschenbush are rooted in Ritschl's thought, carrying his "liberal agenda in new directions" (ibid., p. 51).

[34]   Ibid., p. 63.

[35]   Ibid., p. 64.

[36]   Ibid.

unfulfilled relationship with Regine. Interestingly, they also suggest a tripartite structure to his authorship: (1) writings dealing mainly with his relationship to Regine; (2) writings focused on the difficulty of becoming a Christian following his conversion experience of 1848; and (3) writings, begun in 1854 after "a bishop of the Danish state church praised a departed colleague," that bitterly attacked the State Church.[37] Following this rather idiosyncratic summation of the authorship, Grenz and Olson return to more familiar grounds in noting the controversy between Kierkegaard and the contemporary Hegelian "intelligentsia." Highlighting the relationship between the "collectivism that arose from the Hegelian link between human spiritual progress and the historical self-development of Absolute Spirit," Grenz and Olson introduce Kierkegaard as the one who emphasized the individual.[38]

In the most direct engagement with the thought of Kierkegaard—and introducing the single text of *Philosophical Fragments* as representative[39]—Grenz and Olson conclude and bridge back to Barth:

> Themes announced by the nineteenth-century Danish philosopher—the transcendence of the God who speaks the ineffable truth to the individual in the moment of divine encounter—became the foundation on which the theologians of neo-orthodoxy in the twentieth century built and the theses that they expanded in their theological deliberations.[40]

Specifying this indebtedness further, Grenz and Olson return to Kierkegaard while summarizing Barth's early theology. Two themes quickly emerge as central: the "leap of faith by the finite human mind" and the "infinite qualitative distinction" between time and eternity.[41] And, with that, Kierkegaard's relationship with Barth is set, at least until Grenz revisited it six years later.

In the remaining pages of *20ᵗʰ-Century Theology*, Kierkegaard appears five more times. All of these references link one aspect of Kierkegaard's thought to significant theologians. Brunner is linked to the triad of Tertullian, Pascal, and Kierkegaard, all of whom asserted the fundamental incompatibility of the God of philosophical Theism and the God of biblical revelation.[42] Bultmann is tied back to Barth's and Kierkegaard's shared belief concerning the "infinite qualitative distinction" between God and humanity. Kierkegaard's concept of anxiety briefly reappears when addressing Reinhold Niebuhr's description of the rise of sin.[43] And, Kierkegaard

---

[37]   Ibid.

[38]   Ibid.

[39]   *Concluding Unscientific Postscript* also lies behind the account of Kierkegaard's thought attributed to *Philosophical Fragments*, as evidenced both by a quotation from the text—"An objective certainty held fast in an appropriation-process of the most passionate inwardness is the truth"—and the introduction of the categories of Religiousness A and Religiousness B. The quotation is drawn from *Concluding Unscientific Postscript*, trans. by David F. Swenson and Walter Lowrie, Princeton: Princeton University Press 1968, p. 182 (corresponds to *SKS* 7, 186 / *CUP1*, 203).

[40]   Grenz and Olson, *20ᵗʰ-Century Theology*, p. 65.

[41]   Ibid., p. 67.

[42]   Ibid., p. 79.

[43]   Ibid., p. 104.

is again mentioned as the source of Paul Tillich's understanding of the fall from the state of "dreaming innocence."[44] None of these comments are substantive; none include references to Kierkegaard's texts; all seem to assume that the reference to Kierkegaard is sufficiently uncontroversial or familiar enough that it is understood by an educated reader.

Lest one be too critical of the seemingly superficial presentation of Kierkegaard in the text, it is important to remember that, for Grenz and Olson, the grand narrative of the contest between immanence and transcendence is the focus of the text. To this end, Kierkegaard obviously lines up on the side of transcendence with every appearance except when he is linked to Tillich. But, there is one more idiosyncratically evangelical element yet to be introduced. If *20ᵗʰ-Century Theology* begins with a narrative of the attack on the "classical balance" held in medieval and Reformed theology, the text ultimately presents a restoration narrative, a narrative that returns to Barth's corrective in an evangelical vein. The last character to appear in this story is Bernard Ramm (1916–92), a leading evangelical theologian of the 1970s.

Although the explicit link between Kierkegaard and Ramm is minimalized by Grenz and Olson—they note that Ramm understands his apologetics, like that of Brunner and Pascal, as grounded in "subjective immediacy" which moves from the inward experience of grace through the gospel[45]—the role played by Ramm is essential for the text to work:

> Ramm's concern to set forth credible theology in the post-Enlightenment situation as expressed in his work in apologetics, the interface of Bible and science, and in the doctrine of revelation eventually led him to Karl Barth. In 1983 his lifelong intrigue with the writings of the Swiss theologian climaxed with his controversial open embracing of Barth's approach as the paradigm for evangelicalism in the contemporary world.[46]

Of course, Ramm did not have all the answers. He provided a foundation for younger evangelicals to "think critically and engage in positive dialog with modern culture," yet he, too, had "drunk too deeply from the traditional theological well with its employment of the now discredited spatial metaphor of transcendence and immanence."[47] So, in short, he had paved the way for evangelicals to engage postmodernism, leaving younger theologians, like Grenz and Olson, to take evangelical theology forward.

---

[44]   Ibid., p. 127.

[45]   The particular issue of apologetics is important for linking Ramm with Kierkegaard, as Bernard Ramm's *Types of Apologetic Systems: An Introductory Study to the Christian Philosophy of Religion*, Wheaton, Illinois: Van Kampen Press 1953, devotes an entire chapter to Kierkegaard. And, Ramm is well aware of Kierkegaard's legacy, as he introduces Kierkegaard with the following comments: "Others regard Kierkegaard 'as a major turning-point in the spiritual history of modern Europe.' If this is not enough there is the readily acknowledged indebtedness to Kierkegaard by such theological giants as Barth, Brunner, and Niebuhr" (p. 39). The direct quotation in this passage is drawn from Denzil G.M. Patrick, *Pascal and Kierkegaard*, vols. 1–2, London: Lutterworth 1947 (*Lutterworth Library*, vols. 23–4), vol. 2, p. 159.

[46]   Grenz and Olson, *20ᵗʰ-Century Theology*, p. 307.

[47]   Ibid., p. 309.

The positive vision articulated here at the conclusion of *20ᵗʰ-Century Theology* finds its subsequent trajectory in *Revisioning Evangelical Theology* (1993), *A Primer on Postmodernism* (1996), and *Beyond Foundationalism* (2001). Given the outline of the anti-modern Kierkegaard sketched above and given Kierkegaard's widely recognized contributions to postmodernity,[48] it would come as no surprise if Kierkegaard found an honored place in Grenz's post-modern non-foundationalist project. What is surprising, however, is that Kierkegaard is given absolutely no place in this project—neither positive nor negative—in the ensuing years.[49] He is simply passed over in silence during this phase of Grenz's constructive project. Why? An examination of Grenz's second summary of twentieth-century theology seems to suggest an answer.

In 1998, Grenz wrote the *Fortress Introduction to Contemporary Theologies* with Ed Miller. It does not include the Enlightenment preamble that was included in *20ᵗʰ-Century Theology*, nor does it include the evangelical turn in conclusion. The emphasis is shifted away from the traditional giants of the twentieth century toward the latter half of the century, toward theologians such as Thomas J.J. Altizer, John B. Cobb, Jr., Pannenberg, Gustavo Guttiérez, Rosemary Radford Ruether, and George Linkbeck. At one level, the text traces Grenz's maturing interest in the twentieth-century trajectory toward post-foundational theology. At another related level, the poles around which the narrative turns have also changed. The contest between the individual and the social as the context for theology gives this later text its shape and direction. And, in this narrative, Kierkegaard is not exactly one of the good guys.

In the *Fortress Introduction to Contemporary Theologies*, Grenz and Miller begin by making the familiar link between Barth and Kierkegaard, but the terms of the conversation are slightly different. In this later account, the narrative is somewhat simplified:

> The impact and controversy generated by *Epistle to the Romans*, along with other contributions Barth was making, resulted in the offer of professorships in German universities....It was during these years, 1921–35, that the systematic character of Barth's theology really took shape. Even so, it involved a false start. It was during this time that Barth discovered a kindred spirit in the nineteenth-century Danish thinker Søren Kierkegaard (1813–55), often called the father of existentialism.[50]

---

[48]   To name just one example, see *Kierkegaard in Post/Modernity*, ed. by Martin J. Matuštík and Merold Westphal, Bloomington and Indianapolis: Indiana University Press 1995.

[49]   The one exception here can be found in Stanley J. Grenz, *The Moral Quest: Foundations of Christian Ethics*, Downers Grove, Illinois: InterVarsity Press 1997, where Kierkegaard's knight of faith is used to illustrate the Lutheran priority of obedient faith over reason, effectively affirming Luther's opening of the door for modern, autonomous individualism "stripped of all social relations, standing continually and immediately before God" (p. 160). Grenz's conclusion here fits well with the sketch of an increasingly anti-social and individualistic Kierkegaard provided in Miller and Grenz, *Fortress Introduction to Contemporary Theologies*, which was published one year later.

[50]   Miller and Grenz, *Fortress Introduction to Contemporary Theologies*, p. 6.

Two warning signs emerge in this later account: the first is a reference to an alleged "false start" in Barth's theology and the second is the resurfacing reference to existentialism, rarely a designation with positive connotations among evangelicals. Beginning with Kierkegaard's existentialism, Grenz and Miller identify this term with the claim that "subjectivity must be the starting point," and they follow with Kierkegaard's claim that "Truth is subjectivity," the claim that forces a recognition that the sphere of intellectual abstractions is not the same sphere of faith as passionate assimilation.[51] Grenz and Miller reference both *The Sickness unto Death* and the *Concluding Unscientific Postscript* in the endnotes and also mention Kierkegaard's use of pseudonymity, his use of indirect communication, and the offense of Christianity in their brief summation. Perhaps most central to their introduction of Kierkegaard, however, is a direct quotation from the *Concluding Unscientific Postscript* concerning the polemical relationship between faith and intellectual doctrines: "But faith is a sphere of its own, and the immediate identifying mark of every misunderstanding of Christianity is that it changes it into a doctrine and draws it into the range of intellectuality."[52] This is followed immediately with: "It should be no surprise that such talk played right into Barth's hands."[53]

The Barth referred to here, however, is the Barth engaged in the misdirected "false start," the Barth of *The Epistle to the Romans*, the Barth indebted to Kierkegaard's "infinite qualitative distinction" between God and humanity. Grenz and Miller then highlight Barth's later regret concerning this foundation, his attempt to remove any possible foundation in existentialism, and his negative characterization of Kierkegaard's "holy individualism."[54] Then they introduce the little-known comments Barth made in 1963 upon reception of the Sonning Prize: "I regard [Kierkegaard] as a teacher through whose school every theologian must pass at some time. Woe to anyone who has failed to do that. But he should not remain in it, and he will do better not to return to it."[55] Turning to the theme that had come to preoccupy Grenz by this time, Barth continues:

> Where in his teaching are the people of God, the congregation, the Church: where are her diaconal and missionary charge, her political and social charge?...How strange that we, who were just coming from an intense preoccupation with the relation of Christianity to the social question, did not immediately become suspicious at the point of Kierkegaard's pronounced holy individualism.[56]

---

[51]   Ibid., p. 7.

[52]   See *SKS* 7, 297 / *CUP1*, 326–7.

[53]   Miller and Grenz, *Fortress Introduction to Contemporary Theologies*, p. 7. The tone in this narrative is very different from the earlier account which described Kierkegaard as a theological inspiration for and not merely an affirmation of Barth.

[54]   Ibid., p. 8. This is not the first reference to Kierkegaard's individualism. In his earliest article, Grenz describes how one's individual and unmediated relationship with God is an essential element of Christianity. Later, however, Grenz seems to value this emphasis less and less.

[55]   Ibid. See Karl Barth, *Fragments Grave and Gay*, ed. by Martin Rumscheidt, trans. by Eric Mosbacher, London: Collins 1971, pp. 100–1.

[56]   Miller and Grenz, *Fortress Introduction to Contemporary Theologies*, p. 9.

And, with that, Grenz and Miller approve of the shift from the initial trajectory of Barth's *Christian Dogmatics* to the content of his subsequent *Church Dogmatics*. As the *Introduction to Contemporary Theology* proceeds, Kierkegaard is again identified in relation to the same theologians. Evoking the passion of faith, Kierkegaard and Buber are named as forerunners to Brunner's "theology of encounter."[57] Niebuhr's language of finite and infinite is said to echo Kierkegaard.[58] Barth's criticism of Bultmann is paralleled to his criticism of Kierkegaard: "faith was an inner directed, privatized faith that seemed out of step with social responsibility, the sense of community, and even the doctrine of the church as a communion of believers."[59] And, in their closing comments concerning Tillich, they remind us that Kierkegaard taught us a long time ago that "risk is a measure of faith's intensity."[60] At this point, Kierkegaard disappears from the story of contemporary theology, apparently left as a modern theologian who remained too dependent on the autonomous and individualized self to contribute constructively to the late twentieth-century conviction that "theological reflection is inescapably linked with a specific historical, social situation."[61]

The *Introduction to Contemporary Theologies* ends with a chapter devoted to George Lindbeck (b. 1923). Olson notes that Grenz was not "especially enamored" with Lindbeck's *The Nature of Doctrine*,[62] and it is clear that Grenz worried about the possibility that Lindbeck's vision could lead to a fragmenting of theology that

---

[57]   Ibid., p. 17.

[58]   Ibid., p. 27.

[59]   Ibid., p. 52. Here, too, we see a definitive shift from Grenz's earlier account. In 1992, Bultmann, Barth, and Kierkegaard are identified together in their shared belief concerning the "infinite qualitative distinction" between God and humanity; in 1998, Barth is opposed to both Kierkegaard and Bultmann because of their shared "privatization" of the Christian faith. Barth, in both narratives, remains the steadfast starting-point of the best in twentieth-century theology.

[60]   Ibid., p. 68.

[61]   Ibid., p. 147. This comment is made by Grenz and Miller in the context of liberation theology, but its tone rings steady throughout the latter half of the text as the trajectory moves through narrative theology to end with Lindbeck who argued that people are thoroughly social beings that are given shape through their cultural context and experience of the world, even going so far as claiming that one cannot have an experience apart from the dynamic working of one's social context (p. 211). Two years later, in what could be understood as an indirect repudiation of Kierkegaard, Grenz wrote: "Viewed from a Christian perspective, postmodernism has simply laid bare the bankruptcy of the modern narrative with its anthropocentric orientation. Moreover, the debate between modern progressivists and their postmodern detractors provides Christian theology with an opportunity to present a third way. Theology can only do so, however, if it jettisons its flirtation with the anthropocentrism of modernity and recaptures its moorings in the theocentric narrative of Scripture with its eschatological orientation....Indeed, Christian theology is by definition the teaching about the understanding of the God of the Christian community, the community that finds its identity through the biblical narrative." See Stanley J. Grenz, "Eschatological Theology: Contours of a Postmodern Theology of Hope," *Review and Expositor*, vol. 97, 2000, p. 345.

[62]   Olson, "Stanley J. Grenz's Contribution to Evangelical Theology," p. 28.

he seemed to see in Stanley Hauerwas.[63] That being said, however, his substantial *Theology for the Community of God*[64] clearly travels some of the same roads that he points to as the *Introduction to Contemporary Theologies* comes to a conclusion. And, as one might suspect, *Theology for the Community of God*, too, simply passes over Kierkegaard in silence. Clearly, Grenz has shifted his understanding of Kierkegaard from one of the positive contributors to the twentieth century's reassertion of God's transcendence to one of the misguided theologians of the nineteenth century that remained essentially modern in their assumption of autonomous and individualistic selfhood despite their anti-Enlightenment intentions.[65] This Kierkegaard, the second Kierkegaard of twentieth-century theology, has no place in Grenz's constructive and communal agenda, and he is simply passed over as a useful resource.[66]

III. An Unfinished Return: Kierkegaard and the Relational Self

In the final pages of *The Moral Quest*, Kierkegaard appears very quietly in a couple of endnotes to the chapter describing an ethic of love. In these notes, Grenz uses *Works of Love* for the first time in a significant way. The notes indicate that Grenz identifies Kierkegaard in the same vein as Anders Nygren's (1890–1978) *Agape and Eros*,[67] but Kierkegaard's position is labeled both "intriguing" and "interesting."[68] Interesting and intriguing do not say much about Grenz's evolving understanding of Kierkegaard, but they do indicate that he was continuing to read beyond the texts that had previously determined the contours of his Kierkegaard. Proving that he had not yet finished with Kierkegaard, Grenz returns to Kierkegaard in *The Social God and the Relational Self*.[69] Granted, Kierkegaard's appearance in this later text is limited, but its import is significant.

---

[63]   Miller and Grenz, *Fortress Introduction to Contemporary Theologies*, p. 216.

[64]   Stanley J. Grenz, *Theology for the Community of God*, Nashville, Tennessee: Broadman and Holman 1994.

[65]   In response to my argument that Grenz changes his mind about Kierkegaard in the years between the publications of these two narratives, one might want to suggest that it is the change in co-authors that accounts for this difference. Although this may be partially true, there are three reasons why it appears Grenz is directly involved in articulating the difference: (1) he is the constant in the generation of both accounts; (2) formally, Kierkegaard appears in almost identical fashion, both in reference to Barth and in reference to precisely the same subsequent interlocutors, with the exception of Ramm, who does not appear in the second text; and (3) the shift in Grenz's interpretation of Kierkegaard coheres well with the evolution of his own authorship.

[66]   In Kierkegaard research, the destruction of this caricature has begun many years ago, perhaps most notably with the appearance of *Foundations of Kierkegaard's Vision of Community: Religion, Ethics, and Politics in Kierkegaard*, ed. by George B. Connell and C. Stephen Evans, Atlantic Highlands, New Jersey: Humanities Press 1992.

[67]   Anders Nygren, *Agape and Eros*, trans. by Philip S. Watson, Philadelphia: Westminster Press 1953. (Original Swedish: *Eros och Agape*, vols. 1–2, Stockholm: Verbum 1966.)

[68]   Grenz, *The Moral Quest*, pp. 347–8.

[69]   Stanley J. Grenz, *The Social God and the Relational Self: A Trinitarian Theology of the* Imago Dei, Louisville, Kentucky: Westminster John Knox Press 2001.

In his turn towards accentuating and developing a sensitivity to social and cultural contributions to theology, Grenz began a multi-volume constructive project under the series title, *The Matrix of Christian Theology*. The first volume in this series—*The Social God and the Relational Self*—is wide-ranging and indebted to Barth's "rediscovery" of the doctrine of the Trinity. One of the central issues in the text is understanding the *imago dei* in a Trinitarian perspective, and it is in this context that Kierkegaard is reintroduced. Following a survey of the "substantial" or "structural" interpretation of the image of God—the dominant historical perspective that understands the image of God as attributes or capacities within a person—the "relational" view is introduced as a minority position. Grenz states:

> In the modern era, several Protestant theologians sought to build from the insights of the Reformers in reasserting a relational understanding of the *imago dei*. One more immediate theological impulse for this attempt came through the writings of Søren Kierkegaard. In Kierkegaard's estimation, more crucial than the question of how the divine image exists in humankind is the concern *that* a person exists in the divine image. With this concern in view, Kierkegaard devotes his attention to determining under what conditions such existence in the *imago dei* occurs.[70]

According to Grenz, there are two conditions in which the existence of the *imago dei* occurs. The first, drawn from "The Gospel of Suffering," occurs in the act of worship when the worshipper consents "to be nothing." In essence, the image of God is not something that God and humanity share since God and humanity are infinitely different. Rather, "only when God has infinitely become the eternal and omnipresent object of worship, and man always a worshipper, do they resemble one another."[71] Grenz does not elaborate or explain this quotation further, preferring to turn to the second condition under which the existence of the image of God occurs. As a second example, Grenz returns to *Works of Love*: "As Christianity's glad proclamation is contained in the doctrine about man's kinship with God, so its task is man's likeness to God. But God is love; therefore we can resemble God only in loving."[72] Although it may be possible to interpret this passage as an example of the "substantial" or "structural" interpretation of the image of God, Grenz seeks to emphasize the *imago dei*-constituting element in both of these examples is the relation, or response-ability, humans have with God.

In truth, however, the position of the image of God as relationship is tied more strongly to two of Kierkegaard's heirs than it is to Kierkegaard himself. Referring to the ethicist Paul Ramsey (1913–88) as "one important disciple of Kierkegaard," Grenz illustrates how Ramsey links the image of God to active love for God and

---

[70]   Grenz, *The Social God*, p. 174.

[71]   Grenz, *The Social God*, p. 174. Grenz is citing Søren Kierkegaard, *The Gospel of Suffering and the Lilies of the Field*, trans. by David F. Swenson and Lillian Marvin Swenson, Minneapolis: Augsburg 1948, p. 211 (corresponds to *SKS* 8, 290 / *UD*, 193).

[72]   Grenz, *The Social God*, p. 174. Grenz is citing Søren Kierkegaard, *Works of Love: Some Christian Reflections in the Form of Discourses*, trans. by Howard and Edna Hong, New York: Harper and Row 1962, p. 74 (corresponds to *SKS* 9, 69 / *WL*, 62–3).

neighbor.[73] Looking briefly at Ramsey's *Basic Christian Ethics* reveals that Grenz's debt to Kierkegaard lies here, as Ramsey cites precisely the same text from "The Gospel of Suffering" and also the text from *Works of Love*.[74] Further, Ramsey points forward to Emil Brunner's theology of encounter, and Brunner's anthropology resurfaces in Grenz's text immediately following Paul Ramsey, an anthropology "in keeping with the concerns of his Danish predecessor," an anthropology in which "Man is destined to answer God in believing, responsive love, to accept in grateful dependence his destiny to which God has called him."[75]

Ultimately, Grenz is not interested in pushing the relational view of the image of God forward. Rather, he is interested in proposing a third option, an option more in line with his theological debts to Pannenberg: the *imago dei* as goal. As he shifts to this third option, Grenz drops Kierkegaard from his narrative one more time.

With this disappearance, Grenz's diverse appropriations and interpretations of Kierkegaard's thought come to an end. It is clear that there are some elements that remain stable in his interpretation of Kierkegaard, and some elements become volatile. And, it is also clear that some of the elements that remain stable are volatilized because of Grenz's own development and evolution as a theologian. In sum, it is probably accurate to say that, to Grenz as a young evangelical, Kierkegaard initially appeared to be an attractive ally against modernism and dogmatism, both secular and religious. As Grenz pressed deeper into the theological conversation, however, he appears to have discovered that personal piety—including the form he found in Kierkegaard—was insufficient to account for the rich communal and ecclesial shape of Christianity he began to champion in subsequent years. He continued to acknowledge that Kierkegaard played an important role in twentieth-century theology, but he was also careful to adjust his evaluation of this role. Further, based on his limited interaction with Kierkegaard's texts, it appears that Grenz's interpretation of Kierkegaard is governed primarily by secondary sources. Therefore, his interpretation of Kierkegaard is almost always—especially in the later years—determined by the contours of his larger theological agenda. Kierkegaard has no role in determining this agenda, but is merely a role-player in the furtherance of Grenz's agenda when useful, and a silent observer when not.

Kierkegaard's continued reappearance, however, illustrates that he cannot be ignored indefinitely. Grenz, almost begrudgingly, continues to return to Kierkegaard on various occasions. And, it is these occasions that continue to introduce new dimensions of Kierkegaard's thought into Grenz's *corpus*. When he died suddenly

---

[73]   See Paul Ramsey, *Basic Christian Ethics*, Louisville, Kentucky: Westminster/John Knox 1950, which Grenz quotes: "Jesus' pure humility and prompt obedience to God and his actions expressing pure and instant love for neighbor: these were in fact the same thing, the same image, the very image of God. Standing wholly within the relationship of imaging God's will, 'with unveiled face, reflecting as a mirror the glory of God,' and fully obedient love: these are in reality the same. There is no obedience, no response to God, there are no religious duties beyond this: Thou *shalt* love." (p. 259).

[74]   Ramsey, *Basic Christian Ethics*, pp. 258–9.

[75]   Grenz, *The Social God*, p. 176. Grenz is citing Emil Brunner, *Man in Revolt: A Christian Anthropology*, trans. by Olive Wyon, London: Lutterworth 1939, pp. 98–9. Also see Ramsey, *Basic Christian Ethics*, p. 261.

in 2005, Grenz left much unfinished. Among the engagements that remain open-ended and unfinished is his interpretation of Kierkegaard. Perhaps Grenz would have remained constant in his latest interpretation of Kierkegaard. But, if history is any indication of the future, I doubt it. It would be interesting to see how Grenz would have reacted to some of the recent trends in Kierkegaard scholarship, trends which have begun to interpret and use Kierkegaard for socially and culturally situated theologies and philosophies, trends that would have considerable sympathy for Grenz's postmodern and non-foundational convictions. That task, unfortunately, remains unfinished, waiting for a student as loyal to her mentor as Grenz was to his.

Bibliography

I. References to or Uses of Kierkegaard in Grenz's Corpus

"The Flight from God: Kierkegaard's *Fear and Trembling* and Universal Ethical Systems," in *Christian Freedom: Essays in Honor of Vernon C. Grounds*, ed. by Kenneth W.M. Wozniak and Stanley J. Grenz, Lanham, Maryland: University Press of America 1986, pp. 69–85 (republished in *Perspectives in Religious Studies*, vol. 14, no. 2, 1987, pp. 147–59).

Reason for Hope: The Systematic Theology of Wolfhart Pannenberg, Oxford: Oxford University Press 1990, pp. 126–9.

Together with Roger E. Olson, *20th-Century Theology: God & the World in a Transitional Age*, Downers Grove, Illinois: InterVarsity Press 1992, pp. 64–5.

The Moral Quest: Foundations of Christian Ethics, Downers Grove, Illinois: Inter Varsity Press 1997, pp. 155–60; pp. 347–8.

Together with Ed L. Miller, *Fortress Introduction to Contemporary Theologies*, Minneapolis: Fortress Press 1998, pp. 6–9.

The Social God and the Relational Self: A Trinitarian Theology of the Imago Dei, Louisville, Kentucky: Westminster John Knox Press 2001, pp. 174–6.

II. Sources of Grenz's Knowledge of Kierkegaard

Barth, Karl, *Fragments Grave and Gay*, ed. by Martin Rumscheidt, trans. by Eric Mosbacher, London: Collins 1971, pp. 95–101.

Brunner, Emil, *Man in Revolt: A Christian Anthropology*, trans. by Olive Wyon, London: Lutterworth Press 1939, pp. 140–4; pp. 315–16; pp. 400–3; pp. 486–9; pp. 542–6.

Collins, James Daniel, *The Mind of Kierkegaard*, Chicago: Henry Regnery Company 1965.

Croxall, Thomas Henry, *Kierkegaard Studies*, London: Lutterworth Press 1948.

— *Kierkegaard Commentary*, New York: Harper and Brothers 1956.

Geisler, Norman L., *Ethics: Alternatives and Issues*, Grand Rapids, Michigan: Zondervan 1971, pp. 28–32; pp. 121–2.

Grimsley, Ronald, *Kierkegaard: A Biographical Introduction*, New York: Charles Scribner's Sons 1973.

Lowrie, Walter, *Kierkegaard*, vols. 1–2, New York: Harper and Brothers 1962.

Malantschuk, Gregor, *Kierkegaard's Way to the Truth*, trans. by Mary Michelsen, Minneapolis: Augsburg Publishing House 1963.

— *Kierkegaard's Thought*, trans. by Howard V. Hong and Edna H. Hong, Princeton: Princeton University Press 1971.

Niebuhr, Reinhold, *The Nature and Destiny of Man: A Christian Interpretation, Volume I: Human Nature*, Louisville, Kentucky: Westminster John Knox Press 1996, pp. 170–1; pp. 242–5; pp. 251–4.

Pannenberg, Wolfhart, *Anthropology in Theological Perspective*, trans. by Matthew J. O'Connell, Philadelphia: Westminster Press 1985, pp. 56–8; pp. 96–104; pp. 130–3; pp. 146–50; pp. 254–5.

Ramm, Bernard, *Types of Apologetic Systems: An Introductory Study to the Christian Philosophy of Religion*, Wheaton, Illinois: Van Kampen Press 1953, pp. 39–61.

Ramsey, Paul, *Basic Christian Ethics*, Louisville, Kentucky: Westminster/John Knox 1950, pp. 92–103; pp. 255–9.

Tillich, Paul, *Systematic Theology, Volume II: Existence and The Christ*, Chicago: University of Chicago Press 1957, pp. 33–5; pp. 51–3.

III. Secondary Literature on Grenz's Relation to Kierkegaard

None.

John Alexander Mackay:
The *Road* Approach to Truth

Mariana Alessandri

John Alexander Mackay (1889–1983) first became acquainted with the thought of Søren Kierkegaard in December 1915, during a visit to the larger-than-life Spanish thinker and personality Miguel de Unamuno (1864–1936). "It was from [Unamuno's] lips that I heard for the first time the name of Sören Kierkegaard,"[1] Mackay loyally remembers. As he was in the habit of doing, Unamuno introduced his guest to his copy of Kierkegaard's *Samlede Værker*, perhaps so as not to miss the opportunity to boast of having taught himself Danish to read it.[2] After this initial introduction by Unamuno, Mackay credits Harald Høffding (whose *Søren Kierkegaard als Philosoph* (1896) he read in Spanish translation) with inciting a desire to read Kierkegaard in German,[3] and Mackay names Karl Barth (1886–1968) as the final push toward that goal. In other words, Mackay's interest in Kierkegaard was sparked by Unamuno in 1915, kindled by Høffding and Barth in 1930, and fanned into flame in the years that immediately followed.

---

[1] John Alexander Mackay, "Miguel De Unamuno," in *Christianity and the Existentialists*, ed. by Carl Michalson, New York: Scribner 1956, pp. 45–6. Mackay often reminded his readers that, at the time, it was Unamuno who was at the center of intellectual thought: "Before German scholars had discovered Kierkegaard, before Karl Barth had come under his influence, that great Danish thinker, father of modern existentialists, was known to a Spaniard who lived quietly by the slow-flowing Tormes, in a medieval city on the Castilian plain" (ibid.).

[2] This is not entirely true, but Unamuno was seldom interested in facts. Unamuno learned Norwegian (which he often equates with Danish) in order to read Ibsen, and it was through Brandes, their mutual commentator, that he learned about Kierkegaard. See "Ibsen y Kierkegaard" (1907) in Miguel de Unamuno, *Obras Completas*, vols. 1–9, ed. by Manuel García Blanco, Madrid: Escelicer 1966–71, vol. 3, p. 289.

[3] Harald Høffding, *Søren Kierkegaard als Philosoph*, Stuttgart: Frommann 1896, and Harald Høffding, *Sören Kierkegaard*, Madrid: Revista de Occidente 1930. Mackay's Spanish copy of this book, which contains heavy marginalia, has been conserved in the John A. Mackay Archive at Princeton Theological Seminary Library. I would like to extend my thanks to Isobel Metzger, Mackay's daughter, who granted me access to Mackay's papers, and to John Metzger, Mackay's grandson, who graciously conversed with me about Mackay. I would also like to thank Kenneth Henke, the collection's archivist, without whose efficient help I never would have found the unpublished gems of Mackay's thought.

In the article that follows I (1) offer an historical account of the reception of Kierkegaard by Mackay, (2) analyze Mackay's major references to Kierkegaard during his career, and (3) conclude that Mackay in part interpreted Kierkegaard as a kind of missionary. More specifically, Mackay considered Kierkegaard's vocation as bringing Christianity to Christendom, and he read the mature Kierkegaard's attack on Christendom as the fulfillment of the young Kierkegaard's desire to find an idea worth committing to for life. Later in his career, although the seeds were planted early, Mackay argued that truth can only be found on the *Road*, where one is engaged with life, instead of on the *Balcony*,[4] where one is a mere spectator to life, and credits Kierkegaard with attempting the same kind of "de-balconizing" theology. Mackay saw Kierkegaard as a theologian who tried to bring Christianity to the Road—the level of substantive engagement with the world itself—in order that Christians might make real commitments to live out God's calling. In short, I understand Mackay to have read Kierkegaard as a missionary theologian, one whose project (like Mackay's own) was primarily, though not exclusively, to spread Christianity through depictions of genuine Christian behavior rather than through arguments about Christian theory.

I. History and Reception

Mackay was born in Inverness, Scotland, on May 17, 1889 to a Presbyterian family. In 1907 he entered the King's College branch of the University of Aberdeen. It was in 1910 that he met Robert E. Speer (1867–1947), who had journeyed to Scotland from Princeton on behalf of the American Presbyterian Mission. Speer planted in Mackay's mind the seed of missionary work in Latin America, as well as an interest in attending Princeton. After graduating from Aberdeen with honors in philosophy in 1912, Mackay traveled across the Atlantic to attend Princeton Theological Seminary, from which he graduated in 1915. Now certain of his vocation to be a missionary in Latin America, Mackay traveled back across the Atlantic to Spain, to learn Spanish for his upcoming work. The academic year 1915–16 awakened Mackay's love for Spain and the Spanish language, a love which persisted throughout his career. It was in Madrid, at the *Residencia de Estudiantes* (students' living quarters) that Mackay first met Unamuno, but it was not until his Christmas visit to Unamuno's home in Salamanca that Mackay learned about Kierkegaard. After this momentous year, Mackay and his bride, Jane Logan Wells (1886–1987), headed for Peru on behalf of the Free Church of Scotland. The Mackays lived in Peru from 1916 to 1925, and in that time founded a school, the Colegio Anglo-Peruano, now called the Colegio San Andres.[5] Mackay was awarded a doctorate in literature in 1918 for his dissertation *Don Miguel de Unamuno: His Personality, Work, and Influence*[6] from the University

---

[4]   Mackay imagines a typical Spanish balcony in this image. See John Alexander Mackay, *A Preface to Christian Theology*, New York: Macmillan 1941, p. 5.
[5]   Samuel Escobar, "Mackay, John Alexander," in *Biographical Dictionary of Christian Missions*, ed. by Gerald H. Anderson, New York: Macmillan Reference 1998, pp. 116–22.
[6]   John Alexander Mackay, *Don Miguel De Unamuno: Su Personalidad, Obra e Influencia*, Lima: E.R. Villaren 1919.

of San Marcos, where he would later occupy the chair of philosophy.[7] The Mackays moved to Montevideo, Uruguay, in 1926 and began writing and lecturing there on behalf of the Asociación de Cristianos Jóvenes, or the South American YMCA.[8] The Mackays then spent the years 1930–32 in Mexico City, at the beginning of which time Mackay published his first book *But, I Say Unto You* (1927)[9] and in the middle of which time he fell fully under the spell of Kierkegaard.[10]

From 1929 to 1930, Mackay spent nine months in Europe, visiting Unamuno in Hendaye, France, and spending four months (April–July, 1930) in Bonn with Karl Barth "to study German in order to read Kierkegaard and to meet and listen to a man who had come under Kierkegaard's influence."[11] While tutoring Barth in English and attending his lectures, Mackay also spent time with Emil Brunner (1889–1966), Rudolf Bultmann (1884–1976), and Friedrich Gogarten (1887–1968).[12] From that time forward, Mackay considered Barth an intimate friend, though he never considered himself a *Barthian*. Mackay considered himself more drawn to the *personal* than Barth, whom Mackay read as somewhat uncomfortable with subjectivity. The difference between he and Barth, Mackay explained, was that he himself longed for a philosophy of *life* rather than a philosophy of *light*.[13] Mackay would soon find a like mind in Kierkegaard.

---

[7]   Mackay was the first individual to write a dissertation on Unamuno. See "Memorial Minute," *Theology Today*, vol. 40, no. 4, 1984, pp. 453–6; Escobar, "Mackay, John Alexander"; and Juan Fonesca Ariza, "Unamuno y la Intelectualidad Protestante en el Perú: el Caso de John A. Mackay (1916–1925)," in *La ira y la quimera: actas del Coloquio internacional Centenario de la generación del 98: España y América*, ed. by Eduardo Hopkins Rodriguez, Lima: Pontificia universidad católica del Perú. PUCP, Departamento de humanidades 2001, pp. 169–83.

[8]   See Escobar, "Mackay, John Alexander," and "Memorial Minute."

[9]   John Alexander Mackay, "*Mas Yo Os Digo*," Buenos Aires: Editorial Mundo Nuevo 1927.

[10]   See "Memorial Minute."

[11]   John Alexander Mackay, "Bonn 1930—and After: A Lyrical Tribute to Karl Barth," *Theology Today*, vol. 13, no. 3, 1956, p. 288, and Escobar, "Mackay, John Alexander."

[12]   Mackay claims that though he first heard the name Karl Barth in 1925 from a lecture given by the Swiss churchman Adolf Keller (1872–1963), it was Count Hermann Keyserling who began to popularize Barth in the US, beginning the following year, 1926. According to Mackay (via Unamuno), Keyserling first heard about Barth from Unamuno in 1926 during Unamuno's exile in Hendaye, France, where Mackay, too, would visit him later in the winter of 1929. As Mackay re-narrates the encounter between Unamuno and Keyserling, "[Unamuno] suggested, in the course of their conversation, that [Keyserling] would do well to visit a young German-Swiss theologian who was then teaching in Göttingen, and who, in Unamuno's judgment, was a person of great significance." Mackay knew and was delighted that it was Unamuno who sent Keyserling to Barth. All written correspondence between Keyserling and Unamuno and between Mackay and Unamuno is preserved at the Casa-Museo de Unamuno in Salamanca, Spain. See Mackay, "Miguel de Unamuno" p. 51, Mackay, "Bonn 1930—and After: A Lyrical Tribute to Karl Barth," pp. 287–8, and John Alexander Mackay, "Don Miguel De Unamuno y la Crisis De la Cultura Contemporánea," *Época—Revista de Historia Eclesiástica*, vol. 1, no. 1, 1995, p. 143.

[13]   Mackay wrote a long letter to a friend in Buenos Aires in October 1930, shortly after his return from Germany; which he then copied and sent to several other friends. In this letter

II. Mackay's Lectures and Written Works

The evidence of Mackay's burning enthusiasm for Kierkegaard can most readily be pinned to the years 1931–32, from which we find notes for two distinct lecture series that he gave. The first set of notes form the first two in a series of course lectures that Mackay created and called "Pensadores Proféticos de la Nueva Era" [Prophetic Thinkers of the New Era], and which he delivered to a YMCA audience in Mexico in 1931. The second set of lecture notes form the first of five "Merrick Lectures" that Mackay was invited to deliver by the Ohio Wesleyan University in 1932.[14]

(written in Spanish), Mackay outlined his general points of agreement and contention with Barth and the other German thinkers that he met in Europe, including the Swiss Emil Brunner. Briefly, Mackay approved of the move away from subjectivity and idealism, and he celebrated the resurrection of Kierkegaard and Dostoevsky. Mackay said that Kierkegaard's influence on Barth took the form of the qualitative difference between God and man, and between religion (theology, doctrine, etc.) and revelation. Mackay applauded Barth's reinterpretation of the Bible as Hebraic, rather than Hellenic, calling it the "de-Hellenization of Christianity." Mackay also supported Barth's re-conceptualization of faith and sin. However, in this letter, Mackay disapproved of Barth's neglect or dismissal of the importance of the historical Jesus, which is reflected also in a letter to Barth himself from December 24, 1931, where Mackay attempted to clear up a misunderstanding. Barth thought Mackay called Barth's religion "cold," but Mackay claims to have been referring to Barth's consideration for the historical Jesus, although, "even this a better understanding of your viewpoint would incline me to modify." Additionally, Mackay regretted Barth's disdain toward mysticism, which Barth may well have taken from Kierkegaard. Recall that Mackay was heavily influenced by Unamuno, who was enamored with the mystics, so this point of contention may go back to Unamuno and Kierkegaard instead of Barth and Mackay. Stanton Wilson later said that Mackay helped Barth accept experience as a foundation for religious belief, and helped Barth overcome disparaging comments about mysticism. In support of this, Mackay wrote: "I rejoice in the evidence that Karl Barth has moved beyond the abstract Kierkegaardian doctrine of the divine transcendence which dominated entirely his early thought, and has come to appreciate that form of subjectivity which emerges when a Christian can say with Paul, in profound self-abasement, "It is no longer I who live, but Christ who lives in me." See Stanton Rodger Wilson, *Studies in the Life and Work of an Ecumenical Churchman*, Ph.D. Thesis, Princeton Theological Seminary, Princeton: New Jersey 1958, p. 28, and Mackay, "Bonn 1930—and After: A Lyrical Tribute to Karl Barth," pp. 293–4.

[14]   What survives of Mackay's lecture notes on Kierkegaard are four sets of distinct final-draft-type notes, two typed in Spanish and two in English, and a notebook full of English-language handwritten notes, simply entitled: "Kierkegaard." The Spanish sets of lecture notes seem to be lectures I and II of the same series, "Pensadores Proféticos de la Nueva Era." The first is comprised of 13 pages and is marked "I," while the second is 14 pages and is marked "II." One of the two English sets is 31 pages long, entitled "Kierkegaard, The Existential Thinker," and is presumably the first of the Merrick Lectures, of which there are also some obvious drafts. The other typed set of notes in English is 12 pages long but missing the first page. As this set is most ambiguous, I will refer to it as Mackay's "Untitled Notes." From the content of these four sets, in addition to the information garnered from the letters, I gather that the two Spanish lectures were given on two different occasions, most likely in two consecutive weeks, while the 31-page English lecture was given on a single night. The 12 pages of Mackay's "Untitled

In the fall of 1930, Mackay returned to Mexico City and stayed there until June 1932 (with the exception of May–August 1931 and the winter of 1931–32, when he was in the United States). During these two years in Mexico, under the auspices of the YMCA Mackay delivered three courses simultaneously, which he writes about in letters to various friends.[15] The most relevant of these three courses for the purpose of this study Mackay taught in 1931, and it provides the first locus of his interpretation of Kierkegaard as a kind of missionary. Aimed at the "student and intellectual class," Mackay titled the course: "Pensadores Proféticos de la Nueva Era" ("Prophetic Thinkers of the New Era").[16] About this course, Mackay explained:

> One evening a week I intend lecturing on what I call "modern prophets." In this course I will take up Kierkegaard, Dostoyevski, Unamuno, Albert Schweitzer and Karl Barth. By dealing with the personality and thought of these men I hope to come to grips with the most vital problems of Christianity and civilization.[17]

Mackay wrote this same refrain, with only slight variations, to some twenty different men between November 18, 1930 and February 11, 1931,[18] slowly working out the title, timeline,[19] and figures covered.[20]

Notes" contain different information on Kierkegaard, and remain unaccounted for at present. All subsequent translations of the Spanish lectures are mine.

[15]   The first course that Mackay describes took place on Sundays, and covered the Gospel of John, and was designed for non-churchgoers, Mackay says, as a "substitute for the present at least for a church service." The third course that he describes in these letters was a seminar on the "Sermon on the Mount and Modern Life." See Mackay's December 18, 1930 letter to W.A. Visser 't Hooft. From a flier printed by the Asociación Cristiana de Jóvenes, we know that this series was set to begin on Sunday, February 8, 1931. The flier is dated January 30, 1931.

[16]   See Mackay's April 1 letter to F.W. Ramsey.

[17]   See Mackay's December 18, 1930 letter to W.A. Visser 't Hooft.

[18]   See the following letters: November 18, 1930 to Karl Barth, November 26 to Robert E. Speer, November 27 to John R. Mott, December 3 to S.G. Inman, December 3 to Ortiz Gonzalez, December 4 to J.C. Field, December 10, to Cleveland McAfee, December 13 to Herman Schingensepen, December 13 to H.E. Ewing, December 16 to Rev. J. Foster Stockwell, December 20 to C.H. Robertson, December 27 to John Ritchie, December 27 to Rev. Pierre Maury, December 27 to Rev. Williams Ewen, January 10, 1931 to Rev. John Timothy Stone, January 28 to Charles J. Ewald, January 28 to Rev. James Wright, February 6 to Thomas Cochrane, February 11 to John R. Mott, February 11 to W.S. Rycroft, and February 11 to Robert E. Speer.

[19]   Though Mackay originally wanted twenty weeks for this series, a trip to the US made this impossible. He broke the course into two sets, the first of which contained Kierkegaard. In a letter from April 1 to F.W. Ramsey, Mackay says that he has already "dealt with" Kierkegaard and Dostoevsky. From this, and also from the fact that the first page of these notes is a general gloss on what it means to be a prophet, I gather that Kierkegaard was the first thinker Mackay dealt with in this course. Additionally, a flier for this lecture series advertises that Mackay has discussed Kierkegaard, and that the next lecture will be on Dostoevsky. See the undated flyer marked "Conferencia Sobre Kierkegaard en la Asociación Cristiana de Jóvenes." At least these first lectures ran on Thursdays at 8 pm at Balderas 87, according to the flyer. See the undated flier marked "Conferencia Sobre Kierkegaard en la Asociación Cristiana de Jóvenes" in the Mackey Archive at Princeton Seminary.

[20]   Mackay eventually added Nietzsche to his "Big Five."

In preparation for the course, Mackay requested "first-class" books about Kierkegaard in French and German from friends and booksellers in Europe.[21] In Bonn, Mackay picked up enough reading knowledge of German to tackle Kierkegaard's own texts.[22] Multiple letters also confirm that Mackay read Kierkegaard in German at this time.[23] So, apart from the Spanish translation of Høffding's *Kierkegaard als Philosoph*, the bulk of Mackay's knowledge of Kierkegaard unsurprisingly came filtered through Germany.[24]

Letters written in March and April clearly reflect Mackay's having fallen under Kierkegaard's enchantment. For instance, Mackay writes: "I am at present reveling in the thought of Kierkegaard. I have come to the conclusion that he is the real giant on whose shoulders Barth and Unamuno and many others besides who in themselves are no mean men, are relatively pigmies."[25] Mackay's wild enthusiasm

---

[21]   From Rev. Pierre Murray, Mackay asks for "copies of the three articles by Delacroix and two by Höffding which you mention." I assume that Mackay is referring to Henri Delacroix (1873–1937), and the following articles: Henri Delacroix, "Søren Kierkegaard, Le Christianisme Absolu à Travers le Paradoxe et le Désespoir," *Revue de Métaphysique et de Morale*, vol. 8, 1900, pp. 459–84 and Harald Høffding, "Pascal et Kierkegaard," *Revue de Métaphysique et de Morale*, vol. 30, no. 2, 1923, pp. 221–46. See Mackay's letter to Pierre Maury from March 31, 1931. On a loose sheet of paper in his notes, Mackay has a handwritten note that references the two above mentioned articles, along with "Höffding année 1913." The only thing that Høffding published in 1913 was a Danish work, and since Mackay could not read Danish, we must conclude that he was referring to a different year. This is the 1913 Danish work: Harald Høffding, *Mindre Arbejder*, Copenhagen: Det Nordisk Forlag 1913.

[22]   On April 1, 1931 (presumably in the middle of his lectures on Kierkegaard), Mackay told George Irving that his weekly courses had involved "an extraordinary amount of reading, most of it in German." See Mackay's April 1 letter to George Irving. In terms of how much original material Mackay read, it seems feasible that throughout the course of his career, he would have read the entire Kierkegaard *corpus*.

[23]   For instance, on March 16, Mackay writes the following to Rev. William Paton: "I have recently been reveling in Kierkegaard, whose works I have lately got from Germany. He is the real spiritual and intellectual giant behind the so-called dialectical theological movement, and he possesses, I feel, what many of his modern successors and henchmen lack."

[24]   Mackay habitually commented on the lack of English translations of Kierkegaard, and it is unclear whether he knew about the 1923 Hollander *Selections* (*Selections from the Writings of Kierkegaard*, trans. by L.M. Hollander, Austin: University of Texas 1923 (*University of Texas Bulletin*, no. 2326, *Comparative Literature Series*, no. 3)), because in March he asks his bookseller in Scotland if he had heard of any English translation, to which the bookseller replies in the negative. At this time, Mackay predicted that there would soon be translations into English, so it is unclear whether he was aware of Hollander. See Mackay's March 10 letter to W.A. Visser 't Hooft. The first English translation after Hollander's appeared in 1936: Søren Kierkegaard, *Philosophical Fragments or a Fragment of Philosophy*, trans. by David F. Swenson, Princeton: Princeton University Press 1936. The second was Walter Lowrie's (1868–1959) Søren Kierkegaard, *Christian Discourses, and the Lilies of the Field and the Birds of the Air, and Three Discourses at the Communion on Fridays*, trans. by Walter Lowrie, London: Oxford University Press 1939.

[25]   See Mackay's March 10 letter to W.A. Visser 't Hooft. On April 1, Mackay writes this to Rev. James Taylor: "I am convinced that Kierkegaard and Dostoyevski have not only

for Kierkegaard at this time is significant because it reveals that he has (at least some kind of) a personal connection to Kierkegaard. In addition, that Mackay is living the life of a missionary when he begins reading Kierkegaard is highly relevant and in part explains why Mackay might pick up on a missionary thread in Kierkegaard.

From the Spanish lecture notes, it seems clear that not only was Kierkegaard the first of the five figures covered, but that Mackay dedicated to him two lectures in two consecutive weeks. In the first of these two lectures, Mackay for the most part interprets Kierkegaard's thought biographically, claiming four moments which influenced Kierkegaard's life and work above all others: (1) Kierkegaard's learning about his father's having cursed God on a Jutland hilltop as a small boy, paired with the impact of his father's death on Kierkegaard;[26] (2) The broken engagement to Regine, which Mackay claims pushed Kierkegaard to depths of sorrow rarely experienced by others;[27] (3) The scandal of the *Corsair*, in which Kierkegaard was caricatured publicly, and which led, in Mackay's reading, to Kierkegaard's abandoning the use of pseudonyms;[28] and 4) Kierkegaard's attack on Christendom, which Mackay calls Kierkegaard's mission in life, the idea for which Kierkegaard lived and died.[29] This fourth biographical point is the one which Mackay uses to launch his interpretation of Kierkegaard as a missionary.

After running through some familiar Kierkegaardian themes—the existential spheres, the "leap" of faith, "paradox as the passion of thought," etc.—Mackay cites one of Kierkegaard's journal entries from Gilleleje, 1835. This is the passage that will later become the cornerstone of Mackay's interpretation of Kierkegaard:

> What I really need is to get clear about what I am to do, not what I must know, except insofar as knowledge must precede every act. What matters is to find my purpose, to see what it really is that God wills that I shall do; the crucial thing is to find a truth that is truth for me, to find the idea for which I am willing to live and die..What is truth but to live for an idea?[30]

Mackay ends not only the first night of the Kierkegaard lectures, but the first night of the entire course on prophetic thinkers with these pregnant lines, and so begins what I consider to be his identification with Kierkegaard and his reading of Kierkegaard as a missionary. In reciting this poetic text penned by a 22-year-old Kierkegaard, Mackay also seems to be saying: "What I really need is to get clear about what I must do rather than what I must know." Reading this deliberation that yearns for a life lived in truth and for truth, Mackay seems to be asking with Kierkegaard: "What is truth but to live for an idea?" We may speculate that, in this emotional meditation on what it means to do God's will, in this prayer to live a life that is worthy of his

---

a message for Christianity at the present time, but that they present a viewpoint which must form our point of departure for a new beginning in constructive thought."

[26]   John Alexander Mackay, *Pensadores Proféticos De la Nueva Era I*, Mexico City: Asociación de Cristianos Jóvenes 1931, p. 5.

[27]   Ibid., p. 6.

[28]   Ibid., p. 7.

[29]   Ibid., p. 8.

[30]   *SKS* 17, 26, AA:12–12.10 / *KJN* 1, 13.

purpose, Mackay agrees that "What matters is to find my purpose, to see what it really is that God wills that I shall do."[31] It is in this passage, reserved for the end of not only the first of the two Kierkegaard lectures, but also the first lecture of the entire series on prophetic thinkers, that Mackay enacts a kind of continuity between Kierkegaard's purpose and his own.[32] In other words, it is in front of a Mexican YMCA audience that Mackay's identification with Kierkegaard and his reading of Kierkegaard as a missionary are revealed and run together. It is not a stretch to imagine Mackay reading his own life in Kierkegaard's journal entry, and, at least at this early stage, considering Kierkegaard a kindred spirit.

In what is presumably the second week of the course, Mackay picks up with Kierkegaard's category of Religiousness, but gets there through an early version of his own metaphor of "the Balcony" and "the Road." Mackay claims that writers typically deal with religion in two different ways: as *spectators* or as *actors*. The spectator is primarily a thinker, and for this person the problems of religion are theological problems that they themselves do not face, but watch others face.[33] Actors, on the other hand, are those for whom the problem of religiousness is persistent.[34] In this lecture, Mackay considers Kierkegaard an actor because he took up his calling from God to "purify the religion of his country."[35] This is not to say that missionary work is the only kind of valuable action and that everyone who is not a missionary is reduced to being a spectator, but the difference between spectators and actors does help make sense of what Mackay meant by a Kierkegaardian kind of religiousness. Mackay interprets the difference between Kierkegaard's religious and ethical spheres as the difference between having a personal destiny, that is, a mission, and not having one. For Mackay's Kierkegaard the ethical has to do with norms and general laws—the relative,[36] and the religious with a personal unmediated relationship to God (for which Mackay cites the problem of Abraham).[37] Mackay calls the religious an "adventure," in which an individual chooses to obey a higher power who creates a personal mission for the individual. This idea of a personal destiny recalls the same Gilleleje journal entry which Mackay used at the end of the first lecture, and he uses it here to bolster his conception of Christianity as a

---

[31]   Ibid.

[32]   Mackay recounts having received his call to the missionary life in his youth, a call which defined him for life. I believe that Mackay's vocation as a missionary plays a crucial role in his reading of Kierkegaard as a kind of missionary theologian. See *God's Order: The Ephesian Letter and This Present Time*, New York: Macmillan 1953.

[33]   As examples of spectators on the religious problem Mackay points to Ernest Renán (1823–92) and William James (1842–1910). In later writings, Mackay absolves James, but Renán continues to get the brunt of Mackay's criticism. See Mackay, *A Preface to Christian Theology*, and John Alexander Mackay, *Pensadores Proféticos De la Nueva Era II*, Mexico City: Asociación de Cristianos Jóvenes 1931, p. 1.

[34]   Mackay, *Pensadores Proféticos De la Nueva Era II*, p. 2.

[35]   Ibid.

[36]   Ibid., p. 3.

[37]   Mackay calls the problem of Abraham one of the most tragic in terms of moral behavior. Paraphrasing *Fear and Trembling*, Mackay says that if the ethical is highest, then Abraham is lost, but if the religious is highest, then Abraham is saved (in ibid., p. 4).

missionary enterprise. In other words, all Christians are missionaries for Mackay, and it is their job to find out what mission Christ will send them on, as the young Kierkegaard personally articulated.

In this same lecture Mackay argues that it is not love, not understanding, but obedience to God's call that is the key to religiousness, and he uses the person of Kierkegaard to support this point.[38] Mackay names two exemplars of obedience to God: the apostle Peter, whose whole life was a mission from God and who obeyed readily, and Kierkegaard, in whose thought the highest expression of Christianity consisted in the direct relationship between a soul and God, and in whose life Mackay read a consistent obedience to the call of God.[39] Mackay saw Kierkegaard as living out the particular religious life that God called him to—his mission—obediently. Again, it is reasonable to conclude that Mackay identified all the more so with Kierkegaard for this reason.

In the closing passages of this second lecture, Mackay discusses Kierkegaard's attack on Christendom, which took the radical form of proclaiming that the church had murdered Christianity. Mackay sees Kierkegaard as bringing the sword down on the church, which had unfortunately become a source of comfort and consolation, and rejoices in the fact that Kierkegaard's God is not *Uncle Frank.*[40] However, while Mackay understands Kierkegaard's mission to speak out against the dilution of Christianity and agrees that Christian peace does not consist in theological bunnies and unicorns, he nonetheless worries that Kierkegaard's vitriolic message would inadvertently turn people away from the church.[41] At times like this Mackay takes issue with the effectiveness of Kierkegaard's sword. As I see it, this criticism of Kierkegaard reflects Mackay's own life-long effort to strike a balance between

---

[38]   For Mackay there are three types of religiousness: the first is a loving union with the divine, the second results in an understanding of the divine, and the third involves obeying the divine. As an example of the first, Mackay gives us St. Theresa, for the second, Buddhism, and for the third, the apostle Peter. Surely Mackay's appreciation for St. Theresa came from Unamuno, who wrote that the Saint is "worth any *Critique of Pure Reason.*" See Miguel de Unamuno, *Tragic Sense of Life*, trans. by J.E. Crawford Flitch, New York: Dover 1954, p. 323.

[39]   Mackay, *Pensadores Proféticos De la Nueva Era II*, pp. 5–7.

[40]   Kierkegaard's Climacus says: "In our day, however, when it looks as if one is actually a Christian even as a week-old child, whereby in turn Christ has been changed from the sign of offense into a friend of children *à la* Uncle Frank, Goodman, or a teacher at a charity school." See *SKS* 7, 534 / *CUP1*, 588.

[41]   In general, Mackay considers Kierkegaard too polarizing, and his message too strong. In *God's Order* (1953) Mackay coins the phrase "between order and ardor" to explain what position he believes that Christians ought to take in the world. By *ardor*, Mackay means Kierkegaard's propensity towards Christian revolt and anarchy, while by *order* he means obeying the status quo, neither of which are good without the other. Mackay believes Kierkegaard is too extreme in his anti-Christendom message, and that ardor, without being tempered by order, would presently do more damage than good for Christianity. Jaroslav Pelikan Jr. says this: "in what John Mackay has aptly called the battle between "order and ardor," Kierkegaard had relatively little feeling for the necessity of order as the only framework within which ardor is possible without anarchy. See Mackay, *God's Order*, pp. 176–83 and Jaroslav Pelikan Jr., "The Lord's Hack: A Memorial Tribute to Soren Kierkegaard," *The Cresset*, November 1955.

spurring Christians to action and alienating them. To this point, Mackay ends his discussion of Kierkegaard with what he calls Christ's "paradoxical peace."[42] In (hesitant) agreement with Kierkegaard, Mackay here claims that the peace of Christianity is like the fierce peace of a river, which, though it run fast and rough, contains an order of its own.[43]

We have no information on how these Mexico lectures were received or how many people sat in the YMCA audience, but we do know that in July of that year Mackay received a letter from Phillip Edwards, the assistant to the president of the Ohio Wesleyan University, formally inviting him to give the Merrick Lectures in the Fall of 1932.[44] Mackay agreed to give five nights of lectures (November 20–24) preceded by a church sermon that first Sunday morning. The lectures would cover five thinkers—Kierkegaard, Dostoevsky, Nietzsche, Unamuno and Barth—and would be called "Wilderness Voices of Yesterday and Today."[45] This series was to be published with Abingdon Press after its delivery, a plan which unfortunately never came to fruition.[46]

In terms of his preparation for the Merrick Lectures, Mackay once again ordered books from Germany in October 1931.[47] In March and April 1932, Mackay said that he was "immersed" in Kierkegaard's "Diary," "taken with" Geismar,[48] and that he would soon begin to write the Merrick Lectures for delivery on November 20, 1932.[49]

---

[42]   Mackay, *Pensadores Proféticos De la Nueva Era II*, p. 14.

[43]   Ibid.

[44]   See the letter to John A. Mackay from July 21, 1931, from which it seems that Mackay had already made it clear that he could not give the lectures until the Fall of 1932.

[45]   See Mackay's June 10, 1932 letter to Philip Edwards.

[46]   See Mackay's April 1, 1932 letter to Frank V. Slack. Mackay later remembers: "In 1932, the year I changed my residence and chief sphere of labor from Latin American to the United States, the opportunity came to me to interpret before an American university audience a group of thinkers whose thought, whether Christian or anti-Christian, had provided me with an approach to the intensely secular academic mind of Latin America. In November of that year I delivered the Merrick Lectures at Ohio Wesleyan University. Under the general title of 'Prophetic Thinkers,' I dealt with Kierkegaard, Dostoyevsky, Nietzsche, Unamuno, and Barth." See Mackay, "Bonn 1930—and After: A Lyrical Tribute to Karl Barth."

[47]   In October 1931, Mackay reports that he has ordered the following books: Eduard Oswald Geismar, *Sören Kierkegaard. Seine Lebensentwicklung und seine Wirksamkeit als Schriftsteller*, trans. by Lina von Przyjemski Geismar and E. Krüger, Göttingen: Vandenhoeck & Ruprecht 1929; Anders Gemmer and August Messer, *Sören Kierkegaard und Karl Barth*, Stuttgart: Strecker und Schröder 1925; Friedrich Adolf Voight, *Søren Kierkegaard im Kampfe mit der Romantik der Theologie und der Kirche. Zur Selbstprüfung unserer Gegenwart anbefohlen*, Berlin: Furche-Verlag 1928.

[48]   See Mackay's letter to Professor Douglas Steere from March 18, 1932 and his April 6 letter to Visser 't Hooft. His copy of the "Diary" is the following: Søren Kierkegaard, *Die Tagebücher*, trans. by Theodor Haecker, vol. 2, Innsbruck: Brenner-Verlag 1923.

[49]   See Mackay's April 1, 1932 letter to Frank V. Slack. Concerning English translations, at this point Mackay seems to be aware of the 1923 Hollander English translation of Kierkegaard selections, though it is unlikely that he read it: "no part of Kierkegaard's work has appeared so far in English save a few selections translated in 1923 and published as a

The 31 pages of lecture notes that follow the title "The Existential Thinker" are full of the same themes as "Pensadores Proféticos de la Nueva Era," including an emphasis on personal vocation and living over and against mere thinking. Though they technically debuted in the Spanish lectures, the themes of sin and suffering play an important role in this one. Mackay breaks his lecture into three parts, the first bearing the title "The Return of Job," the second is untitled and the third he calls "Thinking Things." Like the 1931 YMCA lectures, the first section is unsurprisingly dedicated to the biographical influences on Kierkegaard's life, but this time emphasizes more strongly Kierkegaard's mission to attack the established church, again citing Kierkegaard's Gilleleie journal entry for support.[50] The second section rehearses Mackay's earlier argument that Kierkegaard used indirect communication in the form of pseudonyms to teach people the truth because he had considered direct communication futile. Tellingly, Mackay calls Kierkegaard's problem of how to teach people the truth when they do not want to hear it a "missionary problem,"[51] and roughly halfway through this lecture suggests that we think of Kierkegaard as a kind of missionary on the "road" of life. Evidently, Mackay's 1931 implication that Kierkegaard can be read as a missionary becomes a fully explicit suggestion in 1932.

In the third section of the lecture, Mackay reinforces this reading by claiming that Kierkegaard is primarily an existing man and only secondarily a thinker. It seems clear that for Mackay, only existing people can be missionaries. Although it may appear tangential or even trivial, Mackay's associating the term "existing" with Kierkegaard is more significant than one might at first imagine. It is crucial to realize that Mackay's calling Kierkegaard "The Existential Thinker,"[52] is new and weighty in 1932. It is precisely by thinking of Kierkegaard as an existential thinker

---

University of Texas bulletin." See Kierkegaard, *Selections from the Writings of Kierkegaard*, 1923.

[50]   *SKS* 17, 26, AA:12 / *KJN* 1, 13; See also the unpublished notes entitled "Kierkegaard, the Existential Thinker," pp. 6–13.

[51]   At the end of this passage, Mackay remarks that, while Barth was not sensitive to the problem of living rather than thinking, he calls Brunner "intensely sensitive" to it. In many ways it seems that Mackay preferred Brunner's theology to Barth's, and he even predicted in 1930 that Brunner would go "farther than Barth in the end." Brunner also clearly respected Mackay, and wrote this in a dedicatory edition of *Theology Today*: "I met John Mackay for the first time when he visited me on his way back from Bonn, where he had been studying with Karl Barth....Although there was as yet peace between the theology of Barth and my own, my visitor sensed that we were moving on different tracks. John Mackay, however, did not want to play one against the other. He wanted to take the good from each and leave the rest aside. The second time we met at Oxford as we took part in that now historic ecumenical aspect. It was then that Mackay urgently invited me to come to Princeton as professor of systematic theology. I accepted his call, quite as he wished. Hitler came in between. I had to go my own country after only one year of teaching at Princeton. It was during that year, however, that we became good friends. I have admired and even envied one thing particularly in John Mackay, namely, his great wisdom in handling men and in solving situations that seemed insoluble." See Mackay's June 21, 1930 letter to John R. Mott; see also John Baillie et al., "A Thesaurus of Tributes," *Theology Today*, vol. 16, no. 3, 1959, pp. 360–72, see pp. 361–2; and Mackay, "Kierkegaard, the Existential Thinker," p. 15.

[52]   Mackay, "Kierkegaard, the Existential Thinker," p. 5; p. 19.

that one can best see him as a missionary. Recall that 1932 is before the post-World War II existentialist revolution of the 1960s and 1970s in the United States. Mackay called Kierkegaard an existential thinker before "existentialism" was the name of a philosophical school, before the age of Sartre and Camus, before Nietzsche's "death of God" was in vogue, and even before Lowrie,[53] whose volume would not be published for another seven years.[54] No, Mackay invoked Kierkegaard as an existential thinker before an audience of the depression era, of the post-World War I era, and so deserves to be analyzed separately from any subsequent interpretations of Kierkegaard as an existentialist.

Perhaps what Mackay considers revolutionary about Kierkegaard and what reinforces the picture of Kierkegaard as primarily existing is his having asked the question "What shall I do?" instead of "What can I know?" If there is one line that ties Mackay's missionary work with his theological project, it is this. Paraphrasing Kierkegaard, Mackay clearly agrees that "the most important thing about man is that he should live, truly live, not merely think."[55] Though his thought is consistent between the two lectures, in this later one Mackay marries the idea of existence with the idea of living out one's mission. So begins Mackay's emphasis on Kierkegaard's concern with the behavior of Christians over the thought of Christians. This is the full sense of what I am calling the missionary element in Kierkegaard's thought.

In part to explain this point, Mackay introduces what will become the metaphor of his career—"the balcony and the road"—which will be explained more fully in *A Preface to Christian Theology* (1941). In this lecture Mackay distinguishes between a thinker on the balcony and one on the road:

> A thinker on the balcony is the patron of truth, a thinker on the road become's truth's servant. And what truth needs is not patrons but servants, servants in whose life, thought and action, theory and practice are one, thinkers who think not concepts but things.... The man who makes truths for himself on the balcony is a pure impressionist in his thinking and a pure opportunist in his living. The man who has been made by a truth which has met him on the road will be ready to die for the truth that found him.[56]

---

[53]   Lowrie recounts that it was in Mexico City that he met Mackay: "I have known him longer—longer than anyone in Princeton, for I knew him before he came to the United States. I knew him in Mexico when he was under the YMCA, after his propitious work in South America....When I reached Mexico City I called on John Mackay and found that "he was well worth knowing." See John Baillie et al., "A Thesaurus of Tributes," pp. 360–1.

[54]   Søren Kierkegaard, *Christian Discourses, and the Lilies of the Field and the Birds of the Air, and Three Discourses at the Communion on Fridays*, trans. by Walter Lowrie, London and New York: Oxford University Press 1939. In 1942, Lowrie dedicated his *A Short Life of Kierkegaard* to Mackay, with these words: "To John A. Mackay, Doctor of Theology, President of Princeton Seminary, At Home on Both American Continents, and Before Becoming American, a Kierkegaardian, This Little Book is Affectionately Dedicated." See Walter Lowrie, *A Short Life of Kierkegaard*, Princeton: Princeton University Press 1942.

[55]   Mackay, "Kierkegaard, the Existential Thinker," p. 20.

[56]   Ibid., p. 20; p. 5. Mackay begins this lecture by calling Kierkegaard a "wayfarer on the road."

From *actor*, in the Spanish lecture, to *thinker on the road*, in this Merrick lecture, Mackay's portrayal of Kierkegaard has changed mainly in name. Following Kierkegaard, Mackay concludes that if a "truth" does not lead to action then it is not a real truth. But, Mackay quickly clarifies that Kierkegaard does not mean that just any "truth," any idea for which one is willing to live and die is true, or is as good as any other. "No, existence for Kierkegaard is related to the impact of God upon a man's life,"[57] meaning that existence itself is wholly contingent upon God, and Mackay agrees with Kierkegaard that it is only in responding to the call of God that a person can be said to truly exist: "For Kierkegaard, therefore, true thought begins only when one has discovered one's vocation, one's mission in life, when one comes to exist in the true sense of the term."[58] For Mackay (interpreting Kierkegaard), to follow one's vocation is to find and live in the truth. Mackay says that the road is where we learn truth, because the road is where we encounter God and can respond to that call: "When the eternal makes that kind of impact on my life that I, in my finitude and in the concrete situation in which I find myself, strive to let it dominate me utterly in every phase of my being, I exist. By responding utterly to God, I achieve personality."[59] In my reading, Mackay considers Kierkegaard the existential thinker because Kierkegaard marries the concept of existence to the concept of truth. Truth is not akin to fact for Kierkegaard, nor is existence given; and, in Mackay's words, we must find our God-given truth on the road. Once we accept that truth obediently, says Mackay, we can begin to exist. From the balcony, on the other hand, Mackay would say that all one can do is watch the world and think about it—perhaps accumulating facts about reality—but one can never live in it truthfully.[60] Mackay is so far making two radical claims about the nature of truth, both arguably found in Kierkegaard: (1) that any genuinely true concept must in some sense provoke one to act, and (2) that truth or call to action is sent by God, and so ought to be accepted obediently, the acceptance of which is intimately tied to existence.[61] Mackay ends this discussion by saying that active obedience to God's call is each person's mission in life, thereby equating Kierkegaard's "subjective thinking" or "thought that originates in a man's conscious response to the eternal" with his own concepts of the *road, mission,* and *existence.*[62] This discussion is the closest that Mackay comes to explicitly calling Kierkegaard a missionary, aside from his calling what Kierkegaard is dealing with, a

---

[57]   Ibid., p. 22.

[58]   Mackay underlines the term "exist"; see ibid., p. 21.

[59]   Again, Mackay underlines the term "exist"; see ibid., p. 23.

[60]   Ibid., p. 24.

[61]   In a related point, Mackay clarifies that it is an individual's being known by God, instead of his knowing God, that is the basis of existence. In other words, for Mackay, it is not only when I respond to God's call, but when I recognize that I am known by God that I can begin to exist. Mackay goes so far as to change the Cartesian "I think, therefore I am," to "I am known—known of God—therefore I am," ibid., p. 23.

[62]   Mackay moves from here to Kierkegaard's three "stages or levels of existence," and this section is more or less a repetition of the Spanish lectures on the stages. Mackay includes the biographical aspect of Kierkegaard's having been a dandy, though he says it was just an "epoch in Kierkegaard's own life." The aesthete lives for pleasure, and the ethical individual relies on discipline and obedience. Mackay claims that the ethical, though valuable, still

"missionary problem," that is, how to tell people the truth when they do not want to hear it, which we saw earlier and will also encounter later.

Mackay's suggestion that we see Kierkegaard as a missionary makes the most sense in light of two other discussions—suffering and sin. These are both topics that Mackay appreciates Kierkegaard for having addressed, because in Mackay's experience these are the topics which are usually approached reticently by Christians and missionaries. Kierkegaard's views on (and willingness to address) suffering and sin enhance the interpretation of Kierkegaard as a missionary.

Mackay laments what he perceives as a general reluctance on the part of Christians to talk about suffering, and salutes Kierkegaard for his willingness to face the fact that suffering is a necessary part of the Christian life. Unfortunately, says Mackay, the Christianity that once induced a healthy fear of God in people has been replaced by "a religion that exists to give sweetness and consolation,[63] a turn of events which Kierkegaard himself bemoaned. Mackay regrets that Christianity has "been eviscerated of its most characteristic and heroic role" and adds that "true Christianity never makes anyone comfortable or complacent."[64] True Christianity, for Mackay, involves suffering insofar as that suffering can be purifying. Mackay calls God a consuming fire, and says that even (and perhaps especially) when one does respond to the call of God, it is important to understand that suffering will persist. He goes as far as to suggest that Kierkegaard would change Descartes' *Cogito, ergo sum* to *pugno, ergo sum* ("I struggle, therefore I am"). Mackay uses Christ's injunction—"if any man will come after me, let him deny himself"[65]—to remind his readers that the religious life is characterized by pain.[66] Suffering, for Mackay (and presumably Kierkegaard) is the Christian's way back to Christ, so in refusing to discuss it, Christian leaders are to a great extent crippling the Christian community.

In Mackay's understanding, the suffering caused by sin creates a particularly important bridge between the human and the divine. Sin is the way to God, for Mackay, because it is in the throes of repentance that one latches onto Christ (whom Kierkegaard calls *the paradox*):

> The man, says Kierkegaard, who truly knows himself as a sinner, cries out instinctively for the incarnation, for a definite, historic revelation of God, that is, for the absolute paradox. He cries out, like Pascal, for the God of Abraham, Isaac and Jacob, for the face of Jesus Christ....Kierkegaard grounds the necessity of Incarnation in the nature of man as a sinner.[67]

We can assume that Mackay agrees with Kierkegaard that the suffering that accompanies knowing oneself to be a sinner can prompt the acceptance of Christ as both God—the divine power who saves souls—and man—the sympathetic sufferer.

---

belongs to the realm of the relative. In the religious sphere, "the eternal impinges directly upon the temporal and makes an unconditional claim upon the individual." Ibid., pp. 25–6.

[63]   Ibid., p. 28.
[64]   Ibid.
[65]   Luke 9:23; Mackay, "Kierkegaard, the Existential Thinker," p. 27.
[66]   Ibid., p. 22.
[67]   Ibid., p. 30.

Though he calls it "harsh and extreme,"[68] Mackay ultimately applauds Kierkegaard's description of the meeting between the human and the absolute. Far from providing "comfort and sweetness,"[69] Kierkegaard delivers pain and suffering in the image of a burning purification from sin. Mackay not only respects Kierkegaard's candor, but he uses the description of purging evil to emphasize the resulting holiness. Kierkegaard's negativity helps Mackay emphatically proclaim that where sin exists, salvation thrives.[70]

In Mackay's reading, paying attention to and preaching about the saving power of sin is what a good missionary does, and in this case, Kierkegaard is that missionary who tries to lead souls back to Christ. It is because he is willing to dive into the theological trenches of suffering and sin that Mackay regards Kierkegaard as a Christian missionary, and considers him an exemplary philosopher and theologian. By way of a conclusion to this lecture, Mackay lyrically compares Kierkegaard's philosophy to Hegel's:

> We have now arrived at the frontier of Kierkegaard's philosophical position. It stands bold and rugged and mist-clad in its uplands over against a very different type of landscape, a series of gentle hills and valleys, all bathed, in sunshine, extending to the far horizon, reason's fairest empire, the philosophy of Hegel.[71]

Mackay's preference for the "rugged" frontier of Kierkegaard's thought is clear, and it fits into his belief that philosophy and theology must be done on the road, an image which recurs in the next set of Mackay's writing on Kierkegaard.

Mackay's "notes," which presumably either constitute a continuation of the Merrick Lectures on Kierkegaard, or notes for a book, support the reading that Mackay is thinking of Kierkegaard as a missionary. Once again, Mackay invokes the balcony image, claiming that those Christians who live on the balcony must be brought down, be "de-balconized," by Christians on the road. De-balconization is Mackay's answer to what he earlier called the "missionary problem," which is how to bring the truth to those who already think they are in the truth. Mackay's Kierkegaard responded to the missionary problem by using indirect communication in the form of pseudonyms. Mackay writes: "The first step to take in confronting anyone with eternity is to produce within him a sense of sin. That means to de-balconize him to set his feet upon the highway obliging him to raise for himself the question of the meaning of life, of the will of God, not in general, but for him."[72] A *Christian*, for Mackay, lives on the road, and by his example can lead people to Christ.[73] Kierkegaard was an example of this kind of Christian because he

---

68   Ibid., pp. 30–1.
69   Ibid.
70   Ibid.
71   Ibid., p. 31. The last page of this lecture is obviously from an earlier draft, and I have transcribed the handwritten corrections to the typed text.
72   See Mackay's "Untitled Notes," p. 3.
73   Mackay explains: "one who suffers with Christ in life, one who has said "no" to self and "yes" to Christ, one who follows Christ along the road of his own time bearing the cross such loyalty imposes upon him." See Mackay's "Untitled Notes." p. 4.

emphasized the importance of living over thinking. On the other hand, the one whom Kierkegaard calls the *professor* is he who lives on the balcony and leads people away from living like Christ precisely by inverting those values. Kierkegaard and then Mackay viciously refer to the professor as one who values reflective thought over action, who prefers to live on the balcony rather than on the road.

Mackay latches onto Kierkegaard's description of the "professor," and in this set of "notes" points to a separate, two-page document entitled "The Professor," which is none other than a translated passage (presumably done by Mackay), of a Kierkegaard journal entry from 1850.[74] In this "violent" and "priceless" passage,[75] Kierkegaard's professor is the balcony thinker *par excellence*: the professor is a mere spectator, content to study the life of the apostles, but unwilling to live it. What the professor teaches is not Christianity, and Mackay agrees with Kierkegaard that as long as the professors are regarded as the highest authorities, we can know that Christianity is not Christianity.[76]

Mackay's choice to focus on this passage from Kierkegaard's journal is perhaps the strongest evidence in support of the claim that Mackay primarily thinks of Kierkegaard as a missionary. Far from considering Kierkegaard a paralyzed cerebral thinker, Mackay reads him as a Christian actively trying to spread Christianity, through not only his writings, but through his commitment to attack the established church. Mackay's Kierkegaard consistently rails against the professor and tackles Mackay's missionary problem of how to bring Christianity to those who already think they are Christians.

Reading Mackay's 1931–32 lectures, it seems clear that Kierkegaard supplied him with a theology that corresponded to his own missionary work, one that placed personal vocation at its center. Indeed, Kierkegaard's tremendous effect on Mackay is evident on at least three counts. First, in Mackay's interpretation, Kierkegaard was a thinker on the *road*. Kierkegaard placed living higher than thinking, and implied that all thinking ought to be at the service of living. Second, Kierkegaard was not afraid to talk about suffering and sin, both of which are integral to Christianity. He did not offer Christians a comforting or sweet message, and Mackay found this approach new and appropriate to his own missionary life. Third, for Kierkegaard, existence itself hinges on responding to the personal call of God. Mackay's vocation to be and live as a missionary impelled him toward a philosophy which would stress, as he said, *life* over *light*, and in the case of Kierkegaard, existence became synonymous with Christianity itself. Mackay did take issue with Kierkegaard on a few key issues: on his perceived neglect of the social sphere, on the qualitative difference between man and God, and on the vigorousness with which Kierkegaard attacked Christendom, but on the whole, Mackay considered Kierkegaard a theological giant. All of his lectures on Kierkegaard were Mackay's own attempt to bring Christianity back to Christendom in Kierkegaardian fashion.[77]

---

[74]   *SKS* 22, 179, NB12:67 / *JP* 3 3566. *SKS* 23, 301–2, NB18:72 / *JP* 3, 3571.
[75]   See Mackay's "Untitled Notes," pp. 4–5.
[76]   *SKS* 22, 179, NB12:67 / *JP* 3, 3566.
[77]   See Mackay, *A Preface to Christian Theology*.Years later, he reflected on them in his book *Ecumenics: The Science of the Church Universal*, Englewood Cliffs: Prentice-Hall

Though the influence of Kierkegaard on Mackay is most clear during his 1931–32 lectures, the embers of Kierkegaardian thought continue to glow throughout Mackay's career,[78] revived by the publication of *A Preface to Christian Theology* (1941),[79] by which time it is undeniable that his interpretation of Kierkegaard as a missionary is still active. By this time, Mackay has refined his metaphor and devotes an entire chapter to "The Balcony and the Road," claiming that Kierkegaard's "thought and life are the best illustration of the Road approach to truth."[80] Over

---

1964, p. 184: "Some of the lectures were given at times of religious crisis, or where religion was anathema, or at least, was considered unworthy of academic attention. But invariably, whatever the topic, thought would move, in a natural, logical manner, to the figure of Jesus Christ and His relevancy to the question under discussion. The theme might be 'The Vocation of Man,' 'The Meaning of Existence,' 'Intellectuals and the New Era,' 'Metaphysics and life,' 'This revolutionary Springtime,' 'The Concept of freedom in contemporary culture,' or it might be a discussion of Kierkegaard, Nietzsche, Dostoyevsky, Unamuno, or 'The Spanish Mystics.' But there was always one refrain, and it was he, he who was the creator of the lecturer's life passion. And the audience responded, and some saw Christ, God and Christianity, and life in a new perspective."

[78] In *The Presbyterian Way of Life*, Englewood Cliffs: Prentice-Hall 1960, p. xv, Mackay writes: "it was in the late twenties and early thirties of the century, while I roved the Latin-American world endeavoring to interpret Christ and Christianity in the university centers, that I discovered the Lutheran, Søren Kierkegaard. During those same years I became acquainted with the writings of that son of Russian Orthodoxy, Feodor Dostoyevski. Both of these writers opened up for me new insights into the human and the Divine, into Christ and the Church." In *Ecumenics: The Science of the Church Universal*, p. 144, Mackay writes: "the intellectual insight that came to the great Danish thinker, Søren Kierkegaard—that man can fulfill his human destiny and can achieve true existence only when he makes a decision to become God's man—is challenging, in diverse manners, traditional forms of Idealism and Humanism. Existentialism, at its truest and best, as represented by Kierkegaard, and such recent thinkers such as the Spaniard, Unamuno, and the German, Bonhoeffer, calls upon man to wake up, to respond to the awakeness of God, and to live for something bigger than himself." See also ibid., p. 98.

[79] This book was the result of Mackay's 1940 "Sprunt Lectures," given at the *Union Theological Seminary in Virginia,* though I have not come across any explicit lecture notes. As for other lectures on the same theme, from a letter we know that Mackay was planning to give another set of lectures in November 1932 in Nashville, Tennessee, entitled "Life at Three Levels," "under the inspiration of Kierkegaard's *Entweder-Oder* and the *Stadien.*" It is unclear whether these lectures ever took place. See the April 6 letter to Visser 't Hooft. We do know from *That Other America* (1935), that Mackay did give another series of lectures like this in Chile in 1933, though there is not much evidence of its having taken place. Mackay writes: "in the months of May and June 1933, I was in the city of Santiago, Chile. On successive evenings, I lectured on Kierkegaard, the famous Dane, who took issue with Hegel and stands behind the Barthian movement of today, on Dostoyevski, the Russian novelist, who foresaw the Russian revolution and in his works explored the abyss of human nature as no writer had ever done before; and on Miguel de Unamuno, the greatest of contemporary men of letters, whom Kierkegaard had influenced while Barth was yet a schoolboy and who has been called the Dostoyevski of Spain." John A. Mackay, *That Other America*, New York: Friendship Press 1935, p. 121.

[80] Mackay, *A Preface to Christian Theology*, p. 45.

the intervening ten years, Mackay developed his description of the road approach, though it remained fundamentally the same: "knowledge of things divine can be obtained only by those people in whom personal concern has been born and an absolute commitment produced."[81] Mackay repeats his earlier refrain that a man becomes a man when he becomes known, or in this case becomes "God's man," and insists that, for Kierkegaard, being known by God is the key to existence.

III. Conclusion: Kierkegaard Today

Whether Mackay interpreted Kierkegaard correctly or incorrectly (Mackay's *what*), is of secondary concern to the manner in which he delivered his lectures and writings (Mackay's *how*). His early lecture notes reveal something remarkable about the climate in which Mackay was working, which serves as a (rather Kierkegaardian) reminder to Kierkegaard scholars today. In both of these lectures, in Mexico and Ohio, Mackay introduced Kierkegaard's thought as if to suspicious ears. The tone of both lectures is subtly defensive, and he often interjects phrases like: "There is a lot to disagree with in the thought of Kierkegaard, but even despite all of his exaggerations, he calls into question the fundamental problems that our age is called upon to answer."[82] In both Mexico and the US, Mackay delivered these lectures to people who had most likely never heard of Kierkegaard, and before Kierkegaard's message became popular, it sounded rather exaggerated, and even offensive. Recall that his lectures from 1931 and 1932 make Mackay one of the first English speakers to bring Kierkegaard to the Americas. In 1936, David Swenson (1876–1940) published his translation of selections of Kierkegaard's work, and in March of that year, Eduard Geismar (1871–1939) was invited to give the Stone Lectures at Princeton Theological Seminary exclusively on the thought of Kierkegaard; the series would be published in 1938.[83] In addition, Mackay became president of Princeton Theological Seminary in 1936 and served until his retirement in 1959. In 1939, Lowrie introduced his translation of Kierkegaard, for which Mackay wrote a glowing review[84] (but which is problematic if for no other reason than that his more biographical interpretation of Kierkegaard's writings and overall gentler Kierkegaard became authoritative for a long time). Until his death in 1983, Mackay watched the reception of Kierkegaard in the United States grow and change, but his early lectures on Kierkegaard presented an interpretation which was green, and decidedly provocative. Mackay's Kierkegaard was a sword

81   Ibid., p. 49.
82   Mackay, *Pensadores Proféticos De la Nueva Era II*, p. 14. Mackay also writes: "it is easy to say that Kierkegaard had a martyr's complex and that he brought trouble upon himself, and also that his view of Christianity does not tally with that abundance of life about which we hear so much." See Mackay's "Untitled Notes." p. 5.
83   Eduard Geismar, *Lectures on the Religious Thought of Søren Kierkegaard Given at Princeton Theological Seminary in March, 1936*, ed. by David F. Swenson, Minneapolis: Augsburg 1938. See also Swenson's translation from 1936: Kierkegaard, *Philosophical Fragments or a Fragment of Philosophy*.
84   See "The Kierkegaard Renaissance" among Mackay's papers in the Princeton Seminary archive.

in 1931, but I am not sure that we can say the same about the way Kierkegaard's message gets delivered today.

One could have predicted that over time, scholars would cease calling Kierke-gaard's message "exaggerated" or "offensive," and that it might lose its edge. Mackay's worry for Kierkegaard was that he would get into the hands of professors.[85] If Kierkegaard's message is no longer preached with trepidation today as it was by Mackay, and if it would no longer be considered exaggerated or offensive by an audience of Christian youth in Mexico, then Mackay was right to worry that Kierkegaard would fall into the hands of professors. If this has happened, then we can assume that Kierkegaard's message has lost its bite, and in that case any reading of Kierkegaard as a missionary would sound absurd, and would perhaps be rejected outright.

According to my reading of Mackay, he and Kierkegaard agreed that to be a Christian and a missionary means to hear and accept God's call to become a self, and then it means to become a witness to the truth by doing God's work in the world. Mackay made Kierkegaard existentially relevant for himself, his lecture audiences, and his readers. He provocatively interpreted Kierkegaard as advocating a life devoted to God. Mackay would not have read Kierkegaard so thoroughly and would not have kept coming back to Kierkegaard if he had not read in him a call to action, a creative response to a "missionary problem." His lectures and writings suggest that Mackay believed (and believed Kierkegaard to have said) that by dutifully obeying the will of God, by joyfully accepting God's captivity, and by lovingly spreading his message to all of humanity, Christians could create a better world.[86] Because he preached that each person is called to be a missionary of a kind, Mackay won the love and respect of his colleagues, students, friends, and readers. Mackay, in part, used Kierkegaard to spread a message of hope and action in a theological wasteland,[87] and for this reason and others his Kierkegaardian-missionary message is worth retaining.

---

[85]   Mackay writes: "the danger is now that Kierkegaard's oft expressed dread that he would one day fall into the hands of 'professors and wise people,' individuals living detached from life, more interested in thinking life than in living it, may be fulfilled." See Mackay, "Kierkegaard, the Existential Thinker," p. 5.

[86]   Mackay, *A Preface to Christian Theology*, p. 120; p. 78.

[87]   See "Memorial Minute," p. 456. Though no one author takes credit for having written this tribute to Mackay, it is reasonable to assume that it was written by the journal's editor, Hugh T. Kerr.

Bibliography

I. References to or Uses of Kierkegaard in Mackay's Corpus

Don Miguel de Unamuno: Su Personalidad, Obra e Influencia, Lima: E.R. Villaren 1919, p. 7.

The Other Spanish Christ: A Study in the Spiritual History of Spain and South America, London: Student Christian Movement Press 1932, p. 147; p. 224.

That Other America, New York: Friendship Press 1935, p. 121; p. 185.

A Preface to Christian Theology, New York: Macmillan 1941, p. 45.

"Unamuno, Miguel de," *An Encyclopedia of Religion*, ed. by Vergilius Ferm, New York: The Philosophical Library 1945, p. 801.

God's Order: The Ephesian Letter and This Present Time, New York: Macmillan 1953, pp. 176–83.

"Bonn 1930—and After: A Lyrical Tribute to Karl Barth," *Theology Today*, vol. 13, no. 3, 1956, p. 288.

"Miguel De Unamuno," in *Christianity and the Existentialists*, ed. by Carl Michalson, New York: Scribner 1956, p. 45–6.

"Religious Concern and Christian Commitment," *Princeton Seminary Bulletin*, vol. 50, no. 3, 1957, p. 3.

"Theological Triennium: for What?," *Princeton Seminary Bulletin*, vol. 52, no. 3, 1959, p. 8.

The Presbyterian Way of Life, Englewood Cliffs, New Jersey: Prentice-Hall 1960, p. xv.

Ecumenics; the Science of the Church Universal, Englewood Cliffs, New Jersey: Prentice-Hall 1964, p. 98; p. 144; p. 184.

"Unamuno, Miguel de," in *New 20th-Century Encyclopedia of Religious Knowledge*, ed. by J.D. Douglas, Robert G. Clouse, et. al., Grand Rapids, Michigan: Baker Book House 1955, pp. 836–7.

Unpublished Lectures and Notes from the John A. Mackay Archive:

"Pensadores Proféticos de la Nueva Era." I and II. Lecture notes, Mexico City 1930.

"Kierkegaard, The Existential Thinker," Presumed notes from the "Merrick Lectures" given at Ohio Wesleyen University in November 1932.

"Notes," written in English, presumably between 1930 and 1932.

"Conferencia Sobre Kierkegaard en la Asociación Cristiana de Jóvenes." Undated flier summarizing the Kierkegaard lecture given by Mackay the week before and announcing a Dostoevsky lecture for the following week."

"Kierkegaard," English-language Composition notebook, presumably created in 1930–32.

"The Kierkegaard Renaissance" Reviews of *The Point of View* and *Christian Discourses*. 1939.

Letters from the John A. Mackay Archive:

October 13, 1930 to Sr. Dr. don Julio Navarro Monzó
November 2, 1930 to Robert E. Speer
November 18, 1930 to Karl Barth
November 27, 1930 to John R. Mott
December 3, 1930 to S.G. Inman
December 3, 1930 to Ortiz Gonzalez
December 4, 1930 to J.C. Field
December 10, 1930 to Cleveland McAfee
December 13, 1930 to Herman Schingensepen
December 13, 1930 to H.E. Ewing
December 16, 1930 to Rev. J. Foster Stockwell
December 18, 1930 to W.A. Visser 't Hooft
December 20, 1930 to C.H. Robertson
December 27, 1930 to John Ritchie
December 27, 1930 to Rev. Pierre Maury
December 27, 1930 to Rev. Williams Ewen
January 10, 1931 to Rev. John Timothy Stone
January 28, 1931 to Charles J. Ewald
January 28, 1931 to Rev. James Wright
February 6, 1931 to Thomas Cochrane
February 11, 1931 to John R. Mott
February 11, 1931 to W.S. Rycroft
February 11, 1931 to Robert E. Speer
March 10, 1931 to W.A. Visser 't Hooft
March 16, 1931 to Rev. William Paton
March 31, 1931 to Pierre Maury
April 1, 1931 to F.W. Ramsey
April 1, 1931 to George Irving
April 1, 1931 to Rev. James Taylor
March 18, 1932 to Professor Douglas Steere
April 1, 1932 to Frank V. Slack
April 6, 1932 to Visser 't Hooft
June 10, 1932 to Philip Edwards

II. Sources of Mackay's Knowledge of Kierkegaard

Delacroix, Henri, "Søren Kierkegaard, Le Christianisme Absolu à Travers le Paradoxe et le Désespoir," *Revue de Métaphysique et de Morale*, vol. 8, 1900, pp. 459–84.

Geismar, Eduard Oswald, *Sören Kierkegaard. Seine Lebensentwicklung und Seine Wirksamkeit als Schriftsteller*, trans. by Lina von Przyjemski Geismar and E. Krüger, Göttingen: Vandenhoeck & Ruprecht 1929.

— *Lectures on the Religious Thought of Søren Kierkegaard Given at Princeton Theological Seminary in March, 1936*, ed. by David F. Swenson, Minneapolis: Augsburg 1938.

Gemmer, Anders and August Messer, *Sören Kierkegaard und Karl Barth*, Stuttgart: Strecker & Schröder 1925.

Høffding, Harald, *Mindre Arbejder. 1.-3. Række*, Copenhagen: Gyldendal 1905–13.

— "Pascal et Kierkegaard," *Revue de Métaphysique et de Morale*, vol. 30, no. 2, 1923, pp. 221–46.

— *Sören Kierkegaard*, Madrid: Revista de Occidente 1930.

Unamuno, Miguel de, "Ibsen y Kierkegaard" (1907), in Miguel de Unamuno, *Obras Completas*, vols. 1–9, ed. by Manuel García Blanco, Madrid: Escelicer 1966–71, vol. 3, pp. 289–93.

Voigt, Friedrich Adolf, *Sören Kierkegaard im Kampfe mit der Romantik, der Theologie und der Kirche. Zur Selbstprüfung unserer Gegenwart anbefohlen*, Berlin: Furche-Verlag 1928.

III. Secondary Literature on Mackay's Relation to Kierkegaard

Barker, Barbara Graham, *His Becoming Popular: Establishing Søren Kierkegaard in the English-Speaking World*, Ph.D. Thesis, University of Washington, Seattle 1989, p. 149; pp. 173–4.

Cintrón, Pedro, *The Concept of the Church in the Theology of John Alexander Mackay*, Ph.D. Thesis, Drew University, Madison, New Jersey 1979, pp. 53–7.

Escobar, Samuel, "The Legacy of John Alexander Mackay," *International Bulletin of Missionary Research*, vol. 16, no. 3, 1992, pp. 116–22.

Goodpasture, Henry McKennie, "The Latin American Soul of John A. Mackay," *Journal of Presbyterian History*, vol. 48, no. 4, 1970, pp. 265–92.

Jurji, Edward Jabra, *The Ecumenical Era in Church and Society: A Symposium in Honor of John A. Mackay*, New York: Macmillan 1959, p. 15.

Kerr, Hugh T., "The Reformed Faith and the World of Today," *Theology Today*, vol. 16, no. 3, 1959, pp. 301–16.

Lowrie, Walter, "A Thesaurus of Tributes," *Theology Today*, vol. 16, no. 3, 1959, pp. 360–1.

Pelikan, Jaroslav, Jr., "The Lord's Hack: A Memorial Tribute to Soren Kierkegaard," *The Cresset*, vol. 19, no. 1 1955, pp. 20–3.

Wilson, Stanton Rodger, and William O. Harris, "John Mackay: Bibliographical Resources for the Period 1914–1992," *Studies in Reformed Theology and History*, vol. 1, no. 4, 1993, p. 30.

Hugh Ross Mackintosh:
Kierkegaard as "a Precursor of Karl Barth"

David J. Gouwens

I. General Introduction

The significance of Hugh Ross Mackintosh (1870–1936) to Anglophone reception of Søren Kierkegaard lies in the fact that, especially in his posthumously published book, *Types of Modern Theology* (1937), he gave Kierkegaard a central place in the history of German religious thought from the beginning of the modern period to Karl Barth (1886–1968). Mackintosh saw Kierkegaard as "in some degree a precursor of Karl Barth."[1]

Well known in his own day in English-speaking theology, Mackintosh not only introduced English-speaking readers to a wide range of modern German theology and philosophy, but he also shaped a narrative of that theology as a history of responses to the Enlightenment, culminating, in his view, in the Word of God theology of Karl Barth, a picture that has dominated the historiography of nineteenth- and twentieth-century theology.[2] Mackintosh's treatment of Kierkegaard and Barth reveals too his own ongoing theological development, which one student of his thought calls a "theology of transition," not only from his early Ritschlianism to his later sympathies with Kierkegaard and Barth, but a transition reflecting his own relation not only to Barth but also to Emil Brunner (1889–1966).[3]

After theological studies at New College, Edinburgh, and in Germany, Mackintosh soon made himself one of the premier communicators of German

---

The author thanks Joseph McDonald for his assistance in research for this article.

[1] Hugh Ross Mackintosh, *Types of Modern Theology: Schleiermacher to Barth*, London: Nisbet 1937, p. 218. The book "represents in an expanded form the lectures delivered under the Croall Trust…in the autumn of 1933." See Mackintosh, *Types of Modern Theology*, p. vii, the preface by A.B. Macaulay, who brought the book to publication after Mackintosh's death.

[2] Claude Welch calls Mackintosh's *Types of Modern Theology* "undoubtedly the most widely read history of modern theology in English." Claude Welch, *Protestant Thought in the Nineteenth Century, Volume I: 1799–1870*, New Haven and London: Yale University Press 1972, p. 9.

[3] James W. Leitch, *A Theology of Transition: H.R. Mackintosh as an Approach to Barth*, London: Nisbet 1952.

theological thought to Great Britain in his generation.[4] In 1904 at the age of 34 he became Professor of Systematic Theology at New College, Edinburgh, a position he held until his death in 1936. Throughout his career, he maintained close contacts with German theologians, and became "one of the first British theologians to draw attention to the 'dialectical theology' of Brunner, Barth and Gogarten."[5]

Mackintosh's contributions included his involvement in translations of central German theological texts, including Albrecht Ritschl (1822–89), Friedrich Schleiermacher (1768–1834), Brunner, and Barth.[6] His work as a translator mirrors as well his own theological development.

Mackintosh's theological career can be described as finding a way from philosophical idealism and Schleiermacher's liberalism, which he thought had lost sight of divine transcendence. Yet Mackintosh's desire to speak of God as a "personal being in relationship" also went beyond what he judged to be Ritschlian rationalistic moralism, its aversion to metaphysics, and its historical positivism. Like the Ritschlians, he was critical of traditional Christology, particularly Chalcedon, since the Chalcedonian two-natures Christology appeared to Mackintosh to import a "thoroughgoing dualism" into Christology.[7] But Mackintosh sought to rework classical Christology in personalist metaphysical, not only Ritschlian moral, categories, stressing incarnation, pre-existence, and kenosis, with a strong emphasis upon resurrection. In his kenoticism, Mackintosh shared interests with James Denney (1856–1917) and Peter Taylor Forsyth (1848–1921).[8]

Given Mackintosh's developing thought, it is not surprising that beginning in the 1920s and until his death in 1936 he found himself increasingly attracted to dialectical theology. He sought to combine a personalist understanding of God with an affirmation of God's initiative in revelation in Jesus Christ that is open to kenoticism and a strong sense of the believer's experiential participation in Christ. His encounter with the theology of "the Swiss Group," especially Karl Barth, is the primary context for Mackintosh's own appreciative yet critical reception of Kierkegaard.

---

[4]		Robert R. Redman, Jr., *Reformulating Reformed Theology: Jesus Christ in the Theology of Hugh Ross Mackintosh*, Lanham, Maryland: University Press of America 1997, pp. 11–12.
[5]		Ibid., pp. 21–2. The reference is to Friedrich Gogarten (1887–1967).
[6]		Relevant to our topic is his involvement in the translations of Brunner and Barth: Emil Brunner, *The Word and the World*, New York: Charles Scribner's Sons 1931; Emil Brunner, *The Mediator: A Study of the Central Doctrine of the Christian Faith*, trans. by Olive Wyon, Foreword by Canon J. K. Mozley, Foreword by Prof. H.R. Mackintosh, London and Redhill: Lutterworth 1934 (*Lutterworth Library*, vol. 3); Karl Barth, *Church Dogmatics*, vol. I, part 1, trans. by G.T. Thomson, Edinburgh: T. & T. Clark 1936.
[7]		Redman, *Reformulating Reformed Theology*, p. 40.
[8]		Ibid., pp. 22–3. Mackintosh's major treatise on kenotic Christology, *The Doctrine of the Person of Jesus Christ*, New York: Charles Scribner's Sons 1912, uses Forsyth in support of his own position, but while Forsyth quotes Kierkegaard, Mackintosh himself never refers to Kierkegaard.

II. Overview of Places where Kierkegaard is Mentioned or Used

While Mackintosh first notes Kierkegaard's thought appreciatively in 1902, it is not until over twenty years later that he begins to give Kierkegaard a central role in his own theological thought. Given the depth of Mackintosh's familiarity with the German theological scene, it is surprising to see how rarely Mackintosh refers to or quotes from Kierkegaard's works. We can review the history of that growing interest by examining some of Mackintosh's reviews, articles, and lecture notes where, prior to *Types of Modern Theology*, he makes explicit use of Kierkegaard's work.[9]

Mackintosh has the distinction of publishing the first British consideration of Kierkegaard as theologian, "A Great Danish Thinker," in the *Expository Times* of June 1902, a brief review of a German translation of Kierkegaard's *Two Ethical-Religious Essays*. Mackintosh says that "Kierkegaard has come to his kingdom slowly," that he "was almost unknown beyond the Danish frontier," and asks, "Will some one not translate a selection of his shorter pieces into English?"[10]

It is not until over twenty years later, however, that, in addition to passing reference to Kierkegaard in two reviews of books by Joachim Wach,[11] Mackintosh

---

[9]   Mackintosh never refers to Kierkegaard's texts in Danish, and, like P.T. Forsyth, almost certainly worked with the available German translations, although often without clear citation. In *Types of Modern Theology*, Mackintosh cites English books by Werner Brock and E.L. Allen that both include bibliographies of the current Danish editions and of German translations, including those of Christoph Schrempf (1860–1944) and Theodor Haecker (1879–1945). In *Types of Modern Theology*, p. 219, note 1, p. 227, note1, Mackintosh refers to Werner Brock, *An Introduction to Contemporary German Philosophy*, London: Cambridge University Press 1935, pp. 72–86, who, on pp. 129–30, lists both Kierkegaard's *Samlede Værker*, vols. 1–14, Copenhagen: Gyldendal 1901–06, and "the new edition since 1920," and the 1909 edition of Kierkegaard's *Papirer*. Brock also lists Schrempf's and Haecker's translations. In *Types of Modern Theology*, p. 220, note 1, Mackintosh first cites E.L. Allen, *Kierkegaard: His Life and Thought*, London: Stanley Nott 1935. Allen's bibliography on p. 207 lists the Schrempf and Haecker German translations, and three other translations: *Die Reinheit des Herzens. Eine Beichtrede*, trans. by Lina Geismar, Munich: Chr. Kaiser Verlag 1924; *Religion der Tat, Sein Werk in Auswahl*, trans. by Eduard Geismar and Rudolf Marx, Leipzig: A. Kröner 1930, and *Über den Begriff der Ironie*, trans. by Hans Heinrich Schaeder, Munich: R. Oldenbourg 1929. Mackintosh in 1902 reviewed the German translation, Sören Kierkegaard, *Zwei ethisch-religiöse Abhandlungen*, trans. by Julie von Reincke, Giessen: J. Ricker'sche Verlagsbuchhandlung 1902. Finally, in *Types of Modern Theology*, p. 254, Mackintosh says that Kierkegaard "proposed to name his diary *The Book of the Judge*," evidence that perhaps he knew Hermann Gottsched, *Buch des Richters, Seine Tagebücher, 1833–1855 im Auszug*, Jena and Leipzig: Diederichs 1905.

[10]   H.R. Mackintosh, "A Great Danish Thinker," *Expository Times*, vol. 13, October 1901–September 1902, p. 404, reviewing Sören Kierkegaard, *Zwei ethisch-religiöse Abhandlungen*. *SKS* 11, 49–111 / *WA*, 47–108.

[11]   H.R. Mackintosh, "Review of Joachim Wach, *Der Erlösungsgedanke und seine Deutung*," *Expository Times*, vol. 35, October 1923–September 1924, pp. 74–5. Mackintosh mentions Kierkegaard as an example of Wach's "ego-negating" (*Ichverneinung*) type of personality. Mackintosh mentions Kierkegaard again in "Review of Joachim Wach, *Religionswissenschaft*," *Expository Times*, vol. 36, October 1924–September 1925, pp. 376–7.

gives evidence of greater familiarity with Kierkegaard.[12] In his November 1924 review, "The Swiss Group," on Emil Brunner's *Erlebnis, Erkenntnis, und Glaube* and *Die Mystik und Das Wort*, Mackintosh does not mention Kierkegaard, but both of Brunner's books deal extensively with Kierkegaard, revealing Mackintosh's appreciation of dialectical theology, and thus indirectly his awareness of Kierkegaard.[13] Mackintosh says that Brunner "is probably the ablest of the Swiss group, including Kutter, Barth, and Gogarten."[14] He sees in it the beginnings of a movement counter to Ritschlianism, and also against Schleiermacher's "psychologism" (*Erlebnis*). Against "mysticism and intellectualism," Mackintosh welcomes Brunner's stress on "the God who confronts us in the majesty of the Gospel rather than dwells inarticulately within the arcanum of the soul."[15]

More extensive attention to Kierkegaard appears the next year, in Mackintosh's brief March 1926 notice of Emil Brunner's *Philosophie und Offenbarung*, for "in him and others of his group the spirit of Kierkegaard has risen again."[16] Brunner's book, which Brunner himself later acknowledges is strongly influenced by *Philosophical Fragments*, is full of Kierkegaardian language seeing revelation in terms of paradox, dialectic, wonder, and the noetic effects of sin.[17]

Two years after the review of Brunner, Mackintosh mentions Kierkegaard in another article in September 1928 on "Leaders of Theological Thought," focusing now on Karl Barth.[18] Mackintosh treats the early Barth sympathetically, citing the *Romans* commentary and *The Word of God and the Word of Man*, reporting Barth's famous claim that "the line of ancestry to which he wishes to belong goes back through Kierkegaard, Luther and Calvin, Paul, Jeremiah. The name conspicuously

---

[12]   There are, however, Kierkegaardian echoes in Mackintosh's earlier work. Without citing Kierkegaard in his 1912 *The Doctrine of the Person of Jesus Christ*, he states that "antinomy, paradox, contradiction…must meet us at 'every point where we touch the relations of eternity and time.'" Mackintosh, *The Doctrine of the Person of Jesus Christ*, p. 503. Quoting this passage from Mackintosh, Leitch comments that "this dialectic stands much nearer to that of Kierkegaard and of Barth than to the Hegelian." Leitch, *A Theology of Transition*, p. 25.
[13]   H.R. Mackintosh, "The Swiss Group: Review of Emil Brunner, *Erlebnis, Erkenntnis, und Glaube*," Tübingen: Mohr 1923, and *Die Mystik und Das Wort*, Tübingen: Mohr 1924," *Expository Times*, vol. 36, October 1924–September 1925, pp. 73–5.
[14]   Ibid., p. 73. The reference is to Hermann Kutter (1863–1931).
[15]   Ibid., p. 74.
[16]   H.R. Mackintosh, "Review of Emil Brunner, *Philosophie und Offenbarung*, Tübingen: J.C.B. Mohr 1925," *Expository Times*, vol. 37, October 1925–September 1926, pp. 282–3, see p. 282.
[17]   Emil Brunner, *Philosophie und Offenbarung*, Tübingen: J.C.B. Mohr 1925, p. 17, p. 22, p. 25, pp. 37ff. See Brunner's later book, *Der Mittler, zur Besinnung über den Christusglauben*, Tübingen: J.C.B. Mohr (Paul Siebeck) 1927, p. 178, note 1 (*The Mediator*, p. 204, note), where he notes the importance for him of Kierkegaard's *Philosophical Fragments* on how sin is an entity for the theory of knowledge, concluding "cf. my work *Philosophie und Offenbarung*, pp. 37ff."
[18]   H.R. Mackintosh, "Leaders of Theological Thought. Karl Barth," *Expository Times*, vol. 39, October 1927–September 1928, pp. 536–40.

absent here is that of Schleiermacher."[19] Mackintosh's commends Barth's dialectic in *Romans*. "We cannot apply the loved principle of 'continuity' and speak as if God were just the superlative of man, man and something more….We need this broken, mobile, many-dimensioned thinking, the name for which is 'dialectic,' if we are to bear witness to the truth."[20] "Behind all of this, again as with Kierkegaard, is a radically dualistic conception of the relation of God to man,"[21] with God as wholly other, and, alluding to Kierkegaard, "an infinite qualitative difference" between God and humanity. Yet for Barth, he adds, "this primordial dualism is overcome in and by Christ."[22]

Mackintosh here reviews the early Barth positively, but probes two issues in Barth's thought. First, despite his sympathy with Barth's attack upon psychologism, Mackintosh strives yet to relate grace to experience, including the experience of forgiveness.[23] Thus he criticizes Barth's hostility to all "psychological interpretation."[24] Second, Mackintosh appreciates the "primordial dualism" he sees in both Kierkegaard and Barth in their vision of God as "wholly other." Yet he applauds how, referring to Barth without mentioning Kierkegaard, this dualism is overcome in Christ.[25]

Mackintosh's growing interest in Kierkegaard culminates in his extended 1929 essay, "The Theology of Kierkegaard," where he also continues to engage both Barth and Brunner.[26] This essay presents the essentials of his settled judgment of Kierkegaard and will serve as a first draft of his chapter on Kierkegaard in *Types of Modern Theology*.

Since we will examine that later chapter shortly, only two comments are in order on this 1929 essay. First, Mackintosh develops especially his critical reflection upon the "absolute dualism" that he finds in Kierkegaard. Whereas he wrote in his 1928 review of Barth of the "primordial dualism" found in both Barth and Kierkegaard, which, he added, Barth overcomes, in the 1929 Kierkegaard essay, Mackintosh makes clear that he sees Kierkegaard's dualism as "absolute," a fact that is "wholly inconsistent with Kierkegaard's initial principle of subjectivity or inwardness."[27] He

---

[19]   Ibid., p. 536, citing Karl Barth, "The Word of God and the Task of Ministry," in *The Word of God and the Word of Man*, trans. by Douglas Horton, London: Hodder and Stoughton 1928, pp. 183–217, see pp. 195–7.

[20]   Mackintosh, "Leaders of Theological Thought. Karl Barth," p. 537.

[21]   Ibid., p. 538.

[22]   Ibid.

[23]   On experience, see H.R. Mackintosh, *The Christian Experience of Forgiveness*, London: Nisbet 1927, especially pp. 232ff. Mackintosh does not discuss Barth or Kierkegaard in this book.

[24]   Mackintosh, "Leaders of Theological Thought. Karl Barth," p. 539.

[25]   Ibid., p. 538.

[26]   H.R. Mackintosh, "The Theology of Kierkegaard," *Congregational Quarterly*, vol. 7, no. 3, 1929, pp. 282–96.

[27]   Mackintosh, "The Theology of Kierkegaard," p. 282, pp. 288ff., p. 291, p. 292. Mackintosh does not in this essay give sources for this dualistic interpretation of Kierkegaard. The theme of dualism has a long history, of course, in Kierkegaard reception. The themes of Kierkegaard's stress on the infinite qualitative distinction between God and humans,

complains that in Kierkegaard the Incarnation so focuses on the paradox of eternity and time that it destroys the "naturally human," so that in *Concluding Unscientific Postscript* "any degree of continuity, even the minimum, between what we now are and what we were, is proof that we are not in fact living in faith, and that to the miracle of regeneration we as yet are strangers."[28] As in his earlier critical comment on Barth, here too Mackintosh is concerned, against Kierkegaard, to preserve continuity rather than a complete emphasis on discontinuity.

Second, in this 1929 Kierkegaard essay, Mackintosh sees in "the Augustinian doctrine of the total corruption of human nature" "a dubious line of descent from certain features of Augustinianism to [Kierkegaard's] view that, for the Christian, moral life consists in a torturing and sustained act of self-annihilation."[29] As we will see, while Mackintosh later will maintain his critical view that Kierkegaard runs the risk of a Manichaean identification of sin and finitude, in the revision of the 1929 Kierkegaard essay that appears in *Types of Modern Theology*, this earlier essay's negative reference to "certain features of Augustinianism" will drop out, as Mackintosh engages more sympathetically with the understanding of sin in Barth, Brunner, and in Kierkegaard's *The Concept of Anxiety* and *The Sickness unto Death*.[30]

After his own Kierkegaard essay of 1929, Mackintosh continues to engage Brunner and Barth in the 1930s. This included personal contact, involvement in translations of their books, and further reflection especially on Kierkegaard's understanding of sin. Brunner lectured in Great Britain in March 1931, including at New College, Edinburgh, on "Dialectical Theology" or "Theology of Crisis," defending the movement against charges of "having perception only for the transcendence of God, not for His immanence."[31] When Brunner's lectures were published in 1931 as *The Word and the World*, Brunner thanks Mackintosh in the Preface as one of two friends "who revised my English text and assisted me in reading proof."[32] A good example of his eristics, in this book Brunner makes the case for a natural, negative point-of-contact in humanity, making extensive use of Kierkegaard, with Brunner calling him "in my judgment the greatest of all Christian psychologists."[33] It is easy to see why Mackintosh would find Brunner's book of

---

the intellectualism of his alleged irrationalism, and the consequent dualism between his intellectualism and his "initial principle of subjectivity or inwardness" (Mackintosh, "The Theology of Kierkegaard," p. 291) suggest Torsten Bohlin's (1889–1950) *Kierkegaards dogmatische Anschauung: in ihrem geschichtlichen Zusammenhange*, Gütersloh: C. Bertelsmann 1927. As we will see, Mackintosh will indirectly give evidence of Bohlin's influence when he revises his 1929 essay for *Types of Modern Theology*.

[28]   Mackintosh, "The Theology of Kierkegaard," pp. 288–9, p. 292.

[29]   Ibid., p. 292. Here again Mackintosh gives no citations for these views. These are widespread understandings of Kierkegaard in the 1920s and 1930s, and accord closely with Torsten Bohlin's views.

[30]   Contrast Mackintosh, "The Theology of Kierkegaard," p. 288, p. 292, with *Types of Modern Theology*, p. 234, and the expanded discussion of sin in *Types of Modern Theology*, pp. 236–8.

[31]   Emil Brunner, *The Word and the World*, New York: Charles Scribner's Sons 1931, p. 7.

[32]   Ibid., p. 8.

[33]   Ibid., p. 70.

great interest, since it addresses Mackintosh's central concern for maintaining the divine immanence as well as transcendence, continuity within discontinuity, over against dualism. Anticipating his own later reflections on the *imago Dei*, Brunner writes in his Preface to *The Word and the World* that "Much nonsense has been talked about the 'Barthian Theology' having perception only for the transcendence of God, not for His immanence," and that the basis for seeing God and humanity in contradiction is that humanity is created in God's own image.[34]

Three years later, in 1934, Mackintosh, with John Kenneth Mozley (1883–1946), wrote one of the two Forewords to Olive Wyon's (1881–1966) English translation of Brunner's *The Mediator*. Brunner uses Kierkegaard extensively to develop his doctrine of sin, "the gulf between man and the Divine Will...which man cannot bridge....the 'gaping world of human existence' (Kierkegaard)."[35] But Brunner also criticizes Kierkegaard for seeing the "stumbling-block" of Christ as only for the intellect, which echoes Mackintosh's concern in his 1929 Kierkegaard essay that Kierkegaard sees the paradox as "theoretic" and "a new form of intellectualism."[36]

Mackintosh also shared correspondence with Karl Barth, and the two briefly met in Edinburgh in the summer of 1930.[37] Mackintosh had an important role also in the first English translation of Karl Barth's *Church Dogmatics*, volume I, part 1.[38]

In addition to his encounters with Brunner and Barth, Mackintosh also engaged more deeply with Kierkegaard's own thought, particularly on sin. In his unpublished Lecture Synopses (some revised in 1935–36) Mackintosh accentuates his earlier critique of a Ritschlian understanding of sin as ignorance, and, following Kierkegaard, views sin even more as an essentially " 'religious conception' rather than simply an ethical one," namely "godlessness."[39] Thomas F. Torrance (1913–2007), who became his student in 1934, later succeeding him at Edinburgh, writes: "Nowhere had Professor Mackintosh been more critical of himself than in respect of his lecture summaries on sin....Kierkegaard's sharp distinction in *Fear and Trembling* and in

---

[34]   Ibid., p. 7.

[35]   Brunner, *The Mediator*, p. 130.

[36]   Ibid., p. 42; Mackintosh, "The Theology of Kierkegaard," p. 290. See also John W. Hart, *Karl Barth vs. Emil Brunner, The Formation and Dissolution of a Theological Alliance, 1916–1936*, New York: Peter Lang 2001 (*Issues in Systematic Theology*, vol. 6), p. 85.

[37]   Leitch, *A Theology of Transition*, p. v, where Barth in his Foreword writes of his meeting with Mackintosh: "His personality made an unforgettable impression on me. It was not until later that I also came to know his books....His work filled me with interest because, for one thing, I found him engaged quite independently in a movement which, in its general direction, was very like my own."

[38]   The translator of *Church Dogmatics*, vol. I, part 1, G.T. Thomson, writing in Christmas 1934, says of Mackintosh that he "crowned his encouragement of the...[translation] by reading the whole of it in typescript. The magnitude and the thoroughgoing nature of this service some may guess at, I alone can judge...." Barth, *Church Dogmatics*, vol. I, part 1, p. v.

[39]   Redman, *Reformulating Reformed Theology*, p. 156, citing the unpublished Lecture Synopsis, p. 30, "The Nature of Sin." Redman continues that "In his lectures Mackintosh frequently referred to the German edition of *Sickness unto Death*," and to Walter Künneth's *Die Lehre von der Sünde dargestellt an dem Verhältnis der Lehre Sören Kierkegaards zur neuesten Theologie*, Gütersloh: C. Bertelsmann 1927.

Training in Christianity between an ethical and a religious (that is a distinctively Christian) view of sin had clearly struck home to Mackintosh...."[40]

Mackintosh's work on Kierkegaard culminates in Chapter VII of his posthumously published *Types of Modern Theology*, which had such impact on English-speaking theology linking Kierkegaard so closely with Barth.[41] The Kierkegaard chapter, revised from the earlier 1929 version, is organized into five sections.

In the first section, "His Early Life and Training," Mackintosh presents his overall interpretation of Kierkegaard in which Kierkegaard's "infinite qualitative difference between time and eternity," as quoted by Barth, is central. Mackintosh rehearses the familiar events of Kierkegaard's life, focusing upon his relation with his father, his education and engagement, and his sense of guilt, penitence, and solitude before God.[42]

The second section, "Some Fundamental Assumptions," highlights the themes of spiritual inwardness, subjectivity, and passion, defending Kierkegaard against the charge of subjectivism, and commending his distrust of Hegelian philosophy, with particular attention to "qualitative dialectic."[43]

The third section, "The Successive Levels of Human Life," reviews Kierkegaard's literature, and the three stages of life. This section includes new material, carried over to the fourth section, expanding upon his earlier 1929 Kierkegaard essay.[44] Against the charge that Kierkegaard's paradox is nonsense, Mackintosh cites Brunner's *The*

---

[40]   T.F. Torrance, "Hugh Ross Mackintosh: Theologian of the Cross," *Scottish Bulletin of Evangelical Theology*, vol. 5, 1987, pp. 171–2. See Redman, *Reformulating Reformed Theology*, pp. 154–5.

[41]   Mackintosh revised most of this book before his death on June 8, 1936, leaving unrevised only part of the final chapter on Karl Barth, which was edited by A.B. Macaulay, who wrote that for these closing pages (*Types of Modern Theology*, pp. 306–19) he used "a manuscript which was to form the basis of the final version." Mackintosh, *Types of Modern Theology*, p. vii. On the importance of the Kierkegaard chapter for English-speaking theology, see J. Heywood Thomas, "Influence on English Thought," *The Legacy and Interpretation of Kierkegaard*, ed. by Niels Thulstrup and Marie Mikulová Thulstrup, Copenhagen: C.A. Reitzel 1982 (*Bibliotheca Kierkegaardiana*, vol. 8), pp. 166–7.

[42]   The first section is in Mackintosh, *Types of Modern Theology*, pp. 218–23.

[43]   The second section is in Mackintosh, *Types of Modern Theology*, pp. 224–8. Mackintosh's citations of Kierkegaard include: *Types of Modern Theology*, pp. 226–7: on speculation, sin and the individual: *SKS* 11, 230–1 / *SUD*, 119–20; *Types of Modern Theology*, p. 227: on qualitative dialectic: e.g., *SKS* 7, 353 / *CUP1*, 388–9; *Types of Modern Theology*, p. 228: on a system of logic versus a system of being, *SKS* 7, 105–14 / *CUP1*, 109–18.

[44]   The third section is in Macintosh, *Types of Modern Theology*, pp. 228–35, with the new material in sections 3 and 4 covering pp. 234–8. In addition to a general discussion of Kierkegaard's literature, Mackintosh's citations of Kierkegaard in this section include: *Types of Modern Theology*, p. 229: "in interpreting the sign": *SKS* 12, 129ff. / *PC*, 124ff.; *Types of Modern Theology*, p. 231: "the aesthetic life is like a stone thrown across a pool....": *SKS* 2, 131 / *EO1*, 129–30; *Types of Modern Theology*, p. 233: The absurd...with God all things are possible: *SKS* 4, 141 / *FT*, 46; *Types of Modern Theology*, p. 233: "In the power of the absurd, Abraham clung to the certitude that he would receive Isaac back again....": *SKS* 4, 143 / *FT*, 49; *Types of Modern Theology*, p. 234: on paradox in view of Leibniz's distinction between what is above reason and what is against reason: *SKS* 19, 390, Not13:23 / *KJN* 3, 388.

Word and the World in support of paradox, antinomy, and dialectic as a legitimate part of the discontinuity upon which faith rests over against dispassionate, non-paradoxical speculative reason.[45]

The fourth section, "His Reading of the Christian Religion," is the lengthiest section and the heart of the chapter. Mackintosh continues in this section his new material on sin, relating it to the Bible and the Reformers, and drawing upon Kierkegaard's psychological writings.[46] Nonetheless, Mackintosh returns to his earlier fear that it is "only by the narrowest margin" that Kierkegaard escapes "downright Manichaeism," again contrasting this with Barth.[47] Despite his new sympathetic reading of Kierkegaard on sin, he still sees an "absolute dualism between God and man," resolved only in "the leap of pure passion," in which the "relative must be sacrificed to the Unconditioned."[48]

Mackintosh sees this absolute dualism affecting Kierkegaard's thought on God, humanity, and Christ. First, this dualism results in merely negative descriptions of God as "the absolutely Unknown," the mere "Limit," which he finds at odds with personalist language for God in Scripture. Second, with regard to humanity, this dualism obliterates the image of God in humans, to which Mackintosh counters that "The image of God in man is broken, yet not utterly destroyed....What remains of it is not kept in being by man himself....It owes its being, of course, simply to the patient and infinitely merciful grace of God."[49] More seriously, this "unqualified dualism" can lead to seeing finitude as itself guilt, so that "sin and human nature are one and the same."[50] Third, Mackintosh claims that in Kierkegaard's Christology the "paradox assumes its most baffling form," since "Christ is *constituted* by sheer essential contradiction."[51] Mackintosh does again defend Kierkegaard against the charge that the paradox is "nonsense"; to say that the doctrine of the Incarnation is "irrational" stresses the provocativeness in "what the New Testament calls 'the *offence* of the cross.' "[52] Hence, for Kierkegaard "the Person of Jesus is not absurd or irrational for God, but only for us."[53] Nonetheless, Mackintosh, who always stressed the primacy of "immediate utterance of faith" in confessing Christ's deity and humanity, is troubled by Kierkegaard's elevating of the "dogmatic formularies" of the

---

[45]   Mackintosh, *Types of Modern Theology*, pp. 234–5; Brunner, *The Word and the World*, pp. 6–7.

[46]   Mackintosh, *Types of Modern Theology*, pp. 236–8.

[47]   Ibid., pp. 237–8, and citing Künneth, *Die Lehre der Sünde*.

[48]   Ibid., pp. 238–9.

[49]   Ibid., p. 239, p. 241. In the context of the Barth–Brunner debate on natural theology, Mackintosh's language here on the image of God and elsewhere in this chapter (*Types of Modern Theology*, p. 249) is ambiguous, reflecting both Brunner's stress on the formal image of God that remains after sin, yet also showing awareness of Barth's critique. In the chapter on Barth, he will try to mediate the difference between them (*Types of Modern Theology*, p. 316).

[50]   Ibid., p. 242.

[51]   Ibid., pp. 243–4.

[52]   Ibid., p. 245.

[53]   Ibid., pp. 244–5.

two-nature doctrine to make this a "blind acceptance of a Christological paradox."[54] For Kierkegaard, "Sacrifice of the intellect is imperative," and while antinomy is to be defended, Kierkegaard wrongly calls for "the simple crucifixion of intelligence,"[55] "a compulsory theoretical assent at the centre of the religious act."[56] "For the paradox in question, though incomprehensible to reason, is none the less theoretical; and Kierkegaard drives it through with an all but Roman intransigence. But we must not so misuse the method of antinomy that instead of religious sense it yields only logical nonsense."[57] Occasionally, however, Mackintosh grants, Kierkegaard's "violent and exclusive emphasis, in Christology, on the canon *finitum non est capax infiniti*—the finite cannot contain the Infinite—began to trouble him."[58]

Mackintosh here finds Kierkegaard to be insufficiently dialectical. In particular, echoing his earlier work in *The Doctrine of the Person of Jesus Christ*, Mackintosh argues that the two-nature doctrine is not the supreme example of paradox; indeed, historically the doctrine functioned rather as the rationalization of paradox, explaining Christ's human nature impersonally, or, as in Anselm, distributing the experiences of Christ between the two natures. Mackintosh says that "we best keep the paradox or mystery by saying that in Jesus Christ, the man, God is personally present; or, more briefly with Luther: 'This Man is God.' "[59] In this manner Mackintosh remains true to his longstanding personalist understanding of the incarnate divine nature.[60]

In the fifth and concluding section of the chapter, "The Last Phase," Mackintosh turns to Kierkegaard's final years, the *Corsair* affair, and his attack upon the established church, where Mackintosh sees a decline into asceticism and negation

---

[54]   Ibid., p. 250, p. 246.

[55]   Ibid., p. 246, p. 247.

[56]   Ibid., p. 247, see p. 247, note 1, quoting Allen, *Kierkegaard*, p. 22.

[57]   Ibid., pp. 247–8.

[58]   Ibid., p. 248. In the following chapter on Barth, Mackintosh will see Barth giving a place for experience of the Word of God in faith, beyond the incapacity and sin of the finite creature (*Types of Modern Theology*, p. 284).

[59]   Ibid., pp. 250–1; see also Mackintosh, *The Doctrine of the Person of Jesus Christ*, p. 294.

[60]   The fourth section is in *Types of Modern Theology*, pp. 235–51. In addition to a general discussion of Kierkegaard's literature, Mackintosh's citations of Kierkegaard in this section include the following works of Kierkegaard: *Types of Modern Theology*, pp. 235–6: "how to become and be a Christian": e.g., *SKS* 7, 554–9 / *CUP1*, 610–6; *Types of Modern Theology*, p. 236, note 1: "the *blessedness* of the thought that we are always in the wrong as against God": *SKS* 3, 315–32 / *EO2*, 335–54; *Types of Modern Theology*, p. 237: "As doctors could tell us….": *SKS* 11, 138 / *SUD*, 22; *Types of Modern Theology*, p. 237: "Sin…cannot be predicated of God….": *SKS* 11, 233/ *SUD*, 122; *Types of Modern Theology*, p. 238: "Take away the alarmed conscience….": *SKS* 20, 69, NB:79 / *JP* 3, 2461; *Types of Modern Theology*, p. 239: "The Unknown, the Limit": *SKS* 4, 249–50 / *PF*, 44–5; *Types of Modern Theology*, p. 242: on Christ as *incognito*: *SKS* 12, 132–7 / *PC*, 127–33; *Types of Modern Theology*, p. 243: "that in such and such a year": *SKS* 4, 300 / *PF*, 104; *Types of Modern Theology*, p. 244, note 1: on contemporaneity: *SKS* 4, 258–71 / *PF*, 55–71; *Types of Modern Theology*, pp. 244–5: on the absurd no longer absurd for the believer: *Pap.* X–6 B 79 / *JP* 1, 10; cf. *Pap.* X–6 B 68 / *JP* 6, 6598; *Types of Modern Theology*, p. 246: the two Teachers: *SKS* 4, 230–42 / *PF*, 23–36.

of life (including "growing sympathy with Schopenhauer"), and an interpretation of Christianity ending in "shrill defiance."[61] In the chapter's summary, Mackintosh nonetheless defends the "didactic hyperbole" in Kierkegaard's attack, and his rejection of "all efforts to bring faith and speculative philosophy into agreement."[62] Yet here are "new distortions of belief so violent and perverse as gravely to imperil our hold on the New Testament conception of God and of the life His children are called to lead," such as Kierkegaard's extreme individualism that has no place for church and family in relation to "the interior fact of piety," revealing the "same utter dualism between God and man, eternity and time."[63]

Mackintosh's concluding judgment is that at the heart of Kierkegaard's faith are two warring conceptions of God and of the Christian's relation to God: God as Holy Love over against another in which God's love is a "purely formal attribute."[64] Finally, quoting Pascal, Mackintosh says of Kierkegaard that "In great men everything is great—their faults as well as their merits."[65] Thus Mackintosh concludes his chapter on Kierkegaard.[66]

As we have seen, Mackintosh often does not cite sources and so gives little direct indication of the background of his dualistic understanding of Kierkegaard. But in this chapter, Mackintosh expresses appreciation for E.L. Allen (1893–1961), *Kierkegaard, His Life and Thought* of 1935, which he cites three times, with additional allusions.[67] While not the source of Mackintosh's views of Kierkegaard, Allen's book confirms them, and aids also in seeing their sources.[68]

---

[61]   Mackintosh, *Types of Modern Theology*, pp. 251–4, see p. 253, p. 254.

[62]   The chapter summary is in Mackintosh, *Types of Modern Theology*, pp. 254–62. The quotations are from Mackintosh, *Types of Modern Theology*, p. 255, p. 256.

[63]   Ibid., p. 257, p. 258.

[64]   Ibid., pp. 259–60.

[65]   Ibid., p. 262.

[66]   The fifth section, including "The Last Phase" and the untitled summary, is in Macintosh, *Types of Modern Theology*, pp. 251–62. In addition to a general discussion of Kierkegaard's literature, Mackintosh cites in this section the following works of Kierkegaard: *Types of Modern Theology*, p. 251: on suffering: *SKS* 7, 392–477 / *CUP1*, 431–525; *Types of Modern Theology*, p. 252: on 70,000 fathoms: e.g., *SKS* 7, 187 / *CUP1*, 204; *Types of Modern Theology*, p. 253: on the absolute relation to the absolute: *SKS* 7, 352–92 / *CUP1*, 387–431; *Types of Modern Theology*, p. 253: Schopenhauer: e.g., *SKS* 25, 389–90, NB30:12 / *JP* 4, 3881; *Types of Modern Theology*, p. 258, note 1: the apostles administering baptism after Pentecost to thousands: *SKS* 25, 397–8, NB30:19 / *JP* 2, 2056; *Types of Modern Theology*, p. 261: "dying to immediacy": *SKS* 7, 438 / *CUP1*, 483; *Types of Modern Theology*, p. 262: Archimedean point: *SKS* 19, 200, Not6:24 / *KJN* 3, 196.

[67]   Mackintosh, *Types of Modern Theology*, p. 220, note 1, p. 243, note 1, p. 247, note 1.

[68]   Allen, *Kierkegaard*, pp. 144–5; quoted in Macintosh, *Types of Modern Theology*, p. 220, note 1. Allen cites Torsten Bohlin on the intellectualism of Kierkegaard's thought on the Paradox, and to the effect that there is in Kierkegaard "absolutely no continuity between the natural life and the new one" (Allen, *Kierkegaard*, p. 202, citing Bohlin, *Kierkegaards dogmatische Anschauung*, p. 270). Allen accepts also Bohlin's stress that for Kierkegaard the Absolute Paradox is best understood in relation to philosophical categories of the opposition of time and eternity, combined with an intellectualistic understanding of the traditional

Finally, to understand Mackintosh's reception of Kierkegaard as a precursor to Barth in *Types of Modern Theology*, it is important to examine the final chapter, "The Theology of the Word of God: Karl Barth," where Mackintosh relates Kierkegaard not only to the early Barth of *Romans*, but also the Barth of *Church Dogmatics*, vol. I, part 1.[69] For Mackintosh, the new turn in Barth's theology in *Church Dogmatics*, vol. I, part 1, is an abandonment of "existentialism," but "We cannot say that similarly he [Barth] has got beyond dialectical or paradoxical thinking."[70] Moving to a Theology of the Word of God, Barth retains dialectic, and while he makes "more sparing use" of paradox maintains nonetheless Kierkegaard's struggle against reducing God's transcendence to immanence, theology to anthropology.[71] In particular, in Barth's turning to the Trinity, Mackintosh sees the basis for one of his own central theological concerns, affirming a fully personalist understanding of God over against what he sees as Kierkegaard's Absolute, one that secures divine transcendence without sacrificing divine immanence.[72]

It is in this sense that Mackintosh sees Kierkegaard as a precursor of Barth, for while Mackintosh saw both thinkers protesting the immanentism of theology since Schleiermacher, Mackintosh held that Kierkegaard never overcame a profound dualism that afflicted his conception of God and humanity, time and eternity. It is this dualism that Mackintosh sees Barth overcoming in his theology of the Word of God, a theology that at the same time preserves what Mackintosh finds most valuable in Kierkegaard, an appreciation of paradox and qualitative dialectic.

III. General Interpretation of Mackintosh's Use of Kierkegaard

Mackintosh places Kierkegaard within a narrative seeing him as an important precursor to Barth. Particularly in his encounter with "the Swiss Group," but also from his own ongoing "theology of transition" from Idealism to Ritschlianism to dialectical theology, Kierkegaard's importance for Mackintosh is that, over against the main stress of Western theology since the Enlightenment, he rediscovers the Godness of God.

In league with the early Barth and Brunner, Mackintosh values the importance of Kierkegaard on qualitative dialectic, the infinite qualitative difference between God and humanity, and divine transcendence that avoids Schleiermacher's "psychologism," Hegel's "intellectualism," and Ritschl's "rationalistic moralism." At the same time, Mackintosh strongly criticizes Kierkegaard for his "absolute dualism,"[73] resulting in a God seen only as the absolutely unknown, a stress

---

Athanasian doctrine of the two persons (Allen, *Kierkegaard*, p. 196; Mackintosh, *Types of Modern Theology*, p. 250).

[69]   Mackintosh, *Types of Modern Theology*, pp. 263–319.

[70]   Ibid., p. 268.

[71]   Ibid., quoting Barth, *Church Dogmatics*, vol. I, part 1, p. 189.

[72]   Ibid., pp. 299–301; Leitch, *A Theology of Transition*, p. 175, argues for the importance to Mackintosh of Barth's focus on the Trinity.

[73]   Mackintosh, "The Theology of Kierkegaard," p. 288; Mackintosh, *Types of Modern Theology*, p. 238.

on transcendence that threatens the possibility of God's free revelation, denies immanence, confuses finitude with sin, risks seeing incarnation as, if not nonsense, a "crucifixion of intelligence,"[74] intellectualizes the doctrine of the Incarnation, undercuts Christian experience of forgiveness, disparages sociality, and denies God's redemptive power. All of this, for Mackintosh, shows Kierkegaard to be, ironically, insufficiently dialectical.

Mackintosh's engagement with Kierkegaard may best be seen as his attempt, nonetheless, to retrieve what he finds valuable in Kierkegaard's thought, beyond that "dualism," which in turn led Mackintosh to wrestle with Brunner's and Barth's very different appropriations of Kierkegaard.[75] Most students of Mackintosh ignore Brunner's influence, but it is clear that Brunner strongly shapes Mackintosh's positive appropriation of Kierkegaard. With Brunner, Mackintosh appreciates Kierkegaard's interest in human subjectivity and experience, including Kierkegaard's exploration of the psychology of faith and the awareness of guilt and despair, the leap, and the movement through the stages. So too, Mackintosh's interest in subjectivity opened him to Brunner's eristics and Brunner's attempt beyond "dualism" to forge a Kierkegaardian analysis of subjectivity that included continuity as well as discontinuity, allowing a continuing presence of a formal image of God in the sinner. With Barth, however, Mackintosh also appreciated especially Kierkegaard's stress on paradox and dialectic. Indeed, Mackintosh found Kierkegaard in his dualism to be not dialectical enough, whereas Barth was even more dialectical than Kierkegaard, affirming "that man is unlike God, yet also like Him."[76] While Barth discarded "existentialism," Mackintosh claims, "We cannot say that similarly he has got beyond dialectical or paradoxical thinking."[77] And Barth's further development of dialectic firmly establishes for Mackintosh what he himself sought throughout his own theological career: to account for the transcendent God's freedom not only from, but for, immanence, affirming also his own longstanding interests in seeing God as personal and self-giving in *kenosis*, resulting in a soteriology stressing the continuity of Christian experience of forgiveness and union with Christ, and even the capacity of the finite for the infinite.[78]

---

[74]   Mackintosh, *Types of Modern Theology*, p. 247.

[75]   On Brunner's and Barth's different uses of Kierkegaard, see Hart, *Karl Barth vs. Emil Brunner*, pp. 216–17.

[76]   Mackintosh, *Types of Modern Theology*, p. 241.

[77]   Ibid., p. 268, and citing Barth: "The Word of God alone…fulfils the conception of paradox," Barth, *Church Dogmatics*, vol. I, part 1, p. 189. Mackintosh's positive affirmation of the continuing place of dialectical or paradoxical thinking in Barth anticipates recent criticisms of the view that the later Barth abandoned dialectic for analogy. Bruce L. McCormack, *Karl Barth's Critically Realistic Dialectical Theology: Its Genesis and Development 1909–1936*, Oxford: Oxford University Press 1995, p. ix.

[78]   As we have seen, Mackintosh criticized Kierkegaard for "his violent and exclusive emphasis, in Christology, on the canon *finitum non est capax infiniti*," although granting that this "began to trouble" him (*Types of Modern Theology*, p. 248). Mackintosh (*Types of Modern Theology*, p. 284) quotes Barth: "In faith men have an actual experience of the Word of God; and no *finitum non capax infiniti*, nor any *peccator non capax verbi divini* ought now to prevent us from taking this affirmation seriously, with all its consequences." (Mackintosh

At the same time, at the end of *Types of Modern Theology*, Mackintosh sought to mediate between Brunner's and Barth's conflicting appropriations of Kierkegaard. In the Barth essay, Mackintosh shows that he is of course aware of the recent conflicts between Brunner and Barth, especially Barth's discarding of "existentialism" in *Church Dogmatics*, vol. I, part 1, and the dispute with Brunner on the image of God.[79] As we saw, Mackintosh's own reflections on the image of God stand perhaps closer to Brunner, yet toward the end of the Barth chapter Mackintosh wonders whether even in Barth's *Romans* commentary there might be "left room for ultimate agreement between" Barth and Brunner on the formal image of God, for even in *Romans* Barth speaks of God's "relationship...with us which is not broken by sin."[80]

Mackintosh's theology is indeed a theology of transition, drawing alike from both Brunner's and Barth's appropriations of Kierkegaard. Several of Mackintosh's friends and students saw his theology on a trajectory from Ritschlianism through Kierkegaardian existentialism, to a strong Barthian position, and perhaps away from Brunner as well. Mackintosh's friend A.W. Hastings, reviewing *Types of Modern Theology*, reports their conversation shortly before Mackintosh's death, suggesting that the last pages of the Barth chapter, including the pages where Mackintosh suggests a mediation between Barth and Brunner on the image of God, may not reflect Mackintosh's final thoughts on Barth:

> Just before he left for Lewis upon his last mortal journey, he consulted the reviewer as to what he ought to say about Barth, because he found himself so much in agreement with the Swiss doctor. It is, therefore, regrettable that he was prevented...from revising the last twenty pages or so of this book....He was glad for the pungent Reformation savour in the teaching of one who could clothe what was sound in Kierkegaard's reaction in Christian garb, without losing "the whole of Christianity."[81]

So too, his student T.F. Torrance suggests that Mackintosh may have been moving increasingly from Brunner's affirmation of existential continuity to Barth's more dialectical stress on God's free initiative in grace. Torrance claims that Mackintosh tended to link a stress on God's initiative to "an innate hunger or craving or need of man for God which he held to be 'a true point of contact for the gospel of Jesus Christ—a point of contact not created by man but kept in being by God.' "[82] Torrance

---

cites this quotation from Barth as "*Church Dogmatic*, I., p. 250," which is actually the page number in the original German edition. In G.T. Thomson's 1936 English translation, this passage, worded slightly differently, is in *Church Dogmatics*, vol. I, part 1, p. 272.)

[79]   Mackintosh, *Types of Modern Theology*, pp. 263–4, p. 272, p. 316.

[80]   Ibid., p. 316, quoting Karl Barth, *The Epistle to the Romans*, trans. from the sixth edition by Edwyn C. Hoskyns, London: Oxford University Press 1932, p. 170.

[81]   A.W. Hastings, "Review of H.R. Mackintosh, *Types of Modern Theology*," *Expository Times*, vol. 48, October 1936–September 1937, pp. 445–6, see p. 446. The "last twenty pages or so" Mackintosh did not revise are in *Types of Modern Theology*, pp. 306–19.

[82]   Torrance, "Hugh Ross Mackintosh: Theologian of the Cross," p. 171. Torrance does not identify the source of his quotation from Mackintosh, but it closely parallels Mackintosh, *Types of Modern Theology*, p. 241: "The image of God in man is broken, yet not utterly destroyed....It owes its being, of course, simply to the patient and infinitely merciful grace of God...." Compare Mackintosh, *Types of Modern Theology*, pp. 248–50.

suggests, however, that "It was precisely to such a line of thought (the deadly *analogia entis*!) that Barth traced the subtle naturalism that had steadily corrupted and compromised the gospel in Germany—a point which Mackintosh must have taken to heart."[83]

If Hastings and Torrance are correct, Mackintosh might well have moved even further from Brunner's existential employment of Kierkegaard toward Barth's "Theology of the Word of God." Be that as it may, Mackintosh claimed in his Barth chapter—in pages that he did edit before his death—that he saw in Barth not a rejection but a continuation of Kierkegaard's "dialectical or paradoxical thinking," and in that sense Kierkegaard was indeed "in some degree a precursor of Karl Barth."[84]

---

[83]   Torrance, "Hugh Ross Mackintosh: Theologian of the Cross," p. 171.
[84]   Mackintosh, *Types of Modern Theology*, p. 268, p. 218.

Bibliography

I. References to or Uses of Kierkegaard in Mackintosh's Corpus

"A Great Danish Thinker," *Expository Times*, vol. 13, October 1901–September 1902, p. 404.

"Review of Joachim Wach, *Der Erlösungsgedanke und seine Deutung*," *Expository Times*, vol. 35, October 1923–September 1924, pp. 74–5, see p. 74.

"The Swiss Group: Review of Emil Brunner, *Erlebnis, Erkenntnis, und Glaube* and *Die Mystik und Das Wort*," *Expository Times*, vol. 36, October 1924–September 1925, pp. 73–5.

"Review of Joachim Wach, *Religionswissenschaft*," *Expository Times*, vol. 36, October 1924–September 1925, pp. 376–7, see p. 377.

"Review of Emil Brunner, *Philosophie und Offenbarung*," *Expository Times*, vol. 37, October 1925–September 1926, pp. 282–3, see p. 282.

"Leaders of Theological Thought. Karl Barth," *Expository Times*, vol. 39, October 1927–September 1928, pp. 536–40, see p. 536; p. 537; p. 538.

"The Theology of Kierkegaard," *Congregational Quarterly*, vol. 7, no. 3, 1929, pp. 282–96.

Lecture Synopses (some revised 1935–36), unpublished, Lecture 30, "The Nature of Sin," New College Library, New College, Edinburgh.

"The Theology of Paradox: Sören Kierkegaard," in *Types of Modern Theology: Schleiermacher to Barth*, ed. by A.B. Macaulay, London: Nisbet 1937, pp. 218–62.

"The Theology of the Word of God: Karl Barth," in *Types of Modern Theology. Schleiermacher to Barth*, ed. by A.B. Macaulay, London: Nisbet 1937, pp. 263–319, see p. 267; p. 270.

II. Sources of Mackintosh's Knowledge of Kierkegaard

Allen, E.L. [Edgar Leonard], *Kierkegaard: His Life and Thought*, London: Stanley Nott 1935.

Barth, Karl, *Der Römerbrief*, Munich: Christian Kaiser 1922, p. vii; p. xiii; p. 73; p. 91; p. 93; p. 112; p. 234; pp. 262–3; p. 323; p. 379; pp. 424ff. p. 453; pp. 479ff.

— *Das Wort Gottes und die Theologie. Gesammelte Vorträge*, Munich: Christian Kaiser Verlag 1925, p. 164.

— *The Word of God and the Word of Man*, trans. by Douglas Horton, London: Hodder and Stoughton 1928, pp. 195–6.

— *The Epistle to the Romans*, trans. from the 6th ed. by Edwyn C. Hoskyns, London: Oxford University Press 1932, p. 4; p. 10; pp. 98–9; pp. 116–17; p. 136; p. 252; pp. 279–80; p. 338; p. 395; pp. 439ff.; p. 468; pp. 495–6; p. 498.

— *Die Kirchliche Dogmatik,* vol. I, part 1, *Die Lehre vom Wort Gottes: Prolegomena zur Kirchlichen Dogmatik,* Zürich: Zollikon 1932, p. 19; p. 115.

— *Church Dogmatics,* vol. I, part 1, *The Doctrine of the Word of God,* trans. by G.T. Thomson, Edinburgh: T. & T. Clark 1936, p. v; p. 21; p. 126.

Bohlin, Torsten, *Kierkegaards dogmatische Anschauung in ihrem geschichtlichen Zusammenhange,* trans. by Ilsa Meyer-Lüne, Gütersloh: C. Bertelsmann 1927.

Brandes, Georg, *Sören Kierkegaard. Ein literarisches Charakterbild,* trans. by Adolf Strodtmann, Leipzig: J.A. Barth 1879.

Brock, Werner, *Introduction to Contemporary German Philosophy,* London: Cambridge University Press 1935, pp. 72–86; pp. 129–30; and passim.

Brunner, Emil, *Erlebnis, Erkenntnis, und Glaube,* Tübingen: J.C.B. Mohr 1923, p. 6; p. 77; pp. 79–80; p. 79, note 1; p. 97, note 1; p. 110.

— *Die Mystik und das Wort,* Tübingen: J.C.B. Mohr 1924, p. 168; p. 224; p. 322.

— *Philosophie und Offenbarung,* Tübingen: J.C.B. Mohr 1925, p. 17; pp. 22ff.; pp. 37ff.

— *Der Mittler, zur Besinnung über den Christusglauben,* Tübingen: J.C.B. Mohr (Paul Siebeck) 1930, p. 22; p. 106; p. 159; p. 178, note; p. 192, note; p. 195, note; p. 297; pp. 387–8, note.

— *The Word and the World,* New York: Charles Scribner's Sons 1931, passim, see especially p. 6; p. 62; p. 70; p. 74.

— *The Mediator: A Study of the Central Doctrine of the Christian Faith,* trans. by Olive Wyon, Foreword by Canon J.K. Mozley, Foreword by Prof. H.R. Mackintosh, London and Redhill: Lutterworth 1934 (*Lutterworth Library*, vol. 3), p. 42; p. 130; p. 185; p. 204, note; p. 219, note; p. 222, note; p. 332; p. 430 note.

Forsyth, Peter Taylor, *The Work of Christ,* London: Hodder and Stoughton 1910; London: Independent Press 1948, p. xxxii.

Grieve, Alexander, "Kierkegaard," *Encyclopaedia of Religion and Ethics,* ed. by James Hastings, Edinburgh: T. & T. Clark 1908–26, vol. 7, 1914, pp. 696–700.

Heim, Karl, *Der evangelische Glaube und das Denken der Gegenwart, Grundzüge einer christlichen Lebensanschauung,* vol. 1, *Glaube und Denken, Philosophische Grundlegung einer christlichen Lebensanschauung,* Berlin: Furche 1931, p. 93.

Künneth, Walter, *Die Lehre von der Sünde dargestellt an dem Verhältnis der Lehre Sören Kierkegaards zur neuesten Theologie,* Gütersloh: C. Bertelsmann 1927.

Wach, Joachim, *Der Erlösungsgedanke und seine Deutung,* Leipzig: J.C. Hinrichs 1922, pp. 3–4; pp. 21–2; p. 22, note 1; p. 29, note 1; p. 33; p. 62, note 4; p. 70, note 4, p. 88, note3.

— *Religionswissenschaft. Prolegomena zu ihrer wissenschaftstheoretischen Grundlegung,* Leipzig: J.C. Hinrichs 1924, p. 29; p. 31; p. 158, note 2; p. 201.

III. Secondary Literature on Mackintosh's Relation to Kierkegaard

Baillie, D.M., *God Was in Christ,* New York: Charles Scribner's Sons 1948, p. 110.

Baillie, John, *Our Knowledge of God,* New York: Charles Scribner's Sons 1939, p. 101.

Croxall, T.H., *Kierkegaard Commentary*, New York: Harper and Brothers 1956, p. 31; p. 210.

Gardiner, T.W., "Tribute to Professor H.R. Mackintosh," *Scottish Journal of Theology*, vol. 5, no. 3, Spring 1952, pp. 225–36, see p. 227.

Hastings, A.W., "Review of H.R. Mackintosh, *Types of Modern Theology*," *Expository Times*, vol. 48, October 1936–September 1937, pp. 445–6.

Henderson, Ian, *Myth in the New Testament*, London: SCM Press 1952, p. 21.

Hennig, Karl, "Review of H.R. Mackintosh, *Types of Modern Theology*," *Zeitschrift für Theologie und Kirche*, new series, vols. 18–19, 1937–38, pp. 375–8, see p. 377.

Heywood Thomas, J., *Subjectivity and Paradox*. Oxford: Basil Blackwell 1957, p. 110; p. 110, note 5; p. 124; p. 124, note 1; p. 174.

— "The Relevance of Kierkegaard to the Demythologising Controversy," in *Essays on Kierkegaard*, ed. by Jerry H. Gill, Minneapolis: Burgess 1969, pp. 175–85, see p. 179. (Reprinted from *Scottish Journal of Theology*, vol. 10, issue 3, September 1957, pp. 239–52.)

— "Influence on English Thought," *The Legacy and Interpretation of Kierkegaard*, ed. by Niels Thulstrup and Marie Mikulová Thulstrup, Copenhagen: C.A. Reitzel 1982 (*Bibliotheca Kierkegaardiana*, vol. 8), pp. 160–77, see p. 163; pp. 166–7; p. 168.

Leitch, James W., *A Theology of Transition: H.R. Mackintosh as an Approach to Barth*, with a Foreword by Professor Karl Barth, London: Nisbet 1952, p. v; p. 25.

Lewis, Edwin, "Mountain Peaks of Religious Thought: Review of H.R. Mackintosh, *Types of Modern Theology*," *Christian Century*, vol. 54, November 3, 1937, pp. 1359–60.

Lønning, Per, *Samtidighedens Situation, en studie i Søren Kierkegaards kristendomsforståelse*, Oslo: Land og Kirke 1954, pp. 118–54.

— "Kierkegaard's 'Paradox,'" *Orbis Litterarum*, vol. 10, nos. 1–2, 1955, pp. 156–6, see p. 158.

Malik, Habib C., *Receiving Søren Kierkegaard: The Early Impact and Transmission of His Thought*, Washington, D.C.: Catholic University of America Press 1997, p. 326; p. 326, note 22.

Mozley, John Kenneth, *Some Tendencies in British Theology: From the Publication of "Lux Mundi" to the Present Day*, London: SPCK 1952, p. 141.

Muller, Richard A., "Karl Barth and the Path of Theology into the Twentieth Century: Historical Observations," *Westminster Theological Journal*, vol. 51, no. 1, Spring 1989, pp. 25–50, see pp. 25–7; pp. 30–1.

Pattison, George, "Great Britain: From 'Prophet of the Now' to Postmodern Ironist (and after)," in *Kierkegaard's International Reception*, Tome I, *Northern and Western Europe*, ed. by Jon Stewart, Aldershot: Ashgate 2009 (*Kierkegaard Research: Sources, Reception and Resources*, vol. 8), pp. 237–69, see pp. 248–50.

Redman, Robert R., Jr., *Reformulating Reformed Theology: Jesus Christ in the Theology of Hugh Ross Mackintosh*, Lanham, Maryland: University Press of America 1997, p. 25; pp. 154–6; pp. 159–60.

Skarsten, Trygve R., "Danish Contributions to Religion in America," *Lutheran Quarterly*, vol. 25, no. 1, February 1973, pp. 42–53, see pp. 52–3.

Smith, The Rev. J. Weldon, III, "Religion A/Religion B: A Kierkegaard Study," *Scottish Journal of Theology*, vol. 15, no. 3, 1962, pp. 245–65, see pp. 255–6, note 7.

Torrance, T.F., "Hugh Ross Mackintosh: Theologian of the Cross," *Scottish Bulletin of Evangelical Theology*, vol. 5, 1987, pp. 160–73, see pp. 170–1.

Ward, Reverend Rodney A., "The Reception of Søren Kierkegaard into English," *Expository Times*, vol. 107, October 1995–September 1996, pp. 43–7, see p. 46, note 31.

Welch, Claude, *Protestant Thought in the Nineteenth Century, Volume I: 1799–1870*, New Haven and London: Yale University Press 1972, p. 9.

John Macquarrie:

Kierkegaard as a Resource for Anthropocentric Theology

David R. Law

I. The Life and Work of John Macquarrie

John Macquarrie (1919–2007) was born on June 27, 1919 in Renfrew, Scotland. After leaving Paisley Grammar School, he began his university studies in 1936 at the University of Glasgow, where in 1940 he was awarded an M.A. in Mental Philosophy. He then embarked on the study of theology, also at the University of Glasgow, gaining his Bachelor of Divinity in 1943. From 1945 to 1948 Macquarrie served as chaplain in the British Army before becoming minister at St. Ninian's Church, Brechin, where he remained until 1953. Macquarrie described his return to academic theology as "almost accidental."[1] The visit of one of his former theology professors to his parish led to his being persuaded to embark on doctoral studies on Bultmann and Heidegger. By the time Macquarrie completed these studies he was on the teaching staff of the University of Glasgow, having been appointed Lecturer in Systematic Theology in 1953. His doctoral dissertation was published in 1955 under the title of *An Existentialist Theology*.[2] This was followed in 1960 by *The Scope of Demythologizing: Bultmann and His Critics*.[3] During this period Macquarrie was also working with Edward Robinson on the translation of Heidegger's *Being and Time*,[4] which was published in 1962.

In 1962 Macquarrie was appointed Professor of Systematic Theology at Union Theological Seminary, New York, where he converted from Presbyterianism and was ordained to the Anglican priesthood in 1965.[5] During this period Macquarrie

---

[1]   John Macquarrie, "Pilgrimage in Theology," in *Being and Truth: Essays in Honour of John Macquarrie*, ed. by Alistair Kee and Eugene Thomas Long, London: SCM Press 1986, pp. xi–xviii; p. xiii.

[2]   John Macquarrie, *An Existentialist Theology*, London: SCM Press 1955.

[3]   John Macquarrie, *The Scope of Demythologizing: Bultmann and His Critics*, London: SCM Press 1960.

[4]   Martin Heidegger, *Being and Time*, trans. by John Macquarrie and Edward Robinson, Oxford: Basil Blackwell 1962.

[5]   Macquarrie, "Pilgrimage in Theology," p. xiv.

became increasingly unhappy with Bultmann's "almost pure existentialism,"[6] and turned to the theology of Karl Rahner, in whose work he found "that synthesis of catholic faith and philosophical thought for which I had been searching."[7]

During his American period Macquarrie wrote several major works, notably the first edition of his *Twentieth-Century Religious Thought* (1963), *Studies in Christian Existentialism* (1965), *Principles of Christian Theology* (1966), *God-Talk* (1967), *God and Secularity* (1967), and *Martin Heidegger* (1968).[8] *Twentieth-Century Religious Thought* was prompted in part by Macquarrie's "desire to break out of a narrow existentialism."[9] This desire led to Macquarrie's "existential-ontological" period, heralded by the publication of *Principles of Christian Theology*. In this work Macquarrie draws on Heidegger's thought in order to give an ontological grounding to the insights of existentialism and to rethink Christian doctrine in terms of Being as "letting-be" and "Holy Being."

In 1970 Macquarrie left New York to take up the Lady Margaret Chair of Divinity at the University of Oxford. Macquarrie continued to publish prolifically, developing in more detail topics that he had been able to treat only briefly in *Principles*.[10] In the 1970s he published *Three Issues in Ethics* (1970), *Paths in Spirituality* (1972), *Existentialism* (1972), *The Faith of the People of God* (1972), *The Concept of Peace* (1973), *Mystery and Truth* (1973), *Thinking about God* (1975), *Christian Unity and Christian Diversity* (1975), *The Humility of God* (1978), and *Christian Hope* (1978).[11] In 1977 Macquarrie produced a substantially revised second edition of *Principles of Christian Theology*,[12] which attempted to address the criticisms that had been leveled at the first edition and adopted a more positive attitude to natural theology.[13] In his description in "Pilgrimage in Theology" of how his thinking was moving forward in this period, Macquarrie singles out *The Humility of God*

---

[6]   Ibid. Cf. John Macquarrie, *On Being a Theologian: Reflections at Eighty*, ed. by John H. Morgan with Georgina Morley and Eamonn Conway, London: SCM Press 1999, p. 35.

[7]   Macquarrie, "Pilgrimage in Theology," p. xiv.

[8]   See John Macquarrie, *Twentieth-Century Religious Thought*, London: SCM Press 1963; John Macquarrie, *Studies in Christian Existentialism: Lectures and Essays*, London: SCM Press 1966; John Macquarrie, *Principles of Christian Theology*, London: SCM Press 1966; John Macquarrie, *God-Talk: An Examination of the Language and Logic of Theology*, London: SCM 1967; John Macquarrie, *God and Secularity*, London: Lutterworth Press 1967; and John Macquarrie, *Martin Heidegger*, London: Lutterworth Press 1968.

[9]   Macquarrie, "Pilgrimage in Theology," p. xiv.

[10]   Ibid., p. xvi.

[11]   See John Macquarrie, *Three Issues in Ethics*, London: SCM Press 1970; John Macquarrie, *Paths in Spirituality*, London: SCM Press 1972; John Macquarrie, *Existentialism*, New York: World Publishing Co. 1972 and Harmondsworth: Pelican 1972; John Macquarrie, *The Faith of the People of God: A Lay Theology*, London: SCM Press 1972; John Macquarrie, *The Concept of Peace: The Firth Lectures 1972*, London: SCM Press 1973; John Macquarrie, *Mystery and Truth*, Milwaukee: Marquette University 1973; John Macquarrie, *Thinking about God*, London: SCM Press 1975; John Macquarrie, *Christian Unity and Christian Diversity*, London: SCM Press 1975; John Macquarrie, *The Humility of God: Christian Meditations*, London: SCM Press 1978; and John Macquarrie, *Christian Hope*, London: Mowbrays 1978.

[12]   John Macquarrie, *Principles of Christian Theology*, 2nd ed., London: SCM Press 1977.

[13]   Macquarrie, "Pilgrimage in Theology," p. xvii.

as "represent[ing] a development in my thinking, for while it speaks of God's immanence and down-to-earthness, as do my previous writings, it links this far more definitely with the idea of incarnation."[14] It was during this period that Macquarrie entered his "panentheistic phase."

In 1982 Macquarrie published the first volume of a trilogy. The first book to appear was *In Search of Humanity*, in which Macquarrie advances a theology based on his long-held conviction that "the doctrine of man is the right starting point for a contemporary theology."[15] In the final chapter he puts forward a defense of the *analogia entis* and argues that the open-ended character of human existence points towards a panentheistic God, who while transcendent of his creation is nevertheless profoundly involved in its history. At this point, Macquarrie observes, "the search for humanity merges into the search for deity," which is the theme of the second volume in the trilogy, namely, *In Search of Deity* (1984),[16] which was based on Macquarrie's Gifford Lectures at the University of St Andrews in 1983–84. Although he has not abandoned the notion of panentheism, in this phase of his thinking Macquarrie prefers to speak of *dialectical theism*. This is thought about God which attempts to hold together such opposites as transcendence and immanence, eternity and temporality, impossibility and possibility, and knowability and incomprehensibility.

In the *Festschrift* published to mark his retirement in 1986, Macquarrie states his intention to use the time that remains to him to "carry on my quest for a Christian theology truly catholic and truly critical."[17] This determines the themes of his work in his retirement years. In 1986 Macquarrie published *Theology, Church and Ministry*.[18] This was followed in 1990 by the third work of his trilogy, namely, *Jesus Christ in Modern Thought*.[19] In this work—the winner of the 1991 Collins Religious Book Award—Macquarrie provides a historical survey of Christology, before advancing his own position, where, as he puts it in his later *Christology Revisited*, he has "opted for the humanistic approach, the one that begins from the human Jesus."[20] He notes, however, that this approach has encountered resistance in some quarters and cites Kierkegaard and Barth as its opponents. This important book was followed by a plethora of works in which Macquarrie developed many of the themes he had touched upon in earlier works: *Mary for all Christians* (1991), *Heidegger and Christianity* (1994), *The Mediators* (1995), *A Guide to the Sacraments* (1997), *On Being a Theologian* (1999), *Stubborn Theological Questions* (2003), and *Two Worlds Are Ours* (2004).[21] John Macquarrie died on 28 May 2007.

---

[14]   Ibid.

[15]   Ibid. See also John Macquarrie, *In Search of Humanity: A Theological and Philosophical Approach*, London: SCM Press 1982, p. vii.

[16]   Macquarrie, *In Search of Humanity*, p. 261.

[17]   Macquarrie, "Pilgrimage in Theology," p. xviii.

[18]   John Macquarrie, *Theology, Church and Ministry*, London: SCM Press 1986.

[19]   John Macquarrie, *Jesus Christ in Modern Thought*, London: SCM Press 1990.

[20]   John Macquarrie, *Christology Revisited*, London: SCM Press 1998, p. 19.

[21]   See John Macquarrie, *Mary for all Christians*, London: HarperCollins 1991; John Macquarrie, *Heidegger and Christianity*, London: SCM Press 1994; John Macquarrie, *The Mediators*, London: SCM Press 1995; John Macquarrie, *A Guide to the Sacraments*, London: SCM Press 1997; John Macquarrie, *Stubborn Theological Questions*, London: SCM Press

Macquarrie seems to have become acquainted with Kierkegaard through his reading of Heidegger and Bultmann, who were the main subjects of *An Existentialist Theology* and *The Scope of Demythologizing*. In the course of these studies Macquarrie sometimes draws Kierkegaard into the discussion. This discussion, however, is anchored to Macquarrie's study of Heidegger and Bultmann, and does not focus on Kierkegaard for his own sake. In his subsequent works, however, Macquarrie often devotes more attention to Kierkegaard. As we shall see, Macquarrie considers Kierkegaard in the context of his studies of the history of theology and philosophy, but also draws on Kierkegaard to illustrate, unfold, or support various points in his own thought.[22]

II. Kierkegaard's Place in the History of Western Thought

In his existentialist phase Macquarrie regards Kierkegaard primarily as an existentialist philosopher. This view is prominent in *Existentialism*, where he describes Kierkegaard as the father of existentialism[23] or as the first of the existentialists,[24] and places Kierkegaard in the category of "Christian" or "theistic" existentialists.[25] Macquarrie also regards Kierkegaard as a proto-phenomenologist and cites *The Concept of Anxiety* as an example of pre-Husserlian phenomenology.[26] Finally, by the time he came to write *Two Worlds Are Ours* Macquarrie had come to regard Kierkegaard also as a type of mystic.[27]

Macquarrie frequently makes connections between Kierkegaard and other thinkers. These connections are of two types. Firstly, Macquarrie draws attention to Kierkegaard's influence on subsequent thinkers, notably Barth, Bultmann, Niebuhr, R.D. Laing, and John Milbank.[28] Secondly, Macquarrie draws parallels and contrasts between Kierkegaard and other thinkers or cites Kierkegaard in order to elaborate a point made by another thinker. Here Macquarrie's intention is not to

---

2003; and John Macquarrie, *Two Worlds Are Ours: An Introduction to Christian Mysticism*, London: SCM Press 2004.

[22]   Macquarrie uses the older Princeton Lowrie–Swenson translations of Kierkegaard's works. The only exception to this is his use of Alastair Hannay's translation of *Fear and Trembling* (Harmondsworth: Penguin 1985) in Macquarrie, *Jesus Christ in Modern Thought*, p. 243.

[23]   Macquarrie, *Existentialism*, p. 53; p. 118; p. 279.

[24]   Ibid., p. 65, cf. p. 53; p. 62; and p. 220. Cf. also Macquarrie, *Principles of Christian Theology*, 2nd ed., p. 77 and Macquarrie, *Jesus Christ in Modern Thought*, p. 236.

[25]   Macquarrie, *Existentialism*, p. 19; p. 164; p. 251.

[26]   Ibid., p. 23; Macquarrie, *In Search of Humanity*, pp. 216–17.

[27]   Macquarrie, *Two Worlds Are Ours*, pp. 224–5. Macquarrie bases this view in part on David R. Law's doctoral dissertation on Kierkegaard's apophaticism, which Macquarrie supervised and which was later published as *Kierkegaard as Negative Theologian*, Oxford: Clarendon Press 1993.

[28]   See Macquarrie, *The Scope of Demythologizing*, p. 55; Macquarrie, *Existentialism*, p. 271; Macquarrie, *Faith of the People of God*, p. 106; Macquarrie, *Jesus Christ in Modern Thought*, p. 236; p. 279; and Macquarrie, *Stubborn Theological Questions*, p. 217.

argue for Kierkegaardian influence but to point out where Kierkegaardian themes and approaches are evident in the thought of other theologians and philosophers.[29]

Despite his attempts to draw connections between Kierkegaard and other thinkers, Macquarrie was conscious of the difficulty of situating Kierkegaard in the broader currents of Western thought. Thus he later came to doubt the validity of describing Kierkegaard as a philosopher, since "such designations seem to imply the author of some coherent or systematic body of thought."[30] Kierkegaard's thought, however, is "too diffuse and voluminous to admit of summary,"[31] and any attempt to summarize it risks making Kierkegaard's thought more systematic than it really is.[32] The difficulty of finding a neat classification for Kierkegaard leads Macquarrie in *Jesus Christ in Modern Thought* to place Kierkegaard in a category of his own. In a section entitled "A Lone Protestor" he calls Kierkegaard "a lonely eccentric" and describes him as "the best-known of all these mid-century religious thinkers who were swimming against the stream."[33]

---

[29]   Macquarrie finds points of contact, parallels, and contrasting themes between Kierkegaard and Socrates (*Existentialism*, p. 42); Ignatius (*Jesus Christ in Modern Thought*, p. 151); Gregory of Nyssa (*Two Worlds Are Ours*, p. 228); Augustine (*Existentialism*, p. 48); Pseudo-Dionysius (*Jesus Christ in Modern Thought*, p. 379 and *Christology Revisited*, p. 25); Bonaventura (*Christology Revisited*, p. 25); Eckhart (*Christology Revisited*, p. 25); Nicholas of Cusa (*In Search of Deity: An' Essay in Dialectical Theism*, London: SCM Press 1984, pp. 99–100); Wycliffe (*Stubborn Theological Questions*, p. 16; p. 24); Luther (*Principles of Christian Theology*, 2nd ed., p. 185); Pascal (*Principles of Christian Theology*, 2nd ed., p. 185 and *Christology Revisited*, p. 25); Lessing (*Jesus Christ in Modern Thought*, p. 178); Hamann (*Existentialism*, p. 260); Kant (*Two Worlds Are Ours*, p. 226); Hölderlin (*Heidegger and Christianity*, p. 89); Hegel (*In Search of Deity*, p. 99; p. 125; pp. 127–8 and *Jesus Christ in Modern Thought*, p. 212; p. 236; pp. 238–40), where Macquarrie cites the *Concluding Unscientific Postscript*, trans. by David F. Swenson and Walter Lowrie, Princeton: Princeton University Press 1941 p. 79 and p. 107 and Niels Thulstrup, *Kierkegaard's Relation to Hegel*, trans. by George L. Stengren, Princeton: Princeton University Press 1980; *Stubborn Theological Questions*, p. 16); John McLeod Campbell (*Thinking about God*, p. 172, quoting *The Concept of Dread*, trans. by Walter Lowrie, Princeton: Princeton University Press 1944, p. 35, corresponding to *SKS* 4, 345 / *CA*, 38); Gottfried Thomasius (*Jesus Christ in Modern Thought*, p. 246); John Keble (*Two Worlds Are Ours*, p. 224); John Henry Newman (*Stubborn Theological Questions*, p. 165); Harnack (*Principles of Christian Theology*, 2nd ed., p. 185); Kafka (*Existentialism*, p. 260); Buber (*Existentialism*, p. 112); William Temple (*Stubborn Theological Questions*, p. 29); Troeltsch (*Jesus Christ in Modern Thought*, p. 266); Unamuno (*Existentialism*, p. 276); Berdyaev (*Stubborn Theological Questions*, p. 66; p. 74; *Christology Revisited*, p. 25); Heidegger (*Stubborn Theological Questions*, p. 189); Jaspers (*Existentialism*, p. 141); Bultmann (*Stubborn Theological Questions*, p. 213); Sartre (*Existentialism*, p. 72; p. 113; p. 165; p. 170); Popper (*In Search of Humanity*, p. 63; p. 164); Ricoeur (*Stubborn Theological Questions*, p. 189); Bonhoeffer (*Christology Revisited*, p. 25); Ian Henderson (*Thinking about God*, p. 204); Michael Ramsey (*Stubborn Theological Questions*, p. 182); Moltmann (*Thinking about God*, p. 227; *Jesus Christ in Modern Thought*, p. 321).

[30]   Macquarrie, *Jesus Christ in Modern Thought*, p. 236.

[31]   Macquarrie, *Existentialism*, p. 53.

[32]   Macquarrie, *Jesus Christ in Modern Thought*, p. 236.

[33]   Ibid.

III. Macquarrie's Appropriation and Use of Kierkegaard's Thought

Macquarrie had a high opinion of Kierkegaard. He writes of Kierkegaard's "brilliant insights,"[34] and draws on Kierkegaard in developing his own theology. Often these are only passing references. Thus Macquarrie briefly cites Kierkegaard in discussions of the will,[35] selfhood,[36] embodiedness,[37] language,[38] immortality,[39] boredom,[40] commitment,[41] love,[42] the stages of existence,[43] the aesthetic and the ethical,[44] the moment,[45] the crowd,[46]

---

[34]   Ibid.

[35]   Macquarrie, *Existentialism*, p. 216, quoting *The Last Years: Journals 1853–55*, ed. and trans. by Ronald Gregor Smith, London: Fontana 1968, p. 226, which corresponds to *SKS* 26, 254–5, NB33:13.

[36]   Macquarrie, *Existentialism*, pp. 217–18, quoting a passage cited inaccurately as *The Last Years. Journals 1853–55*, ed. and trans. by Smith, p. 156, and Heidegger's comments on Kierkegaard's understanding of temporality and eternity in *Being and Time*, p. 497.

[37]   Macquarrie, *Existentialism*, p. 167 and *In Search of Humanity*, p. 48, where Macquarrie quotes *The Concept of Dread*, trans. by Lowrie, p. 39, which corresponds to *SKS* 4, 349 / *CA*, 43. In *Existentialism* Macquarrie cites Kierkegaard and Heidegger's distrust of the body as evidence for the Gnostic tendencies of existentialist philosophy (*Existentialism*, p. 93).

[38]   Macquarrie, *Existentialism*, pp. 147–8, quoting *The Last Years. Journals 1853–55*, ed. and trans. by Smith, p. 262, which corresponds to *SKS* 26, 318, NB34:6.

[39]   Macquarrie, *Existentialism*, p. 253.

[40]   Ibid., p. 172.

[41]   Macquarrie, *In Search of Humanity*, p. 146.

[42]   Macquarrie, *Studies in Christian Existentialism*, p. 266; p. 273; Macquarrie, *Principles of Christian Theology*, 2nd ed., pp. 348–50; Macquarrie, *In Search of Humanity*, p. 186. In all of these discussions Macquarrie cites the statement in *Works of Love* that "God becomes the third party in every relationship of love" (*The Works of Love*, trans. by Howard V. and Edna H. Hong, New York: Harper & Row 1944, p. 124, which corresponds to *SKS* 9, 123 / *WL* 121).

[43]   Macquarrie, *Existentialism*, p. 175, referring to *Either/Or* and *Stages on Life's Way* and quoting *The Journals of Kierkegaard 1834–1854*, ed. and trans. by Alexander Dru, London: Fontana 1958, p. 45 and p. 44 (mistakenly cited as 44 and 46 respectively), which corresponds to *SKS* 17, 27 and 24, AA:12 / *KJN* 1, 21 and 19.

[44]   Macquarrie, *In Search of Humanity*, pp. 191–2, quoting *Either/Or*, vols. 1–2, trans. by David F. Swenson, Lillian Marvin Swenson, and Walter Lowrie, Princeton: Princeton University Press 1941, vol. 1, p. 95 (which corresponds to *SKS* 2, 100 / *EO2*, 96); p. 97 (which corresponds to *SKS* 2, 102 / *EO2*, 99); p. 363 (which corresponds to *SKS* 2, 356 / *EO2*, 367); *Either/Or*, trans. by Swenson, Swenson, and Lowrie, vol. 2, p. 10 (which corresponds to *SKS* 2, 20 / *EO2*, 10) and p. 161 which corresponds to *SKS* 3, 169 / *EO2*, 157).

[45]   Macquarrie, *Studies in Christian Existentialism*, p. 68 and *Existentialism*, pp. 217–18, citing *Training in Christianity*, trans. by Walter Lowrie, Princeton: Princeton University Press 1944, p. 117 (which corresponds to *SKS* 12, 123 / *PC*, 115); See also Macquarrie, *Principles of Christian Theology*, 2nd ed., p. 77; Macquarrie, *Christian Hope*, p. 100; and Macquarrie, *In Search of Humanity*, p. 176.

[46]   Macquarrie, *An Existentialist Theology*, p. 91; Macquarrie, *Existentialism*, pp. 118–19, quoting *The Point of View for My Work as an Author*, trans. by Walter Lowrie, New York and London: Oxford University Press 1939, p. 114 (which corresponds to *SV1* XIII, 593–4 / *PV*, 107), mistakenly cited as *The Point of View for My Work as an Author*, trans. by Lowrie, p. 193; and *Fear and Trembling and The Sickness unto Death*, trans. by Walter

the Church,[47] and Mary.[48] More significant is Macquarrie's use of ideas drawn from Kierkegaard to support and develop his own theological and philosophical position. As we shall see, however, Macquarrie holds that many of Kierkegaard's ideas are one-sided and need to be corrected before they can be employed in constructive theology.

A. Existence and Thought

Throughout his works Macquarrie cites passages from Kierkegaard critical of modes of thinking that ignore the concrete reality in which human beings live their lives.[49] In *Existentialism* he cites *Fragments* and *Postscript* as examples of the existentialist denial that "reality can be neatly packaged in concepts or presented as an interlocking system,"[50] and quotes passages from *Postscript* where Kierkegaard states that abstract thought ignores the concreteness, temporality, contingency, and particularity of human existence, and neglects the existential process in which human beings live.[51] Macquarrie makes a similar point in *Jesus Christ in Modern Thought*, where he notes that such titles as *Philosophical Fragments*, *Concluding Unscientific Postscript*, *Practice in Christianity*, *Fear and Trembling*, and *Either/Or* indicate that Kierkegaard "wishes to have nothing to do with system-building." For Macquarrie, however, Kierkegaard is not presenting us with a rival intellectual system to abstract

---

Lowrie, Garden City, New York: Doubleday 1954, p. 193 (which corresponds to *SKS* 11, 229 / *SUD*, 118).

[47]   See Macquarrie, *Existentialism*, p. 31; p. 54; p. 55 (citing *The Last Years: Journals 1853–1855*, ed. and trans. by Smith, p. 266, which corresponds to *SKS* 26, 323–6, NB34:13); Macquarrie, *Existentialism*, p. 119 (citing *Fear and Trembling and The Sickness unto Death*, trans. by Lowrie, p. 165, which corresponds to *SKS* 11, 216 / *SUD*, 102); Macquarrie, *Existentialism*, p. 225 (citing *The Last Years: Journals 1853–1855*, ed. and trans. by Smith, p. 143, which corresponds to *SKS* 26, 42–3, NB31:57 and *SKS* 26, 45, NB31:61); Macquarrie, *Jesus Christ in Modern Thought*, p. 244 (citing *Attack upon "Christendom,"* trans. by Walter Lowrie, Princeton: Princeton University Press 1944, p. 156, where Lowrie has inserted a passage from Kierkegaard's journal, namely, that which corresponds to *SKS* 26, 43–4, NB31:59); Macquarrie, *Principles of Christian Theology*, 2nd ed., pp. 377–8; Macquarrie, *Two Worlds Are Ours*, p. 224.

[48]   Macquarrie, *Principles of Christian Theology*, 2nd ed., p. 397, citing *The Last Years: Journals 1853–1855*, ed. and trans. by Smith, pp. 38–40 (which corresponds to *SKS* 25, 284, NB28:94 and *SKS* 25, 287–8, NB28:99) and quoting a passage from *The Last Years: Journals 1853–1855*, ed. and trans. by Smith, p. 111 (which corresponds to *SKS* 25, 468–9, NB30:101).

[49]   Macquarrie, *Existentialism*, p. 66. Macquarrie attributes Kierkegaard's emphasis on "the connection between life and thought" to Kierkegaard's strict religious upbringing, broken engagement, and introspective and melancholy disposition. In support of this claim he cites journal passages where Kierkegaard speaks of being "inwardly torn asunder" and "without any expectation of leading a happy earthly life" (*The Journals of Kierkegaard 1834–1854*, ed. and trans. by Alexander Dru, New York: Peter Smith 1959, p. 40). Cf. *Existentialism*, p. 54.

[50]   Macquarrie, *Existentialism*, p. 13, cf. ibid., p. 140 and p. 241.

[51]   See *Concluding Unscientific Postscript*, trans. by Swenson and Lowrie, p. 267, which corresponds to *SKS* 7, 275 / *CUP1*, 301; Macquarrie, *Existentialism*, pp. 140–1; cf. ibid., p. 72.

thought, but has "turned away toward the problems of life with all its discontinuities and its refusal to fit neat logical patterns."[52]

Kierkegaard's insistence that existence cannot be grasped by thought has led to his being charged with irrationalism. Macquarrie believes that there is some truth in this claim,[53] and cites Kierkegaard's knight of faith and Unamuno's Don Quixote as evidence that the existentialist call for passionate participation can "lead to a state of mind which conflicts with the philosopher's obligation to reason."[54] Despite this, however, Macquarrie defends Kierkegaard against the charge of irrationalism,[55] condemning as a caricature the view that Kierkegaard affirmed an arbitrary leap of faith. Such a view ignores Kierkegaard's explicit affirmation "that the believer must use his understanding and that he cannot believe nonsense."[56] Macquarrie quotes with approval Louis Pojman's comment that Kierkegaard was "a highly rational person, he saw that reason had severe limits, and that for many of our deepest beliefs there were no full justifications."[57] For Macquarrie, Kierkegaard's "concern was not to downgrade reason, but to combat the narrow rationalism that separates reason from the personal existence within which it functions, and so to reintegrate reason with the whole person." As evidence, Macquarrie quotes Kierkegaard's comment in *Postscript* that "in existence thought is by no means higher than imagination and feeling, but coordinate."[58] Macquarrie sums up Kierkegaard's position as follows: "If one eventually comes to believe in a paradox, it is not because it is absurd, but because the drive of reason itself has brought the thinker to a limit or a point of collision where he is impelled to go beyond the reach of reason."[59] In support of this Macquarrie quotes Kierkegaard's comment in *Philosophical Fragments* that "The supreme paradox of all thought is the attempt to discover something that thought cannot think."[60] For Macquarrie, "This implies that thought and reason themselves include a faith that carries them beyond themselves, and without such a faith they lose their drive and becomes lifeless."[61] As evidence, Macquarrie quotes the comment

---

[52]   Macquarrie, *Jesus Christ in Modern Thought*, p. 236.
[53]   Macquarrie, *Existentialism*, p. 141.
[54]   Ibid., p. 276, cf. ibid., p. 144.
[55]   Notably against Herbert James Paton, *The Modern Predicament: A Study in the Philosophy of Religion*, London: Allen & Unwin 1955. Macquarrie, *In Search of Humanity*, p. 163.
[56]   Ibid. Macquarrie is referring to *Concluding Unscientific Postscript*, trans. by Swenson and Lowrie, p. 504, which corresponds to *SKS* 7, 516 / *CUP1*, 567–8.
[57]   Louis P. Pojman, *Kierkegaard as Philosopher*, Swindon: Waterleaf Press 1978, p. 34; cf. Macquarrie, *Jesus Christ in Modern Thought*, p. 237, where Macquarrie refers to Louis P. Pojman, *The Logic of Subjectivity*, Tuscaloosa, Alabama: University of Alabama Press 1984, p. 144.
[58]   See *Concluding Unscientific Postscript*, trans. by Swenson and Lowrie, p. 310, which corresponds to *SKS* 7, 317 / *CUP1*, 346–7.
[59]   Macquarrie, *In Search of Humanity*, pp. 163–4.
[60]   See *Philosophical Fragments, or a Fragment of Philosophy*, trans. by David F. Swenson, Princeton: Princeton University Press 1936, p. 29, which corresponds to *SKS* 4, 243 / *PF*, 37.
[61]   Macquarrie, *In Search of Humanity*, p. 164.

in *Fragments* that "The thinker without a paradox is like a lover without feeling: a paltry mediocrity."[62] Macquarrie returns to this theme in *Two Worlds Are Ours*, where he states his view that Kierkegaard "does make a good case for believing that the powers of reason are limited," above all in relation to the question of God's existence.[63]

Macquarrie, however, while recognizing the importance of Kierkegaard's critique of modes of thought which do not take reality seriously,[64] disagrees with the conclusion that this necessitates the abandonment of metaphysics. On the contrary, for Macquarrie:

> The very fact that human existence is the theme of existentialism leads into questions of a metaphysical kind, for the existentialist denies that this existence is an objectifiable empirical phenomenon....There is in existence an inexhaustibility and a transcendence, and to probe into these in any depth is to engage in some kind of metaphysical inquiry.[65]

Macquarrie makes similar points in later works. After citing Kierkegaard in *In Search of Deity* as someone who was profoundly suspicious of philosophical theism,[66] Macquarrie insists that "there is something to be said on the other side, too. There are minds which cannot rest unless they have inquired, as far as their powers allow, into the very foundations of belief. They would consider it irresponsible not to conduct such an inquiry."[67]

For Macquarrie, Kierkegaard's critique is aimed not at metaphysics as such but at the distorted form of metaphysics and narrow intellectualism prevalent in contemporary thought.[68] Thus although Kierkegaard, Unamuno, and others sometimes make use of "extravagant statements that suggest that thought is being abandoned and that feeling and willing are to take its place,"[69] Macquarrie insists that "the main thrust of existentialism is in the direction not of abandoning thought... but of recognizing that it has many forms."[70] Macquarrie, however, "would wish to go much further than Kierkegaard in recognizing the role of critical understanding in belief," a point he reiterates in *Thinking about God*.[71] Above all, Macquarrie "find[s] Kierkegaard's scorning of probability unacceptable."[72] Although he accepts

---

[62]   See *Philosophical Fragments*, trans. by Swenson, p. 29, which corresponds to *SKS* 4, 243 / *PF*, 37.

[63]   Macquarrie, *Two Worlds Are Ours*, p. 225, quoting *Philosophical Fragments*, trans. by Swenson, p. 35, which corresponds to *SKS* 4, 251 / *PF*, 44.

[64]   Macquarrie, *Principles of Christian Theology*, 2nd ed., p. 185.

[65]   Macquarrie, *Existentialism*, p. 241.

[66]   Macquarrie, *In Search of Deity*, p. 24.

[67]   Ibid., p. 25.

[68]   Macquarrie, *Existentialism*, pp. 13–14. In support of this view Macquarrie quotes Hermann Diem, *Kierkegaard: An Introduction*, trans. by David Green, Richmond, Virginia: John Knox Press 1966, p. 81; Paul Sponheim, *Kierkegaard on Christ and Christian Coherence*, New York: Harper & Row 1968, p. 14. Cf. Macquarrie, *Existentialism*, pp. 140–1.

[69]   Macquarrie, *Existentialism*, p. 141.

[70]   Ibid.

[71]   Macquarrie, *Thinking about God*, p. 135.

[72]   Macquarrie, *In Search of Humanity*, p. 164.

Kierkegaard's claim that empirical evidence can never prove a transcendent belief, he holds that probability can nevertheless lead a person to the point where he or she may make the imaginative leap necessary for committing himself or herself to such a belief.[73]

This means that we cannot stop at Kierkegaard's critique of metaphysical thought, but must search for a mode of thinking that takes on board Kierkegaard's critique and yet allows us to do justice to the metaphysical questions thrown up by the concrete reality of existence. Macquarrie sees Heidegger as providing a way of steering a course between metaphysical speculation and the outright rejection of metaphysics.[74] The implication, then, is that Heidegger is able to provide a metaphysics that meets the anti-metaphysical critique advanced by Kierkegaard and others.

B. Individualism, Subjectivism, and Collectivism

Macquarrie regards individualism as a weakness of existentialism in general and of Kierkegaard in particular, whose individualism he considers to be exaggerated.[75] Macquarrie holds that Kierkegaard "never broke out of individualism," a fact which "has remained significant for the whole subsequent development of existentialism."[76] In the final chapter of *Existentialism* Macquarrie provides a detailed discussion of the charge that "existentialism is infected with an undesirable degree of individualism," a criticism that is closely allied with the complaint that existentialism is a subjectivism.[77] As the pre-eminent example of individualism and subjectivism run riot Macquarrie cites Kierkegaard, quoting the comment in *Practice in Christianity* that " 'fellowship' is a lower category than the 'single individual,' which everyone can be and should be."[78]

Macquarrie ascribes Kierkegaard's individualism and subjectivism to two factors. Firstly, they stem from the autobiographical character of Kierkegaard's thought. For Macquarrie, this is a weakness, for "the philosopher has an obligation to transcend as far as he can a narrowly personal point of view."[79] Macquarrie cites H.J. Paton in support of this point, commenting that in his criticism of Kierkegaard's extreme self-centeredness and elevation of the inwardness of his personality over objective thinking,[80] "H.J. Paton is unduly harsh in his judgement, yet not entirely wide of the mark."[81] Secondly, Macquarrie attributes Kierkegaard's individualism

---

[73]   Ibid.

[74]   Macquarrie, *Principles of Christian Theology*, 2nd ed., pp. 185–6.

[75]   Macquarrie, *Existentialism*, p. 103; Macquarrie, *In Search of Deity*, p. 129; cf. Macquarrie, *Two Worlds Are Ours*, p. 224.

[76]   Macquarrie, *Existentialism*, p. 224, cf. ibid., p. 220 and p. 280.

[77]   Ibid., p. 279.

[78]   See *Training in Christianity*, trans. by Lowrie, p. 218, which corresponds to *SKS* 12, 217 / *PC*, 223. Macquarrie, *Existentialism*, p. 280; cf. Macquarrie, *In Search of Humanity*, p. 84.

[79]   Macquarrie, *Existentialism*, p. 280.

[80]   Paton, *Modern Predicament*, p. 120.

[81]   Macquarrie, *Existentialism*, p. 280.

to his "reaction against a false collectivism,"[82] which has "tried to fit everyone to a uniform pattern."[83] At such times there has always arisen someone "to champion the right of the individual to be himself."[84] Kierkegaard is such a champion.[85]

Macquarrie raises several objections to Kierkegaard's individualism. Firstly, emphasis on the individual is now less important than it was in Kierkegaard's day, for "In our own time, conscious as we are of the interdependence of mankind, we are more concerned with the social implications of faith."[86] Furthermore, existentialism provides few resources for dealing with "the most pressing problems of the contemporary world," namely, those which "concern the relations between groups or corporate entities—national and international bodies, corporations, races, trade unions and the like."[87] Although Macquarrie concedes "that the political role of existentialism may be simply that of criticizing all dehumanizing forms of collectivism," he holds that "we need some positive guidance in these areas, and it is doubtful if existentialism has much to offer."[88]

Secondly, Macquarrie criticizes Kierkegaard's view that "the other can be a barrier to a relation with God,"[89] and observes that Buber and many Christian theologians would take issue with Kierkegaard on this point. Macquarrie claims that behind this suspicion of the other lies Kierkegaard's broken engagement, which he attributes to Kierkegaard's belief that "it conflicted with God's claim on him as an extraordinary individual."[90] Macquarrie warns against "any point of view that consistently advocated detachment from other (finite) persons for the sake of a supposed relation to God,"[91] and draws a parallel between Kierkegaard's position and Sartre's comment in *No Exit* that "Hell is other people."[92] In making such a comparison, however, Macquarrie seems to have been conscious of doing Kierkegaard an injustice, for he qualifies his remarks with the statement that "in fairness to Kierkegaard, we have to remember that there is much more to his teaching, and the relation to the other is affirmatively evaluated and finely described in such a book as *Works of Love*."[93]

Macquarrie's third objection is that Kierkegaard's emphasis on the individual results in an abstract notion of the human being, because human beings cannot

---

[82]   Macquarrie, *Principles of Christian Theology*, 2nd ed., p. 68; cf. Macquarrie, *Faith of the People of God*, p. 29.

[83]   Macquarrie, *Faith of the People of God*, p. 28.

[84]   Ibid.

[85]   Ibid., p. 29.

[86]   Macquarrie, *Principles of Christian Theology*, 2nd ed., p. 68.

[87]   Macquarrie, *Existentialism*, p. 280.

[88]   Ibid.

[89]   Macquarrie, *Existentialism*, p. 112. Cf. Macquarrie, *Two Worlds Are Ours*, p. 224, where he states that Kierkegaard "believed that each human person must define his or her own relation to God."

[90]   Macquarrie, *Existentialism*, p. 112.

[91]   Ibid.

[92]   Ibid., p. 113.

[93]   Ibid., pp. 112–13.

exist apart from their social context.[94] As an example of an isolated self-sufficient individual who resists the need to be taken up and brought to completion in the larger whole of the community Macquarrie cites Hegel's discussion of Abraham, pointing out that Hegel's negative assessment of Abraham "contrasts very sharply with the praise which he receives from Kierkegaard in *Fear and Trembling*."[95] Macquarrie takes Hegel's side on this issue, who he believes "has the deeper insight at this point."[96] The task, then, is to find some way of holding individual and society, individualism and collectivism in balance. For Macquarrie, "Kierkegaard's philosophy of the person requires to be corrected by Buber's, according to which there can be no 'I' without a 'thou.' "[97]

For Macquarrie, Kierkegaardian individualism is justified in opposing the submerging of human beings into an anonymous collective mass, but it must be tempered by an equal emphasis on sociality.

C. Freedom, Decision, and Choice

In *Existentialism* Macquarrie notes that the theme of freedom "is present in all the existentialist writings," and that "it is prominent in Kierkegaard, for whom to exist and to be free are almost synonymous expressions."[98] A few pages later Macquarrie compares Berdyaev's distinction between irrational and rational freedom with the connection Kierkegaard makes "between the primordial anxiety that comes before the exercise of freedom and the subsequent anxiety of care that accompanies man throughout his life."[99] Macquarrie also touches on Kierkegaard's understanding of freedom when he cites the definition in *Either/Or*, Part Two of the self as "the most abstract of all things, and yet at the same time it is the most concrete—it is freedom."[100] Macquarrie agrees with this definition, but draws attention to the fact that Kierkegaard says that this is only the *first* answer to the question of what it is to be a self, which Macquarrie takes to imply that "much more remains to be said after one has opened the question of freedom."[101]

Closely connected to the notion of freedom are the concepts of decision and choice. In *Existentialism* Macquarrie describes Kierkegaard's understanding of these concepts as being that "we touch reality in the intense moments of existence, especially moments of painful decision." In support of this view Macquarrie quotes the statement in *Either/Or*, Part Two that the personality is consolidated through

---

[94]   Macquarrie, *Faith of the People of God*, p. 29; Macquarrie, *In Search of Humanity*, p. 84; Macquarrie, *In Search of Deity*, p. 129.

[95]   Macquarrie, *In Search of Deity*, p. 129.

[96]   Ibid.

[97]   Macquarrie, *Faith of the People of God*, p. 29.

[98]   Macquarrie, *Existentialism*, p. 177.

[99]   Ibid., p. 180.

[100]   See *Either/Or*, trans. by Swenson, Swenson, and Lowrie, vol. 2, p. 218, which corresponds to *SKS* 3, 205 / *EO2*, 214.

[101]   Macquarrie, *In Search of Humanity*, p. 9.

the earnestness and pathos with which the individual chooses.[102] Later, Macquarrie focuses on *Either/Or*'s treatment of decision in relation to marriage, friendship, and vocation, which are all decisions that "have lasting consequences for the whole life of the individual who makes the choices."[103]

Macquarrie observes, however, that "nowadays the seriousness of decision of which Kierkegaard wrote will scarcely be understood by many people."[104] For Macquarrie, Kierkegaard's employment of marriage as an example of the earnestness of decision runs up against the problem of the decline of Christian marriage and the rise of serial monogamy. Similarly, the commitment Kierkegaard associates with friendship has been weakened by the mobility of modern society, which "makes more difficult the development of permanent friendships at the deeper levels." Finally, Macquarrie points out, "the ideal of lifelong vocation is probably the one that has declined most," for "the changing of jobs has become part of the modern economy." Macquarrie makes the further observation that Kierkegaard's distinction between a mere job and a vocation "may once again reflect an aristocratic tendency in existentialism that is not particularly relevant to an age of mass-existence." For Macquarrie, "in such an age the kind of choices of which Kierkegaard wrote may not be possible for the great bulk of mankind."[105] The key issue is, then, not so much the concrete subject matter of an individual's decision, but *the very act of making a decision*. As Macquarrie puts it in *Jesus Christ in Modern Thought*, "for Kierkegaard it was the freedom and intensity of choice that gave an action its worth and dignity, rather than the content."[106] It is the act of choosing rather than the subject matter that is chosen which is decisive.

According to Macquarrie, it is this emphasis on decision and the continued reaffirmation of this initial decision that leads the existentialists to deprecate action which does not arise from "conscious, even agonizing, decision." This view in turn leads the existentialists to be critical of what they regard as conventional and habitual forms of behaviour and action. Macquarrie points out that "Again, this type of criticism goes back to Kierkegaard,"[107] namely to Kierkegaard's critique of habitual, conventionalized Christianity or "Christendom."[108]

D. Subjectivity and Truth

Kierkegaard's understanding of truth as subjectivity is a theme to which Macquarrie devotes some attention in *Existentialism*, *Principles of Christian Theology*, and *Thinking about God*. Macquarrie warns against understanding the notion of subjective

---

[102]   Incorrectly citing *Either/Or*, trans. by Swenson, Swenson, and Lowrie, vol. 2, p. 171 (which corresponds to *SKS* 3, 164 / *EO2*, 167) as *Either/Or*, trans. by Swenson, Swenson, and Lowrie, vol. 2, p. 141. Macquarrie, *Existentialism*, p. 54.
[103]   Macquarrie, *Existentialism*, p. 183; cf. Macquarrie, *Christian Unity and Christian Diversity*, p. 84.
[104]   Macquarrie, *Existentialism*, p. 184.
[105]   Ibid.
[106]   Macquarrie, *Jesus Christ in Modern Thought*, p. 243.
[107]   Macquarrie, *Existentialism*, p. 186.
[108]   Ibid., pp. 186–7.

truth to indicate that existentialism is solipsistic or has an arbitrary conception of truth.[109] Rather, the notion of truth as subjectivity denotes *existential* or *lived* truth as distinct from propositional truth.[110] Macquarrie attributes Kierkegaard's development of this subjective notion of truth to religious influence and points specifically to Christ's statement in John 14:6, "I am the truth," a passage which identifies truth with a personal life.[111] Macquarrie then cites Climacus' comment in *Postscript* that the *relationship* to the truth determines whether the individual is related to the truth, even when that individual is related to what is not true.[112]

Macquarrie complains, however, that it is difficult to know what Kierkegaard means by subjective truth.[113] He considers Kierkegaard's terminology to be "unfortunate," pointing out that truth, almost by definition, is objective and universal,[114] while in *Thinking about God* he states his preference for "the more sober remarks of Heidegger."[115] Macquarrie also holds "that it is possible to criticize Kierkegaard's account of truth as too individualistic," a tendency which he claims "is corrected in some of the later existentialist philosophers, notably Berdyaev and Marcel."[116] He notes that because truth has a communal dimension this Kierkegaardian notion of existential truth "tends to be developed into an existential-ontological truth."[117] He returns to the problematic character of Kierkegaard's notion

---

[109]   Ibid., p. 81.

[110]   Ibid., pp. 137–8, mistakenly quoting *Concluding Unscientific Postscript*, trans. by Swenson and Lowrie, p. 178 (which corresponds to *SKS* 7, 182 / *CUP1*, 199) as *Concluding Unscientific Postscript*, trans. by Swenson and Lowrie, p. 319. See also Macquarrie, *Principles of Christian Theology*, 2nd ed., p. 146, quoting *Training in Christianity*, trans. by Lowrie, p. 201 (which corresponds to *SKS* 12, 203 / *PC*, 205); Macquarrie, *Thinking about God*, pp. 17–20, citing *Training in Christianity*, trans. by Lowrie, pp. 198ff. (which corresponds to *SKS* 12, 199ff. / *PC*, 202ff.) and *Concluding Unscientific Postscript*, trans. by Swenson and Lowrie, pp. 173ff. (which corresponds to *SKS* 7, 177ff. / *CUP1*, 193ff.); *Concluding Unscientific Postscript*, trans. by Swenson and Lowrie, p. 182 (which corresponds to *SKS* 7, 186 / *CUP1*, 203); *Concluding Unscientific Postscript*, trans. by Swenson and Lowrie, p. 217 (though this is an incorrect reference); Macquarrie, *Jesus Christ in Modern Thought*, p. 238. Macquarrie cites Kierkegaard, as well as Heidegger, as subscribing to the view that "man… has an untidiness that does not conform to clear and distinct ideas" (Macquarrie, *Thinking about God*, p. 39).

[111]   Macquarrie, *Existentialism*, p. 137; Macquarrie, *Thinking about God*, p. 17, where Macquarrie mistakenly cites this passage as John 14.7; Macquarrie, *Thinking about God*, pp. 19–20, citing *Training in Christianity*, trans. by Lowrie, p. 199 (which corresponds to *SKS* 12, 200 / *PC*, 203) and *Training in Christianity*, trans. by Lowrie, p. 200 (which corresponds to *SKS* 12, 201–3 / *PC*, 205).

[112]   *Concluding Unscientific Postscript*, trans. by Swenson and Lowrie, p. 178, which corresponds to *SKS* 7, 182 / *CUP1*, 199. Macquarrie mistakenly cites this passage as *Concluding Unscientific Postscript*, trans. by Swenson and Lowrie, p. 319. Macquarrie, *Existentialism*, pp. 137–8.

[113]   Macquarrie, *Jesus Christ in Modern Thought*, p. 238.

[114]   Macquarrie, *Existentialism*, p. 137, cf. Macquarrie, *Thinking about God*, p. 20.

[115]   Macquarrie, *Thinking about God*, pp. 20–1.

[116]   Macquarrie, *Existentialism*, p. 138.

[117]   Macquarrie, *Principles of Christian Theology*, 2nd ed., p. 146.

of truth in *Two Worlds Are Ours*, where he interprets Climacus' definition of truth as "the objective uncertainty held fast in the appropriation of the most passionate inwardness"[118] to indicate that Kierkegaard had reached "the 'mature' stage of giving up the passion for certainty and acknowledging the vulnerability of faith." Macquarrie further suggests that Kierkegaard may be "saying about truth something like what Gregory of Nyssa said about perfection: it is not so much a goal as the passionate pursuit of that goal."[119]

In *Existentialism* Macquarrie argues that the problematic elements of Kierkegaard's assertion of the subjective character of truth fall away, however, if we understand his language "in terms of his protest against what he took to be the abstractness of 'objective' truth. The fullness of truth implies its inwardness. It is not something impersonal to be bandied about in propositions, but something to be inwardly appropriated."[120] Macquarrie makes a similar point in *Jesus Christ in Modern Thought*, where he emphasizes the importance of placing Kierkegaard's view of truth as subjectivity in the context of contemporary Denmark, where in Kierkegaard's view everyone was supposedly a Christian merely as a matter of course.[121]

E. Conscience

Macquarrie distinguishes between two notions of conscience, namely, conscience as "a person's awareness of the moral code accepted in his society," and "the kind of moral conviction that will sometimes lead a person to reject the accepted standards of his society in response to what he believes to be a more deeply founded imperative."[122] According to Macquarrie, "Existentialists tend to be critical of conscience in the first of the two senses and to hold that only the second is important."[123]

As an example of the distinction between two types of conscience Macquarrie cites *Fear and Trembling* and its notion of a teleological suspension of the ethical.[124] Macquarrie quotes George Price's comment that what is at stake in *Fear and Trembling* "is Abraham's self, his struggle to *be*, to exist as the individual he knew he ought to be."[125] As Macquarrie puts it in *In Search of Humanity*, for Kierkegaard Abraham's

---

[118]   *Concluding Unscientific Postscript*, trans. by Swenson and Lowrie, p. 182, which corresponds to *SKS* 7, 186 / *CUP1*, 203.

[119]   Macquarrie, *Two Worlds Are Ours*, p. 228.

[120]   Macquarrie, *Existentialism*, p. 137.

[121]   Macquarrie, *Jesus Christ in Modern Thought*, p. 238. Macquarrie inaccurately quotes *Training in Christianity*, trans. by Lowrie, 71, which corresponds to *SKS* 12, 79 / *PC*, 67.

[122]   Macquarrie, *Existentialism*, p. 210.

[123]   Ibid.

[124]   Ibid. Cf. Macquarrie, *Theology, Church and Ministry*, pp. 119–20, citing *Fear and Trembling and The Sickness unto Death*, trans. by Lowrie, p. 75, which corresponds to *SKS* 4, 148 / *FT*, 54.

[125]   George Price, *The Narrow Pass: A Study of Kierkegaard's Concept of Man*, New York: McGraw-Hill 1963, p. 192.

"duty to God was identical with his duty to himself."[126] For Macquarrie, Price's expression "the individual he knew he ought to be" corresponds to the second sense of conscience.[127] Macquarrie sees this struggle between two senses of conscience as a feature of Kierkegaard's own life, holding that Kierkegaard's dissolution of his engagement to Regine Olsen constituted a setting aside of conscience understood as obedience to the universal ethic in order to respond to conscience as unconditional obedience to the divine will.[128]

There are, however, dangers in the existentialist notion of conscience. Firstly, "no individual conscience ever speaks with complete purity," and "it is easy to manipulate conscience."[129] To illustrate this peril, Macquarrie asks whether Abraham and Kierkegaard were right in believing that they knew God's will, and that it took precedence over the ethical imperative. The problem is that "An appeal to 'God's will' can be made the excuse for the most outrageous kinds of conduct,"[130] and can become a means of disguising elitism and egoism.[131] Macquarrie wonders whether Kierkegaard's behaviour towards his fiancée was really his response to a higher vocation or merely an egotistical desire to avoid the responsibilities of marriage.[132] The problem is knowing whether one is indeed genuinely responding to the "call of Being" or the "voice of God," or is guilty of self-deception or of indulging a latent selfishness.[133]

A second danger is that the existentialist notion of conscience seems to abolish conventional morality without putting anything in its place, and arguably reduces morality to a matter of subjective preference. Macquarrie warns that "if every individual claimed the right to set aside his ordinary moral obligations for the sake of the ultimate demands of his own authentic selfhood, surely we would soon find ourselves in moral chaos."[134] The existentialist notion of conscience can lead to amoralism or even immoralism.[135]

---

[126]   Macquarrie, *In Search of Humanity*, p. 131. Macquarrie refers to *Fear and Trembling and The Sickness unto Death*, trans. by Lowrie, p. 70 (which he cites as *Fear and Trembling and The Sickness unto Death*, trans. by Lowrie, p. 75) in *In Search of Humanity*, p. 269, note 20. See also Macquarrie, *Jesus Christ in Modern Thought*, pp. 243–4, where Macquarrie makes a similar point and quotes the same passage, though this time from Alastair Hannay's translation of *Fear and Trembling*, p. 88.

[127]   Macquarrie, *Existentialism*, p. 210.

[128]   Ibid., p. 211.

[129]   Ibid., p. 213.

[130]   Ibid.

[131]   Macquarrie, *In Search of Humanity*, p. 131.

[132]   Ibid., p. 133. Cf. Macquarrie, *Existentialism*, pp. 183–4.

[133]   See also Macquarrie, *Jesus Christ in Modern Thought*, pp. 243–4.

[134]   Macquarrie, *Existentialism*, p. 213.

[135]   Ibid., p. 277.

F. Anxiety

One of the most prominent Kierkegaardian concepts in Macquarrie's writings is "anxiety," particularly the notion of anxiety as the "dizziness" of freedom.[136] In *Existentialism* Macquarrie describes how Kierkegaard employs the Genesis fall account to trace the factors involved in every human being's transition from innocence to sin. Macquarrie describes the anxiety that leads to the positing of the first sin as "primordial anxiety," which he breaks down into three aspects.

Firstly, primordial anxiety "is inherent in the state of innocence,"[137] in support of which Macquarrie quotes Vigilius Haufniensis' comment that "This is the profound secret of innocency, that at the same time it is anxiety."[138] The second aspect of primordial anxiety is its link with freedom, which Macquarrie understands as "a kind of instability prior to action." Macquarrie notes Kierkegaard's use of the metaphor of the "vertigo" or "dizziness" of freedom, but prefers to suggest his own metaphor: "one might say that freedom is by its very nature pregnant with possibility; and it is the stirring of possibility in the womb of freedom that is experienced as the primordial anxiety." The third aspect of primordial anxiety is the tension that arises from the human being's constitution as a synthesis of body, soul, and spirit.[139] It is the combination of these three aspects of primordial anxiety that creates the context in which the individual makes the transition from innocence to sin.

Macquarrie notes that for Kierkegaard anxiety is not only the precondition of sin, but is also the *effect* of sin, "for fallen man lives amid ever deepening anxiety." Anxiety is not directed at an object, but is, as George Price puts it, "a complex of presentiments which, though nothing in themselves, develop themselves by reflecting themselves in themselves."[140]

Macquarrie claims that his brief summary of Kierkegaard's concept of anxiety shows that Kierkegaard's "concept is by no means clearcut. Indeed, it may not even be entirely self-consistent."[141] The only "inconsistency" that Macquarrie discusses, however, is Kierkegaard's description of anxiety as both a negative and a positive phenomenon. On the one hand, anxiety is "the precondition of sin and also the characteristic of man's fallen existence."[142] On the other hand, "Kierkegaard is willing to assign a positive role to anxiety as a propaedeutic to faith." Macquarrie himself, however, shows how this alleged inconsistency can be overcome: "To endure anxiety is to have one's eyes opened to the reality of the human condition, and so to see the need for grace."[143] Anxiety thus functions as the precondition of

---

[136]   Macquarrie, *Existentialist Theology*, pp. 69–71; Macquarrie, *Existentialism*, p. 54; p. 170; Macquarrie, *In Search of Humanity*, pp. 19–20, where Macquarrie cites *The Concept of Dread*, trans. by Lowrie, p. 55 (which corresponds to *SKS* 4, 366 / *CA*, 61).

[137]   Macquarrie, *Existentialism*, pp. 166.

[138]   See *The Concept of Dread*, trans. by Lowrie, p. 38, which corresponds to *SKS* 4, 348 / *CA*, 41.

[139]   Macquarrie, *Existentialism*, p. 167.

[140]   Ibid., p. 67. See Price, *Narrow Pass*, p. 46.

[141]   Macquarrie, *Existentialism*, p. 167.

[142]   Ibid., pp. 167–8.

[143]   Ibid., p. 168.

sin, the characteristic of the human being's fallen existence, and the propaedeutic of faith, because it is through the sin committed by the anxious individual that that individual becomes aware of his need for divine forgiveness.

In *In Search of Humanity* Macquarrie introduces the notion of anxiety into his discussion of post-Enlightenment attempts to interpret religion from the perspective of human experience. After discussing Schleiermacher, Otto, and James, Macquarrie turns to "negative" and "positive" types of religious experience. For Macquarrie, "The negative type is primarily determined by a sense of the fragmentariness of human existence. It takes its rise from awareness of finitude and even of sinfulness."[144] Among the proponents of this negative type of religious experience Macquarrie cites Kierkegaard, the starting point of whose thought "is the mood of anxiety, the deep-seated malaise which reveals the fundamental instability of the human existent as it faces the existential task of synthesizing body and soul."[145] God is the power which enables human beings to overcome these negative phenomena.[146]

It is, however, in the chapter on alienation that Macquarrie provides his fullest discussion of anxiety. For Macquarrie, although "alienation" is not a Kierkegaardian term, Kierkegaard's "whole philosophy can be seen as an attempt to break out of such alienating forms of existence as pretence and superficiality to a genuinely human mode of being."[147] To support this claim, Macquarrie cites Kierkegaard's contrast between objective and subjective truth in *Postscript*, the teleological suspension of the ethical of *Fear and Trembling*, and Kierkegaard's attack on Christendom. In Macquarrie's opinion: "Since truth, morality and religion are close to the centre of human life, Kierkegaard's contention that we meet them for the most part in alienated forms in the modern world must be considered just as revolutionary as Marx's assault on the political and economic fabric of society."[148]

It is in the context of this discussion of alienation that Macquarrie turns to Kierkegaard's concept of *anxiety*, which he sees as "a classic analysis of the duality of human existence."[149] According to Macquarrie, "What emerges in Kierkegaard's analysis is not yet alienation in the full sense, but rather, what makes alienation possible." Kierkegaard's treatment of original sin in *The Concept of Anxiety* is a study of the "original breach or duality in human existence that makes sin possible." It corresponds to what Macquarie calls "alienation in the natural sense of the term."[150]

Macquarrie then discusses the connection Kierkegaard makes between innocence and ignorance. Innocence, Macquarrie writes, "is really a pre-human condition, in which the human being has not yet emerged as spirit with freedom and responsibility, but is still determined in a natural condition." Although there is peace and repose

---

[144]   Macquarrie, *In Search of Humanity*, p. 207.
[145]   Ibid.
[146]   In support of his discussion Macquarrie cites Peter Rohde, *Søren Kierkegaard*, London: George Allen & Unwin 1963, p. 65.
[147]   Macquarrie, *In Search of Humanity*, p. 111.
[148]   Ibid.
[149]   Ibid., p. 113.
[150]   Ibid., p. 114.

in this state of innocence, "There is a stirring, a malaise, a sense of instability."[151] Macquarrie also draws attention to Kierkegaard's view that "anxiety is not guilt, but perhaps it is the premonition of the possibility of guilt." For Macquarrie, such passages indicate that "we can recognize in Kierkegaard's descriptions of what I have called the sense of otherness or alienation in its neutral sense, the anxiety attendant on being launched out of the given into the insecurity of freedom."[152]

Macquarrie is critical, however, of the connection Kierkegaard makes between the transition from innocence and the awakening of sexuality, although he recognizes that Kierkegaard is following the Genesis fall narrative. For Macquarrie, "this introduction of sexuality into the analysis may be unfortunate, since it could easily mislead us into supposing that Kierkegaard is moving in the direction of a dualism of body and soul, and is advocating a form of asceticism."[153] Macquarrie holds, however, that this was not Kierkegaard's intention, and as evidence cites Kierkegaard's declaration in *The Concept of Anxiety* that "the human task is to accomplish the synthesis of soul and body."[154] "Such a synthesis," Macquarrie points out, "is the very opposite of any dualism."[155]

In *Two Worlds Are Ours* Macquarrie draws on Kierkegaard in support of his claim that "emotions or feelings…carry with them something like perception of direct awareness." As an example he cites anxiety, at which point he brings Kierkegaard into the discussion, commenting that "anxiety or *angst*, as analyzed by Kierkegaard and others, is a feeling which forcefully makes us aware of human finitude."[156] He later describes Kierkegaard's notion of "angst" as denoting a state of mind which is "a mood of questioning which is also a searching."[157] It is a "deep-seated sense of insecurity and finitude which carries an intuition of our ontological status as contingent beings who owe their existence to the self-subsistent Being of God."[158]

G. Paradox

Throughout his works Macquarrie emphasizes the importance for theology of the notion of paradox, which he describes as the attempt "to hold together two sides of a truth though we may understand only imperfectly how these two sides can be reconciled."[159] The paradox is a "coincidence of opposites" in which "we find ourselves situated between two truths which appear to be incompatible, yet each

---

[151]   Macquarrie cites *The Concept of Dread*, trans. by Lowrie, p. 38: "This is the profound secret of innocence, that at the same time it is anxiety" (which corresponds to *SKS* 4, 348 / *CA*, 41).

[152]   Macquarrie, *In Search of Humanity*, p. 114.

[153]   Ibid.

[154]   Ibid.

[155]   Ibid.

[156]   Macquarrie, *Two Worlds Are Ours*, p. 10.

[157]   Ibid., p. 56.

[158]   Ibid., p. 226.

[159]   Macquarrie, *The Scope of Demythologizing*, p. 26; cf. Macquarrie, *Jesus Christ in Modern Thought*, p. 239.

of which appears to have a powerful claim."[160] In theologizing, "we must run into paradoxes,"[161] for there is an "inescapable element of paradox that enters into all theological language, and so of the need for a dialectical method which allows for the possibility that every statement made may need to be corrected by a statement of apparently opposite tendency."[162] Indeed, "the presence of paradox may well be a healthy sign in theology"[163] and "a theology without paradox would be suspect."[164] It is in such contexts that Macquarrie draws on Kierkegaard, for he sees Kierkegaard as someone who helps prevent the tendency to suppress the paradoxical character of theological language and who reminds us of the inadequacy of our attempts to conceive of God.[165]

Macquarrie emphasizes, however, that "the paradox is not nonsense,"[166] nor should it lead us to conclude that Kierkegaard rejects thought outright. Macquarrie points out that "Paradox is not plain contradiction, which would be the rejection of thought." In support of this claim, Macquarrie quotes the passage from *Fragments* where Climacus states that reason and the paradox encounter one another in the happy passion that is faith.[167] For Macquarrie, Kierkegaard's view is that "Each side of the paradox asserts a truth which, taken in isolation, would become an untruth. They are not combined but they correct one another."[168]

Although Macquarrie recognizes the importance of the notion of paradox, he is concerned that it should not be misused and warns against "the unrestrained use of paradox or opening the door to a flood of unexplained inconsistencies."[169] Macquarrie identifies two wrong attitudes towards paradox, namely, the temptation "to glory in paradox,"[170] and the temptation to "make the paradoxes of theology vanish altogether."[171] Those writers who glory in paradox "rejoice in self-contradiction and seeming absurdity, and go out of their way to stress oppositions in their thought."[172] For Macquarrie, "The example which comes most readily to mind is that of Kierkegaard with his contention that 'humanly speaking, the knight of faith

[160] Macquarrie, *Christology Revisited*, p. 14. Macquarrie refers the reader to *Philosophical Fragments*, trans. by Swenson, p. 29 (which corresponds to *SKS* 4, 243 / *PF*, 37). Cf. Macquarrie, *Principles of Christian Theology*, 2nd ed., p. 306, where he quotes *Concluding Unscientific Postscript*, trans. by Swenson and Lowrie, pp. 194–5, which corresponds to *SKS* 7, 198 / *CUP1*, 217.

[161] Macquarrie, *The Scope of Demythologizing*, p. 27.
[162] Macquarrie, *Principles of Christian Theology*, 2nd ed., p. 306.
[163] Macquarrie, *The Scope of Demythologizing*, p. 26.
[164] Ibid., p. 27.
[165] Macquarrie, *God-Talk*, p. 229.
[166] Macquarrie, *Jesus Christ in Modern Thought*, p. 239.
[167] See *Philosophical Fragments*, trans. by Swenson, p. 47, which corresponds to *SKS*, 257–8 / *PF*, 54.
[168] Macquarrie, *Jesus Christ in Modern Thought*, p. 239.
[169] Macquarrie, *The Scope of Demythologizing*, p. 27.
[170] Ibid.
[171] Ibid., pp. 27–8.
[172] Ibid., p. 27.

is crazy, and cannot make himself intelligible to anyone.' "[173] He further complains: "Doubtless Kierkegaard's paradoxes served a very useful purpose in their day as a protest against excessive rationalism in theology, but they are sometimes confusing and even irritating to the reader who rightly expects that the business of theology is to clarify rather than to mystify."[174] Macquarrie, then, is prepared to acknowledge the usefulness of Kierkegaardian paradoxes as an antidote to excessive rationalism, but believes that, in one-sidedly emphasizing the paradoxical, Kierkegaard muddies the waters and hinders the theological enterprise, which Macquarrie sees first and foremost as that of *clarification*. "It is not enough," he states, "just to present the paradox and leave it."[175]

The second wrong attitude towards paradox is to explain it away. Macquarrie acknowledges that Kierkegaard's one-sided treatment of paradox arose from his concern to expose the error of thinkers who annul the paradoxes of theology. Such thinkers "had made Christianity something inoffensive but in doing so they had drifted away from the existential reality."[176] In so far as the paradoxes of theology draw our attention to the need of existential commitment, they serve a useful function, and we should not attempt to do away with them by means of reason.

Both of these approaches—the glorification of paradox and the rational dissolution of paradox—are inadequate, and "we must try to avoid both of these ways, for in the first case we are offered an unintelligible picture and in the second case a distorted one."[177] According to Macquarrie, there is a third way which avoids the excesses of the other two approaches. He calls this "the vindicating of the paradox," and describes it as a procedure which "would neither leave us with a blank unexplained opposition nor explain the opposition away by suppressing one side in the interests of consistency but would show how the opposition has its rights."[178] Macquarrie makes a similar point in *Two Worlds Are Ours*, where he argues in opposition to Kierkegaard's notion of paradox that "any alleged revelation is strengthened if it can be shown to have the support of rational reflection, though it is not founded on reason or reason alone."[179]

H. History

In *Existentialism* Macquarrie states that although Kierkegaard's focus on the individual rather than on the history of the human race meant that he wrote little on the subject of history, "there are at least two ideas in Kierkegaard that reappear

---

[173]   Ibid. Macquarrie is citing *Fear and Trembling and The Sickness unto Death*, trans. by Lowrie, p. 115 (which corresponds to *SKS* 4, 167 / *FT*, 76). Cf. Macquarrie, *Studies in Christian Existentialism*, p. 22.

[174]   Macquarrie, *The Scope of Demythologizing*, p. 27. Cf. Macquarrie, *Studies in Christian Existentialism*, p. 22.

[175]   Macquarrie, *The Scope of Demythologizing*, p. 27.

[176]   Ibid., p. 28.

[177]   Ibid.

[178]   Ibid.

[179]   Macquarrie, *Two Worlds Are Ours*, p. 227.

(though in altered guise) in later existentialist reflection on history."[180] The first of these is "the idea that history tends to be a neutralizing process, in which everything that is great and distinctive gets watered down and rendered harmless."[181] Macquarrie points out how untypical this view of history was for the nineteenth century, and attributes it on the one hand to Kierkegaard's opposition to the Hegelian view of history and on the other hand to his understanding of Christianity as the paradoxical entry of God into time.[182]

The second of Kierkegaard's ideas which influenced subsequent existentialist thinking about history is "repetition," which, according to Macquarrie, modifies Kierkegaard's view of history as a neutralizing process. There are *authentic* and *inauthentic* forms of repetition. The inauthentic form corresponds to the diluting effect of the historical process described above. The authentic form of repetition, however, "is a form of repetition that holds out the promise of a completion in Christ."[183] In explicating this point Macquarrie quotes Kierkegaard's comment in *Repetition* that "Repetition and recollection are the same movement, only in opposite directions; for what is recollected has been, is repeated backwards; whereas repetition, properly so-called, is recollected forwards."[184] Macquarrie finds this passage to be "a very obscure statement,"[185] but ventures the following interpretation: "The idea seems to be that a primordial state of existing is repeated, in the sense of being restored, through the act of faith made in the moment of decision."[186] Macquarrie notes that Kierkegaard discusses repetition in relation to Abraham and Job, and comments that, "Once again, it will be noticed that Kierkegaard's discussion is related to the individual, and history is, indeed, precisely the way in which that primordial fullness of being gets lost in the first place, to be finally restored in repetition."[187]

Macquarrie then explains why he has introduced Kierkegaard's notion of repetition into his discussion of existentialist views of history. His first reason "is the importance of the idea of repetition...in later existentialist writers, notably Nietzsche and Heidegger,"[188] though he concedes that later thinkers have understood the notion differently from Kierkegaard. The second reason is "the affinity between Kierkegaard's notion and the idea of repetition in early Christian thought, where it had a definitely historical and universal reference."[189] Macquarrie claims that there

---

[180]   Macquarrie, *Existentialism*, p. 224.
[181]   Ibid. Macquarrie quotes a late journal entry (*The Last Years. Journals 1853–55*, ed. and trans. by Smith, p. 151, which corresponds to *SKS* 26, 82, NB31:110).
[182]   Macquarrie, *Existentialism*, p. 224.
[183]   Ibid., p. 225.
[184]   See Søren Kierkegaard, *Repetition: An Essay in Existential Psychology*, trans. by Walter Lowrie, Princeton: Princeton University Press 1944, p. 4, which corresponds to *SKS* 4, 9 / *R*, 131.
[185]   In *Theology, Church and Ministry*, p. 135, Macquarrie reiterates this point, describing *Repetition* as "one of Kierkegaard's most obscure works," citing *Repetition*, trans. by Lowrie, p. 52, which corresponds to *SKS* 4, 9 / *R*, 131.
[186]   Macquarrie, *Existentialism*, p. 225.
[187]   Ibid., pp. 225–6.
[188]   Ibid., p. 226.
[189]   Ibid.

is an affinity between Kierkegaard's notion of repetition and Irenaeus' concept of recapitulation, which "describes on the cosmic-historical scale what Kierkegaard has restricted to individual experience."[190]

I. God

In developing his notion of God Macquarrie draws on Kierkegaard in three ways. Firstly, in *Thinking about God* Macquarrie briefly cites Kierkegaard in his discussion of God's relation to time. He writes: "Even the finite existing person is, as Kierkegaard put it, 'an atom of eternity' in time. Our own experience of time therefore may afford us some glimpse of God's double relation to time."[191] For Macquarrie, then, Kierkegaard's understanding of the human beings as a synthesis of the temporal and the eternal provides an analogy that may help us to grasp how God may be involved in time without being subject to it, just as human beings "are in time and subject to its flux" and yet possess "a capacity to transcend time as mere succession."[192]

Secondly, Macquarrie cites Kierkegaard, along with Pascal, Heidegger, and Barth, when discussing the problematic status of arguments for the existence of God.[193] These thinkers "have usually suggested that faith is made even more insecure by so-called 'proofs,' the cogency of which we begin to doubt when they are no more plainly before our minds."[194] Macquarrie has some sympathy for this view, pointing out if an incontrovertible proof were found for God's existence this would spell the end of faith and the search for deity would be over. This, however, would be an absurdity, "for what we had found would not be deity. The true deity is always ahead of us and we never catch him up with even our ingenious and subtle arguments."[195] Kierkegaard is important as one of the thinkers who exposes the inappropriateness of proofs for God's existence and promotes a conception of God that takes account of divine elusiveness.

Macquarrie's main consideration of Kierkegaard's understanding of God, however, occurs in *In Search of Deity*, where he co-opts Kierkegaard into the service of his development of "dialectical theism," that is, thinking about God that attempts to hold together in dialectical tension the opposing divine attributes of infinitude and finitude, transcendence and immanence, eternity and time. In his chapter on "Dialectical Theism and Theology" Macquarrie explains his reason for not including Kierkegaard among the "eight representative figures whose religious philosophies illustrated the major features of what I have been calling 'dialectical,' " as being that Kierkegaard "was quite specifically a Christian thinker who did not practise an abstract natural theology but prized the particular expression of truth that he found

---

[190]   Ibid.
[191]   Macquarrie, *Thinking about God*, p. 114.
[192]   Ibid., quoting *The Concept of Dread*, trans. by Lowrie, p. 79 (which corresponds to *SKS* 4, 392 / *CA*, 88). Although Vigilius Haufniensis applies the phrase "atom of eternity" to the moment, Macquarrie takes it as a description of the nature of human beings.
[193]   Macquarrie, *Thinking about God*, p. 114, quoting *The Concept of Dread*, trans. by Lowrie, p. 125, which corresponds to *SKS* 4, 441 / *CA* 140.
[194]   Macquarrie, *In Search of Deity*, p. 207; Macquarrie, *Two Worlds Are Ours*, p. 227.
[195]   Macquarrie, *In Search of Deity*, p. 207.

in Jesus Christ."[196] Despite this, however, Macquarrie holds that Kierkegaard's "emphasis on paradox is clearly related to dialectic and to the *coincidentia oppositorum*, and though he was a severe critic of Hegel, there is considerable affinity between the two."[197] Macquarrie sets himself the task of "working from the other side" in order "to show that Kierkegaard's thinking about the incarnation points towards a dialectical theism."[198]

Macquarrie takes as his starting point for this venture the parable of the king and the lowly maiden of *Philosophical Fragments*. After quoting the passage in which Climacus states that the god appeared in the form of a servant,[199] Macquarrie states that "Perhaps one could interpret this in a 'death of God' sense, as some have interpreted (though probably wrongly) Hegel, that God has fully poured himself out into the creation and emptied himself of his transcendent otherness."[200] This, however, was not Kierkegaard's intention, which Macquarrie sees rather as being the disavowal of "the monarchical view of God." As evidence he quotes the *nota bene* of *Fragments* that "We have believed that in such and such a year God appeared among us in the humble figure of a servant, that he lived and taught in our community, and finally died."[201] Macquarrie interprets this passage to mean that, for Kierkegaard, "God is not the celestial monarch that he has been represented to be, even in classical theism, but a God deeply involved in the strivings and sufferings of his creatures, so that he would be better represented in servant-form."[202] Macquarrie goes on to comment that Kierkegaard's language "is dramatic and pictorial, and has its own one-sidedness," but claims that "it would not be unfair to claim that just as dialectical theism draws us towards a concept of incarnation, so Kierkegaard's reflections on incarnation point us towards a form of dialectical, not to say paradoxical, theism."[203]

Macquarrie insists, however, that Meister Eckhart is "a far more typical representative of dialectical theism than Kierkegaard."[204] After citing Eckhart's more macaber version of Kierkegaard's parable of the king and the lowly maiden, Macquarrie points out that both men speak of God's humbling himself and suffering with his creatures. Nevertheless, Macquarrie points out that

> it cannot be denied that there is a wide gap between Kierkegaard's *existential* apprehension of the incarnation and Eckhart's *mystical* understanding of it. For Kierkegaard, incarnation is quite definitely and specifically the incarnation of the Word in Jesus Christ. For Eckhart, incarnation often has a much more general sense.

---

[196]   Ibid., p. 234.
[197]   Ibid.
[198]   Ibid.
[199]   See *Philosophical Fragments*, trans. by Swenson, pp. 24–5, which corresponds to *SKS* 4, 238–9 / *PF*, 31–2.
[200]   Macquarrie, *In Search of Deity*, p. 235.
[201]   See *Philosophical Fragments*, trans. by Swenson, p. 87, which corresponds to *SKS* 4, 274 / *PF*, 104.
[202]   Macquarrie, *In Search of Deity*, p. 235.
[203]   Ibid.
[204]   Ibid.

It is the birth of God in the soul that has prepared itself through emptying out worldly attachments.[205]

In *Two Worlds Are Ours* Macquarrie suggests that, although Kierkegaard rejects the traditional arguments for the existence of God, his notion of sin-consciousness as the prerequisite of the God-relationship constitutes a negative form of Kant's moral argument for God's existence. Whereas Kant reinstates God as a postulate of moral experience, for Kierkegaard "it is not the summons to righteousness or to transcendence that leads the mind to God, but the consciousness of sin."[206] Both thinkers are, for Macquarrie, making the same point, namely, "that although pure reason, even if spurred by passion, cannot find the way to God, there are other aspects of our complex human nature which can find that way."[207]

J. Belief

In unfolding the nature of belief Macquarrie introduces the notion of "transcendent beliefs," by which he means "beliefs that transcend the level at which empirical evidences could, at least in principle, be decisive for establishing the truth or falsity of the beliefs, or even for establishing a very high degree of probability or improbability."[208] To explain the character of transcendent beliefs Macquarrie makes use of Kierkegaard's discussion of the limitations of reason and his notion of the leap of faith. Macquarrie begins by quoting Vigilius Haufniensis' comment in *The Concept of Anxiety* that the stronger the alleged evidence for the existence of God appears to be, the more the certitude that God exists seems to diminish.[209] Macquarrie identifies three noteworthy points in Kierkegaard's argument.

Firstly, "Kierkegaard was acutely aware of the limitations of human experience and knowledge" and the impossibility of arriving at incontrovertible answers to transcendent or ultimate questions. Such questions ask about the world as a whole. Precisely because human beings can never stand outside of the world as a whole, they can never attain certainty concerning beliefs about the nature of the world in its entirety.[210]

---

[205]   Ibid., pp. 236–7.

[206]   Macquarrie, *Two Worlds Are Ours*, p. 226, inaccurately quoting *Training in Christianity*, trans. by Lowrie, 71 (which corresponds to *SKS* 12, 80 / *PC*, 67–8) and referring to *The Concept of Dread*, trans. by Lowrie. Macquarie attributes this negative form of the argument from moral experience to Kierkegaard's "melancholy outlook on life, inherited from a gloomy father."

[207]   Macquarrie, *Two Worlds Are Ours*, p. 226.

[208]   Macquarrie, *In Search of Humanity*, p. 159.

[209]   See *The Concept of Dread*, trans. by Lowrie, p. 125, which corresponds to *SKS* 4, 441 / *CA*, 140. Macquarrie, *In Search of Humanity*, p. 161.

[210]   Macquarrie, *In Search of Humanity*, p. 161.

Secondly, Macquarrie singles out for consideration Kierkegaard's claim that "the more excellent proof, the less sure we seem to be!"[211] Macquarrie asks whether this really is the case. He answers his own question with the comment that

> I suppose one could say that if the very attempt to prove God's existence is fundamentally an error because it rests on a failure to distinguish transcendent beliefs from everyday and scientific beliefs, then it can in the long run produce only confusion and bewilderment, so it shakes rather than establishes belief in God's reality.[212]

The third noteworthy point is Kierkegaard's insight that "belief is not just an approximation to knowledge,"[213] that "transcendent belief is not an inferior or provisional form of knowledge," and that consequently it is a mistake to attempt to convert this type of belief into knowledge." Macquarrie concludes that belief has an essential role to play in human existence "in its own right, and not merely as a substitute for something else," for it "stretches the human being beyond himself, it sets before him visions or speculations that do not let him settle down in the comfortable assurance of the familiar and the well-known."[214]

According to Macquarrie, these Kierkegaardian insights allow us to begin "to see the connection between transcendent beliefs and transcendence as a basic human characteristic."[215] Kierkegaard was ahead of his time in anticipating the dynamic view of human nature affirmed by modern philosophical anthropologies from existentialism and neo-Marxism to transcendental Thomism.[216] These philosophical anthropologies share the insight that human existence "was to be lived in risk, as it is constantly projecting itself into the region of the new and untested," and "in such an existence, belief rather than knowledge must be our guide." The nature of this risk-laden existence is illustrated for Macquarrie by Kierkegaard's notion of the leap and his metaphor of the believer swimming over seventy thousand fathoms of water, both of which are risky ventures that go beyond "the secure region of proofs and evidence" and make clear the qualitative difference between transcendent beliefs and our ordinary, everyday modes of thought.[217] The significance of these Kierkegaardian insights is that they allow us to get away from inadequate ways of understanding transcendent beliefs. Kierkegaard helps us to recognize that "transcendent beliefs are not static ancient metaphysical prejudices inherited from the past and inhibiting further thought," but "are part of the human search for a vision that will make sense of human life and give it the dignity that we feel belongs to it."[218]

---

[211]   See *The Concept of Dread*, trans. by Lowrie, p. 125, which corresponds to *SKS* 4, 441 / *CA*, 140.

[212]   Macquarrie, *In Search of Humanity*, p. 162; cf. Macquarrie, *Two Worlds Are Ours*, p. 227.

[213]   Macquarrie, *In Search of Humanity*, p. 162.

[214]   Ibid.

[215]   Ibid.

[216]   Ibid.

[217]   Ibid., pp. 162–3.

[218]   Ibid., p. 163.

K. Faith and Offense

In *Existentialism* Macquarrie argues that it is his emphasis on paradox that makes Kierkegaard a *Christian* existentialist. Kierkegaard is a Christian existentialist, because he believes that human beings' finitude and sin mean that they do not possess the resources for solving the dilemma of existence. Consequently, Macquarrie continues, "The only answer to the paradox of human existence is a still greater paradox—the absolute paradox of Christianity, and above all, the paradox of the incarnation, God's gracious condescension to man."[219] To shed light on this notion Macquarrie introduces Lessing's view that "contingent truths of history cannot afford the basis for eternal truths of reason." From the standpoint of reason this claim is indeed correct. It is, however, precisely the *incapacity* of reason to deal with the truth of Christianity that Kierkegaard takes as his starting point. Macquarrie points out that "In the line of Tertullian, Kierkegaard holds that Christianity is an offence to reason. It is to be embraced by an act of will in spite of reason. This is the 'leap' of faith."[220]

Macquarrie returns to Kierkegaard's understanding of the relation between faith and offense in his later works. In *Jesus Christ in Modern Thought* he cites offense as one of the distinctive features of Kierkegaard's Christology and claims that Kierkegaard has taken the notion of offense directly from the New Testament. He further notes that in contrast to Christian apologists' attempts to remove the paradox, Kierkegaard has no use for apologetics, holding that "the paradox of the God-man is bound to be an offence to reasonable people."[221]

The only way to overcome offense at the paradox of the God-man is by *faith*. Macquarrie points out that Kierkegaard rejects Hegel's view of faith as an inferior form of knowledge and attributes Kierkegaard's rejection of arguments for the existence of God to this position. For Kierkegaard, "Faith is not the result of argument or a calculation of probability, but is, in Kierkegaard's language, a leap."[222] By the term "leap" Macquarrie understands Kierkegaard to be designating "the achievement of a new stance such that we cannot explain or analyse how we have come to that point."[223] For Macquarrie, it is appropriate to describe Kierkegaard's "leap" as a "stance," "for it is not just an intellectual conviction but an attitude of the complete person, in which not only thought but the will and even the passions are involved." Macquarrie claims that in Kierkegaard's view faith "has a participatory character which gives its own certitude, even in the face of objective uncertainties."[224]

---

[219] Macquarrie, *Existentialism*, p. 217.
[220] Ibid.
[221] Macquarrie, *Jesus Christ in Modern Thought*, p. 244.
[222] Ibid.
[223] Ibid.
[224] Ibid.

L. Christology

Macquarrie occasionally touches on Kierkegaard's Christology when discussing other issues. In *Studies in Christian Existentialism* Macquarrie briefly mentions the notion of Christ's sinlessness and cites Kierkegaard's description in *Works of Love* of Christ's sinlessness as the "'limitless love" whereby Christ overcomes the separation of sin.[225] Macquarrie's most sustained treatment of Kierkegaard's Christology, however, occurs in *Jesus Christ in Modern Thought*, although he concedes that he finds it "difficult to talk about a 'christology' in Kierkegaard," because there is "hardly a coherent body of teaching one would call a 'christology' in the conventional sense."[226] Nevertheless, Macquarrie sets down seven points he believes are at the heart of Kierkegaard's Christological thinking, although he emphasizes that in doing so he is not attempting to impose a system on Kierkegaard's thought. These seven points are those features of Kierkegaard's thought "which we shall find being revived when Kierkegaard was rediscovered (or even discovered for the first time) in the earlier part of the twentieth century."[227] Macquarrie considers these seven points to be "more like a shopping list than the summary of a coherent theological position" and suspects that this is the way Kierkegaard would have wanted it. Because not all of Macquarrie's seven points are strictly speaking Christological and have been dealt with under other headings, we shall focus here only on Macquarrie's discussion of the overtly Christological elements of Kierkegaard's thought.

The first of Macquarrie's seven points is that "The foundation is Jesus Christ, the God-man, the Absolute Paradox."[228] This is an issue Macquarrie touches on in several of his works. For example, he cites Kierkegaard in his discussion of the paradoxical character of the Incarnation in *Principles of Christian Theology*, where he quotes Climacus' statement in *Postscript*: "That God has existed in human form, has been born, grown up and so forth, is surely the paradox *sensu strictissimo*, the absolute paradox."[229]

In several of his works Macquarrie cites Kierkegaard's view that it is not possible to know Christ from history and his denial that the contemporary disciple had an advantage over later followers who never knew the historical Jesus.[230] In

---

[225]   Macquarrie, *Studies in Christian Existentialism*, p. 240.

[226]   Macquarrie, *Jesus Christ in Modern Thought*, p. 237.

[227]   Ibid., p. 240.

[228]   Ibid.

[229]   See *Concluding Unscientific Postscript*, trans. by Swenson and Lowrie, pp. 194–5, which corresponds to *SKS* 7, 198 / *CUP1*, 217. Macquarrie, *Principles of Christian Theology*, 2nd ed., p. 306. See also Macquarrie, *Thinking about God*, p. 12; Macquarrie, *Humility of God*, p. 64; Macquarrie, *Jesus Christ in Modern Thought*, p. 165; and Macquarrie, *Christology Revisited*, p. 14. In the two latter works Macquarrie cites *Philosophical Fragments*, trans. by Swenson, p. 29, which corresponds to *SKS* 4, 243 / *PF*, 37.

[230]   See Macquarrie, *The Scope of Demythologizing*, p. 92, citing *Philosophical Fragments*, trans. by Swenson, pp. 44ff., which corresponds to *SKS* 4, 258ff. / *PF*, 55ff.; Macquarrie, *Faith of the People of God*, p. 87, citing *Philosophical Fragments*, trans. by Swenson, p. 44, which corresponds to *SKS* 4, 258 / *PF*, 55; Macquarrie, *Jesus Christ in Modern Thought*, p. 51; p. 237 (referring to *Philosophical Fragments*, trans. by Swenson, pp. 37–48 and quoting

Macquarrie's opinion, "Kierkegaard seems to have been even more dismissive of the historical than Kant was."[231] For Kierkegaard, "the great event in all history was God's condescension to man in the incarnate Christ." As far as Kierkegaard is concerned, "this is all the history one need know, and yet it is not history in the sense of something past, but a contemporary truth."[232] This dismissal of history is due not to Kierkegaard's doubting the historical reports concerning Jesus, in relation to which Macquarrie holds Kierkegaard "could be quite naive," but is due rather to Kierkegaard's conviction that "the event of Jesus Christ was more than history,"[233] and "belongs to a different realm of discourse."[234] For Kierkegaard, Jesus Christ "was the appearance of the eternal in time, and debates over historical questions trivialized the issue."[235]

Macquarrie agrees with Kierkegaard that even the most detailed historical evidence is insufficient to prove that Jesus Christ is the incarnate Word of God, for this assertion is of a different order from an accurate historical account of his life.[236] Macquarrie disagrees, however, "with the very sharp disjunction which is made here between the historical Jesus and the Christ of faith, or that between knowledge and faith,"[237] and cites several arguments against Kierkegaard's position.

Firstly, Macquarrie questions Anti-Climacus' claim that history cannot teach us anything about Christ because he is the paradox which exists only for faith.[238] For Macquarrie, such a claim "raises the standard question addressed to docetic Christologies: of what relevance to the human race is a Christ who is 'really' not human, or possibly at best half-human?"[239]

A second objection Macquarrie levels against Kierkegaard's view that history cannot teach us about Christ is "how can one believe in someone or something if one *knows nothing* about the object of belief?"[240] Macquarrie quotes with approval Donald Baillie's point that "we must have some knowledge of Jesus if he is to

---

Philosophical Fragments, trans. by Swenson, p. 87, which corresponds to *SKS* 4, 274 / *PF* 104); and p. 351, quoting inaccurately *Training in Christianity*, trans. by Lowrie, 27, which corresponds to *SKS* 12, 40 / *PC* 25.

[231]   Macquarrie, *Jesus Christ in Modern Thought*, p. 237. Before considering Kierkegaard's view of the historical Jesus, Macquarrie briefly sums up the distinction made in *Fragments* between Socrates and Christ, the notion of reason's collision with something beyond its grasp when encountering Christ, and the choice to leap out beyond reason into faith, or else take offense and turn away. Macquarrie, *Jesus Christ in Modern Thought*, p. 237, citing *Philosophical Fragments*, trans. by Swenson, p. 35, which corresponds to *SKS* 4, 243 / *PF*, 37.

[232]   Macquarrie, *Existentialism*, p. 224.

[233]   Macquarrie, *Jesus Christ in Modern Thought*, p. 237.

[234]   Ibid., p. 351.

[235]   Ibid., p. 237.

[236]   Macquarrie, *Christology Revisited*, pp. 24–5. Macquarrie refers the reader to *Training in Christianity*, trans. by Lowrie, p. 28, which corresponds to *SKS* 12, 40 / *PC*, 25–6.

[237]   Macquarrie, *Christology Revisited*, p. 25.

[238]   *Training in Christianity*, trans. by Lowrie, p. 28, which corresponds to *SKS* 12, 40 / *PC*, 25–6.

[239]   Macquarrie, *Jesus Christ in Modern Thought*, p. 241.

[240]   Ibid.

mean anything to us,"[241] and later cites Baillie's comment that if we affirm Christ's incognito in "the extreme form advanced by Kierkegaard, then there would be no revelation of God in Christ and no point to the incarnation."[242] Macquarrie asks: "Again, if God is qualitatively different from man, and Christ is really God, not really man, are we not reduced to complete incomprehension?[243] He later makes a similar point in *Two Worlds Are Ours*, where he asks whether it is possible to continue to speak of *revelation*, if Christ is hidden behind an incognito. For Macquarie, if we had no historical information, "Jesus Christ would be only an empty name."[244] For Macquarrie, the *nota bene* of *Fragments* "would certainly not be enough" to provide the basis for an individual's decision about Christ, for "It tells us virtually nothing about the kind of human life that Jesus lived." In Macquarrie's opinion, "Here Kierkegaard seems to be going from paradox into sheer incoherence.'"[245]

Macquarrie wonders if Kierkegaard himself did not eventually become aware of this problem and quotes Climacus' remarks in *Fragments* that, despite his incognito, Christ did not intend to live his life completely unnoticed by human beings.[246] For Macquarrie, historical evidence about Jesus is able to "point us in the direction of a certain estimate of his character and significance and that this might induce some people to make the leap to the assertion that 'God was in Christ' or to an equivalent assertion in an appropriate idiom." The importance of probability for faith becomes even more apparent when we consider what the impact would be of evidence proving that Jesus was a hypocrite or a mythical invention. Macquarrie notes that such evidence "would surely deter us from embracing the church's transcendent beliefs about him." For these reasons, Macquarrie asserts that "It is probability rather than improbability that must be our guide, and even the paradox which is initially improbable must be shown to be not a sheer contradiction."[247]

Thirdly, Kierkegaard makes the gulf between divinity and humanity too deep, and Macquarrie warns that "it is important…that we do not make the problem even more difficult than it actually is."[248] Indeed, Macquarrie suggests that "the root of the trouble may well be Kierkegaard's notion of an 'infinite qualitative difference' between God and man."[249] Macquarrie classifies Kierkegaard and the early Barth as examples of theologians who have intensified the difficulty by assuming "a concept which separates [God] so absolutely from the created order that the gulf can never

---

[241]   Ibid., p. 328; cf. ibid., p. 351.

[242]   Donald Baillie, *God was in Christ*, London: Faber & Faber 1948, pp. 49–50.

[243]   Macquarrie is guilty of a misunderstanding here. Kierkegaard nowhere affirms that Christ is "not really man." Indeed, it would negate Kierkegaard's notion of paradox if Christ were not human.

[244]   Macquarrie, *Two Worlds Are Ours*, pp. 227–8.

[245]   Ibid., p. 228.

[246]   Macquarrie, *In Search of Humanity*, p. 165; Macquarrie, *Two Worlds Are Ours*, p. 228, quoting *Philosophical Fragments*, trans. by Swenson, p. 44, which corresponds to *SKS* 4, 259 / *PF*, 56.

[247]   Macquarrie, *In Search of Humanity*, p. 165; cf. Macquarrie, *Two Worlds Are Ours*, p. 227.

[248]   Macquarrie, *Jesus Christ in Modern Thought*, p. 376.

[249]   Ibid., p. 352.

be bridged."[250] Kierkegaard's "infinite qualitative difference" and Barth's concept of God as "the wholly other" mean "that incarnation must be not only the 'absolute paradox' but a sheer impossibility."[251]

Macquarrie goes on to claim that Kierkegaard and Barth "were able to speak of incarnation only because in the course of their dialectical thinking they profoundly modified their stress on the otherness of God."[252] According to Macquarrie, Kierkegaard and Barth undertook this modification by finding in God "a humanity and even a humility which made contact across the gulf."[253] With regard to Kierkegaard, Macquarrie cites as evidence the parable of the king and lowly maiden in *Fragments*. Nevertheless, despite such modifications, Macquarrie holds that both Kierkegaard and Barth "lacked an adequate doctrine of the divine immanence, and without such a doctrine, the difficulties in the way of thinking of an incarnation are enormously increased."[254]

Macquarrie claims that implicit in Kierkegaard's notion of Christ as the absolute paradox is the view that "Any thinking about Jesus Christ will get nowhere if it begins with his humanity."[255] Kierkegaard's commitment to the infinite qualitative difference between God and humanity leads him to reject Schleiermacher's view of Christ as the completion of the creation of humanity and the notion of a transition from affirming Christ's goodness to the claim that he is God. Such a transition, Macquarrie points out, would be a μετάβασις εἰς ἄλλο γένος, and he cites *Practice in Christianity* in support of this view.[256] Macquarrie comments: "So here Kierkegaard decisively rejects the so-called 'christology from below,' though it is precisely in this context that he reveals the naivete mentioned above, for he says that Christ told us he was God."[257] For Macquarrie, Kierkegaard "seems to hold that the human historical Jesus is not the 'real' Christ. The real Christ is God, God appearing in history, but not historical, for this is the eternal in history."[258] Macquarrie wonders "whether one can make any sense of this or whether it would be wrong even to try."

A further distinctive feature of Kierkegaard's Christology is the "incognito." Macquarrie suggests that this notion "perhaps had its roots in the teaching of some early Lutheran theologians that there was a κρύψις or hiddenness of the divine attributes of the divine attributes of Christ."[259] In advancing this notion of the Incarnation, Kierkegaard draws attention to an important problem: "The problem is, basically, how is revelation possible." Macquarrie claims that "Kierkegaard seems to have boxed himself in at this point, for he has denied that we can learn anything

---

250   Ibid., p. 376.
251   Ibid., p. 376; cf. ibid., p. 352.
252   Ibid., p. 376.
253   Ibid.
254   Ibid.
255   Ibid., p. 240.
256   *Training in Christianity*, trans. by Lowrie, pp. 28–31, which corresponds to *SKS* 12, 40–3 / *PC*, 26–9. Macquarrie also quotes, slightly inaccurately, *Training in Christianity*, trans. by Lowrie, p. 31, which corresponds to *SKS* 12, 43 / *PC*, 29.
257   Macquarrie, *Jesus Christ in Modern Thought*, p. 238.
258   Ibid., p. 240.
259   Ibid., p. 241.

about the 'real' Christ from historical information about the career of Jesus."[260] The one assertion that Kierkegaard repeatedly makes about Jesus which "does break the incognito…is the assertion that Jesus himself declared that he was God."[261] Macquarrie points out, however, that the view that the historical Jesus claimed to be God would be accepted by few scholars today. In Kierkegaard's defense, Macquarrie points out that there are elements in Kierkegaard's teaching which "save him from thoroughgoing docetism and also point to a very profound view of God on his part."[262] The elements to which Macquarrie is referring are the parable of the king and the maiden in *Fragments*. Macquarrie believes, however, that these elements "may be inconsistent with [Kierkegaard's] more robust affirmations of the divine incognito."[263]

Connected with Kierkegaard's notion of the incognito is Kierkegaard's use of indirect communication. Macquarrie raises the question of "how indirect is it possible for a communication to be, without its ceasing to be a communication? If the Christ appears incognito, what is the point or where is the revelation?"[264] Macquarrie points out that Kierkegaard himself raises this question when he states in *Fragments* that the god did not assume the form of a servant to mock humans and that the god "will therefore doubtless give some sort of sign."[265] Macquarrie holds, however, that Kierkegaard fails to inform the reader of the nature of this sign and merely indicates that it may just as easily provoke offense as faith. Macquarrie then turns to the discussion in *Practice of Christianity* of Matthew 11.6, which Kierkegaard takes as an indirect answer to John the Baptist's question whether Jesus is the messiah. Macquarrie focuses on Anti-Climacus' statement that Jesus could not give John the Baptist a direct answer because John was absent, but he could have given a direct answer to someone who was present. Macquarrie finds this puzzling and turns for help to Walter Lowrie's explanation in his notes to *Training in Christianity* that "Kierkegaard was at this time giving up his attachment to 'indirect communication.' "[266]

Macquarrie goes on to link Kierkegaard's theory of indirect communication with Kant's notion of the archetype. Macquarrie points out that we would not be able to recognize Jesus Christ as the person "well-pleasing to God" if we did not already have some image or archetype of such a person in our minds. Macquarrie then contrasts *Philosophical Fragments* and *Fear and Trembling*. In *Fragments* "Jesus is the teacher to whom we owe everything, in contrast to Socrates who awakens what is

---

[260]   Ibid., p. 242; cf. ibid., pp. 351–2, where Macquarrie inaccurately quotes Anti-Climacus' comment in *Practice in Christianity* that in Christ God appeared "in a strict incognito, an incognito impenetrable to the most intimate observation" (*Training in Christianity*, trans. by Lowrie, p. 27, which corresponds to *SKS* 12, 40 / *PC*, 25).

[261]   Macquarrie, *Jesus Christ in Modern Thought*, p. 242. Macquarrie refers the reader to *Training in Christianity*, trans. by Lowrie, p. 33, which corresponds to *SKS* 12, 46 / *PC*, 30.

[262]   Macquarrie, *Jesus Christ in Modern Thought*, p. 242.

[263]   Ibid.

[264]   Ibid., p. 243.

[265]   See *Philosophical Fragments*, trans. by Swenson, p. 44, which corresponds to *SKS* 4, 259 / *PF*, 56.

[266]   Macquarrie, *Jesus Christ in Modern Thought*, p. 243.

already hidden in our minds."[267] In his treatment of Abraham in *Fear and Trembling*, however, Kierkegaard seems to assume the existence of some innate capacity within Abraham that enables him to recognize the commandment to sacrifice Isaac as coming from God. This conflicts with *Fragments*, where Kierkegaard seems to deny the presence of such a capacity and to place the initiative entirely with God.

Macquarrie picks up on Kierkegaard's description of himself as a gadfly and comments that "we can recognize that he made an important contribution by asking so many awkward questions of nineteenth-century thinkers."[268] Despite this, however, Macquarrie ultimately finds Kierkegaard's thinking about Christ unsatisfactory, precisely because Kierkegaard is, in Macquarrie's opinion, not prepared to apply reason to some of the important Christological questions. He comments: "Kierkegaard teaches us to have misgivings about the humanistic and immanentist thrust of early nineteenth-century Christology, and we do well to ponder some of his warnings. But he does not himself offer us a Christology in which we can rest."[269] Macquarrie holds that Kierkegaard is himself unable consistently to sustain his paradox Christology. He points out that Kierkegaard fails to elucidate his claim that Christ is the eternal in time and "even seems to be saying that it cannot be elucidated."[270] Despite this lack of elucidation, however, Macquarrie argues that Kierkegaard's introduction of the notion of the eternal means that Kierkegaard "does admit metaphysics into his work." Macquarrie sees this as an important point, "because it shows the inadequacy of a purely existentialist Christology."[271] Existentialist Christology appeals to immediate experience such as anxiety and sin as prerequisites for the emergence of faith. For Macquarrie, however, this is insufficient, for "Christology, as a part of theology, needs reflection as well as experience."[272] In this respect Macquarrie holds that Hegel's criticism of Schleiermacher is also applicable to Kierkegaard, namely, "Why have faith in Christ?" For Macquarrie Kierkegaard provides an answer to this question in his assertion that the eternal has become present in history in Christ, but "he does not or rather he will not explain the answer."[273] If we wish to make progress in our thinking about Christ, then, we cannot remain with Kierkegaard's paradox Christology, but must look for other guides.

IV. Conclusion

Macquarrie's treatment of Kierkegaard takes three basic forms. Firstly, Macquarrie considers Kierkegaard in the context of his studies of the history of theology and philosophy, especially existentialism. Here Macquarrie takes Kierkegaard as the example of the Christian existentialist *par excellence* and cites his works in order to illustrate the character of Christian existentialism. This treatment of Kierkegaard

---

[267]   Ibid.
[268]   Ibid., p. 244.
[269]   Ibid., pp. 244–5.
[270]   Ibid.
[271]   Ibid.
[272]   Ibid.
[273]   Ibid., p. 241.

is particularly prominent in *Studies in Christian Existentialism* and *Existentialism*. Macquarrie also discusses Kierkegaard in his historical studies of Christian theology. Thus Macquarrie frequently mentions Kierkegaard as an influential figure on the thinkers he deals with in his *Twentieth-Century Religious Thought* and devotes a section to Kierkegaard in his *Jesus Christ in Modern Thought*.

Secondly, Macquarrie draws on aspects of Kierkegaard's thought in order to expose the weaknesses of one-sided existentialist approaches to theology. If existentialist approaches are to be of service to theology, they must be corrected by approaches which draw on the resources of rationality and are prepared to think through as deeply as possible the profound metaphysical questions raised by Christianity's claims that the Word became flesh and dwelt among us. This is why Macquarrie's own thinking moved away from a purely existentialist approach to "existential-ontological theology," "panentheism," and, finally, "dialectical theism."

Thirdly, in developing his own anthropologically based approach to theology Macquarrie finds Kierkegaard a useful resource in shedding light on those features of human existence that point the human being towards God. Here he adopts an appreciative but critical attitude towards Kierkegaard. For Macquarrie, Kierkegaard is a quarry containing valuable building materials for the theological enterprise and for his own anthropocentric theology. The materials Kierkegaard provides, however, are not sufficient to construct a free-standing edifice in their own right, but must be supplemented with additional resources. This is why Macquarrie is drawn to Heidegger rather than Kierkegaard, for Heidegger's thought has an ontological dimension lacking in Kierkegaard. It also accounts for why Macquarrie, particularly in his early period, views Kierkegaard through a Heideggerian lens.

There are, however, problems with Macquarrie's treatment of Kierkegaard. His knowledge of Kierkegaard's thought seems to be based primarily on *Fear and Trembling*, *The Concept of Anxiety*, *Philosophical Fragments*, *Concluding Unscientific Postscript*, and *Practice in Christianity*. There is a cluster of quotations from these works that Macquarrie returns to time and again throughout the fifty years of his authorship. Macquarrie does not seem to have been well acquainted with the works which Kierkegaard penned under his own name, the only one of which he occasionally cites being *Works of Love*. There is little development in Macquarrie's thinking concerning Kierkegaard. He seems to have arrived at an assessment of Kierkegaard's thought at an early date in his career and remained true to this view throughout his authorship, even to the extent of repeating the same inaccurate quotations from Kierkegaard's works.

Macquarrie makes no distinction between Kierkegaard and his pseudonyms. Although he recognizes that the most likely explanation for Kierkegaard's use of pseudonyms is to provide "different points of view so as to encourage the reader to make a choice,"[274] Macquarrie generally attributes the views of the pseudonyms directly to Kierkegaard himself. This results in a homogenization and "flattening" of Kierkegaard's thought that erases its dialectical character and arguably tones down the existential decision which Kierkegaard's pseudonyms aim to provoke in the reader.

---

[274]   Ibid., p. 242.

A further issue with Macquarrie's treatment of Kierkegaard arises from his synthesizing tendencies. Macquarrie is constantly searching for points of contacts between thinkers and attempting to synthesize their insights into a coherent and comprehensive theology. Kierkegaard, too, is subjected to this synthesizing treatment. Indeed, it could be argued that Macquarrie subjugates Kierkegaard to the *via media* characteristic of Anglicanism. He is constantly trying to find the middle ground between Kierkegaard and the positions Kierkegaard opposes. This means that Macquarrie tends to play down the most significant features of Kierkegaard's thought, such as his emphasis on paradox, the incognito, and divine transcendence. While recognizing the importance of these Kierkegaardian insights, Macquarrie tones them down—we might even say "tames" them—in order to assimilate them into precisely the sort of systematic theology that was anathema to Kierkegaard. At the same time, however, Macquarrie's subordination of Kierkegaard's thought to the concerns of contemporary systematic theology highlights the continued importance of Kierkegaard as both a theological corrective and a resource for theology.

Bibliography

I. References to or Uses of Kierkegaard in Macquarrie's Corpus

An Existentialist Theology: A Comparison of Heidegger and Bultmann, London: SCM Press 1955, p. 16; p. 68; p. 69; p. 70; p. 91; p. 221; p. 240.

Twentieth-Century Religious Thought, 5th ed., London: SCM Press 2001 [1963], p. 117; p. 120; p. 132; p. 194; p. 199; p. 200; p. 203; p. 319; p. 331; p. 333; p. 339; p. 345; p. 356; p. 370; pp. 374–5; p. 427; p. 428; p. 429; p. 448; p. 451; pp. 453–4; p. 455; p. 457; p. 458; p. 463; p. 468.

Principles of Christian Theology, 2nd ed., London: SCM Press 1977 [1966], p. 68; p. 77; p. 146; p. 185; p. 306; p. 350; p. 377; p. 397; p. 520.

Studies in Christian Existentialism: Lectures and Essays, London: SCM Press 1966, p. 22; p. 68; p. 240; p. 266; p. 273.

God-Talk: An Examination of the Language and Logic of Theology, London: SCM Press 1967, p. 229.

Existentialism, New York: World Publishing Co. 1972 and Harmondsworth: Pelican 1972, pp. 13–14; pp. 18–20; p. 23; p. 31; p. 42; p. 48; p. 52; pp. 53–5; p. 62; pp. 65–6; p. 68; p. 72; p. 77; p. 81; p. 93; p. 103; pp. 112–13; pp. 118–20; p. 136; pp. 137–9; pp. 140–1; pp. 143–4; pp. 147–8; p. 164; pp. 165–8; p. 170; p. 171; p. 175; pp. 177–8; p. 180; pp. 183–7; p. 203; pp. 210–11; p. 213; pp. 216–18; p. 220; pp. 224–6; p. 227; pp. 228–30; p. 241; p. 250; p. 251; p. 253; p. 260; pp. 263–4; p. 271; pp. 275–80; pp. 302–3.

Thinking about God, London: SCM Press 1975, p. 12; p. 17; pp. 19–21; p. 39; p. 144; p. 135; p. 172; p. 206; p. 227.

In Search of Humanity: A Theological and Philosophical Approach, London: SCM Press 1982, p. 9; pp. 19–20; p. 48; p. 55; p. 63; p. 84; p. 98; p. 111; pp. 113–14; pp. 131–3; p. 141; p. 146; pp. 161–5; p. 169; p. 176; p. 186; pp. 190–2; pp. 207–8; p. 216; p. 261; p. 262; p. 264; p. 266; p. 268; p. 269; p. 270; p. 271; p. 272.

In Search of Deity: An Essay in Dialectical Theism, London: SCM Press 1984, p. 24; p. 99; p. 125; p. 127; p. 129; p. 138; p. 207; p. 234; p. 235; p. 252; p. 261; p. 267; p. 268; p. 269.

Jesus Christ in Modern Thought, London: SCM Press 1990, p. 51; p. 151; p. 165; p. 178; p. 212; pp. 236–45; p. 266; p. 279; p. 321; p. 328; p. 351; p. 376; p. 379; p. 430; p. 434; p. 442.

Christology Revisited, London: SCM Press 1998, p. 13; p. 19; p. 24; p. 25; p. 90.

On Being a Theologian: Reflections at Eighty, ed. by John H. Morgan with Georgina Morley and Eamonn Conway, London: SCM Press 1999, p. 62; pp. 132–3.

Stubborn Theological Questions, London: SCM Press 2003, p. 16; p. 23; p. 29; p. 66; p. 74; p.165; p. 182; p. 189; p. 213; p. 216.

Two Worlds Are Ours: An Introduction to Christian Mysticism, London: SCM Press 2004, p. 10; p. 56; pp. 224–9; p. 252.

II. Sources of Macquarrie's Knowledge of Kierkegaard

Diem, Hermann, *Kierkegaard: An Introduction*, trans. by D. Green, Richmond, Virginia: John Knox Press 1966.

Heidegger, Martin, *Being and Time*, trans. by John Macquarrie and Edward Robinson, Oxford: Basil Blackwell 1962.

Kierkegaard, Søren, *Philosophical Fragments, or a Fragment of Philosophy*, trans. by David F. Swenson, Princeton: Princeton University Press 1936.

— *Stages on Life's Way*, trans. by Walter Lowrie, Princeton: Princeton University Press 1940.

— *Concluding Unscientific Postscript*, trans. by David F. Swenson and Walter Lowrie, Princeton: Princeton University Press 1941.

— *Either/Or*, vols. 1–2, trans. by David F. Swenson, Lillian Marvin Swenson, and Walter Lowrie, Princeton: Princeton University Press 1941.

— *Attack upon "Christendom,"* trans. by Walter Lowrie, Princeton: Princeton University Press 1944.

— *The Concept of Dread*, trans. by Walter Lowrie, Princeton: Princeton University Press 1944.

— *Repetition: An Essay in Existential Psychology*, trans. by Walter Lowrie, Princeton: Princeton University Press 1944.

— *The Works of Love*, trans. by Howard V. and Edna H. Hong, New York: Harper & Row 1944.

— *Fear and Trembling and The Sickness unto Death*, trans. by Walter Lowrie, Garden City, New York: Doubleday 1954.

— *Training in Christianity*, trans. by Walter Lowrie, Princeton: Princeton University Press 1944.

— *The Journals of Kierkegaard 1834–1854*, ed. and trans. by Alexander Dru, New York: Peter Smith 1959.

— *The Last Years: Journals 1853–1855*, ed. and trans. by Ronald Gregor Smith, New York: Peter Smith 1959.

— *Fear and Trembling*, trans. by Alistair Hannay, Harmondsworth: Penguin 1985.

Law, David R., *Kierkegaard as Negative Theologian*, Oxford: Clarendon Press 1993.

Paton, H.J., *The Modern Predicament: A Study in the Philosophy of Religion*, London: Allen & Unwin 1955.

Pojman, Louis P., *Kierkegaard as Philosopher*, Swindon: Waterleaf Press 1978.

— *The Logic of Subjectivity*, Tuscaloosa, Alabama: University of Alabama Press 1984.

Rohde, Peter, *Søren Kierkegaard*, London: George Allen & Unwin 1963.

Sponheim, Paul, *Kierkegaard on Christ and Christian Coherence*, New York: Harper & Row 1968.

III. Secondary Literature on Macquarrie's Relation to Kierkegaard

None.

Reinhold Niebuhr:

The Logic of Paradox for a Theology of Human Nature

Kyle A. Roberts

Reinhold Niebuhr (1892–1971) is arguably America's greatest twentieth-century theologian. Niebuhr's father, Gustav Niebuhr, emigrated to the United States from Germany and became a Lutheran pastor. Reinhold, along with his brother H. Richard, followed in his father's footsteps, attending seminary at Eden Theological Seminary in St. Louis. He would go on to take his B.D. and M.A. in theology from Yale University Divinity School. Niebuhr developed an acute sense for social justice issues while serving in his first pastorate in Detroit, during the Great Depression. He advocated on behalf of auto industry workers for whom conditions were unjust and oppressive. His memoir, *Leaves from the Notebook of a Tamed Cynic*, captures his theological reflections during his ministerial tenure in Detroit.[1] After gaining attention for his writing and preaching, Niebuhr accepted a position as professor of theological ethics at Union Theological Seminary, where he remained until 1960.

Among Niebuhr's many books and articles, his most well known include *Moral Man and Immoral Society* (1932), *The Irony of American History* (1952), *The Self and the Dramas of History* (1955), and *Christian Realism and Political Problems* (1953).[2] Niebuhr's indebtedness to Kierkegaard can be seen most clearly in his magnum opus, *The Nature and Destiny of Man: A Christian Interpretation* (1941–43).[3] He borrows heavily from Kierkegaard's innovative integration of theology and psychology in his anthropology and theology of sin. Kierkegaard's articulation of human nature as a paradoxical combination of freedom and limitation became a driving force in Niebuhr's formulation of a theological anthropology and a political theology. While heavily based on *realism* and sensitive to the fallibility of human nature, this theology aimed toward a creative reimagining of society in accordance with God's justice and love. As Langdon Gilkey put it, Niebuhr was an existentialist

---

[1]   Reinhold Niebuhr, *Leaves from the Notebook of a Tamed Cynic*, New York: Willett, Clark and Colby 1929.

[2]   Reinhold Niebuhr, *Moral Man and Immoral Society*, New York: Scribner 1932; Reinhold Niebuhr, *The Irony of American History*, New York: Scribner 1952; Reinhold Niebuhr, *The Self and the Dramas of History*, New York: Scribner 1955; and Reinhold Niebuhr, *Christian Realism and Political Problems*, New York: Scribner 1953.

[3]   Reinhold Niebuhr, *The Nature and Destiny of Man: A Christian Interpretation*, vols. 1–2, New York: Scribner 1941–43.

but one whose concerns tilted to social, more than to individual, issues.[4] In this respect, Niebuhr might be thought of as extending Kierkegaardian subjectivity in the direction of collective, theological ethics.

While deeply appreciative of and heavily influenced by Kierkegaard, Niebuhr held him at arm's length on certain issues. He summed up his measured approach in a 1941 review of the English translation of *Stages on Life's Way*:

> Kierkegaard was at once one of the most profound and one of the most perverse Christian theologians. He was profound in the sense that he explored the psychological facts which lie at the foundation of Christian thought more thoroughly than any theologian since Augustine. He was perverse in the sense that he accentuated some of the most negative aspects of the Protestant Reformation, thus becoming a nexus between Martin Luther and Karl Barth.[5]

I. Kierkegaard's Contribution to Niebuhr's Theology of the Self

Niebuhr's theology can be described as a persistent attempt to apply the insights of the Gospel to the complexities of modern life. In so doing, he focused his theological reflections largely through the lens of the nature of humanity and its implications for sociality. While reflecting many of the impulses of neo-orthodoxy, he had a more positive view regarding the intersection of nature and grace than his trans-Atlantic colleague, Karl Barth (1886–1968). Not surprisingly, he was more optimistic regarding the possibilities of natural theology, while retaining a realistic doctrine of sin. Niebuhr described humanity as existing within a persistent tension of freedom and limitation. Humans desire to exercise their creativity and yet struggle with the temptation to exceed their proper reach, thus asserting their independence in idolatrous ways. For Niebuhr, persistently inadequate philosophies of human nature only contribute to, rather than alleviate, that tension.

Niebuhr located the crisis in modern thought in humanity's attempt to understand itself in either exclusively rationalist or materialist categories. Philosophies of rationalism (whether the idealist or naturalist form) and Romanticism (or what he also called "vitalism") were, for Niebuhr, modern manifestations of perpetually inadequate attempts to explain human nature. Both naturalism and idealism abrogate the individual. Naturalism does so by not accounting for the transcendent dimension of the self as spirit and by defining humanity solely through categories of natural causation. Idealism, on the other hand, loses the self by deifying the spirit and by forcing the shape of individuality to "conform to its pattern of rationality."[6] In sum, both alternatives think either too pessimistically or too optimistically of humanity.

Idealism, for Niebuhr, assumed that the self could connect to universal rationality through consciousness, without remainder; thus the particularities of history and of human individuality are lost in the ocean of transcendent mind. Niebuhr appealed

---

4   Langdon Gilkey, *On Niebuhr*, Chicago: University of Chicago Press 2001, p. 20.

5   Reinhold Niebuhr, "Review of Lowrie's Translation of *Stages on Life's Way*," *New York Herald Tribune Books*, January 26, 1941, p. 17.

6   Niebuhr, *The Nature and Destiny of Man*, vol. 1, p. 81.

to the *Concluding Unscientific Postscript* as an ally in his critique of idealism; in particular, the latter's apparent inclination to subsume all of existence within the category of the eternal or the universal.[7] He quoted: "Before the system completes itself, every scrap of existence must have been swallowed up in the eternal; there must not be the slightest remainder; not even so much as a bit of dingle-dangle represented by the Herr Professor who writes the system."[8] In sum, idealism is a faulty understanding of human selfhood that has negative consequences for the pursuit of truth, ethics, and political progress.

In response to what he perceived as flaws in idealism and naturalism, Niebuhr attempted to establish both the partial transcendence of the self and the contingency of the self as a historical, created (and thus dependent) being. While the self's consciousness can break beyond the bounds of immediate, natural experience, it cannot survey all of reality or link itself to transcendent rationality. Christianity's distinction from idealism was that "it knows of the finiteness of the self and of its involvement in all the relativities and contingencies of nature and history."[9] While the self might reach beyond itself through the exertion of self-consciousness, it remains mortal and finite. Here Niebuhr turned to Kierkegaard, who "interpreted the true meaning of human selfhood more accurately than any modern, and possibly more than any previous, Christian theologian."[10] Niebuhr cited the notion in *The Sickness unto Death* that the task of a human being is to "become a self." For Kierkegaard, the self is a "conscious synthesis of the limited and the unlimited," which in effect involves a continual dialectical movement in which the self "escapes the self" and yet "endlessly returns to the self."[11] Thus, to be a self is to accept the difficult task of approaching life as a rigorous dynamic movement in which one is always working both with and against competing factors inherent to human life—in particular the dual realities of creaturely freedom and finite limitation.

Niebuhr's appropriation of Kierkegaard's theology of selfhood is not without critical reflection. In *Nature and Destiny,* he analyzed the following passage from *Either/Or*:

> Truth [in the human situation] is exactly the identity of choosing and determining and of being chosen and determined. What I choose I do not determine, for if it were not determined I could not choose it; and yet if I did not determine it through my choice

---

[7]   In a review of David F. Swenson's English translation of this work (London: Oxford University Press 1941) Niebuhr claimed that "no work of the Danish philosopher will give the reader a more comprehensive view of his thought world that this 'Postscript.' " Reinhold Niebuhr, "Review of *Concluding Unscientific Postscript*," *New York Herald Tribune Books*, November 30, 1941, p. 33.

[8]   Ibid. Niebuhr's Kierkegaard citation is from a selection of Swenson's translation of *Concluding Unscientific Postscript*, in *An Anthology of Modern Philosophy: Selections for Beginners from the Writings of the Greatest Philosophers from 1500 to 1900*, ed. by Daniel Sommer Robinson, New York: Thomas Y. Crowell 1931, p. 649.

[9]   Niebuhr, *The Nature and Destiny of Man*, vol. 1, p. 170.

[10]   Ibid., vol. 1, p. 171.

[11]   Ibid. Niebuhr's Kierkegaard citation is from *Die Krankheit zum Tode*, Jena: Diederichs 1957, p. 27.

I would not really choose it. It is: if it were not I could not choose it. It is not: but becomes reality through my choice, or else my choice were an illusion…I choose the Absolute? What is the Absolute? I am that myself the eternal personality…but what is this myself?…it is the most abstract and at the same time the most concrete of all realities. It is freedom.[12]

Niebuhr was troubled by a straightforward identification here of the self with the Absolute and with freedom. He suggested a correction of this view of the self with the Christian view in which the self is understood through a Christological lens. For Niebuhr, humanity learns its true nature from Christ—this includes both humanity's "norm" and its limits. As he put it, Christ was at once an historical character and more than an historical character—both transcendent and limited. Here Niebuhr points out a flaw in modern liberal theology's tendency to overemphasize the historical to the neglect of the transcendent dimension of Christ's life. This is a perspective which Kierkegaard himself fully affirms, however. For Kierkegaard, only in Christ do we find the true measure of the human condition; the human creature has an infinite and finite aspect which cannot fully measure up to Christ's unified personhood but which can at least receive grace by following in the way of Christ and accepting the gift of forgiveness. In a number of texts, to which he did not have access, Niebuhr would have discerned a greater correlation between his and Kierkegaard's Christological and theological interpretation of the self.[13] Admittedly, it is odd to read Niebuhr on the one hand praising Kierkegaard as the most accurate interpreter of human selfhood while, on the other hand, raising serious issues with particular passages on the nature of the self. But here again the issue of pseudonymity in Kierkegaard interpretation emerges. Is the speaker of the *Either/Or* passage in question to be taken as Kierkegaard himself? Is the perspective offered to be taken as normative—without qualification?

In an essay first published in 1951, "Coherence, Incoherence and Christian Faith," Niebuhr adopted an explicitly cautious approach to Kierkegaard's philosophy of selfhood.[14] After arguing that an overemphasis on coherence and rationality is dangerous to Christian theology, he suggested that an emphasis in the other direction—toward what he called "hazardous subjectivity"[15]—is equally

---

[12]   Niebuhr, *The Nature and Destiny of Man*, vol. 1, p. 163. The Kierkegaard citation is from *Entweder Oder*, vol. 2, of *Gesammelte Werke*, vols. 1–12, trans. by Hermann Gottsched and Christoph Schrempf, Jena: Eugen Diederichs 1909–22, p. 182.

[13]   Niebuhr had access to both German and English translations of a number of standard Kierkegaard texts available at the time, but several of the works with which Niebuhr would have found most affinity in Christology (for example, *Training in Christianity* and *For Self-Examination*) were not yet available to him.

[14]   Reinhold Niebuhr, "Coherence, Incoherence and Christian Faith," *Journal of Religion*, vol. 31, no. 3, July 1951, pp. 155–68 (also in his *Christian Realism and Political Problems*, New York: Scribner 1953, pp. 175–203 and in *The Essential Reinhold Niebuhr: Selected Essays and Addresses*, ed. by Robert McAfee Brown, New Haven: Yale University Press 1986, pp. 218–36).

[15]   Niebuhr "Coherence, Incoherence and Christian Faith," *Journal of Religion*, vol. 31 no. 3, July 1951, p. 163.

problematic. In this vein, Kierkegaard's critique of Hegelianism led him to discount "all inquiries into essences and universal forms…in order to emphasize the existing particular."[16] Niebuhr sensed that this prioritizing of individual particularity vis-à-vis Hegelian idealism forced Kierkegaard into a subjectivist corner. Furthermore, he viewed Kierkegaard as making the recognition of paradox through passionate subjectivity the "basis of faith."[17] While Niebuhr affirmed that his writings "contain a genuine expression of the Christian faith," Kierkegaard's thought implied that the self saves itself "by choosing itself in its absolute validity."[18] This can sometimes mean that "passionate subjectivity becomes the sole test of truth."[19]

On this point Niebuhr referred to the oft-cited and typically un-contextualized suggestion in the *Concluding Unscientific Postscript* that passionate worship of a false God is preferable to disinterested worship of the true one. Niebuhr was troubled by the notion that "a passionate Nazi could meet Kierkegaard's test."[20] Like many of his contemporaries, Niebuhr did not apparently notice the ways in which pseudonymity complicates interpretation of such texts, in particular here the Climacus literature. Taking Johannes Climacus' perspective into account lessens—at least to some degree—the charge that Kierkegaard is advocating "hazardous subjectivity."[21] Niebuhr's use of Kierkegaard—in both appreciative and critical ways—would have been more consistent and useful to subsequent scholars, had pseudonymity and polyonymity been recognized as significant hermeneutical factors. In fairness, however, Niebuhr's inattentiveness to these aspects simply reflected his times.

In his essay "Love and the Law in Protestantism and Catholicism," Niebuhr levels another kind of critique against Kierkegaard's ethic of love. He charges *Works of Love* with presenting a "legalistic version of universal love" in which the particularities and uniqueness of individual relationships have "nothing to do with 'Christian' love."[22] Christian love, as Niebuhr interprets Kierkegaard, is a universal love which "proves itself by regarding the loved self as anonymously as possible."[23] Niebuhr contrasts Kierkegaard's view of love as duty and as driven by the force of conscience with Emil Brunner's notion that love is only revealed in the particularities of "unique personal and intimate relations."[24] Thus while Brunner focuses on individual relationships to particular people, Kierkegaard articulates a universal, abstract love defined by duty. In a book review of David Swenson's translation of *Works of Love*, Niebuhr suggested that "the entire emphasis in Kierkegaard lies upon one aspect

---

[16]   Niebuhr "Coherence, Incoherence and Christian Faith," p. 162.

[17]   Ibid.

[18]   Ibid., p. 163.

[19]   Ibid.

[20]   Ibid.

[21]   Ibid.

[22]   Reinhold Niebuhr, "Love and the Law in Protestantism and Catholicism," *Journal of Religious Thought*, vol. 9 no. 2, Spring–Summer, 1952, pp. 95–111. Citation is from p. 102 (in *The Essential Reinhold Niebuhr*, p. 149).

[23]   Niebuhr, "Love and the Law in Protestantism and Catholicism," p. 102 (in *The Essential Reinhold Niebuhr*, p. 149).

[24]   Ibid.

of the moral demand: its universality."[25] In a strange reversal, Kierkegaard—who was so acutely conscious of the contingent nature of human existence and history—reflected the universality of idealism in his ethic of love.[26] This critique mirrored Niebuhr's suggestion elsewhere that "Kierkegaard was too indifferent to the communal problem of man and was incapable...of making social judgments which required a weighing of competing claims."[27] Thus while Kierkegaard's anthropology served as a basis for Niebuhr's theology, his definition of love appeared too universal and idealist for Niebuhr's socially-oriented ethical taste.

II. Niebuhr and Kierkegaard on Sin and Anxiety

Nonetheless, Niebuhr's debt to Kierkegaard was not ultimately undermined by these worries regarding the particularity of the self, passionate subjectivity, and an ethic of universal duty. Kierkegaard's greatest contribution to Niebuhr's thought can be seen in his theology of sin. For Niebuhr, above and beyond other alternatives in modern philosophy, Christian revelation offered a more accurate way of holding together the paradox that human beings are both bound and free. Only biblical revelation can adequately explain the mystery of human beings: they bear the image of God and are sinners. Niebuhr's articulation of both the creative and destructive potential of the self in the context of a realistic political ethic was due in no small part to Kierkegaard's influence, in particular *The Concept of Anxiety* and *The Sickness unto Death.* One interpreter of both Niebuhr and Kierkegaard went so far as to question whether it is possible to understand the former apart from the influence of the latter on this point.[28]

Kierkegaard, Niebuhr claimed, interpreted the human self "more accurately than any modern, and possibly than any previous, Christian theologian."[29] Kierkegaard's concept of anxiety as the origin of sin enabled Niebuhr to articulate a doctrine of original sin that both rejected the imputation of Adam and Eve's guilt to all humanity while avoiding Pelagian optimism. Kierkegaard bequeathed to Niebuhr a conceptuality of sin and of evil that embraced its paradoxical nature, located sin and guilt in the freedom of each individual and attuned it more closely to the sensibilities of modern science.[30]

[25] Reinhold Niebuhr, "Kierkegaard and Love," *New York Times Book Review*, vol. 51, no. 33, 1946, p. 8.
[26] Ibid.
[27] Reinhold Niebuhr, " 'The Kierkegaard View': Review of James Collins' *The Mind of Kierkegaard*," *New York Times Book Review*, vol. 29, no. 6, 1954, p. 6.
[28] E.J. Carnell, *The Theology of Reinhold Niebuhr*, Grand Rapids, Michigan: Eerdmans 1951, p. 71.
[29] Niebuhr, *The Nature and Destiny of Man*, vol. 1, p. 171. See also Richard Kroner, "The Historical Roots of Niebuhr's Thought," in *Reinhold Niebuhr: His Religious, Social, and Political Thought*, ed. by Charles W. Kegley and Robert W. Bretall, New York: Macmillan 1956, pp. 177–92.
[30] For an extensive treatment of this point, see Roger A. Badham, "Redeeming the Fall: Hick's Schleiermacher versus Niebuhr's Kierkegaard," *Journal of Religion*, vol. 78, no. 4, October, 1998, pp. 547–70.

For both Niebuhr and Kierkegaard, while sin is not ontologically necessary it is historically inevitable; thus, a doctrine of sin could not escape logical absurdity. Niebuhr appealed to Kierkegaard's suggestion that sin is neither "necessity nor accident."[31] Rather, it emerges inevitably from the human experience of anxiety. Anxiety, Niebuhr says, "is the eternal precondition of sin. It is the inevitable spiritual state of man, standing in the paradoxical situation of freedom and finiteness."[32] Anxiety has a creative and positive function as well as a destructive one. It is the consequence of the freedom of humanity. Sin results from the misuse of creaturely freedom and is the intensification of anxiety into despair. In this respect, Niebuhr claims—in a footnote—that Kierkegaard's "analysis of the relation of anxiety to sin is the profoundest in Christian thought."[33]

The key point, for Niebuhr, was that sin is not an ontological *necessity*; rather, it is "within and by his freedom that man sins."[34] The doctrine of original sin—when correctly understood—captures the idea that while not necessary, sin is historically inevitable.[35] As Niebuhr pointed out, this theology of sin is problematic from a strictly logical perspective. But historically, attempts to solve that dilemma were misguided, in his view. Pelagianism, for example, tried to locate sin and guilt in the unimpeded, free will of mature human beings and thereby posited the theoretical possibility of sinlessness.[36] This view, however, was hampered by a naively optimistic view of human nature and did not account well for sin's pervasiveness and the presence of radical evil. Kierkegaard offered Niebuhr a more satisfactory solution.

While Kierkegaard did not embrace an Augustinian or Calvinist doctrine of original sin, in which Adam's sin and guilt is imputed to every subsequent human being, neither did he explain sin and guilt solely by reference to a libertarianly free will. In the emergence of anxiety and its intensification to despair, when freedom is turned in a negative direction, sin emerges and guilt accrues to each individual—not on the basis of Adam's sin but in the context of a historically inevitable perversion of freedom by finite, limited beings. Freedom gives rise to anxiety, which leads to sin, when the inherent limitations of finitude cause a person to grasp beyond those limits.

For Kierkegaard, while anxiety is not itself sin it lies very close to sin.[37] Temptation—the occasion for the actualization of sin—implies that there is a

---

[31] Niebuhr cites *Der Begriff der Angst*, vol. 5 in *Gesammelte Werke*, vols. 1–12, trans. by Hermann Gottsched and Christoph Schrempf, p. 95, which corresponds to *SKS* 4, 401 / *CA*, 98.

[32] Niebuhr, *The Nature and Destiny of Man*, vol. 1, p. 182. In a footnote, Niebuhr cites Kierkegaard: "Anxiety is the psychological condition which precedes sin. It is so near, so fearfully near to sin, and yet it is not the explanation for sin." Kierkegaard citation from *Der Begriff der Angst* in *Gesammelte Werke*, p. 89, which corresponds to *SKS* 4, 395 / *CA*, 92.

[33] Niebuhr, *The Nature and Destiny of Man*, vol. 1, p. 182. Later in this text, in a sentence which mirrors this footnote, Niebuhr claims that "Kierkegaard's explanation of the dialectical relation of freedom and fate in sin is one of the profoundest in Christian thought" (p. 263).

[34] Ibid., p. 263.

[35] William John Wolf, "Reinhold Niebuhr's Doctrine of Man," in *Reinhold Niebuhr: His Religious, Social, and Political Thought*, p. 315.

[36] Niebuhr, *Nature and Destiny of Man*, vol. 1, p. 245.

[37] Ibid., vol. 1, p. 182.

sense in which humanity "already sinned."[38] Along these lines, Niebuhr argued that wherever sin appears, it has already been present in the form of possibility—due to the very nature of what it means to be human.[39] Niebuhr suggested a more concrete illustration of this idea: the sin of "inordinate self-love" points to "the prior sin of lack of trust in God."[40] Inherited sin, for Kierkegaard (and for Niebuhr), is a way of saying that human beings are creatures who are both free and finite, and inevitably sin as a result. As Niebuhr put it: "This is the meaning of Kierkegaard's assertion that sin posits itself."[41] This left Niebuhr with the logically perplexing—if theologically satisfying—notion that sin is inevitable but not necessary. Furthermore, sin's inevitability in history and in each individual human life does not abrogate responsibility for sin in the lives of those in whom it is actualized.[42]

III. Original Sin, Rebellion, and Feminist Theology

Original sin, for Niebuhr, takes concrete shape primarily as pride or rebellion against God. Freedom, the potential of self-determination in humanity, makes possible the sin of pride. As one commentator put it, Niebuhr's anthropology of the "double environment" of humanity, or the dialectic of freedom and necessity, reflects humanity's temptation to think either too highly of himself or too lowly.[43] Nonetheless, in *The Nature and Destiny of Man* Niebuhr consistently emphasized the former—humanity's tendency toward narcissistic self-assertion and forcefully securing one's place in the world.

In his regard, Wanda Berry has pointed out that Niebuhr's use of Kierkegaard in developing a doctrine of sin suffers from his inattention to the complex and diverse manifestations of sin in Kierkegaard's anthropology. Whereas Kierkegaard makes room for both the "masculine" and the "feminine" forms of sin, or the sin of pride and the sin of self-dissolution, Niebuhr collapses all forms of sin underneath the

---

[38]   Ibid., vol. 1, p. 250. This is Niebuhr's interpretation of Kierkegaard's notion that "sin presupposes itself."

[39]   See also Reinhold Niebuhr, "Mystery and Meaning," in his *Discerning the Signs of the Times: Sermons for Today and Tomorrow*, New York: Scribner 1946, pp. 152–73. Alexander J. Burnstein explains this idea in his "Niebuhr, Scripture, and Normative Judaism," in *Reinhold Niebuhr: His Religious, Social, and Political Thought*, p. 490: "For sin, he holds, with Kierkegaard, always implies 'prior sin'; even 'Adam's sin' is not the first sin, but seems to point to sin running 'farther back than human history.' Here, then, lies the human dilemma: on the one side, man is confronted with the tendency to do evil which is inevitable, unavoidable; and on the other side, he is fully free and responsible for his sin." Roger Baudham, on the other hand, disagrees that Kierkegaard held to a belief in a pre-human sin (for example, cosmic, demonic sin) and suggests that such an interpretation would diminish the uniqueness of Kierkegaard's anthropology for a modern, feasible theodicy. Baudham, "Redeeming the Fall," pp. 566–8.

[40]   Niebuhr, *The Nature and Destiny of Man*, vol. 1, p. 252.

[41]   Ibid. Niebuhr cites here *Der Begriff der Angst*, vol. 5, in *Gesammelte Werke*, p. 89, which corresponds to *SKS* 4, 395 / *CA*, 92.

[42]   Niebuhr, *The Nature and Destiny of Man*, vol. 1, p. 254.

[43]   Carnell, *Theology of Reinhold Niebuhr*, p. 71.

single root category of pride and therefore describes original sin as "the universality of the corruption which results from undue self-regard."[44] For Berry, Niebuhr "removes the dialectical tension" from Kierkegaard's rich, multifarious analysis of sin. Niebuhr takes Kierkegaard's feminine form of sin and defines it in terms of sensuality, rather than that form of despair described in *The Sickness unto Death* as the refusal to will to be oneself. Feminist theology, among other things, bequeaths to contemporary thought the reminder that sin takes on multiple expressions, affecting people differently. Male-dominated theological metaphors tend to highlight that particular form of sin known as pride, an obsession understandable from a male-centric theological perspective. A recovery of Kierkegaard's two forms of sin, including the dissolution and underachievement of the self, "might liberate each soul to the extent that it is oppressed, and humble it to the extent that it is oppressor."[45]

IV. Epistemological Ramifications of the Paradoxical Self: On Coherence, Mystery, and Subjectivity

One of the ways in which humanity attempts to exceed its reach is through the attempt to understand the mysteries of God. As one author puts it: "The attempt to solve the mysteries of Creation and Redemption merely through the instrumentality of reason is itself a formidable occasion for sin."[46] This same author suggests that at this point Niebuhr and Kierkegaard's concerns about the impulses in modernity toward rationalism clearly intersect.[47]

Both Niebuhr and Kierkegaard affirmed a "leap," or the infinite qualitative distinction between God and humanity, which in the final analysis, can only be "traversed by God."[48] Niebuhr referred to Kierkegaard's epistemological framework in developing his own dialectical thought. Nonetheless, Niebuhr was careful to distance himself from Kierkegaard when he felt the latter went too decisively in a subjectivist direction; in particular he contested Kierkegaard's emphasis on paradox and the absurd. His reticence on this point was partly due to the ways in which subsequent thinkers took Kierkegaard's existentialism in an entirely subjectivist direction. Nonetheless, Niebuhr also identified direct problems in Kierkegaard's epistemology, such as a too hasty move from the "incomprehensibility of God to the 'passionate subjectivity' of religious truth."[49] He argued that Kierkegaardian subjectivity could be used as "cover" for the intrusion of error into "the interpretation of the ultimate

---

[44]   Wanda Warren Berry, "Images of Sin and Salvation in Feminist Theology," *Anglican Theological Review*, vol. 60, no. 1, 1978, pp. 25–54, see p. 47. See also Valerie Saiving, "The Human Situation: A Feminine Viewpoint," in *Womanspirit Rising: A Feminist Reader in Religion*, ed. by Carol P. Christ and Judith Plaskow, San Francisco: Harper & Row 1992, pp. 25–42.

[45]   Berry, "Images of Sin and Salvation in Feminist Theology," p. 48.

[46]   Ronald Howell, "Political Philosophy on a Theological Foundation," *Ethics*, vol. 63, no. 2, 1953, pp. 79–99, see pp. 84–5.

[47]   Ibid.

[48]   Kroner, "The Historical Roots of Niebuhr's Thought," p. 260.

[49]   Niebuhr, "Coherence, Incoherence and Christian Faith," p. 163.

issues in social and political life."[50] This was the element of Kierkegaard which Niebuhr identified as containing an element of perversity and which ultimately gave rise to the theology of Karl Barth in theology and existentialism in philosophy (for example, Jaspers and Heidegger).[51] For Niebuhr, some kind of synthesis between faith and reason needs to be maintained in Christian theology.[52] This concern makes perfect sense for a theologian dedicated to the continuing relevance of the Christian message in the public square.

Nonetheless, for Niebuhr, the Christian concept of selfhood cannot be adequately articulated through rational coherence alone. Thus, history (the drama of God's interaction with humanity and creation) "remains morally ambiguous to the end."[53] Faith can neither completely relinquish nor fully elucidate the darkness of mystery. A balance between humility and trust is called for by a biblical, Christian epistemology.[54] For Niebuhr, the absurdity of life must be affirmed, and this is a basic requirement for theology, but it cannot go so far as an "absolute absurdity."[55] Niebuhr affirmed the possibility of faith to apprehend divine revelation; the category of the absurd reflected a too pessimistic view of human comprehension.

Nonetheless, that which human beings can apprehend of God's revelation is appropriated only inwardly through faith, "because it is a truth which transcends the human situation in each individual just as it transcended the total cultural situation historically."[56] Individual human beings must appropriate existential truth, "inwardly through faith."[57] On this level, Niebuhr conceded that the *Concluding Unscientific Postscript* gets it quite right.[58] Christianity does not offer metaphysical, abstract truths which can be objectively understood and rationally assimilated objectively without remainder. Rather, it requires a personal, inward, and passionate

---

[50]   Kroner, "The Historical Roots of Niebuhr's Thought," pp. 260–1.

[51]   Niebuhr, "Review of *Concluding Unscientific Postscript*," p. 33.

[52]   Ibid.

[53]   Niebuhr, "Coherence, Incoherence and Christian Faith," p. 159 (in *The Essential Reinhold Niebuhr*, p. 223).

[54]   Niebuhr, "Mystery and Meaning."

[55]   Niebuhr, *The Nature and Destiny of Man*, vol. 2, p. 38. Niebuhr cites Kierkegaard disapprovingly here: "Anything that is almost probable or probable, or extremely and emphatically probable, is something he [man] can almost know, or as good as know, or extremely and emphatically almost know—but it is impossible to believe. For the absurd is the object of faith, and the only object that can be believed." He quotes from the *Concluding Unscientific Postscript*, trans. by David F. Swenson and Walter Lowrie, Princeton: Princeton University Press 1941, p. 189, which corresponds to *SKS* 7, 195 / *CUP1*, 211.

[56]   Niebuhr, *The Nature and Destiny of Man*, vol. 2, p. 38.

[57]   Ibid., vol. 2, p. 57.

[58]   Quoting Kierkegaard, Niebuhr (ibid., vol. 2, p. 57) says: " 'Forgiveness,' declares K quite rightly, 'is a paradox in the Socratic sense insofar as it involves a relationship between the eternal truth and the existing individual…The individual existing human being must feel himself a sinner; not objectively which is nonsense but subjectively which is the most profound suffering…he must try to understand the forgiveness of sins and then despair of understanding. With the understanding directly opposed to it, the inwardness of faith must lay hold of this paradox." He quotes from the *Concluding Unscientific Postscript*, p. 201, which corresponds to *SKS* 7, 205 / *CUP1*, 224.

involvement. Niebuhr took issue with Kierkegaardian subjectivity wherever its proponents seemed to denigrate the importance of culture in theological knowledge or precluded the possibility of some kind of synthesis of faith and reason.

An unwillingness to recognize this central truth about Christianity can lead to a misunderstanding of the relationship between knowledge and power. A presumed accumulation of correct information and truth in the possession of the elite can lead to oppression or subjugation of the marginalized. The over-reaching of finitude can spawn the collective imperial abuse of power in the name of truth. In *The Self and the Dramas of History*, Niebuhr drew on Kierkegaard's claim that "before God all men are in the wrong,"[59] arguing that, in the interaction between God and the human self, the self is convicted of sin not because it is finite as such but because in its finiteness it claims to be more than it is and to know more than it does. Finitude should serve as a constant reminder to human beings not to claim too much.[60] As one author described it, Niebuhr found in Kierkegaard "a companion of his own inner plight and of his spiritual uncertainty."[61] Furthermore, Kierkegaard gave impetus to the notion so prominent in Niebuhr that the "Christian message cannot be rationalized without losing its deepest meaning and its most precious truth."[62]

---

[59]   Niebuhr, *The Self and the Dramas of History*, p. 65.
[60]   Ibid.
[61]   Kroner, "The Historical Roots of Niebuhr's Thought," p. 258.
[62]   Ibid.

Bibliography

I. References to or Uses of Kierkegaard in Niebuhr's Corpus

"Review of Lowrie's Translation of *Stages on Life's Way*," *New York Herald Tribune Books*, January 26, 1941, p. 17.

"Review of David F. Swenson's Translation of *Concluding Unscientific Postscript*," *New York Herald Tribune Books*, November 30, 1941, p. 33.

The Nature and Destiny of Man: A Christian Interpretation, vols. 1–2, New York: Scribner 1941–43, vol. 1, p. 44; p. 75; p. 81; p. 162; p. 169; p. 182; p. 242; p. 245; p. 250; p. 252; p. 254; p. 263; vol. 2, p. 38; p. 57; p. 61.

"Kierkegaard and Love," *New York Times Book Review*, vol. 51, no. 33, 1946, p. 8.

"Mystery and Meaning," in his *Discerning the Signs of the Times: Sermons for Today and Tomorrow*, New York: Scribner 1946, pp. 152–73 (in *The Essential Reinhold Niebuhr*, ed. by Robert McAfee Brown, New Haven: Yale University Press 1986, pp. 237–49).

"Coherence, Incoherence and Christian Faith," *The Journal of Religion*, vol. 31, no. 3, July 1951, pp. 155–68 (in *The Essential Reinhold Niebuhr*, ed. by Robert McAfee Brown, New Haven: Yale University Press 1986, pp. 218–36).

" 'The Kierkegaard View': Review of James Collins' *The Mind of Kierkegaard*," *New York Times Book Review*, vol. 29, no. 6, 1954, p. 6.

The Self and the Dramas of History, New York: Scribner 1955, p. 65.

"Love and Law in Protestantism and Catholicism," *The Journal of Religious Thought*, vol. 9, no. 2, Spring–Summer, 1952, pp. 95–111 (in *The Essential Reinhold Niebuhr*, ed. by Robert McAfee Brown, New Haven: Yale University Press 1986, pp. 142–59.)

II. Sources of Niebuhr's Knowledge of Kierkegaard

Collins, James, *The Mind of Kierkegaard*, Chicago: Henry Regnery 1953.

Kierkegaard, Søren, *Concluding Unscientific Postscript*, trans. by David F. Swenson and Walter Lowrie, Princeton: Princeton University Press 1941.

— *Works of Love*, trans. by David Swenson and Lillian Marvin Swenson, Princeton: Princeton University Press 1946.

— *Stages on Life's Way*, trans. by Walter Lowrie, Princeton: Princeton University Press 1940.

— *Der Begriff der Angst*, vol. 5, in *Gesammelte Werke*, vols. 1–12, trans. by Hermann Gottsched and Christoph Schrempf, Jena: Eugen Diederichs 1909–22.

— *Entweder Oder, I–II,* vols. 1–2, in *Gesammelte Werke,* vols. 1–12, trans. by Hermann Gottsched and Christoph Schrempf, Jena: Eugen Diederichs 1909–22.
— *Die Krankheit zum Tode*, Jena: Diederich Verlag 1924.

Secondary Literature on Niebuhr's Relation to Kierkegaard

Badham, Roger A., "Redeeming the Fall: Hick's Schleiermacher versus Niebuhr's Kierkegaard," *Journal of Religion*, vol. 78, no, 4, October, 1998, pp. 547–70.

Berry, Wanda Warren, "Images of Sin and Salvation in Feminist Theology," *Anglican Theological Review*, vol. 60, no. 1, 1978, pp. 25–54.

Burnstein, Alexander J., "Niebuhr, Scripture and Normative Judaism," in *Reinhold Niebuhr: His Religious, Social, and Political Thought*, ed. by Charles Kegley and Robert Bretall, New York: Macmillan 1956, pp. 411–28.

Carnell, Edward John, *The Theology of Reinhold Niebuhr*, Grand Rapids, Michigan: Eerdmans 1951.

Gilkey, Langdon, *On Niebuhr*, Chicago: University of Chicago Press 2001, p. 20.

Howell, Ronald, "Political Philosophy on a Theological Foundation," *Ethics*, vol. 63, no. 2, 1953, pp. 79–99.

Kroner, Richard, "The Historical Roots of Niebuhr's Thought," in *Reinhold Niebuhr: His Religious, Social, and Political Thought*, ed. by Charles Kegley and Robert Bretall, New York: Macmillan 1956, pp. 177–92.

Wolf, William John, "Reinhold Niebuhr's Doctrine of Man," in *Reinhold Niebuhr: His Religious, Social, and Political Thought*, ed. by Charles Kegley and Robert Bretall, New York: Macmillan 1956, pp. 229–50.

Gene Outka:

Kierkegaard's Influence on Outka's Writing on Neighbor Love, Equality, Individuality, and the Ethical

Sarah Pike Cabral

Throughout his literary career, Gene Outka (b. 1937) courageously raises and addresses significant theological and philosophical questions, such as "Regarding the love commandment, what does it mean to love each neighbor and oneself equally?" and "Can or must religious and ethical duty conflict?" Outka's reading of Kierkegaard has undoubtedly influenced his awareness of the interrelationship of neighbor love, equality, individuality, and the ethical. A specialist in the areas of Christian ethics and bioethics, Outka is currently the Dwight Professor of Philosophy and Christian Ethics at Yale University Divinity School, where he has taught since 1975, after teaching at Princeton University for 10 years. Outka's published works include *Agape: An Ethical Analysis*, *Norm and Context in Christian Ethics*, co-edited with Paul Ramsey (1913–88), *Religion and Morality* and *Prospects for a Common Morality*, co-edited with John P. Reeder, Jr., as well as over forty scholarly articles, which have appeared in such journals as *Journal of Religious Ethics* and the *Journal of Religion*.

Outka's early work, *Agape: An Ethical Analysis*, remains a highly influential study of the concept of agape, one that brings Kierkegaard together with many figures, including Reinhold Niebuhr (1892–1971), Anders Nygren (1890–1974), Paul Ramsey, and Karl Barth (1886–1968). In *Agape*, Outka interprets Kierkegaard's *Works of Love* as setting friendship and erotic love in opposition to neighbor love.[1] Outka mainly attends to Kierkegaard's treatment of neighbor love and investigates why and how the Christian is to love everyone equally. Referencing *Works of Love*, Outka writes that one is to love every individual as the neighbor, who is a human being and equal, based on the belief that all are equal before God, who loves every individual equally. However, even if one grants that we are to love each individual as an equal and equally, how one is to live out this ideal remains unsettled. Therefore, Outka luminously articulates that while the individual is required to give everyone "equal consideration," she is not asked to practice "identical treatment."[2] In order to

---

[1]   Gene Outka, *Agape: An Ethical Analysis*, New Haven and London: Yale University Press 1972, p. 255.

[2]   Ibid., p. 20.

evidence Kierkegaard's awareness that loving everyone equally also requires loving each person as a particular individual, Outka cites Kierkegaard's *Works of Love*:

> Yet this love is not proudly independent of its object. Its equality [*Ligelighed*] does not appear in love's proudly turning back into itself through indifference [*Ligegyldighed*] to the object—no, the equality appears in love's humbly turning outward, embracing everyone, and yet loving each one individually but no one exceptionally.[3]

Outka reads this passage as supporting his understanding that although we are to love and regard everyone equally, one's *expression* of love will depend on the neighbor and also reflect the neighbor's particular needs.[4]

When meeting the particular needs of the individual neighbor, Outka warns that one must avoid "submission to exploitation."[5] The three reasons for doing so are for the good of the neighbor, for the good of another neighbor (especially innocent third parties), and for the good of oneself.[6] One is to love oneself as one loves the neighbor, so that one can be said to fully recognize that all are equal before God. One has just as much of a responsibility to love oneself as she does the neighbor. Outka refers to Kierkegaard's conviction that one is to have appropriate self-love and quotes Kierkegaard in *Works of Love*:

> When the light-minded person throws himself almost like a non-entity into the folly of the moment and makes nothing of it, is this not because he does not know how to love himself rightly? When the depressed person desires to be rid of life, indeed, of himself, is this not because he is unwilling to learn earnestly and rigorously to love himself?[7]

Even though Outka acknowledges that Kierkegaard's usual view of self-love is "nefarious," he argues that there is a place for "proper or justified self-love" in *Works of Love*.[8]

Although Outka does not explicitly reference Kierkegaard in his chapter "Universal Love and Impartiality" in *The Love Commandments: Essays in Christian Ethics and Moral Philosophy*, which was published 20 years after *Agape*, the same themes found in *Agape* are also taken up here. At the outset of his essay, Outka asks: "How is each of the three loves identified—love for God, love of neighbor, and love of self—like and unlike the others?...Which needs and choices of the neighbor should we generally meet and support? Which neighbors should we aid when we cannot aid them all?"[9] In general, Outka's concern is once again with understanding the practical ramifications of attempting to love all others and oneself equally. What Outka claims is that there is an important distinction to be made between "equal

3   *SKS* 9, 73 / *WL*, 67.
4   Outka, *Agape: An Ethical Analysis*, p. 20.
5   Ibid., p. 22.
6   Ibid., pp. 21–3.
7   *SKS* 9, 30–1 / *WL*, 23.
8   Outka, *Agape: An Ethical Analysis*, p. 23.
9   Gene Outka, "Universal Love and Impartiality," in *The Love Commandments: Essays in Christian Ethics and Moral Philosophy*, ed. by Edmund N. Santurri and William Werpehowski, Washington, D.C.: Georgetown University Press 1992, pp. 1–2.

consideration" or "impartial appraisal" and "equivalent treatment" or "impartial treatment."[10] Outka establishes that impartiality allows or permits dissimilar treatment as opposed to *requiring* either equivalent or dissimilar treatment.[11] Also, if our love is to be universal in scope, then one is to love oneself as one loves the neighbor. In his essay, Outka additionally presents a survey of how "loving oneself" and "loving one's neighbor" have been interpreted in religious and secular contexts.

Both *Agape* and "Universal Love and Impartiality" provide the background for Outka's article, "Equality and Individuality: Thoughts on Two Themes in Kierkegaard," in the *Journal of Religious Ethics*. In this article, Outka discusses the link between equality and individuality in Kierkegaard, focusing on *Works of Love* and "Purity of Heart is to Will One Thing." Outka points out that scholars have treated the concepts of equality and individuality in Kierkegaard separately and that there is a surprising lack of attention given to the relationship between equality and individuality in Kierkegaard's writing. Outka is interested in ascertaining how Kierkegaard's emphasis on universal equality before God may be harmonious with Kierkegaard's understanding that we appear before God as the individual.[12] Outka's first move is to identify the ways in which both philosophers and theologians have responded to the inequalities that exist between individuals. Their replies include claiming that there is nothing anyone can do about existing inequalities, that one is to work as much as possible towards achieving equality, and that respect is not dependent upon equality but rather on some other "shared factual or descriptive or substantive feature."[13] Outka holds that Kierkegaard believes the following: (1) Inequalities do exist but do not affect one's religious or ethical prospects, (2) Normative equality is commanded by God: "You shall love your neighbor as yourself," and (3) Equality is dependent upon the substantive features of grace and everyone's equal access to both God and the conception of the good itself.[14]

Despite his emphasis on equality, Kierkegaard stresses that one must individually choose to enter into a relationship with God. Due to the fact that we must make a free choice, subjectivity or individuality matters. Kierkegaard, as Outka observes, values "authentic individuality" as dependent upon God, as necessary for a relationship with God, and not guaranteed to be actualized by every individual.[15] Outka quotes from Kierkegaard's *Works of Love*: "*before God* to be oneself—the emphasis is on 'before God,' since this is the source and origin of all distinctiveness. The one who has ventured this has distinctiveness; he has come to know what God has already given him."[16] "Authentic individuality," according to Outka, is possible for everyone and to ignore "authentic individuality" leads one to despair, but this universal possibility and consequence does not mean that one will become an individual without choosing to do

[10]   Ibid., p. 11.
[11]   Ibid., p. 21.
[12]   Gene Outka, "Equality and Individuality: Thoughts on Two Themes in Kierkegaard," *Journal of Religious Ethics*, vol. 10, 1982, p. 172.
[13]   Ibid., pp. 175–7.
[14]   Ibid., pp. 177–8.
[15]   Ibid., p. 183.
[16]   *SKS* 9, 270 / *WL*, 271.

so. In light of the role of choice in becoming an individual, Outka draws attention to Kierkegaard's focus on performance. One is able to be in a relationship with God and grasp the "highest," but whether or not one does so depends on if one wills it or not.[17] Outka concludes that the concepts of equality and individuality in Kierkegaard are best understood in relationship to each other. If one attempts to interpret individuality without a belief in equality, then individuality becomes elitist. Belief in equality rules out the elitist claims "that some can *do* more than others, that what some do is *more valuable* than others, and that some can or should be used as a *means* to others' self-realization."[18] Yet, if one interprets equality without a belief in individuality, then one "threaten[s] the high status to be given to individuality *per se*," refuses to acknowledge that one must individually appropriate what is accessible to all, and fails to realize that one's own actions alone will not bring another closer to God.[19] One can help and aid others, but one's choice to enter into a relationship with God will be made independent of another's aid.

Kierkegaard's notion of equality receives further treatment by Outka in the article "Equality and the Fate of Theism in Modern Culture" in the *Journal of Religion*. At the outset of his essay, Outka includes three quotations from Kierkegaard's works. The first is from Kierkegaard's journals and emphasizes a universal capacity for comprehending the highest:

> But I cannot escape the thought that every man, unconditionally every man, no matter how simple he is or how suffering, nevertheless can comprehend the highest, specifically, the religious. If this is not so, then Christianity is really nonsense. For me it is frightful to see the recklessness with which philosophers and the like introduce differentiating categories like genius, talent, etc., into religion. They have no intimation that religion is thereby abolished. Only one consolation have I had, the blessed one that I know something which can console, blessedly console every human being, unconditionally every single one. Take this consolation away, and I would rather not live, then I am splenetic.[20]

The second, from *Works of Love*, stresses a universal capacity for performance or the ability to change. Kierkegaard writes: "eternity, which speaks of the highest, calmly assumes that every person can do it and therefore asks only if he did it."[21] The third, from *Fear and Trembling*, identifies that, in respect to the highest, each generation faces the same task:

> Whatever one generation learns from another, no generation learns the essentially human from a previous one. In this respect, each generation begins primitively, has no task other than what each generation had, nor does it advance further, insofar as the previous generations did not betray the task and deceive themselves.[22]

---

[17]   Outka cites Kierkegaard in *Works of Love*: "basically we all understand the highest," p. 78.
[18]   Outka, "Equality and Individuality," p. 193.
[19]   Ibid.
[20]   *SKS* 23, 19, NB15:19 / *JP* 1, 1017.
[21]   *SKS* 9, 85 / *WL*, 79.
[22]   *SKS* 4, 208 / *FT*, 121.

Outka then poses two questions: "How does the role of Christ as the historical point of departure for an eternal happiness bear on the commitment to religious equality?" and "How does Kierkegaard's emphasis on religious equality fit into discussions about the fate of modern theism?"[23] Outka, in his article, searches for Kierkegaard's answers to the traditional theological questions regarding those who have never heard about Christ and whether or not it is more difficult to believe in Christ now than it was centuries ago.

As to how the role of Christ bears on religious equality, Outka reads Kierkegaard as promoting the universal significance of the *absolute*, not merely *historical*, fact of Christ and his universal "invitation to help all who are heavy-laden."[24] The basis for this interpretation comes from *Philosophical Fragments* and *Practice in Christianity*. Those who hear this message either respond with faith or offense, and either include or exclude themselves by their own actions. Kierkegaard, however, acknowledges that knowledge of the God-man through preaching is unavailable to some, and that this exclusion is not based on disobedience. Outka cites Kierkegaard in the *Concluding Unscientific Postscript*: "The happiness linked to a historical condition excludes all who are outside the condition, and among those are the countless ones who are excluded through no fault of their own but by the accidental circumstance that Christianity has not been proclaimed to them."[25] Outka, like Johannes Climacus, does not go into detail about what "the final religious prospects" are for those who never hear about Christ.[26] On the other hand, Outka does clarify that Climacus is not promoting a doctrine of predestination.

As for the second question regarding religious equality and modern theism, Outka calls attention to both the work of D.Z. Phillips (1934–2006), who predicted the decline of theism, and the fact that theism has declined with the rise of science and the fall of cultural morality. Outka summarizes three distinct views on the relationship between Christian theism and variation: (1) Variation is unavoidable, (2) There remains throughout time a "self-identical core that abides through a comprehensive scheme or story internalized by a set of skills by practice and training," and (3) There is a true development of Christianity through time.[27]

According to Outka, Kierkegaard's own position is that the Christian notion of revelation identifies certain concepts that will not change, despite variations in people, time, and place. Outka explains that if non-believers of a certain culture do not agree with these concepts or if they view Christianity as failing to meet certain epistemological criteria that they have established, then Christianity will "find its location at the periphery of a culture," which alone is not injurious to faith. Kierkegaard believes that anyone can appropriate Christian faith, and one living today can respond in the same way as one living in the first century to the Absolute Paradox. Finally, religious belief, for Kierkegaard, is a "volitional resolution," not

---

23   Gene Outka, "Equality and the Fate of Theism in Modern Culture," *Journal of Religion*, vol. 67, 1987, p. 276.
24   Ibid., p. 277.
25   *SKS* 7, 530 / *CUP1*, 582–3.
26   Outka, "Equality and the Fate of Theism in Modern Culture," p. 279.
27   Ibid., pp. 284–5.

a conclusion, and intellectual history cannot change the fundamental nature of religious belief.[28]

More than in the previous works, Outka devotes great attention to Kierkegaard's conception of the ethical in his chapter "Religious and Moral Duty: Notes on *Fear and Trembling*" in *Religion and Morality*. This essay, in which Outka examines the teleological suspension of the ethical in *Fear and Trembling*, has generated notable debate in Kierkegaard scholarship. Outka's intention is to "examine the complex character of the relation between religion and morality."[29] He raises the significant question: "*Can* or *must* religious duty conflict with moral duty?"[30] Outka challenges the idea that a collision *must* occur, but purports that religious duty *can* "conflict with our antecedent judgments of right and wrong."[31] According to Outka, Kierkegaard, in *Fear and Trembling*, seems to hold that a conflict between religious and moral duty is possible in principle, a position Outka attributes to Hegel.

Outka reads *Fear and Trembling* as characterizing the ethical in three ways: (1) The ethical is "the results of actions"[32] that involve society or the public, (2) Ethical reasons are "universally communicable in principle,"[33] and (3) The ethical is "self-contained,"[34] which means there is "no direct and active reference to God."[35] There are two senses in which ethical judgments are generally held to be universally communicable, in regards to the "universalizability principle test"[36] and also with reference to a metaphysical understanding of the universal. The "universalizability principle test" is to test whether or not a particular moral judgment made by an individual is to be made in all other similar and morally relevant situations. A metaphysical understanding of the "universal" interprets the whole or structure of reality as the "universal."[37] If the ethical is the "universal" in this second sense, then the ethical would require no reference to God as that which is beyond reality and a religious duty would not be able to override an ethical duty. Outka also clarifies what Kierkegaard means by religious duty in *Fear and Trembling*, stating that it is a personal undertaking with direct reference to God that is "incommensurable with any single coherent structure of encompassing reality which the reason can grasp."[38] After analyzing the ethical and religious duty, Outka examines Kierkegaard's notion of the individual, determining that the individual is one who can experience isolation in this world, as she is ultimately responsible to God and has little to do with the opinions of others.

---

28   Ibid., pp. 287–8.
29   Gene Outka, "Religious and Moral Duty: Notes on *Fear and Trembling*," in *Religion and Morality*, ed. by Gene Outka and John P. Reeder, Jr., Garden City, New York: Doubleday Anchor 1973, p. 204.
30   Ibid., p. 205.
31   Ibid., p. 206.
32   Ibid., p. 212.
33   Ibid., p. 213.
34   Ibid., p. 218.
35   Ibid., p. 214.
36   Ibid., p. 213.
37   Ibid., p. 214.
38   Ibid., p. 218.

Having defined the ethical, religious duty, and the individual in the context of *Fear and Trembling*, Outka asks: "Can one make a cogent case that Kierkegaard's account of the trial (of Abraham) passes the universalizability test, regardless of the terminological reasons the reader meets with initially for supposing not?"[39] Outka anticipates the reply that the trial fails the universalizability test on the basis of Abraham's silence and offers five possible reasons for Abraham's silence: (1) Abraham's situation is "exceedingly complex" and God's command is "highly particular," (2) God's command resists being the "subject of an interpersonal argument," (3) Reasonable arguments, in general, may not be effective "when one must decide what to do," (4) Abraham must make the movement of faith on his own, and (5) Abraham may be tacitly acknowledging the limits of human language.[40]

Despite Abraham's silence and his justification for remaining silent, Outka identifies reasons as to why one might be able to view certain conditions of Abraham's trial as universalizable. Kierkegaard gives additional examples of "knights of faith" in *Fear and Trembling*, including Mary, the mother of Jesus. Abraham's trial is referred to as *a*, not *the*, teleological suspension of the ethical. The universalizability test "provides abundant logical room for criticism of conventional moral opinions, and for the importance of making one's own decisions."[41] Finally, there are certain features of the trial that are "repeatable in principle."[42] The specific conditions for Abraham's trial that Outka considers "repeatable in principle" are: (1) One must seriously hold moral and religious beliefs, (2) One cannot hate another in suspending the ethical, and (3) One must rely on oneself and not on other persons. Outka stresses the import of drawing attention to these conditions, for these conditions allow Abraham's trial to be distinguishable from *crimes* committed in the name of God. Outka contrasts Abraham's trial with Charles Manson's serial killing, and he rules out the possibility of the latter being based on a divine command by both referring to the conditions for Abraham's trial and also noting that they do not apply for Manson.

Outka next evaluates how Kierkegaard uses the terms "good," "right," and "duty" as prescriptive in *Fear and Trembling*, since the terms are not used to "simply state a fact about the world."[43] Outka asks if Kierkegaard violates such usage by writing "Duty is precisely the expression for God's will."[44] Has Kierkegaard here opposed "duty" and morality? Outka concludes that it would be illogical for Kierkegaard to be proposing a definition of "duty" as "the expression for God's will," since non-believers use the term "duty" to convey something entirely different. Kierkegaard is using "duty" as others do, but he is not conveying the same thing. Kierkegaard offers a commendation not a definition, the recommendation that "one ought to obey God's will, even when it violates one's own antecedent judgments of those things

---

[39]   Ibid., p. 223.
[40]   Ibid., pp. 223–4.
[41]   Ibid., p. 226.
[42]   Ibid., p. 227.
[43]   Ibid., p. 231.
[44]   Ibid.

which are 'right' and 'wrong.' "[45] "Right" and "wrong" in this context signify "what everyone logically means by right and wrong."[46]

Outka moves from examining the autonomy of the above evaluative words to exploring the autonomy of the agent who is given a divine command. The individual is able to recognize that the command has a divine origin, even if she does not understand the point of the command. She is also free to choose this command, or, in other words, yield to God. However, the origin of the command, for Kierkegaard, ultimately lies beyond the individual, since "something must be told to Abraham which he cannot tell himself."[47] Abraham can only recognize that the command has a divine origin and accept the command. He cannot understand the command, for it "violates his ordinary *ethical* scruples" and "perplexes him *religiously*," since God has also promised Abraham that his descendants will be as numerous as the stars in the sky.[48] Because of his lack of understanding, Abraham experiences suffering. The outcome of his trial is unclear, and he does not have support from others. Abraham accepts "divine elusiveness," since, as Outka highlights, he acknowledges that God's governance exceeds human understanding, that God's commands are to bring one closer to God, and that God would not command something that was unloving.[49] Therefore, Abraham, in obeying God, cannot do anything to Isaac that is unloving.

According to Outka, Abraham's fear and trembling is not based on his uncertainty as to whether or not it is God commanding him to sacrifice Isaac. He *knows* that it is God's command, but he does not *understand* it. Abraham's fear and trembling is the product of his decision to maintain faith in God despite not understanding the purpose behind the divine command given to him. Outka concludes that religious duty can conflict with our ordinary antecedent judgments of "right" and "wrong," but it is not the case that it must. He also discerns that Kierkegaard "allows a 'secular ethic' to stand on its own feet without requiring any referral to God," an ethic that views Abraham as culpable. Outka holds that a "religious ethic," which redefines the "murder" of Isaac in light of it being authorized by God, could prevent a collision between ethical and religious duty.[50] Outka concludes:

> Whether one should call such dispositional openness a teleological suspension of the ethical, or characterize the ethical in such a way that one allows in principle for new universal prescriptions in obedience to divine commands, might seem to Kierkegaard, when pressed, to be after all a subsidiary terminological question. I have tried nonetheless to suggest how a case for the latter alternative might intelligibly go.[51]

One can summarize the objective of Outka's essay as an attempt to imagine how ethical and religious duty could not conflict in *Fear and Trembling*, if one adopted a religious ethic.

---

[45]   Ibid., p. 233.
[46]   Ibid.
[47]   Ibid., p. 237.
[48]   Ibid., p. 238.
[49]   Ibid., p. 240.
[50]   Ibid., p. 251.
[51]   Ibid., p. 253.

Outka's examination and expansion of Kierkegaard's characterization of the ethical in "Religious and Moral Duty: Notes on *Fear and Trembling*" generated two scholarly articles: Edmund Santurri's "Kierkegaard's *Fear and Trembling* in Logical Perspective" and Ronald M. Green's "Enough is Enough! *Fear and Trembling* is *Not* About Ethics." In the first article, Santurri is critical of Outka's "attempt to suggest that Abraham's decision to sacrifice Isaac as presented in *Fear and Trembling* can be characterized relevantly in universal terms and, therefore, admits of moral approval in spite of Kierkegaard's persistent indications to the contrary."[52] Santurri's contention is that "given the formal conditions of our moral reasoning in general and given the particular nature of the Abraham story, the patriarch's act in some manner resists favorable moral judgment."[53] Santurri is concerned with a logical analysis of Abraham's trial, in order that he may show that Kierkegaard views Abraham's trial as *non-ethical*, rather than *ethical* or *unethical*.

Santurri, like Outka, invokes the universalizability test as an aid for determining whether or not a judgment, such as Abraham's decision to sacrifice Isaac, is capable of universalization and moral approbation. One reason that Santurri deems Abraham's decision as unable to be universalized and, thus, as *non-ethical* is due to Abraham's silence and Kierkegaard's interpretation of Abraham's act as unintelligible. Santurri quotes Kierkegaard in *Fear and Trembling*:

> Abraham remains silent—but he *cannot* speak. Therein lies the distress and anxiety. Even though I go on talking night and day without interruption, if I cannot make myself understood when I speak, then I am not speaking. This is the case with Abraham. He can say everything, but one thing he cannot say, and if he cannot say that—that is, say it in such a way that the other understands it—then he is not speaking.[54]

Santurri goes on to explain that since Abraham's silence is a reflection of the unintelligibility of the act, then "a comparison or analogization of Abraham's act with other acts is *a priori* impossible."[55] If there is no possibility of an analogy, then, Santurri concludes, there can be no possibility of "universalizing any favorable moral judgment of Abraham's act."[56]

Abraham might justify, on moral grounds, the act of sacrificing Isaac, by calling the act loving and a trial. These descriptions are "absurd," according to Santurri, since Abraham's love "by definition rules out the possibility of sacrifice." Even if by faith Abraham believes Isaac will be restored to him, Abraham would "be forced to say both that Isaac would be lost and that Isaac would not be lost," which is a contradiction.[57] Santurri also evaluates the act as a trial, arguing that "if one cannot distinguish *a priori* between an egotistically oriented act on the one hand and a divinely inspired act on the other, then *a fortiori* it is impossible to make

---

[52]   Edmund Santurri, "Kierkegaard's *Fear and Trembling* in Logical Perspective," *Journal of Religious Ethics*, vol. 5, 1977, p. 228.
[53]   Ibid., p. 226.
[54]   *SKS* 4, 201 / *FT*, 113.
[55]   Santurri, "Kierkegaard's *Fear and Trembling* in Logical Perspective," p. 231.
[56]   Ibid., p. 232.
[57]   Ibid., p. 235.

such a distinction empirically."[58] Santurri considers Abraham's motivation to be indeterminate, and, therefore, open to the interpretation that it is egoism. According to Santurri, no moral judgment based on the act being described as loving and a trial can be universalized. For this reason, Santurri is at odds with Outka's suggestion that one is "able to specify the descriptive meaning of a favorable moral judgment of Abraham's act."[59] Santurri regards Outka's features as possibly *necessary* but not as *sufficient* conditions for the moral approval of Abraham's act. If one were to universalize Abraham's act on the basis of Outka's three features, then one would be forced to admit the following: "If a person is virtuous, generally speaking, and if he decides without the counsel and support of others to kill his son, then we *must* judge his act of deciding as good or right."[60] Finally, Santurri also denies that the universalization of Abraham's act on the basis of the relevant descriptions offered in the biblical text is possible, since these descriptions are unintelligible or self-contradictory. Therefore, Santurri finds Outka's general thesis to be unsubstantiated.

The second article, which responds to Outka's essay on *Fear and Trembling*, is Ronald M. Green's "Enough is Enough! *Fear and Trembling* is *Not* about Ethics." Green recommends that *Fear and Trembling* be read in relationship to the theme of Christian soteriology, and he interprets the text as symbolically using the Abraham story to promote justification through faith alone, as it is not about "*human* but *divine* conduct."[61] According to Green, *Fear and Trembling* should not be analyzed as a text about ethics, because "doing so produces a serious tension and even a degree of incoherence in the text."[62] Green critiques Outka's attempt "to expand our conception of the universalizable sphere of morality" to include obedience to God, on the basis of Santurri's article, which shows Abraham's act to be absurd, and, therefore, beyond moral approval. The real meaning of *Fear and Trembling*, according to Green, is that human redemption does not depend on one's ethical conduct but rather "on God's merciful suspension of his justice."[63] Green writes that although Abraham was not a sinner, he "stands for all sinners," since he suspends the ethical by way of obedience. Abraham is also considered by Green to be the counterpart to the Merman, who suspends the ethical by way of sin. Green's conclusion is that *Fear and Trembling* is meant "to be an encoded message to all those capable of seeing beyond its surface treatment of Abraham's singular trial to a more universal message concerning our common failure before the stringency of God's moral demands and our shared need for God's grace."[64] In light of this universal message *Fear and Trembling* has to offer, Green determines that an ethical analysis of Abraham's particular act is peripheral, if not impossible.

---

[58]   Ibid., p. 236.

[59]   Ibid., p. 240.

[60]   Ibid., p. 241.

[61]   Ronald M. Green, "Enough is Enough! *Fear and Trembling* is *Not* About Ethics," *Journal of Religious Ethics*, vol. 21, 1993, p. 192.

[62]   Ibid., p. 193.

[63]   Ibid., p. 198.

[64]   Ibid., p. 204.

Outka responds to Green in his article "God as the Subject of Unique Veneration: A Response to Ronald M. Green" in the *Journal of Religious Ethics*. Here Outka acknowledges that the central subject of *Fear and Trembling* is "the vindication of a direct relationship to God" and that other themes, including "obedience to God, the ethical, sin, and so on" are derived from this main idea.[65] Outka, however, argues that one does not need to read *Fear and Trembling* in view of Christian soteriology exclusively in order for it to be recognized as a topic important to Kierkegaard. Outka is critical of Green's particular interpretation of *Fear and Trembling*, which both identifies Abraham as one who is a representative of all sinners and assumes a fixed understanding of ethics. In regards to Green's treatment of Abraham and the Merman, Outka underscores that Green neither adequately clarifies how both can be said to suspend the ethical nor properly justifies why Abraham is to be viewed as standing for all sinners, since the text emphasizes Abraham's obedience to God. Outka also makes a case for why Green cannot easily exclude ethics from his treatment of *Fear and Trembling*, for Outka, in his own essay, explicitly challenges the assumption that "ethics" has a fixed meaning, since what one means by "ethics" varies.[66]

Other references to Outka's work are primarily found in the context of an analysis of *Fear and Trembling* or *Works of Love*. These references are, in general, more brief than what one finds in the Santurri and Green articles. Amy Laura Hall writes in *Kierkegaard and the Treachery of Love* that *Fear and Trembling* supports both Outka and Green's reading, and that the text is about both Christian soteriology and ethics.[67] In his treatment of the ethical in *Fear and Trembling* in *Kierkegaard's Ethic of Love: Divine Commands and Moral Obligations*, C. Stephen Evans affirms Outka's claim that the collision between religious and ethical duties in *Fear and Trembling* could be avoided, if one perceives the ethical differently. Evans is critical, however, of Outka's failure to distinguish Kierkegaard's own view from Johannes de silentio.[68] In *Love's Grateful Striving*, M. Jamie Ferreira cites Outka's examination of the limits of self-sacrifice in relationship to neighbor love in her own analysis of *Works of Love*.[69] Louise Carroll Keeley, in her article "Loving 'No One,' Loving Everyone: The Work of Love in Recollecting One Dead in Kierkegaard's *Works of Love*," discusses Outka's observations on the subject of mutuality and neighbor love based on Kierkegaard's *Works of Love*.[70]

---

[65] Ibid., p. 211.

[66] Green replies to Outka's response in "A Reply to Gene Outka," *Journal of Religious Ethics*, vol. 21, 1993, pp. 217–20. Much of this article reiterates points previously made by Green in "Enough is Enough!" Ultimately, Green writes that the reader must determine whose interpretation of *Fear and Trembling* is best supported by the text.

[67] Amy Laura Hall, *Kierkegaard and the Treachery of Love*, Cambridge: Cambridge University Press 2002, p. 54.

[68] C. Stephen Evans, *Kierkegaard's Ethic of Love: Divine Commands and Moral Obligations*, Oxford: Oxford University Press 2004, pp. 70–1.

[69] M. Jamie Ferreira, *Love's Grateful Striving: A Commentary on Kierkegaard's* Works of Love, Oxford: Oxford University Press 2001, p. 129.

[70] Louise Carroll Keeley, "Loving 'No One,' Loving Everyone: The Work of Love in Recollecting One Dead in Kierkegaard's *Works of Love*," in *Works of Love*, ed. by Robert

In summary, Kierkegaard's influence on Outka is evident in Outka's writing on neighbor love, equality, individuality, and the ethical. In *Agape*, where he makes his earliest reference to Kierkegaard, Outka relies only on the primary text, *Works of Love*, in his consideration of how we are to practice loving oneself and each neighbor equally. In his later essays, Outka's familiarity with both Kierkegaard's *corpus* and Kierkegaard scholarship is readily apparent as he discusses how equality and individuality appropriately balance and limit one another, how each generation faces the identical task of appropriating theism, and how a religious ethic could include divine commands. Kierkegaard scholars continue to note Outka's important work on the concept of neighbor love in *Agape* and to refer to his treatment of ethical and religious duty in "Religious and Moral Duty: Notes on *Fear and Trembling*" in *Religion and Morality*.

L. Perkins, Macon, Georgia: Mercer University Press 1999 (*International Kierkegaard Commentary*, vol. 16), p. 232, note.

Bibliography

I. References to or Uses of Kierkegaard in Outka's Corpus

Agape: An Ethical Analysis, New Haven and London: Yale University Press 1972, p. 2; p. 7; pp. 13–24; pp. 34–5; pp. 37–8; pp. 45–6; pp. 52–3; p. 67; p. 132; p. 159; p. 166; p. 181; p. 193; pp. 209–10; p. 223; p. 255; p. 263; p. 265; p. 268; pp. 280–2; p. 291.

"Introduction," in *Religion and Morality*, ed. by Gene Outka and John P. Reeder, Jr., Garden City, New York: Doubleday Anchor 1973, p. 7; pp. 15–17; p. 19; p. 28.

"Religious and Moral Duty: Notes on *Fear and Trembling*," in *Religion and Morality*, ed. by Gene Outka and John P. Reeder, Jr., Garden City, New York: Doubleday Anchor 1973, pp. 204–54.

"On Harming Others," *Interpretation*, vol. 34, 1980, p. 390.

"Equality and Individuality: Thoughts on Two Themes in Kierkegaard," *Journal of Religious Ethics*, vol. 10, 1982, pp. 171–203.

"Kierkegaardian Ethics," in *The Dictionary of Christian Ethics*, ed. by James F. Childress and John Macquarrie, Philadelphia: Westminster Press; London: SCM Press 1986, pp. 337–43.

"Equality and the Fate of Theism in Modern Culture," *Journal of Religion*, vol. 67, 1987, pp. 275–88.

"Kierkegaard, Søren [Aabye] (1813–1855)," in *Encyclopedia of Ethics*, vols. 1–2, ed. by Lawrence C. Becker, New York: Garland Publishing, Inc. 1992, vol. 1, pp. 678–81.

"Universal Love and Impartiality," in *The Love Commandments: Essays in Christian Ethics and Moral Philosophy*, ed. by Edmund N. Santurri and William Werpehowski, Washington, D.C.: Georgetown University Press 1992, pp. 1–103.

"God as the Subject of Unique Veneration: A Response to Ronald M. Green," *Journal of Religious Ethics*, vol. 21, 1993, pp. 211–15.

II. Sources of Outka's Knowledge of Kierkegaard

Clive, Geoffrey, " 'The Teleological Suspension of the Ethical' in Nineteenth Century Literature," *Journal of Religion*, vol. 34, 1954, pp. 75–87.

Collins, James, *The Mind of Kierkegaard*, Chicago: Henry Regnery 1953.

Coons, John E, and Patrick M. Brennan, *By Nature Equal: The Anatomy of Western Insight*, Princeton: Princeton University Press 1999, pp. 36–7.

Crites, Stephen, *In the Twilight of Christendom*, Chambersburg, Pennsylvania: AAR Studies in Religion 1972, pp. 21–34; pp. 58–95.

Dietrichson, Paul, "Kierkegaard's Concept of the Self," *Inquiry*, vol. 8, 1965, pp. 1–32.

Eller, Vernard, *Kierkegaard and Radical Discipleship*, Princeton: Princeton University Press 1968, pp. 186–200.

Elrod, John, *Being and Existence in Kierkegaard's Pseudonymous Works*, Princeton: Princeton University Press 1975.

Jones, Joe R., "Some Remarks on Authority and Revelation in Kierkegaard," *Journal of Religion*, vol. 57, 1977, p. 240.

Lindström, Valter, "A Contribution to the Interpretation of *The Works of Love*," *Studia Theologica*, vol. 6, 1952, pp. 3–6.

MacIntyre, Alasdair, *A Short History of Ethics*, New York: Macmillan 1966, p. 216.

Mackey, Louis, *Kierkegaard: A Kind of Poet*, Philadelphia: University of Pennsylvania Press 1971.

Malantschuk, Gregor, *Kierkegaard's Thought*, Princeton: Princeton University Press 1971, p. 37.

Ofstad, Harold, "Morality, Choice, and Inwardness," *Inquiry*, vol. 8, 1965, pp. 33–73.

Shmuëli, Adi, *Kierkegaard and Consciousness*, trans. by Naomi Handelman, Princeton: Princeton University Press 1971.

Søe, N.H., *Christliche Ethik*, 3rd ed. Munich: Chr. Kaiser Verlag 1965, pp. 136–40.

Taylor, Mark C., *Kierkegaard's Pseudonymous Authorship*, Princeton: Princeton University Press 1975.

Walker, Jeremy D.B., *To Will One Thing: Reflections on Kierkegaard's 'Purity of Heart'*, Montreal: McGill-Queen's University Press 1972.

Westphal, Merold, "Kierkegaard and the Logic of Insanity," *Religious Studies*, vol. 7, 1971, pp. 205–7.

III. Secondary Literature on Outka's Relation to Kierkegaard

Davenport, John, "Faith as Eschatological Trust in *Fear and Trembling*," in *Ethics, Love, and Faith in Kierkegaard*, ed. by Edward F. Mooney, Bloomington and Indianapolis: Indiana University Press 2008, p. 222.

Evans, C. Stephen, *Kierkegaard's Ethic of Love: Divine Commands and Moral Obligations*, Oxford: Oxford University Press 2004, pp. 70–1.

Ferreira, M. Jamie, *Love's Grateful Striving: A Commentary on Kierkegaard's* Works of Love, Oxford: Oxford University Press 2001, p. 129.

Gouwens, David Jay, *Kierkegaard as a Religious Thinker*, Cambridge: Cambridge University Press 1996, pp. 194–5; pp. 204–5.

Green, Ronald M., "Enough is Enough! *Fear and Trembling* is *Not* about Ethics," *Journal of Religious Ethics*, vol. 21, 1993, pp. 191–209.

— "A Reply to Gene Outka," *Journal of Religious Ethics*, vol. 21, 1993, pp. 217–20.

— " 'Developing' *Fear and Trembling*," in *The Cambridge Companion to Kierkegaard*, ed. by Alastair Hannay and Gordon D. Marino, Cambridge: Cambridge University Press 1998, pp. 264–5; p. 267.

Hall, Amy Laura, *Kierkegaard and the Treachery of Love*, Cambridge: Cambridge University Press 2002, p. 9; p. 54; p. 69; p. 81.

Keeley, Louise Carroll, "Loving 'No One,' Loving Everyone: The Work of Love in Recollecting One Dead in Kierkegaard's *Works of Love*," in *Works of Love*, ed. by Robert Perkins, Macon, Georgia: Mercer University Press 1999 (*International Kierkegaard Commentary*, vol. 16), p. 232, note.

Lippitt, John, *Routledge Philosophy Guidebook to Kierkegaard and* Fear and Trembling, London and New York: Routledge 2003, p. 168.

Mehl, Peter J., "Kierkegaard and the Relativist Challenge to Practical Philosophy (with a New Postscript)," in *Kierkegaard After MacIntyre: Essays on Freedom, Narrative, and Virtue*, ed. by John Davenport and Anthony Rudd, Chicago and La Salle, Illinois: Open Court 2001, p. 25.

Purvis, Sally B., "Mothers, Neighbors, and Strangers: Another Look at Agape," in *Christian Perspectives on Sexuality and Gender*, ed. by Elizabeth Stuart and Adrian Thatcher, Leominster: Gracewing/Fowler Wright Books; Grand Rapids, Michigan: Eerdmans 1996, pp. 233–5; pp. 243–6.

Santurri, Edmund, "Kierkegaard's *Fear and Trembling* in Logical Perspective," *Journal of Religious Ethics*, vol. 5, 1977, pp. 225–47.

Webb, Stephen H., *Blessed Excess: Religion and the Hyperbolic Imagination*, Albany, New York: State University of New York Press 1993, pp. 34–6; p. 38; pp. 48–50; pp. 52–3; pp. 55–6.

Francis Schaeffer:
How Not to Read Kierkegaard

Kyle A. Roberts

Some may wonder whether Francis Schaeffer (1912–84) should be included in a book on Kierkegaard reception among modern theologians. For one, it is questionable whether Schaeffer counts as a major theologian; he was an evangelist who intellectually engaged in cultural and world-view analysis. The extent of Schaeffer's formal education was a degree through Westminster and Faith seminaries in Pennsylvania, founded as conservative alternatives to Princeton and charged with the task of perpetuating the "Princeton theology" of Charles Hodge and B.B. Warfield. Schaeffer's philosophical and theological analyses of modern culture were largely formulated in the subsequent context of his mission work at *L'Abri*, a communal retreat and study center he later instituted in Lausanne, Switzerland.

Schaeffer merits inclusion in this collection not because of an insightful engagement with or constructive use of Kierkegaard, but because his writings, public lectures, and apologetic engagement with modern culture left a deep and lasting impression on evangelical Christianity in America. The mainly negative portrait of Kierkegaard he put forth was widely disseminated and deeply imbibed. Schaeffer's pithy and often insightful musings on philosophy and the arts, his sometimes tenuous interpretations of major thinkers, and his interesting but sometimes unfounded analyses of the history of modern thought have been accepted and transmitted through generations of evangelical Christians. While direct influence of Schaeffer's writings has decreased substantially since the peak of his prominence, the world-view he advocated still reverberates through many of those who studied under him and is still accessible in his books, videos and numerous *L'Abri* communities operating throughout the United States, Europe, Canada, and Asia. The mainly negative and misguided view of Kierkegaard reflective of much early fundamentalist and neo-evangelical theology could be traced in part to Schaeffer's influence in his most significant books, *The God Who Is There*,[1] *Escape from Reason*,[2] *He Is There*

---

[1]   Francis Schaeffer, *The God Who is There*, Downers Grove, Illinois: InterVarsity Press 1968 (also in *The Complete Works of Francis A. Schaeffer*, vols. 1–5, Westchester, Illinois: Crossway 1982, vol. 1). Unless otherwise noted, all subsequent references to Schaeffer's works will be from the first editions.

[2]   Francis Schaeffer, *Escape from Reason*, Downers Grove, Illinois: InterVarsity Press 1968 (in *The Complete Works of Francis A. Schaeffer*, vol. 1).

and He Is Not Silent,[3] and *How Should We Then Live?*[4] To scholars of Kierkegaard, Schaeffer is interesting because he provides both a negative example of how *not* to read Kierkegaard and insight into one source of a widely disseminated and unfounded caricature of him.

I. Preliminary Discussion: From Outright Rejection to Subtle Appreciation

To Schaeffer, Kierkegaard was a fideist and the father of modern existentialism (of both its philosophical and religious versions) who opened the door to the modern split between faith and reason.[5] It is worth noting that any measured admiration Schaeffer expressed toward Kierkegaard develops over time. We can see this development clearly in the progression between the first edition of *The God Who is There* (1968) and the edition later published in the complete works (1982). In this later version, Schaeffer offers a more positive and measured account than can be found in the original. Here he includes the suggestion, noted above, that Kierkegaard's "devotional writings" can be "very helpful," giving as an example that "Bible-believing Christians in Denmark still use these devotional writings."[6] He suggests further that, "We can also be totally sympathetic to his outcry about the deadness of much of the Church in his day."[7] He then switches to his typically more critical tone as he discusses Kierkegaard's "more philosophical writings," through which he becomes "the father of modern thought." These writings, *Fear and Trembling* in particular, give rise to the various existentialisms that follow in the wake of Kierkegaard's supposed complete bifurcation of faith and reason.[8] In a sympathetic moment, Schaeffer speculates whether Kierkegaard would approve of his existentialist successors. In the aforementioned *Complete Works* edition of *The God Who is There,* he suggests:

> I do not think that Kierkegaard would be happy, or would agree, with that which had developed from his thinking in either secular or religious existentialism. But what he wrote gradually led to the absolute separation of the rational and logical from faith. The reasonable and faith bear no relationship to each other.[9]

In the first edition, Schaeffer's speculation was less optimistic. He simply wondered whether, "if he came today, he would be pleased with what had been made of his

---

[3]   Francis Schaeffer, *He Is There and He Is Not Silent*, Carol Stream, Illinois: Tyndale House 1972 (in *The Complete Works of Francis A. Schaeffer*, vol. 1).
[4]   Francis Schaeffer, *How Should We Then Live?* Old Tappan, New Jersey: F.H. Revell Co. 1976 (in *The Complete Works of Francis A. Schaeffer*, vol. 5).
[5]   Schaeffer, *He Is There and He Is Not Silent*, pp. 46–7. See also Schaeffer, *Escape from Reason*, pp. 46–50 and Schaeffer, *The God Who is There*, pp. 21–2.
[6]   Schaeffer, *The God Who is There*, in *Complete Works*, vol. 1, p. 15. (Only the *Complete Works* edition is cited here because this material was not included in the earliest version.)
[7]   Ibid.
[8]   Ibid.
[9]   Ibid., p. 16.

teaching."[10] Furthermore, he suggested that it would be profitable to debate whether Kierkegaard was in fact a "real Christian."[11] Regardless of Kierkegaard's intentions or what he might have thought of his intellectual successors, Schaeffer remained steadfast that Kierkegaard was the first to enter through what Schaeffer called the "line of despair."[12] This line represented the movement from a basically unified Christian world-view, in which reason and existential/religious meaning were connected, to a modern, secular world-view in which they were bifurcated. This split was the interpretive key, for Schaeffer, for the perplexities of modern life and culture. The answer to the problems of the West lay in the resurgence of a unified, Christian world-view in which meaning, truth, rationality, and revelation were joined again in felicitous harmony.

In any case, Schaeffer's measured notes of appreciation in the later edition at least soften the blunter claims of the original, in which he questioned the legitimacy of Kierkegaard's Christianity on the basis of his faulty epistemology: "Kierkegaard came to the conclusion that you could not arrive at synthesis by reason. Instead, you achieved everything of real importance by a leap of faith. The reasonable and faith bear no relationship to each other...."[13] A recent biographical work suggests that the shift toward the slightly more nuanced interpretation and appreciation for Kierkegaard, from the first edition to the complete works, was likely due to corrective criticism Schaeffer received from prominent evangelical philosophers, such as Arthur Holmes and Stephen Evans.[14]

It is worth noting that at least two scholars have defended Schaeffer's interpretation of Kierkegaard on the basis that—at the very least—it was in keeping with a then common scholarly point of view. Evangelical philosopher Ronald Nash pointed to Brand Blanshard, Alastair McKinnon, and Harold DeWolf as examples of thinkers who shared Schaeffer's view that Kierkegaard was essentially an irrationalist; for DeWolf, Kierkegaard's thought also gave rise to the split between faith and reason as perceived in neo-orthodoxy.[15] Indeed, the basics of this view did not originate with Schaeffer. Variations on this reading of Kierkegaard persist today: as fideist,

---

[10]   Schaeffer, *The God Who is There* (1968), p. 22.
[11]   Ibid. Of course, many have wondered whether Kierkegaard was a "real Christian," due to his heightened ambivalence and antipathy toward established Christianity, but this is clearly not what Schaeffer has in mind. Rather, he doubts whether Kierkegaard's belief system counts as sufficiently and legitimately Christian.
[12]   Schaeffer, *Escape from Reason*, pp. 42–5 (in *Complete Works*, vol. 1, pp. 233–6). See also Schaeffer, *The God Who is There*, pp. 20–4 (In *Complete Works*, vol. 1, pp. 14–16.)
[13]   Schaeffer, *The God Who is There*, p. 21.
[14]   Barry Hankins, *Francis Schaeffer and the Shaping of Evangelical America*, Grand Rapids, Michigan: Eerdmans 2008, pp. 99–100.
[15]   Ronald Nash, "The Life of the Mind and the Way of Life," in *Francis A. Schaeffer: Portraits of the Man and His Work,* ed. by Lane T. Dennis, Westchester, Illinois: Crossway Books 1986, pp. 51–70 (citation is on p. 62). Nash lists Brand Blanshard, *Reason and Belief,* London: Allen and Unwin 1974, chapter 6; Alastair McKinnon, "Kierkegaard, 'Paradox' and Irrationalism," in *Essays on Kierkegaard*, ed. by Jerry H. Gill, Minneapolis: Burgess 1969, pp. 102–12; Harold DeWolf, *The Religious Revolt Against Reason,* New York: Harper 1949).

irrationalist, relativist, etc. Nash is right that Schaeffer was at least in the ballpark in terms of available interpretations.

In the same volume in which Nash's essay appears, Lane T. Dennis took on Schaeffer's critics (Evans, in particular), arguing that Schaeffer's view of Kierkegaard was more balanced than they gave him credit for. As support for his argument he referenced the previously mentioned selection from the most recent edition (*Complete Works*) of *the God Who is There*.[16] Neither of these two Schaeffer supporters appear to recognize or acknowledge the disparity between the first edition and the final. They only reference the final edition without acknowledging the shift in tone and the possibility that Schaeffer may have grown in his appreciation of Kierkegaard because of engagement with the very same critics Nash and Dennis were rebuffing.[17]

In any case, for Schaeffer, thereafter the Kierkegaardian concept of a "leap of faith" became a dominant theme in philosophy and theology, irrespective of Kierkegaard's motivations or the Christian (or sub-Christian) nature of his world-view.[18] The leap signaled, to Schaeffer, modernity's desperate attempt to reach beyond the confines of an anthropocentric rationality—which could offer neither meaning nor existentially significant truth—into a "mystical," higher plane of symbolism, metaphor, and theological fiction. The fact that such a leap had to be made belied the presence of a chasm in the modern world between fact and rationality on the one side and meaning, existential truth, and religion on the other. As we noted earlier, Schaeffer based his discussion of the leap in part on a well-known, though misguided, reading of *Fear and Trembling*. In his brief discussion of this text, Schaeffer suggested that, for Kierkegaard, Abraham's willingness to sacrifice Isaac was a groundless, irrational act of faith.[19] Schaeffer held that the biblical concept of faith is always linked to propositional content; this, he claimed, is "the very opposite of a Kierkegaardian leap into the void."[20]

---

[16]   Lane T. Dennis, "Schaeffer and His Critics," in *Francis A. Schaeffer: Portraits of the Man and His Work,* ed. by Lane T. Dennis, p. 115. The endnote incorrectly cites the passage as coming from *Escape from Reason* rather than (correctly) *The God Who is There*, in *Complete Works*, vol. 1, pp. 15–16.

[17]   See Hankins, *Francis Schaeffer and the Shaping of Evangelical America,* pp. 99–100.

[18]   As Jamie Ferreira points out, while Kierkegaard does employ the terminology of a "leap" to speak of a qualitative ethical-religious transition, he never uses the Danish equivalent of the English phrase "leap of faith." See "Faith and the Kierkegaardian Leap" in *The Cambridge Companion to Kierkegaard,* ed. by Alastair Hannay and Gordon D. Marino, Cambridge: Cambridge University Press 1998, p. 207.

[19]   Schaeffer, *The God Who is There*, in *Complete Works*, vol. 1, p. 15. (This does not appear in the original edition.)

[20]   Francis Schaeffer, *Genesis in Space and Time*, Downers Grove, Illinois: InterVarsity Press 1972, p. 110 (in *Complete Works*, vol. 2, p. 79.) Similarly, *The God Who is There*, Schaeffer suggests that "Kierkegaard had not read the Bible carefully enough," because "…before Abraham was asked to move toward the sacrifice of Isaac (which, of course, God did not allow to be consummated), he had much propositional revelation from God, he had seen God, God had fulfilled promises to him. In short, God's words at this time were in the context of Abraham's strong reason for knowing that God both existed and was totally

To fully appreciate Schaeffer's reaction to Kierkegaard, it helps to understand his intellectual background. Schaeffer was deeply influenced by J. Gresham Machen (1881–1937) and Cornelius Van Til (1895–1987), both of whom were his professors during his studies at Westminster Seminary. Through Machen, Schaeffer absorbed the "Princeton theology," associated with Charles Hodge (1797–1878) and B.B. Warfield (1851–1921), which upheld an unflinching view of biblical inerrancy linked to the "objective nature of faith."[21] Theology was to be undertaken as an objective science: a coherent, systematic arrangement of propositional truths derived both from Scripture and the natural world. Personal experience succumbs to the priority of rational reflection on the objective data of biblical revelation. From Van Til, Schaeffer discovered presuppositional apologetics. Influenced by the Reformed theology of Abraham Kuyper (1837–1920), this approach highlighted the centrality of the religious status and world-view of the knower and explained the fundamental difference between the rationalities and world-views of believers and non-believers. Presuppositional theology holds that one must be regenerated by the Holy Spirit and have access to divine revelation in order to truly understand both God and creational reality. As has been pointed out, Schaeffer was not a consistent presuppositionalist because, like the Princetonians (Hodge, Warfield, and Machen), he believed there could be an "objective" starting place for dialogue with unbelievers.[22] This combination of convictions elucidates Schaeffer's zealous apologetic work, sheds light on the inconsistencies of his method and throws into stark relief his misreading of Kierkegaard as little more than an irrational fideist.

II. The Line of Despair and Upper Story Theology

As noted earlier, Schaeffer charged Kierkegaard with being one of the first philosophers to move past what he called the *line of despair*.[23] Hegel, with his elimination of the idea of contradiction and the introduction of relativism in philosophy, had opened the door; Kierkegaard walked through it. Previously, he argued, philosophers had an optimistic view of the capacity of reason to discern truth and meaning. They labored under the assumption that a "unified field of knowledge" was possible,[24] one that incorporated the natural world and the religious world and which utilized reason and faith as partners in the search for knowledge. History, science, religion, and

---

trustworthy." Schaeffer, *The God Who is There*, in *Complete Works*, vol. 1, p. 16. (The original edition does not contain this reflection on *Fear and Trembling*.)
[21]   Forrest Baird, "Schaeffer's Intellectual Roots," in *Reflections on Francis Schaeffer,* ed. by Ronald Ruegsegger, Grand Rapids, Michigan: Zondervan 1986, pp. 45–68.
[22]   See Kenneth Harper, "Francis Schaeffer: An Evaluation" *Bibliotheca Sacra*, vol. 133, no. 530, April–June 1976, pp. 130–42, see p. 138. Cited in Baird, "Intellectual Roots," p. 57.
[23]   Schaeffer, *Escape from Reason*, pp. 42–5 (in *Complete Works*, vol. 1, pp. 233–6). See also Schaeffer, *The God Who is There*, pp. 20–4 (in *Complete Works*, vol. 1, pp. 14–16).
[24]   Schaeffer, *Escape from Reason*, p. 42 (in *Complete Works*, vol. 1 pp. 233–4). Schaeffer wrote, "Kierkegaard is the real modern man because his thinking led to what Leonardo and all other thinkers had rejected. His thinking led to putting aside the hope of a unified field of knowledge" (*Escape from Reason*, p. 42).

spirituality could be explored in tandem, and connections could be made coherently between them. The construction of a philosophical and theological world-view which made use of logic, science, history and biblical revelation was not only possible, but imperative.

According to Schaeffer, Kierkegaard—along with Jean-Jacques Rousseau (1712–1778), Immanuel Kant (1724–1804), and G.W.F. Hegel (1770–1831)—introduced an epistemological crisis in which the quest for meaning became divorced from reason and from epistemological verification.[25] For Schaeffer, Kierkegaard despaired that philosophy could offer a legitimate depiction of reality that would also be religiously and existentially significant. Thus, he rejected epistemological realism in favor of anti-realism. In Schaeffer's terminology, he moved from "lower story" philosophy to "upper story" theology. In upper story theology, language does not purport to refer to reality as it is. Concepts and doctrines are tools for facilitating existential reality. Upper story theology limits itself only to the truth of experience; it avoids the complexities and challenges of rational verification. The problem with bypassing the lower for the upper, according to Schaeffer, is that there are no categories "upstairs" by which to determine what belongs there and what are the right values to hold.[26] Upstairs, in the existential arena, there is no way to distinguish "between reality and fantasy."[27] Thus, Kierkegaardian fideism became the basis of modern existentialist thought. For Schaeffer, not only did Kierkegaard represent the dichotomy of faith and reason in modernity, he caused the break.

While the leap was responsible for dichotomizing faith and reason, Schaeffer blamed Hegel for modernity's rejection of "classical logic." Prior to Hegel, philosophy and theology operated, according to Schaeffer, under the assumption that the law of non-contradiction was sacrosanct. Classical logic, he said, always protected the distinction between a thesis and its antithesis: "If this is true, then its opposite is not true."[28] Hegel's dialectical method, on the other hand, incorporated contradictions within it, paving the way for relativism in philosophy. According to Schaeffer, Kierkegaard's response to Hegel was to take this "a step further" by introducing an "absolute dichotomy between reason and non-reason."[29] He rejected the implications of relativism in Hegel's dialectic but, rather than reintroduce classical logic and epistemological realism into philosophy (which Schaeffer would have preferred), Kierkegaard turned to fideism and to the bifurcation of faith and knowledge.

---

[25]   Schaeffer, *Escape from Reason*, pp. 46–7 (in *Complete Works*, vol. 1, pp. 237–8).

[26]   Schaeffer termed the division into these two "stories" the hallmarks of the "*existential methodology.*" He asserted, "Once people adopt this dichotomy—where reason is separated totally from non-reason—they must then face the fact that many types of things can be put in the area of non-reason. And it really does not matter what one chooses to put there, because reason gives no basis for a choice between one thing or another." Schaeffer, *How Should We Then Live?*, p. 189.

[27]   Schaeffer, *He Is There and He Is Not Silent*, p. 58.

[28]   Ibid., p. 45.

[29]   Ibid., p. 46.

The implications of Kierkegaard's thought were that faith "became a leap without any verification."[30] This existentialist impulse was extended, Schaeffer claimed, in two directions: the secular and the religious. The former category comprised Jean-Paul Sartre (1905–80), Albert Camus (1913–60), Karl Jaspers (1883–1969), and Heidegger (1889–1976) while the latter included Karl Barth (1886–1968), Rudolf Bultmann (1884–1976), and Paul Tillich (1886–1965). Following this existentialist trajectory, theologians could embrace the findings of historical criticism as applied to the Bible, for example, without endangering their faith. If the truth of history and science lies in a sphere completely separate from the truth of religion and existential meaning, then it does not matter whether the history represented in the Bible is accurate.[31] Schaeffer named Barth the first modern theologian to appropriate Kierkegaard's leap.[32] In line with Kierkegaard, Barth's existential theology required no rational verification (in fact it renders it pointless) because it segregated the world of fact from the world of (religious) value. Schaeffer summed up what he viewed as the problem of modernity in philosophy and theology, with Kierkegaard as its cause, in *How Should We Then Live?*

> One must understand that from the advent of Kierkegaardianism onward there has been a widespread concept of the dichotomy between reason and non-reason, with no interchange between them. The *lower story* area of reason is totally isolated from the optimistic area of non-reason. The line which divides reason from non-reason is as impassable as a concrete wall thousands of feet thick, reinforced with barbed wire charged with 10,000 volts of electricity. There is no interchange, no osmosis between the two parts. So modern man now lives in such a total dichotomy, wherein reason leads to despair. "Downstairs" in the area of humanistic reason, man is a machine, man is meaningless. There are no values. And "upstairs" optimism about meaning and values is totally separated from reason. Reason has no place here at all; here reason is an outcast.[33]

It should be pointed out that Schaeffer drew a distinction in a few places between "Kierkegaard" and "Kierkegaardianism." In *How Shall We Then Live?*, he acknowledged a "discussion among scholars as to whether the secular and religious thinkers who built on Kierkegaard did him justice."[34] He concluded that "Kierkegaardianism" brought "to full tide the notion that reason will always lead to pessimism."[35] In *The Church at the End of the Century,* however, Schaeffer was less forgiving, if slightly ambivalent, toward Kierkegaard's direct impact on modernity:

---

[30]   Schaeffer, *Escape from Reason*, p. 51.
[31]   Ibid., pp. 51–2.
[32]   Schaeffer, *How Should We Then Live?*, p. 174. Here Schaeffer wrote: "In addition to the secular existentialism of Sartre, Camus, Jaspers and Heidegger, Kierkegaardianism brought forth another form of existentialism: the *theological* existentialism which began with Karl Barth (1886–1968), especially with his first commentary (1919) on the New Testament book entitled *The Epistle to the Romans*."
[33]   Ibid.
[34]   Ibid., p. 163.
[35]   Ibid.

Some may feel that I attribute to Kierkegaard the attributes peculiar to his followers and not to him and, surely, that is a point that could be argued. But whether Kierkegaard or Kierkegaardianism gave birth to it—I think it was Kierkegaard—we now have a divided universe, something man has not faced in past history. Before this, philosophers and thinkers were always striving for a unified field concept, a concept that would include all of life and all of knowledge.[36]

While acknowledging his critics, Schaeffer remained confident in his assessment that Kierkegaard's philosophy severed the tie between knowledge and faith. Moreover, the reader gets the sense that whether or not Kierkegaard was actually to blame for the split between faith and reason was beside the point. He had at the very least opened the door, which was enough to elicit Schaeffer's critique. Furthermore, he was convinced there was such a split, which was the most important thing; the details of how that came about must have seemed relatively insignificant in the grand scheme of things.

III. Schaeffer on Inerrancy, the Bible, and Epistemology

For Schaeffer, the primary flaw of modernity was the loss of trust in the Bible to provide an infallible connection between "downstairs" and "upstairs," or the realm of fact and meaning. Schaeffer's doctrine of biblical inerrancy, in which Scripture was understood to be God's direct deposit of didactic propositions, was an attempt to bridge the divide. In short, for Schaeffer, the crisis of Christianity was a loss of confidence in Scripture as the epistemological foundation for a coherent world-view. The issue, for Schaeffer was one of faulty presuppositions. Here the apologetic method he learned from Van Til is instructive. The world-view of modern rationalism, according to Schaeffer, assumed the "uniformity of natural causes in a closed system."[37] Naturalism of this sort renders "propositional, verbalized revelation— knowledge that man has from God" an entirely "unthinkable concept."[38] Christians, however, are committed to the "uniformity of natural causes in an open system." In such an open system, God can speak into his creation through the medium of Scripture. He can provide propositional content that can be accessed through rational means. This is, of course, a fundamental assumption for many Christians. For Schaeffer, however, the implications of this assumption are far-reaching: because divine revelation is possible, a Christian "simply does not have a problem with epistemology."[39] The Christian knows that everything that exists "is there because God made it to be there."[40] The Bible provides the principles by which humans can understand the world, and then it confirms those principles by narrating how God works within it.

---

[36]   Francis Schaeffer, *The Church at the End of the 20th Century*, Downers Grove, Illinois: InterVarsity Press 1970, p. 17.

[37]   Schaeffer, *He Is There and He Is Not Silent*, p. 63.

[38]   Ibid.

[39]   Ibid., p. 72.

[40]   Ibid.

Only a truly regenerated believer, however, can rightly interpret the Bible and the reality it depicts. The infallibility of the interpreter, optimistically assumed in Schaeffer's Christian epistemology, hinges on the spiritual status and correlative presuppositions of the perceiver. Persons must first be convinced that, while they are created in the image of God, they are sinners in need of redemption and of the objective revelation God has provided in Scripture. Only then can they be certain they have *true* truth.[41] For Schaeffer, Christianity must insist that there is such a thing as truth and that "it is possible to know that truth, not exhaustively but truly."[42] True Christianity depends on rationally accessible and divinely provided content in the form of universally valid propositions.[43] On this basis, there can be no room for Kierkegaardian fideism in a responsible, Christian epistemology. Schaeffer derided what he called "evangelical Kierkegaardianism." As he put it, "Patting people on the head, they say, 'Don't ask questions, dear, just believe.' "[44] Ironically, however, the presuppositionalism undergirding Schaeffer's methodology has itself been used as a prime example of irrational fideism.[45] This contradiction will be explored in the following section.

IV. Schaeffer's Reception of Kierkegaard: An Assessment

Several issues are immediately raised by Schaeffer's reception of Kierkegaard. One wonders how Schaeffer could so confidently lay the blame for the emergence of existentialism and the "line of despair" in modern thought at the feet of Kierkegaard when there is little evidence in his writing that he actually read Kierkegaard. Among the several references to Kierkegaard in his writings there are no actual quotations from any of Kierkegaard's works. The closest Schaeffer came to quoting Kierkegaard is his several allusions to the "leap of faith" and his two references to Abraham's near-sacrifice of Isaac.[46] In his brief introduction to Kierkegaard in *How Shall We Then Live?* Schaeffer names three of his works: *Either/Or*, *Philosophical Fragments*, and the *Concluding Unscientific Postscript*.[47] Aside from naming their titles, however (and that without acknowledgement of the pseudonymous authorship), one looks in vain for textual engagement with Kierkegaard's ideas. It is well known that Schaeffer developed his world-view communally and conversationally in his context as director

---

[41]   Ibid., p. 47.

[42]   Schaeffer, *The Church at the End of the 20th Century*, p. 105.

[43]   Ibid., p. 103.

[44]   Ibid.

[45]   In contrast to Schaeffer's analysis, Evans proposes Van Til's presuppositional apologetics (which Schaeffer advocated) as an example of "irrational fideism," while arguing that Kierkegaard's is a version of "responsible fideism" because he affirms a positive role for rationality in religious belief and justification. Stephen Evans, *Faith Beyond Reason: A Kierkegaardian Account*, Grand Rapids, Michigan: Eerdmans 1998, pp. 18–24.

[46]   Schaeffer, *Genesis in Space and Time*, p. 110; Schaeffer, *The God Who is There*, in *Complete Works*, vol. 1, p. 15. (The original edition does not include this Kierkegaard reference.)

[47]   Schaeffer, *How Should We Then Live?*, p. 163.

and lecturer of *L'Abri*. One wonders if his analysis of Kierkegaard emerged more through these informal discussions than through close readings of the texts. While it cannot be proven, this speculation is supported by a recent biographical assessment:

> While there is no certainty on this point, it is highly unlikely that Schaeffer ever actually read Hegel, Kant, Kierkegaard and the other modern thinkers he would later critique in his lectures and books....Schaeffer was a voracious reader of magazines and the Bible, but some who lived at L'Abri and knew him well say they never saw him read a book. It appears highly likely, therefore, that Schaeffer learned western intellectual history from students who had dropped out of European universities where secular thinkers from the eighteenth through the early twentieth centuries were believed to have eclipsed traditional Christian ways of thinking about important issues.[48]

Whether or not he directly engaged the works he mentions, the confidence with which he dubbed Kierkegaard the father of existentialism, the source of the demise of modern culture, and the cause of the split between reason and faith should have merited a more thorough exegesis of Kierkegaard's authorship. If Kierkegaard was the key to modernity's self-destruction and to the undermining of a Christian world-view, he would have been worth at least a close reading.

A related problem in Schaeffer's reading of Kierkegaard was his neglect of the hermeneutical implications of Kierkegaard's pseudonyms. To name only one example, the pseudonymous nature of *Philosophical Fragments* and the *Concluding Unscientific Postscript* calls for an appreciation of the "author's" explicitly sub-Christian stance and of its literary nature as a thought experiment.[49] Climacus' emphasis on the contradictory and paradoxical nature of Christianity must be framed in the context of his perceiving himself outside of the experience of faith. For the non-believer, the central concepts of Christianity (in particular the notion that God became a single, historical human being), appear to be irrational and irreducibly paradoxical. One cannot, through the employment of reason alone, reconcile its paradoxes. For Climacus and, on this point for Kierkegaard also, Christianity cannot be directly appropriated via rational conceptuality or, as Schaeffer would have it, through cognitive acceptance of propositional doctrines. Nonetheless, Climacus' emphasis on subjectivity does not preclude a role for objective approaches to knowledge, when appropriate to the nature of the object. He states:

> If Christianity is essentially something objective, it behooves the observer to be objective. But if Christianity is essentially subjectivity, it is a mistake if the observer is objective. In all knowing in which it holds true that the object of cognition is the inwardness of the subjective individual himself, it holds true that the knower must be in that state. But the

[48]   Hankins, *Francis Schaeffer and the Shaping of Evangelical America*, p. 43.
[49]   See C. Stephen Evans, *Kierkegaard's Fragments and Postscript: The Religious Philosophy of Johannes Climacus,* Atlantic Highlands, New Jersey: Humanities Press 1983, pp. 17–21. See also the insightful article by Ron Ruegsegger, "Schaeffer on Philosophy," *Christian Scholars Review,* vol. 10, no. 3, 1981, pp. 238–54. Evans, *Faith Beyond Reason*, p. 12.

expression for the utmost exertion of subjectivity is the infinitely passionate interest in its eternal happiness.[50]

Christianity deals with immense matters of life, death, and eternal salvation. Climacus, advised anyone who would attempt to truly understand these matters to be passionately involved rather than dispassionately "objective." True, genuine faith cannot emerge from "scholarly deliberation." As he said, "on the contrary, in this objectivity one loses that infinite, personal, impassioned interestedness, which is the condition of faith, the *ubique et nusquam* (everywhere and nowhere) in which faith can come into existence."[51]

Climacus did not reject the epistemological importance of objectivity in its proper place; rather, he emphasized the importance of the order in knowing religious truth: the "how" (subjectivity) renders the "what" (objective content).[52] Thus, appropriation of objectively true religious notions is only possible through passionate, subjective involvement.[53] Climacus, who as an outsider to faith highlighted its paradoxical nature, understood that Christianity does not reject reason or objectivity altogether. Rather, it requires that the one who would be truly involved with it and thereby truly understand it must enter through the passion of faith rather than through scholarly deliberation.

As has been pointed out elsewhere, Schaeffer's charge that Kierkegaard was an irrational fideist reflected the former's faulty conflation of metaphysical realism and epistemological realism.[54] Kierkegaard was a metaphysical realist, in that he affirmed the objective reality of the metaphysical world. However, the quest for objective certainty regarding the truth of that world betrayed faulty assumptions about the nature of the object (God), the subject (the knower), and the potential of the subject to access the object with epistemological infallibility. Kierkegaard emphatically pointed out the noetic impact of sin and the fallibility of human reason. As Evans noted, for Kierkegaard, sin creates a tension between faith and reason and drastically impacts a person's ability to appropriate the essential truth of Christianity.[55] A new way of perceiving reality is required which is only possible with the assistance of divine revelation and the corresponding development of authentic subjectivity.

One might even say that for Climacus (and for Kierkegaard), Christianity can be neither properly understood nor put into action apart from a qualitative shift in

---

[50]   *SKS* 7, 58 / *CUP1*, 53.

[51]   *SKS* 7, 36 / *CUP1*, 29.

[52]   As Kierkegaard put it, "In all the usual talk that Johannes Climacus is mere subjectivity, etc. it has been completely overlooked that in addition to all his other concretions he points out in one of the last sections that the remarkable thing is that there is a 'How' with the characteristic that when the 'How' is scrupulously rendered the 'What' is also given, that this is the How of 'faith.' " *SKS* 22, 414, NB14:121 / *JP* 4, 4550.

[53]   Evans, *Kierkegaard's Fragments*, p. 129.

[54]   Arthur Holmes, *All Truth is God's Truth*, Downers Grove, Illinois: InterVarsity Press 1997, p. 47. See also Ron Ruegsegger, "Schaeffer on Philosophy," *Christian Scholars Review*, vol. 10, no. 3, 1981, pp. 238–54.

[55]   Evans, *Faith Beyond Reason*, p. 12.

vision, or what Jamie Ferreira has analogously referred to as a "Gestalt" shift. So Kierkegaard:

> Here as everywhere we must pay attention to the qualitative leap, that there is no direct transition (for example, as from reading and studying in the Bible as an ordinary book— to taking it as God's word, as Holy Scripture), but everywhere a μετάβασις εἰς ἄλλο γένος, a leap, whereby I burst the whole progression of reason and define a qualitative newness, but a newness ἄλλο γένος.[56]

Climacus, speaking of the transition of despair between the ethical and the religious spheres of existence, notes that

> in this moment of decision…the individual needs divine assistance, although it is quite correct that one must first have understood the existence-relation between the esthetic and the ethical in order to be at this point—that is, by being there in passion and inwardness, one indeed becomes aware of the religious—and of *the leap.*[57]

Schaeffer had interpreted the leap as exclusively a leap of faith *into* despair. That is, since human beings cannot access the world of meaning and value through rational deliberation, they must make an irrational leap into the void. For Climacus—and for Kierkegaard—however, the leap is not an irrational movement meant to bypass the "rigors" of rationality and verification. Rather, the idea is grounded in a fundamental assumption that human beings cannot *truly* access and therefore appropriate the essence of Christianity (which, in fact, is a person—Christ) apart from "a qualitative transformation, a total character transformation in time."[58]

If Kierkegaard was a fideist, he was a *responsible fideist.*[59] That is, Kierkegaard (and his pseudonyms) did not view faith as being "exempt from rational, critical scrutiny."[60] In this light, he should be viewed as a basically orthodox Christian who accounted for the limitations of finitude and the role of subjectivity in knowledge. God cannot be proven nor can Christ be fully understood through objective rationality and human logic. Upon reflection, Kierkegaard's notion of the "leap" and his concept of subjectivity sounds similar to Schaeffer's stress on the importance of presuppositions and the necessity of faith for accessing the truth about God, humanity and the world.

While Schaeffer did stress the role of subjectivity in several places, he was also convinced that the central medium for accessing divine truth is objective rationality. God reveals himself through propositions—universally valid, didactic principles given in the Bible. These are then read and interpreted by rational human beings who, if they are Christians, enjoy the full restoration of their epistemic (rational) powers to perfectly, though not exhaustively, access these divine propositions. While subjectivity is implicated (one must be a Christian to do so), once one is a Christian and has one's objective capacity fully restored, the powers of objective reason can

---

[56]   *SKS* 22, 40, NB11:63 / *JP* 3, 2358.
[57]   *SKS* 7, 234 / *CUP1*, 258.
[58]   *SKS* 26, 250, NB33:8 / *JP* 3, 3101.
[59]   Evans, *Faith Beyond Reason*, p. 79.
[60]   Ibid., p. 18.

be applied to the object of knowledge. These propositions can then be systemized and framed as a single, coherent world-view.[61] For Kierkegaard, the knowledge of God and Christ require passionate involvement, inward appropriation, and always a measure of objective uncertainty—whether one is a Christian or not. The construction of a final, systematic world-view in which doctrines are assembled and propositions are neatly placed together simply does not fit Kierkegaard's understanding of the Christian faith.

Schaeffer's epistemological optimism (again, for the Christian), hinged on a particular construal of biblical inerrancy in which propositional truth played the central role. As a result, Schaeffer did not feel the weight of what, for many, are burdensome and complex issues of textual criticism, translation, and seemingly conflicting historical records in the Bible.[62] Neither did he appear to consider the difficult notion that, if the Bible is to be primarily understood as a collection of universally valid propositions which serves as the exclusive means of God's revelation, it has been available only to a select minority, relative to the whole of human history. Furthermore, for Schaeffer, there appears to be little consideration, not only of the historical context of the Bible's formation, but of the contextuality of the reader as socially, culturally, and historically located. Kierkegaard's energetic affirmation of the positive role of subjectivity, on the other hand, implicitly highlights the constructive value of context in theology and interpretation.

Schaeffer's presuppositionalism should have heightened his appreciation of the value of subjectivity, of the place of contextuality in knowledge, and even of the importance of Kierkegaard for modern theology. But his equal allegiance to the Princeton theology of his teachers forced his methodology into odd contortions and limited his "reading" of Kierkegaard to a mainly uncharitable and unappreciative one. The glaring contradictions in Schaeffer's methodology are thrown into sharp relief by his heavy critique of Kierkegaard. Perhaps had Schaeffer attended more closely to the texts—or perhaps read them at all—he would have recognized that Kierkegaard's own assumptions about subjectivity, sin, Christianity, and even epistemology (in particular the relation between faith and reason) were closer to his own than he realized. Moreover, Schaeffer's optimistic view of the restoration of full epistemic (and objective) capacities of the Christian through propositional revelation prevented him from recognizing the important place of subjectivity in his own method. In this respect, Kierkegaard's critique of rationalist theological method and of objective approaches to Christianity serves as a compelling challenge to the epistemological assumptions represented by Schaeffer and some versions of fundamentalist Christianity today.

---

[61]   As Holmes has pointed out, Schaeffer did not draw the crucial distinction between reason as medium for understanding (what he calls a basic Christian assumption) and rationality as a reliable (for the Christian) means for articulating and justifying universal truths. Holmes, *All Truth is God's Truth*, p. 47.

[62]   Clark Pinnock, "Schaeffer on Modern Theology," in *Reflections on Francis Schaeffer*, ed. by Ronald W. Ruegsegger, Grand Rapids, Michigan: Zondervan 1986, p. 182.

Bibliography

I. References to or Uses of Kierkegaard in Schaeffer's Corpus

Escape From Reason, Downers Grove, Illinois: InterVarsity Press 1968, pp. 42–52.
The God Who is There, Downers Grove, Illinois: InterVarsity Press 1968, pp. 21–2;
    p. 44; p. 51; p. 54; p. 60.
The Church at the End of the 20th Century, Downers Grove, Illinois: InterVarsity
    Press 1970, p. 17; pp. 103–5.
Genesis in Space and Time, Downers Grove, Illinois: InterVarsity Press 1972, p. 110.
He Is There and He Is Not Silent, Wheaton, Illinois: Tyndale House 1972, pp. 45–7;
    p. 51; p. 58; p. 63; p. 72.
How Should We Then Live? The Rise and Decline of Western Thought and Culture,
    Old Tappen, New Jersey: Fleming H. Revell 1976, p. 89; p. 163; p. 174.

II. Sources of Schaeffer's Knowledge of Kierkegaard

Undetermined.

III. Secondary Literature on Schaeffer' Relation to Kierkegaard

Baird, Forrest, "Schaeffer's Intellectual Roots," in *Reflections on Francis Schaeffer*,
    ed. by Ronald Ruegsegger, Grand Rapids, Michigan: Zondervan 1986, pp. 45–
    68.
Brown, Harold O.J., "Three Thinkers, Two Poets, One Teacher," *Southern Baptist
    Journal of Theology*, vol. 6, no. 2, 2002, pp. 34–41.
— "Kierkegaard's Leap or Schaeffer's Step?" *Christianity Today*, vol. 28, no. 18,
    1984, p. 82.
Dennis, Lane T., "Schaeffer and His Critics," in *Francis Schaeffer: Portraits of
    the Man and His Work*, ed. by Lane T. Dennis, Westchester, Illinois: Crossway
    Books 1986, pp. 99–128; see pp. 114–16.
Holmes, Arthur, *All Truth is God's Truth*, Downers Grove, Illinois: InterVarsity Press
    1997, pp. 47–8; p. 64.
Johnson, Thomas K., "Dialogue with Kierkegaard in Protestant Theology,"
    Communio Viatorum, vol. 46, no. 3, 2004, pp. 284–98.
Nash, Ronald, "The Life of the Mind and the Way of Life," in *Francis Schaeffer:
    Portraits of the Man and His Work*, ed. by Lane T. Dennis, Westchester, Illinois:
    Crossway Books 1986, pp. 51–70; see pp. 61–2.

Pinnock, Clark, "Francis Schaeffer on Modern Theology," in *Reflections on Francis Schaeffer*, ed. by Ronald W. Ruegsegger, Grand Rapids, Michigan: Zondervan 1986, pp. 173–93.

Ruegsegger, Ronald W., "Francis Schaeffer on Philosophy," in *Reflections on Francis Schaeffer*, ed. by Ronald W. Ruegsegger, Grand Rapids, Michigan: Zondervan 1986, pp. 107–30.

— "Schaeffer on Philosophy," *Christian Scholars Review*, vol. 10, no. 3, 1981, pp. 238–54.

PART II

Scandinavian Theology

Gisle Christian Johnson:
The First Kierkegaardian in Theology?

Svein Aage Christoffersen

I. Biography

Gisle Johnson (1822–93) is without doubt the most influential theologian of the latter half of the nineteenth century in Norway. He was born in Fredrikshald (now Halden) on December 10, 1822, but grew up in Kristiansand, where his father became the harbor manager in 1823. On completing his education at Kristiansand Cathedral School, he enrolled at the University of Christiania (now Oslo) in 1839, where he passed his professional theological qualification in 1845. After some years as a private tutor, he received a grant from the university, which made it possible for him to continue his theological studies in Germany in 1847–48. He was appointed Reader in theology at the university in 1849, Professor in 1860, and taught mainly dogmatics and ethics. From 1855 to 1874, he also taught in pedagogy at the Seminary for Practical Theology. In 1874, he handed over his teaching in systematic theology to Fredrik Petersen, whilst he himself went over to teach in church history.[1]

As principal teacher in systematic theology at the only university in the country, Johnson exerted a decisive influence on a number of generations of Norwegian theology students. He made a particularly marked impression in the initial period of his work, until the mid-1860s. After this, he lost some of the personal fervor and intensity that had characterized him as a young university teacher. In his lectures, he mainly dictated the sections of a completely developed system. Although not everyone was equally impressed by Johnson's system, it was nevertheless "standard theology" for all Norwegian priests in the latter half of the nineteenth century.

Johnson's influence was, however, not restricted to his activity as a university teacher but was perhaps just as much a result of his attending to the laity, and his central position in the organization of Norwegian lay activity in this period. Johnson started Bible readings in Christiania early in the 1850s and soon came to stand at the head of a revival movement that spread to large parts of the country. In time, he also traveled around as a revival preacher himself. In 1855, he took the initiative to establish an association for Home Mission in Christiania and was himself the first chairman of the association. The initiative quickly grew to a national movement, and eventually resulted in the establishment of the Norwegian Luther Foundation in

---

[1]   *Norsk Bibliografisk Leksikon*, vols. 1–19, ed. by A.W. Brøgger, Einar Jensen, Oslo: Aschehoug 1923–83, vol. 7, pp. 83–92.

1868. The Luther Foundation later (in 1891) became the Norwegian Lutheran Home Mission Society, which was to be one of the most powerful lay organizations in the Church of Norway in the twentieth century. Johnson thus came to be one of the most important advocates of lay preaching rights in the Church of Norway. He himself, however, believed that lay preaching was only expedient because the spiritual need was so pressing in his country that it could not be met purely through the ministry of the church.

Johnson's desire to exert an influence also expressed itself when he established, and for a long time ran, a series of theological and church journals. From the start in 1846, until 1857, he was on the editorial committee of the *Theological Journal for the Church of Norway* (*Theologisk Tidsskrift for den norske Kirke*). In 1863–71 he published the weekly *Lutheran Church Times* (*Luthersk Kirketidende*), and in 1864–71 *The Old and the New, a Journal for the Enlightenment and Edification of Lutheran Christians* (*Gammelt og Nyt, et Tidsskrift til Oplysning og Opbyggelse for lutherske Kristne*). Together with his colleague, Professor Carl Paul Caspari (1814–92), he also published *The Book of Concord* (*Konkordiebogen*) (1861–66), *The Norwegian-Lutheran Church's Confessional Documents* (*Den norsk-lutherske Kirkes Bekjendelsesskrifter*) (1872) and *Dr. M. Luther's Large Catechism* (*Dr. M. Luthers Store Katekisme*) (1881), all in Norwegian translation.

Johnson's *oeuvre* is primarily connected to the journals he started and ran. It was here that he published, amongst other things, a series of long articles on "What is the Church?" (1863),[2] "In Defence of my Teaching concerning Rebirth and on the Church" (1864),[3] and "Luther's Teaching concerning the Word of God" (1864–68).[4] As an independent work, however, he also published *A Word concerning Infant Baptism* (1857).[5] *Groundwork of Systematic Theology: For Use in Lectures* appeared in 1881 (in a series from 1878).[6] The book includes the first two parts of Johnson's systematic theology, "Christian Pistics" ("Den christelige Pistik") and "Christian Dogmatics" ("Den kristelige Dogmatik"). The third part, *Christian Ethics* (*Den Kristelige Ethik*) was published posthumously in 1898, based on Johnson's lecture manuscripts (1898).[7] Based on lecture notes by students, *Lectures on the*

[2]   Gisle Johnson, "Hvad er Kirken?" *Luthersk Kirketidende*, vol. 1, Christiania 1863, pp. 1–12; pp. 33–8; pp. 65–74; pp. 401–12.

[3]   Gisle Johnson, "Til Forsvar for min Lære om Gjenfødelsen og om Kirken," *Luthersk Kirketidende*, vol. 2, Christiania 1864, pp. 81–94; pp. 129–43; pp. 145–60; pp. 193–215; pp. 257–65; pp. 273–86; pp. 289–303; pp. 384–96.

[4]   Gisle Johnson, "Luthers Lære om Guds Ord, i sine Hovedmomenter fremstillet," *Theologisk Tidsskrift for den evangelisk-lutherske Kirke i Norge*, vol. 8, 1864, pp. 197–253. Gisle Johnson, *Theologisk Tidsskrift for den evangelisk-lutherske Kirke i Norge*, Ny Række, vol. 4, 1968, pp. 486–568.

[5]   Gisle Johnson, *Nogle Ord om Barnedaaben*, Christiania: Dybwad 1857.

[6]   Gisle Johnson, *Grundrids af den systematiske Theologi. Til Brug ved Forelæsninger*, Christiania: Dybwad 1881.

[7]   Gisle Johnson, *Forelæsninger over den kristelige Ethik*. Udgivet efter Forfatterens Død ved Jonathan Johnson, Gjennemseet af S. Odland. Med Forord af A.Chr. Bang, Christiania: Dybwad 1898.

History of Dogma came out in 1897.[8] Gisle Johnson is also reckoned as one of the originators of the "Appeal to Friends of Christianity in Our Country" ("Oprob til Christendommens venner i vårt land") (1884).[9]

II. Johnson's Theological Profile

Johnson's theological profile can be summarized under three points. Firstly, Johnson was a *revival theologian* who preached *conversion* to a new life. He wanted to awaken the Christian life in his students and auditors and to make them real, living Christians. The road to a vivacious, Christian life went via conversion and rebirth. Conversion and rebirth were, however, not one-time events in Johnson's perspective, but processes that could—indeed had to—start again every time the person had turned away from God.

Secondly, Johnson was an *experiential theologian* in the sense that he based his theological system on Christian faith experience. He developed the fundamental theological significance of faith experience in what he called "pistics" (*pistikken*), where the doctrine of the essence of Christian faith and character founds a theological system. In pistics, Johnson attempts to maintain both a subjective and an objective perspective. On the one hand, he establishes the knowing subject's own personal conviction of faith as the sole epistemological source for theology. On the other hand, he makes the conviction of faith dependent on Christian fellowship, that is, the church, and thereby on the church's confession in the form of its confessional documents.

Pistics is Johnson's most original contribution to systematic theology. Its originality, however, does not reside primarily in this combination of subjectivity and objectivity, but in his view of faith as a form of existence: faith, for Gisle Johnson, is "a peculiar form of human personal existence."[10] In this way, he founds his conception of faith, and thereby his systematic theology as a whole, on a particular understanding of existence. In Johnson's conception of existence, the person fundamentally has three different ways of existing, all depending on how one relates to God. In the pistics, he therefore describes human forms of existence as (a) "the human relation to God in its natural condition," (b) "the human relation to God under the law," and (c) the human relation to God "in the Christian faith."[11] The relationship between these forms of existence is such that the human urge to exist leads it from the first, through the second, to the third form of existence. The transition between the forms of existence does not, however, flow as a natural development, but takes place purely in the form of individual decision and one's own choice.[12]

---

8   Gisle Johnson, *Forelæsninger over Dogmehistorien*, ed. by H. Wølner-Hansen, Kristiania: Dybwad 1897.
9   Gisle Johnson, *Gjør døren høy. Kirken i Norge 1000 år*, Oslo: Aschehoug 1995, pp. 425–33.
10   Johnson, *Grundrids*, p. 8.
11   Ibid., p. 9.
12   Ibid., pp. 63–4.

Thirdly, Gisle Johnson was *confessionalist*. As we have seen, "Lutheran" is a word that arises in association with everything he did. The church had to be Lutheran, and the Lutheran church's confession in the form of the *Book of Concord* was the basis for addressing all theological questions. Lutheranism naturally implied that Scripture was held as the highest norm for all church discussion of any theological question, but the Lutheran confessional writings guaranteed a way of using Scripture that maintained the correct balance between the subjective and the objective.

Gisle Johnson's confessional position rendered him an irreconcilable opponent of the emerging Grundvigianism, against which he struggled with practically all means available. His main contention with the Grundtvigian understanding was its view of the word of Scripture. In a long article from 1864, he reviews recent books on Grundtvigianism by the Danish theologians Henrik Nikolai Clausen and Hans Lassen Martensen.[13] Neither book gets any reprieve from his sharp scrutiny, even though he is much more positive concerning Martensen's work than that of Clausen. But not even Martensen was, in Johnson's view, sufficiently clear and consistent in his view of Scripture as "the fundamental source of Christian faith."[14] At the same time, he considered the potential achievements of such theological confrontations to be limited from the start. Grundtvigianism was, in Johnson's opinion, not a religion but a sect. It was a movement that "eats the bread of the church" but "undermines its walls."[15] The road back from Grundtvigian "fanaticism" to "the true church" did not run, according to Johnson, through enlightenment, but through conversion, "a thorough and complete conversion."[16]

III. The Influence of Søren Kierkegaard

A. Direct Evidence of Kierkegaard's Influence

There is broad agreement amongst researchers that Gisle Johnson was influenced by and had received important stimulation from Søren Kierkegaard.[17] However, it is not entirely simple further to specify this influence. Johnson did not himself give an account of his relation to Kierkegaard, and there are no references to Kierkegaard in his printed work. After his death, Johnson's immensely rich library was transferred to Kristiansand Cathedral School. The library includes about 3,200 volumes, but not a single one of Kierkegaard's books. We may nonetheless not conclude *ex silentio* that Johnson never either owned or read a single book by Kierkegaard, since there may be several reasonable explanations for the absence of Kierkegaard's books in

---

[13]   Gisle Johnson, "Boganmeldelse," *Luthers Kirketidende*, vol. 1, Christiania: Dybwad 1863, pp. 308–20.
[14]   Ibid., p. 318.
[15]   Gisle Johnson, "Erklæring," *Norsk Kirketidende*, no. 25, Christiania: Steenske 1857, p. 241.
[16]   Johnson, "Boganmeldelse," p. 320.
[17]   Cf. Andreas Aarflot, *Norsk Kirkehistorie*, vols. 1–3, Oslo: Lutherstiftelsen 1966–71, vol. 2, p. 353. Einar Molland, *Norges Kirkehistorie i det 19. århundre*, vols. 1–2, Oslo: Gyldendal Norsk Forlag 1979, vol. 1, p. 189.

the library today. The library, in other words, does not give us any foothold for a well-grounded opinion concerning what Johnson may have read by Kierkegaard.

Contemporary sources are also extremely sparse as regards precise information on Johnson's relation to Kierkegaard. Nils Hertzberg, who was a student in 1847, describes in his memoirs in 1909 the powerful influence Johnson had over the students in the 1850s.[18] Johnson's lectures were held in such a form as to make it possible for the students to write them down coherently and in clear language, so that they could practically memorize them from start to finish. However, the revival started by Johnson did not come primarily from the lectures, but from the Bible readings, according to Hertzberg.[19] There was no tradition for a theology professor to hold popular Bible readings of this kind, and so many asked themselves naturally enough where the initiative for this came from. Some speculated it was the priest Gustav Adolph Lammers (1802–78), according to Hertzberg, but he himself gives no credence to this theory, even though Lammers certainly was a fiery revival preacher at this time. He rather sets more store in the influence of Søren Kierkegaard. His main proposal is, however, that Johnson's religious breakthrough was not due to any external influence, but to Johnson's own inner growth and development.[20]

As we shall argue later, there is good reason to assume that Hertzberg's assessment of Johnson's development is quite accurate. The most interesting information he gives us is, however, that Johnson's contemporaries were themselves unsure of who his influences were. This is, in other words, not a problem that developed later, but is rather a question raised by Johnson's contemporaries. Not even then could anyone give a well-grounded answer. People have had to speculate—some pointing to Lammers, others to Kierkegaard. The explanation may, of course, be that Johnson was careful to cover his tracks and keep his sources hidden. But just as likely as a solution is that the influence of, for example, Kierkegaard actually only played a minor role for him. So this possibility should be kept in mind when we look more closely at the material that may indicate that Johnson was influenced by Kierkegaard.

How probable is it that Gisle Johnson really was influenced by Kierkegaard? Kierkegaard's attack on the Church in *The Moment* caused furor in Norway in the mid-1850s, particularly amongst young theologians. Hertzberg recalls a large meeting in the Student Union, where he himself introduced the topic, "Is becoming a priest in the state church defensible?" His own conclusion was clear: "When I started from Kierkegaardian premises, I found it indefensible."[21] The Kierkegaardian premises admittedly faded a little with time. Hertzberg later became both director of the Ministry for Church Affairs and Minister for Church Affairs. But for Hertzberg and for other students in the 1850s, it took time to digest Kierkegaard's startling attacks on the State Church, and many of them at least waited a while before they became priests.

Hertzberg also tells us that Gisle Johnson attended the meeting of the Student Union, and he says he remembers that Johnson expressed a good deal of sympathy

18 Nils Hertzberg, *Fra min barndoms- og ungdoms tid*, Christiania: Aschehoug 1909.
19 Hertzberg, *Fra min barndoms- og ungdoms tid*, p. 136.
20 Ibid., pp. 137–8.
21 Ibid., pp. 138–9.

with the young people who were so strongly inspired by Kierkegaard. Hertzberg also remembers that Johnson even let slip a strongly worded remark, saying "that he thanks God that he had not become a priest."[22]

Even if we assume that Hertzberg remembers correctly, more than 50 years after the event, it is by no means clear what Johnson may have meant with his remark. Until we know more about the context in which it was delivered, there is little point in further speculation concerning the thought behind it. What Johnson at least cannot have meant was to reply to the main topic of the meeting that evening. On this point, Hertzberg is crystal clear in his memoirs: Johnson was *not* in agreement with the young people's view that it was indefensible to enter the priesthood of the State Church, for the State Church after all was in possession of "pure Word and pure Sacraments."[23] This is also entirely in keeping with what Johnson said and did as a teacher of priests for more than 40 years. Neither at this point nor later did he support Kierkegaard or the Kierkegaard-inspired student attack on the State Church. We should in addition note that Hertzberg does not remember Johnson explicitly talking about Kierkegaard in the course of the evening, either positively or negatively. Johnson was generally fairly silent in such company, and probably would not have said very much at all.

If Kierkegaard did influence Johnson, he certainly did not do so in connection with Kierkegaard's attack on the church. Scholars also agree that any influence should be looked for further back in time. There are in particular two researchers who have investigated this further, namely, Godvin Ousland[24] and Valborg Erichsen.[25]

Kierkegaard's books were known early in Norway. In Thue's reader of 1846,[26] three texts by Kierkegaard were included: excerpts from *Either/Or*, Part Two, from *Prefaces*, and from *Stages on Life's Way*. According to Valborg Erichsen, Thue's reader was used at all the higher levels in schools.[27] Kierkegaard must therefore have been known and read in Norway as soon as his books were released, and it is not unreasonable to assume that Gisle Johnson was among those who knew Kierkegaard's works at an early stage. In Thue's perspective, however, Kierkegaard was primarily a novelist with acute powers of psychological observation, not least within the field of the erotic.[28] All the pieces he has picked out from the works of Kierkegaard are about the feminine as opposed to the masculine.

According to Godvin Ousland, Johnson devoted steadily greater attention to Kierkegaard's writings in the years 1847–49, and Ousland believes that Johnson

---

[22]   Ibid., p. 139.
[23]   Ibid.
[24]   Godvin Ousland, *En kirkehøvding. Professor Gisle Johnson som teolog og kirkemann*, Oslo: Lutherstiftelsen 1950.
[25]   Valborg Erichsen, *Søren Kierkegaards betydning for norsk aandsliv*, Kristiania: Edda 1923.
[26]   *Læsebog i Modersmaalet for Norske og Danske, tilligemed en Exempelsamling af den svenske Literatur og med æsthetiske og literaturhistoriske Oplysninger*, ed. Henning Junghans Thue, Kristiania: Wulfsberg 1846, pp. 486–90.
[27]   Erichsen, *Søren Kierkegaards betydning for norsk aandsliv*, p. 229.
[28]   *Læsebog i Modersmaalet*, p. 487.

may have been the first theologian in the country to have made a more penetrating study of Kierkegaard.[29] But how does he know this?

Ousland has two references for his claim that Johnson studied Søren Kierkegaard's writings in depth in 1847–49. In a note to the relevant text, he writes "As communicated by Professor Odland, cf. also Th. B. Odland in the 79th Annals of the Norwegian Bible Society, page 78."[30] To take the last first, it refers to an extremely comprehensive and in-depth 80-page-long obituary written by Rector Thor Bernhard Odland on the death of Johnson.[31] The page reference does not, however, lead us to any mention of Kierkegaard, so it is clearly wrong, and if we look at the article as a whole, it contains absolutely nothing to say that Johnson might have studied Kierkegaard in the relevant period. Thor Bernhard Odland is therefore not a source for this information. We might rather say that Thor Bernhard Odland's presentation points us in the opposite direction, since he has nothing to tell us about Johnson's relationship to Kierkegaard.[32]

We are therefore left with an oral communication from "Professor Odland," who must presumably be Professor Sigurd Odland, who was born in 1857 and died in 1937. Odland could certainly have followed the lectures of the ageing Gisle Johnson in the second half of the 1870s, and was doubtless theologically close to Johnson. He followed Johnson as Chairman of the Home Mission Association in 1892 and became Professor of New Testament Studies at the university in 1894. However, he left the university in 1906, in protest at the appointment of the liberal Johannes Ordning as Professor of Theology, and helped to establish the Congregational Faculty of Theology (today the Norwegian School of Theology) in 1907 as a competing institution to the priestly training at the university. Odland, however, also broke with the Congregational Faculty in 1916. Ousland therefore never had Odland as teacher, and the information given him by Odland must reasonably have taken place after Odland's 70th birthday, and certainly long before Ousland started working on his dissertation on Johnson. We must therefore conclude that we do not know when and in what form Ousland may have received this information from Odland, and neither do we know whence Odland himself got his information. In short, Ousland's claim cannot be tested and cannot be confirmed through any other sources either. The conclusion must therefore be, as Ousland himself admits, that sources for this period of Johnson's life are quite incomplete, and that the period lies in historical darkness.[33]

---

[29]   Ousland, *En kirkehøvding*, p. 34.

[30]   Ibid., p. 322.

[31]   Thor Bernhard Odland, "Professor dr.theol. Gisle Johnson," *Det Norske Bibelselskabs 79. Beretning*, Christiana 1894, pp. 67–158.

[32]   It is worth noticing that Kierkegaard is not mentioned in Andreas Brandrud, "Gisle Johnson. 1822–1922," *Norsk Teologisk Tidsskrift*, vol. 23, 1922, pp. 124–8. See, however, Andreas Brandrud, "Teologien ved det norske universitet 1811–1911," *Norsk Teologisk Tidsskrift*, vol. 12, Kristiania: Grøndahl 1911, p. 228.

[33]   Ousland, *En kirkehøvding*, p. 37.

B. Indirect Signs of Kierkegaard's Influence

As a result of the extremely sparse historical information available to us, the most important arguments for claiming that Johnson took significant inspiration from Kierkegaard are of an indirect nature. They build on a further analysis of Johnson's theology, and not least of his pistics, something Ousland makes much of.

As we have seen, Johnson builds the pistics around three human forms of existence: the human in the natural condition, the human under the law, and the human in faith's form of existence. This construction, says Ousland, is strikingly reminiscent of Kierkegaard's stages.[34] In particular, Johnson's emphasis on the break between the three forms of existence and on faith's existentialism point in Kierkegaard's direction. But Ousland admits that this is no more than circumstantial, because Johnson may also have been inspired by Romans 1 and 2, and Lutheran teaching on the law.[35]

A more thorough treatment of Johnson's pistics, however, shows—according to Ousland—a lack of clarity in his view of the ethical stage. The "legal faith" that the human has at this stage is in a way an expression of Christian faith, but at the same time it is not real Christianity after all. Legal faith is not yet Christianity but still has some of the content of the Christian faith.[36] In this way it becomes unclear, according to Ousland, that the power driving the human to break with the aesthetic stage does not come from the persons themselves and their dissatisfaction, but comes from without, that is, from God. This lack of clarity does not stem from the Bible, but is something Johnson has in common with "the great Danish thinker" concludes Ousland, who thereby sees a clear influence from Kierkegaard.[37] This attempt to explain why Johnson's system does not fit with Ousland's own dogmatics is not especially convincing.

Valborg Erichsen also claims that Kierkegaard must have played an important role in Johnson's religious development. What she has in particular focused on is that in his earliest stages as a preacher of repentance, Johnson emphasized suffering as an important condition for being a Christian. The true, confessing Christian must bear the hatred of the world, she quotes from an unnamed source, and claims that it is specifically *Practice in Christianity* of 1850 and the *For Self-Examination* that Johnson must have read.[38] Historical evidence for these claims is, however, not produced.

Erichsen also claims that it is not only possible but even likely that Kierkegaard has contributed a quality to Johnson's Christianity that is not immediately recognizable. When he emphasizes in the printed version of his systematic theology that faith can only be achieved through denial and giving up all of one's own wisdom, she claims to know that in its earliest stage, this was—probably—formulated in the form of a

---

[34]   Ibid., p. 95.

[35]   Ibid., p. 99.

[36]   Ibid., pp. 102–3.

[37]   Ibid., p. 150.

[38]   Erichsen, *Søren Kierkegaards betydning,* p. 281.

paradox. Here she refers to an article by Jens Gleditsch from 1913,[39] who tells that he had heard both from Johnson's oldest disciples and from his opponents that his dogmatics had been focused into the form of paradox point by point.[40]

Gleditsch was born in 1860, and so he certainly did know some of Johnson's students and disciples from the 1850s. But it is difficult to say how much weight to give to this information in particular. Erichsen, for her part, wants to set a great deal of store on it and claims that Johnson from the start ingested more of Kierkegaard's subjectivism than he later maintained. It was Kierkegaard's attack on the church that first showed Johnson the dangers of an unbridled subjectivism and taught him that a system of dogma cannot be maintained without being accompanied by objective faith in authority.[41]

Erichsen's conjectures concerning Johnson's religious development do not build on any in-depth study of sources. Ousland's, however, do. Although Johnson's pistics was not published until the end of the 1870s, there is a series of lecture notes that make it possible to form an impression of Johnson's dogmatics at an early stage. Ousland has gone through several manuscripts of this kind and can declare that Johnson was already building his pistics on the doctrine of the three stages of existence in 1855. According to his understanding, pistics was born in 1852. The first notes from Johnson's dogmatics lectures stem from 1851, and in these lectures, claims Ousland, pistics does not exist. In the lectures on the theological encyclopedia in 1853, the expression "pistics" appears for the first time, and in 1855, systematic theology is presented based on the three stages of existence. So it is in 1852 that Johnson concludes that dogmatics has to build on a doctrine of the appearance and nature of faith, and he combines this thought with the three stages of Kierkegaard, and as a result arrives at pistics as we know it today.[42]

Ousland's thorough work on lecture notes gives no evidence to say that Johnson's dogmatics from the very beginning was to be much more subjectively oriented and Kierkegaard inspired than it later became. His work does not, therefore, support the conjectures of Valborg Erichsen. But did Johnson's pistics really appear for the first time in 1852?

One manuscript not employed by Ousland, or anyone else for that matter, is Karl Roll's lecture notes on Johnson's 1849 lectures on the "Theological Encyclopedia."[43] These were Johnson's very first lectures at the university, as newly employed reader. Roll's records are very careful, making up 150 handwritten A4 pages and thus giving us an extremely interesting insight into Johnson's theological thinking when he started his academic work.

The first thing Roll's records allow us to state is that pistics did not appear for the first time in Johnson's lectures in 1852. On the contrary, pistics appears fully

---

[39]   Jens Gleditsch, "Søren Kierkegaards betydning for teologien," *Kirke og Kultur*, vol. 20, Kristiania: Steen'sche 1913, pp. 268–72.

[40]   Erichsen, *Søren Kierkegaards betydning*, p. 282.

[41]   Ibid., pp. 282–3.

[42]   Ousland, *En kirkehøvding*, p. 109.

[43]   Gisle Johnson, *Theologisk Encyclopædi*, lecture notes by Karl Roll 1849. Det teologiske Menighetsfakultets arkiv.

200 *Svein Aage Christoffersen*

developed in all its primary features already in Johnson's 1849 lectures. In addition, it is not difficult to see a certain influence from Kierkegaard in Johnson's formulations. Faith is called a form of existence, the emergence of faith is described as stages on life's way, and faith itself is a passionate, personal relation to revealed truth. It is also relevant to point out his description of the natural human as captured in finitude and his characterization of this form of life as aesthetic. It also resounds of Kierkegaard when Johnson says that the human cannot "quantify himself into the qualitatively different existence."[44] A break is necessary to realize faith's form of existence.

The differences are, however, also striking. The subjective perspective is firmly connected to an equally marked objective perspective, as is also the case later. Faith is a subjective acquiring of the objectively patent truth, and this objectively patent truth is grounded in church confession. There is no sign of Kierkegaard's "subjectivity is truth." Erichsen's conjecture that Johnson only returns to the dogma as a counterweight to Kierkegaard's subjectivism after his attack on the church is therefore far from the truth.

There is a series of literature references in the manuscript, but Kierkegaard is not mentioned. The central figure is, without a doubt, Schleiermacher. Even though much is made of classical Lutheran dogmatics, Johnson concludes that it has not solved the encyclopedic task, which is to present the various disciplines of theology as a whole, delimited, and closed system, based on cohesive principles. A decisive step along the road to solving this task is Schleiermacher's "Kurze Darstellung,"[45] which in Johnson's view introduces a new era of the history of the theological encyclopedia, and which he did not hesitate to call an "architectonic masterpiece."[46]

Johnson does, however, distance himself from Schleiermacher at some decisive points. He agrees with Schleiermacher that the objectives of theology lie with the practical life, but not that theology as scholarly work exists for the sake of church leadership. Theology exists for the edification of the church. In addition, in spite of his practical orientation, Schleiermacher has a tendency to make Christianity into a speculative construction. Johnson, however, rejects the speculative understanding of Christianity as well as the attempt to understand Christianity as an empirical phenomenon. Christianity is in its immediacy given in the believer's subjective consciousness of faith. Finally, Johnson also refused to accept Schleiermacher's lack of confessional Lutheran profile.

The fact that certain features of Johnson's thought *may* come from Kierkegaard does not thereby mean that they *must* do so. It must be established whether they just as easily may come from other sources. The person with most significance for Johnson's development is without doubt Christian Thistedahl (1813–1876), with whom Johnson came into contact in 1838, when he started at Kristiansand Cathedral School, where Thistedahl was a teacher.[47] Thistedahl was nine years older than Johnson and an extremely gifted man. A very close and personal relation soon

---

[44]   Ibid.
[45]   Ibid.
[46]   Ibid.
[47]   Oluf Kolsrud, *Bibeloversætteren Christian Thistedahl 1813–1876*, Christiania: Det norske Bibelselskap 1913.

developed between teacher and pupil, and Thistedahl was Johnson's first and most important theological teacher and mentor. Thistedahl was a Lutheran scriptural theologian of the orthodox kind, and it is not difficult to see that Johnson's own confessional Lutheranism has its roots in their relationship.

There is, however, one aspect of the relation between Thistedahl and Johnson that has only played a minor role in scholarship, and that is the *practical* significance that theology had in this relationship. It is well documented that Johnson was a sensitive person who was at times disheartened, dejected, and lacking in faith in himself. Particularly in the years 1841–42, he was struggling through a difficult period. The letters Johnson wrote to Thistedahl in this period are lost, but the letters Thistedahl wrote to Johnson are preserved, and they fully document the existential role played by theology in this relationship. Here, theology is not something studied for the sake of church leadership (Schleiermacher) but for the sake of one's own faith. Theology is meant to strengthen one's zest for life and serve as edification in a context where the individual's mental disposition is central. The role played by the mental dispositions in these letters gives them a clear *Romantic* feel, and this Romantic feel has until now been overlooked by scholars.

Of particular interest in this regard is Thistedahl's letter from the day after Whitsun in 1841. It is clear that Thistedahl had just received a gloomy letter from Johnson and was therefore doing all he could to sustain his friend's zest for life. Thistedahl warns against two mental dispositions: frivolity and dejection. The first mental disposition implies that one has lost holy fear for the law of God, and the other that one has lost faith in God's eternal fatherly love in Christ. Both mental dispositions are resisted by thinking about Christ. This is, as Thistedahl himself says, his entire *philosophia practica*.[48]

Against this background, it is unnecessary to turn to Kierkegaard for an explanation of the existential features of Johnson's theology. The most natural explanation is that Johnson's existence-based pistics originates in the Romantic *philosophia practica* that played such an important role in his intimate friendship with Christian Thistedahl as a young man in the 1830s and 1840s.

IV. Conclusion

There is no reason to doubt that Gisle Johnson knew of and certainly also read central works of Kierkegaard, or even received stimulus from Kierkegaard at an early point in his theological development. That he therefore recognized parts of his own existential and psychological interests in Kierkegaard is also a reasonable assumption. But there is little reason to believe that it is the stimulus from Kierkegaard that formed Johnson's own theological thinking. The stimuli that became normative for him from this point of view are more likely to stem from Christian Thistedahl and Schleiermacher. Johnson probably did not consider Kierkegaard primarily as a theologian in the academic meaning of the word, but

---

[48]   Ole Christian Thistedal, "Breve fra Ole Christian Thistedahl til Gisle Johnson," *Luthersk Kirketidende*, Kristiania: Lutherstiftelsens forlag 1909, pp. 280–1.

rather as a preacher of repentance who exhorted people to existential seriousness about life and the requirement to conversion and a break with the worldly life. This perspective of penitence is something Johnson could identify with.[49] The differences between Johnson and Kierkegaard, however, come clearly to light in the view of the church that played such a central role in Johnson's theology. In this respect, there is little he has in common with Kierkegaard.

Translated by Andrew Thomas

---

[49]   Andreas Brandrud, "Teologien ved det norske universitet 1811–1911," *Norsk Teologisk Tidsskrift*, vol. 12, Kristiania: Grøndahl 1911, p. 228.

Bibliography

I. References to or Uses of Kierkegaard in Gisle Johnson's Corpus

Undetermined.

II. Sources of Johnson's Knowledge of Kierkegaard

Undetermined.

III. Secondary Literature on Gisle Johnson's Relation to Kierkegaard

Aarflot, Andreas, *Norsk Kirkehistorie*, vol. 2, Oslo: Lutherstiftelsen 1967, pp. 353–4.

Brandrud, Andreas, "Teologien ved det norske universitet 1811–1911," *Norsk Teologisk Tidsskrift*, vol. 12, Kristiania: Grøndahl 1911, p. 228.

Erichsen, Valborg, *Søren Kierkegaards betydning for norsk aandsliv*, Kristiania: Edda 1923, pp. 281–3.

Gleditsch, Jens, "Søren Kierkegaards betydning for teologien," *Kirke og Kultur*, vol. 20, Kristiania: Steen'sche 1913, pp. 268–72.

Hertzberg, Nils, *Fra min barndoms- og ungdoms tid*, Christiania: Aschehoug 1909, pp. 137–9.

Molland, Einar, *Norges Kirkehistorie i det 19. århundre*, vols. 1–2, Oslo: Gyldendal Norsk Forlag 1979, vol. 1, pp. 189–91.

Ousland, Godvin, *En kirkehøvding. Professor Gisle Johnson som teolog og kirkemann*, Oslo: Lutherstiftelsen 1950, pp. 95–105.

Selmer, L., "Johnson, Gisle Christian," *Norsk Biografisk Leksikon*, ed. by A.W. Brøgger, Einar Jensen. Oslo: Aschehoug 1936, vol. 7, p. 89.

Anders Nygren:

Influence in Reverse?

Carl S. Hughes

The question of the role of Anders Nygren (1890–1978) in the reception of Søren Kierkegaard presents something of an interpretative conundrum. On the one hand, Nygren is a nearly ubiquitous reference in discussions of the theme of love in Kierkegaard's work. His *agape/eros* distinction has shaped how Kierkegaard has been interpreted and translated to such a degree that the two figures' treatments of love are frequently collapsed as though they were the same. On the other hand, with respect to Kierkegaard's influence upon Nygren himself, Nygren is virtually silent— providing only a few superficial references to Kierkegaard's name in his vast authorship. Although Nygren certainly had at least a passing familiarity with Kierkegaard's work, substantial engagement with it is conspicuously absent in his writings. Nygren treats numerous figures throughout the history of theology and philosophy in depth—Augustine, Thomas Aquinas, Immanuel Kant, Friedrich Schleiermacher, Rudolf Otto, to name only a few—yet he attempts no such analysis of Kierkegaard. Thus, although Nygren is indisputably a major figure in the reception of Kierkegaard, he does virtually none of this receiving himself. How can his silence be explained? What does it suggest about his own understanding of the degree to which his thought overlaps with Kierkegaard's? And how might taking stock of his silence begin to reshape how we read Kierkegaard today?

I. Anders Nygren: Philosopher of Religion, Theologian, Bishop

Anders Nygren published extensively on a wide range of philosophical and theological themes over the course of a writing career lasting more than 50 years. His official bibliography spans over 19 pages,[1] and includes works about philosophical and theological method, historical theology, ethics, systematic theology, political theology, ecclesiology, ministry, and ecumenical theory.[2] Even though Nygren's international fame was widespread in the twentieth century, it was generally not

---

[1]   Ulrich E. Mack, "Bibliography of the Publications of Anders Nygren to 1970," in *The Philosophy and Theology of Anders Nygren*, ed. by Charles W. Kegley, Carbondale and Edwardsville: Southern Illinois University Press 1970, pp. 379–97.

[2]   Excellent summaries of Nygren's major publications can be found in Thor Hall, "The Nygren Corpus: Annotations to the Major Works of Anders Nygren of Lund," *Journal of the American Academy of Religion*, vol. 47, no. 2, 1979, pp. 269–89.

based on the full scope of his output. Rather, it was due almost entirely to one book: *Agape and Eros*, the first part of which was published in 1930 and the second in 1936.[3] It is difficult to overstate this book's influence in twentieth-century theologies and philosophies of love. Karl Barth incorporates its *eros/agape* opposition in his *Church Dogmatics*,[4] Martin Luther King Jr. appeals to it as an impetus for social transformation,[5] Irving Singer uses it heuristically in his history of the philosophy of love,[6] and numerous Christian ethicists—notably Gene Outka[7] and Timothy Jackson[8]—take it as a pillar of their ethics. Even figures who criticize Nygren's thesis tend to adopt his terminology and his way of framing the question of love.[9]

Nygren was born in the town of Gothenburg, Sweden in 1890, the son of pious Lutheran parents.[10] He pursued his theological studies at the University of Lund, and was ordained to the ministry in 1912, at the young age of 21. He served as a parish pastor for nine years, during which time he was able to complete a doctoral

[3]   The first part of Nygren's book, *A Study of the Christian Idea of Love*, treats Christian doctrine about love conceptually and abstractly. The second part, *The History of the Christian Idea of Love*, analyzes its concrete historical manifestations. Anders Nygren, *Den kristna kärlekstanken genom tiderna. Eros och Agape*, vols. 1–2, Stockholm: Svenska Kyrkans Diakonistyrelses Bokförlag 1930–6. (English translation: *Agape and Eros*, trans. by Philip S. Watson, London: SPCK 1957.)

[4]   Karl Barth, *Die kirchliche Dogmatik*, vols. I–IV, Zollikon-Zurich: Evangelischer Verlag 1955, vol. IV/2, pp. 831–53. (English translation: *Church Dogmatics*, trans. by G.W. Bromiley, Edinburgh: T. & T. Clark 1957–75, vol. IV/2, pp. 733–51.) Although Barth incorporates Nygren's terminology and general framework, he also criticizes a number of Nygren's specific claims. Many of Barth's criticisms can be interpreted as expressions of a Reformed suspicion of Nygren's hyper-Lutheranism. See Barth, *Die kirchliche Dogmatik*, vol. IV/2, p. 837; pp. 840–1; p. 848; pp. 853–4; p. 902; p. 939. (*Church Dogmatics*, vol. IV/2, pp. 737–8; pp. 740–1; p. 747; p. 752; p. 795; p. 827.)

[5]   For example, Martin Luther King, Jr., "An Experiment in Love," *Jubilee*, September 1958, pp. 11–16. This article is anthologized in *A Testament of Love: The Essential Writings and Speeches of Martin Luther King, Jr.*, ed. by James M. Washington, New York: HarperOne 1990, pp. 16–20.

[6]   Irving Singer, *The Nature of Love: Plato to Luther*, New York: Random House 1966, p. 165, pp. 282–320; pp. 322–3.

[7]   For example, Gene Outka, *Agape: An Ethical Analysis*, New Haven and London: Yale University Press 1972.

[8]   For example, Timothy P. Jackson, *The Priority of Love: Christian Charity and Social Justice*, Princeton: Princeton University Press 2003, p. 8, note 26.

[9]   See, for example, Paul Tillich, *Love, Power, and Justice*, New York and London: Oxford University Press 1954, p. 30. For a complete discussion of Tillich's critical relation to Nygren, see Alexander C. Irwin, *Eros Toward the World: Paul Tillich and the Theology of the Erotic*, Minneapolis: Fortress Press 1991, pp. 22–31. There is, of course, at least as vast a literature critiquing Nygren's paradigm as that embracing it. For example, Anne Bathurst-Gilson, *Eros Breaking Free: Interpreting Sexual Theo-Ethics*, Cleveland: Pilgrim Press 1995 and the essays collected in *Toward a Theology of Eros: Transfiguring Passion at the Limits of Discipline*, ed. by Virginia Burrus and Catherine Keller, New York: Fordham University Press 2006.

[10]   For this and other biographical information in this article, I have relied primarily on Thor Hall, *Anders Nygren*, Waco, Texas: Word Books Publisher 1978.

dissertation in philosophy of religion, which he submitted in 1921. His dissertation is an analysis of the notion of the religious *a priori* in the work of Immanuel Kant, Ernst Troeltsch, and Rudolf Otto. It immediately earned him the position of *docent* at the University of Lund, and he was named Professor of Systematic Theology soon afterward in 1924.

Nygren's tenure at Lund lasted 24 years and was the prime of his writing career. He and his slightly older colleague Gustaf Aulén collaborated closely, published extensively, and became known internationally as exponents of "Lundensian Theology."[11] Both Nygren and Aulén characteristically approach theological history through a method Nygren terms "motif research"—an effort to define and describe the "fundamental motifs" through which a particular theological problem has been approached throughout history. Although they claim such description to be value-neutral,[12] they do not hesitate to distinguish the motifs that they take to be authentically Christian from those that they see as corruptions of Christianity from without. Both figures exalt the theology of Martin Luther as the luminous norm making such differentiation possible. Their work draws upon the so-called Scandinavian "Luther Renaissance" of the early twentieth century, centered around the research of Peter Eklund in Sweden and Albert Rischl in Germany.[13] The book that introduced Aulén to the international stage was his 1931 study of atonement theology *Christus Victor*—a text that manifests significant structural similarities to Nygren's *Agape and Eros*.[14] Both books argue that foreign paradigms have infected theology's presentation of their chosen theme, distorting the original Christian message; both promote new readings of Martin Luther as a means of reclaiming it.

Nygren's writing career moved through a series of distinct periods focused on different themes.[15] His earliest work was concerned with issues of method and epistemology in the philosophy of religion. When he became professor of systematic theology at the University of Lund, he turned to more classical issues in systematic theology and Christian ethics, such as the doctrine of love. In 1948, he left academia to serve as bishop of Lund in the Swedish State Church. He held this position until 1959, and he served concurrently as the first president of the Lutheran World Federation from 1947 to 1952. He continued to publish extensively during this period, but his writings then are more concrete, practical, and pastoral. His retirement beginning in

---

[11]　　Nygren's own account of this methodology can be found in his *Den kristna kärlekstanken*, vol. 1, pp. 8–24. (*Agape and Eros*, pp. 30–48.)

[12]　　Nygren, *Den kristna kärlekstanken*, vol. 1, pp. 16–17. (*Agape and Eros*, pp. 38–40.)

[13]　　Hall, *Anders Nygren*, p. 24.

[14]　　Gustaf Aulén, *Den kristna försoningstanken*, Stockholm: Svenska Kyrkans Diakoni-styrelses Bokförlag 1930. (English translation: *Christus Victor: An Historical Study of the Three Main Types of Atonement*, trans. by A.G. Hebert, London: Society for Promoting Christian Knowledge 1945.) Aulén distinguishes three basic understandings of the atonement: the "Christus Victor" model, which he associates with the early church (and Martin Luther); the substitutionary model, which he associates with Latin fathers such as Anselm; and a "subjective" model of moral exemplarity, which he associates with Peter Abelard and modern figures like Schleiermacher. He advocates reclaiming the first of these models through an original and idiosyncratic interpretation of Luther's theology.

[15]　　Hall traces this progression in much more detail in "The Nygren Corpus."

208 Carl S. Hughes

1959 was an active one, and it provided him the opportunity to return to the abstract questions of theological and philosophical method with which his career began. In 1972, he published a major monograph titled *Meaning and Method: Prolegomena to a Scientific Philosophy of Religion and a Scientific Theology*.[16] He died in 1978.

II. Agape and Eros

Despite the varied course of Nygren's career, it is *Agape and Eros* that secured him his international renown and that has influenced Kierkegaard scholarship so extensively. One finds this book cited most frequently in the context of Christian ethics today, but it is important to recognize that *Agape and Eros* actually has very little to say about intra-human relationships.[17] Its fundamental concern is the source of human fellowship with God: for Nygren, the two love-motifs are two competing doctrines of salvation.[18] Nygren replays the classic Lutheran opposition between human works and divine grace by aligning *eros* with works-righteousness and *agape* with undeserved love.

Nygren presents *eros* and *agape* as diametrically opposed "fundamental motifs" according to which love has been understood throughout Western history. *Eros* is, for him, the love commended by "practically all religious life outside of Christianity,"[19] whereas *agape* is "Christianity's own original basic conception,"[20] that without which "nothing that is Christian would be Christian."[21] He makes clear that when he speaks of *eros*, he is not at all concerned with sexual desire, since he does not think that anyone could ever confuse it with a salvific means of fellowship with God. He is referring instead to the "Heavenly Eros" of Platonic philosophy—*eros* "in its most sublimated and spiritualized form," which is "the born rival of Agape."[22] He finds the classic statements of this "heavenly Eros" in Socrates' recitation of Diotima's teaching in the *Symposium* and his narration of the myth of the charioteer in the *Phaedrus*.[23] Nygren argues that such a conception of love tempts Christians into believing that they can bring about fellowship with God themselves, on the basis of their innate longing for the infinite. He maintains that authentic Christianity, in contrast, teaches that God alone creates this fellowship through freely given *agape*.

---

[16] Anders Nygren, *Meaning and Method: Prolegomena to a Scientific Philosophy of Religion and a Scientific Theology*, trans. by Philip S. Watson, Philadelphia: Fortress Press 1972. (Swedish translation: *Mening och metod: Prolegomena till en vetenskaplig religionsfilosofi och en vetenskaplig teologi*, Åbo: Åbo Akedemia 1982.)
[17] While *Agape and Eros* is principally a theological text, it did grow out of two more ethically oriented studies. Anders Nygren, *Filosofisk och kristen Etik*, Lund: C.W.K. Gleerup 1923 and *Etiska grundfrågor*, Stockholm: Sveriges Kristliga Studentrörelses Förlag 1926.
[18] Nygren, *Den kristna kärlekstanken*, vol. 1, pp. 126–7. (*Agape and Eros*, p. 163.)
[19] Nygren, *Den kristna kärlekstanken*, vol. 1, p. 25. (*Agape and Eros*, p. 49.)
[20] Nygren, *Den kristna kärlekstanken*, vol. 1, p. 24. (*Agape and Eros*, p. 48.)
[21] Ibid.
[22] Nygren, *Den kristna kärlekstanken*, vol. 1, p. 27. (*Agape and Eros*, p. 51.)
[23] Nygren, *Den kristna kärlekstanken*, vol. 1, pp. 130–44. (*Agape and Eros*, pp. 166–81.)

Nygren's understanding of the relationship between the two love-motifs is antipodal and exclusionary; it has rightly been described as "neo-Manichean."[24] He presents each of the defining features of *agape* as standing in opposition to a defining feature of *eros*, and vice versa. *Eros* is fundamentally egocentric, emerging from individuals' lack of and longing for specific goods that they feel they need to be complete. *Agape* is God's gracious and self-sacrificial gift, freely given without hope of return. Whereas *eros* is a human striving, *agape* is fundamentally a divine act, for which humans can at best be an instrument or channel in relation to one another. *Eros* responds to value in the objects it desires, preferring some and ignoring others. *Agape* is "spontaneous" and "unmotivated"; it is extended universally, offered to any and all regardless of their intrinsic worth.[25]

Nygren's goal is to show the mutual independence and opposition of the love-motifs so as to disentangle them from each other once and for all. Two basic convictions guide him in this pursuit: "First, that in Eros and Agape we have two conceptions which have originally nothing whatsoever to do with one another; and second, that in the course of history they have nonetheless become so thoroughly bound up and interwoven with one another that it is hardly possible for us to speak of either without our thoughts being drawn to the other."[26] Repeatedly using imagery that invites a Freudian reading, Nygren depicts *agape* as having "lost its purity" through its unholy intertwinement with *eros*.[27]

In Nygren's telling of theological history, virtually every writer other than the apostle Paul and Martin Luther proves guilty of tainting *agape* with *eros*. As one might expect, Neoplatonic figures such as Origen, Gregory of Nyssa, and Pseudo-Dionysius are lead offenders in Nygren's analysis, but he also provides an extensive critique of Augustine, who is typically received more kindly in Protestant thought.[28] Nygren's ax even falls upon the author of the Gospel of John, whom he reads as instigating "the weakening of the idea of Agape" by enabling "the transition to a stage where the Christian idea of love is no longer determined solely by the Agape motif, but by 'Eros and Agape.' "[29] Nygren gives no indication in this book or elsewhere as to whether Kierkegaard would survive his razor.

---

[24]   Rick A. Furtak, *Wisdom in Love: Kierkegaard and the Ancient Quest for Emotional Integrity*, Notre Dame, Indiana: University of Notre Dame Press 2005, p. 102.
[25]   The most concise summary of these oppositions can be found in Nygren's chart in *Den kristna kärlekstanken*, vol. 1, p. 171. (*Agape and Eros*, p. 210.)
[26]   Nygren, *Den kristna kärlekstanken*, vol. 1, p. 8. (*Agape and Eros*, p. 30.)
[27]   Nygren, *Den kristna kärlekstanken*, vol. 1, p. 30. (*Agape and Eros*, p. 54.)
[28]   Nygren, *Den kristna kärlekstanken*, vol. 1, pp. 33–74. (*Agape and Eros*, pp. 449–562.) This aspect of Nygren's argument distinguishes it sharply from that of a German book on love published just a year before *Agape and Eros*. Heinrich Scholz, *Eros und Caritas, Die platonische Liebe und die Liebe im Sinne des Christentums*, Halle: Niemeyer 1929.
[29]   Nygren, *Den kristna kärlekstanken*, vol. 1, p. 123. (*Agape and Eros*, p. 158.)

III. Nygren and Kierkegaard

That being said, it is not difficult to see why Kierkegaard's readers have been tempted to compare his thought on love—particularly his argument in *Works of Love*—to Nygren's *eros*/*agape* distinction. Both authors highlight what makes Christian neighbor love distinct from ordinary human love. Both emphasize the selfless, sacrificial nature of the Christian ideal. Both construe Christian love as mediated through God, rather than being governed by immediate preference. Because of such similarities, Kierkegaard scholarship frequently assumes an extraordinary degree of overlap between the two thinkers. The Hong translations of Kierkegaard promote this tendency by suggesting that the Danish *Elskov* and *Kjærlighed*[30] equate with Nygren's definitions of *eros* and *agape*. In a footnote that appears several times in the English edition of *Kierkegaard's Works*, the Hongs provide the following explanation of these two words: "*Elskov* is immediate, romantic, dreaming love, as between a man and a woman. *Kjærlighed* is love in a more inclusive and also higher sense. *Elskov* and *Kjærlighed* correspond to 'eros' and 'agape.' "[31] While the first two sentences in this explanation are helpful, the blunt conclusion in the third is (as I will argue in the last section of this article) a major over-reading.

Likely influenced by these translations, subsequent interpreters of Kierkegaard argue for an even more extensive conflation of his thought with Nygren's. On the second page of his book *Agape*, a text that is much indebted to Nygren's paradigm, Gene Outka states that he will sometimes take *Works of Love* "as a substitute for Nygren," because this book—though saying virtually the same thing about love as Nygren does—is "more oriented toward specifically ethical matters."[32] Another example of this conflationary tendency can be found in the Australian Kierkegaard scholar William McDonald. In a recent article, he reproduces the oppositions that Nygren made famous and attributes them wholesale to Kierkegaard. He writes:

> The specific meaning of [Kierkegaard's terms for love] are distributed around two poles: love as *eros*, modeled on the discussion in Plato's *Symposium*, and love as *agape*, modeled principally on the Pauline and Johannine texts of the New Testament. This polar opposition of conceptions of love is underscored by a series of binary oppositions, with the first term elucidating erotic love and the second term elucidating Christian love. These binary oppositions include: psycho-sensual/spiritual, immediacy/ higher immediacy, self/other, recollection/repetition, immortality/salvation, beloved/ neighbor, desire/duty, luck [*Lykke*]/gift [*Gave*], happiness [*Lykke*]/task [*Opgave*], *lex talionis*/redoubling, possession/debt, hiddenness/transparency, visibility/invisibility, immanence/transcendence, and time/eternity.[33]

---

[30]   At Kierkegaard's time, the word could also be spelled *Kjerlighed*, as it is in *Kjerlighedens Gjerninger*. It is today spelled *kærlighed*.
[31]   *EO2*, 32, note 39. Near identical versions of this same explanation can be found in *TD*, 43, note 1 and *CD*, 116, note 40.
[32]   Outka, *Agape: An Ethical Analysis*, p. 2, note 1.
[33]   William McDonald, "Love in Kierkegaard's *Symposia*," *Minerva—An Internet Journal of Philosophy*, vol. 7, 2003, pp. 60–93.

Although this passage is ostensibly an exposition of Kierkegaard's philosophy of love, it is informed at least as much by Nygren as it is by anything in Kierkegaard himself.

Given the degree of alignment between Nygren and Kierkegaard that is frequently claimed, one would expect Nygren to profess a considerable debt to his predecessor. But the references to Kierkegaard in his writings are both scant and superficial. To my knowledge, they all occur in his late book *Meaning and Method.* Nygren mentions Kierkegaard here on four occasions—each time as an example of an "existentialist" thinker. He generally names him together with others like Pascal, Heidegger, Sartre, and Tillich.[34] He never mentions Kierkegaard in *Agape and Eros* or in the two more ethically oriented studies of love that precede it. He does not mention him in his doctoral dissertation,[35] or in the account of his influences in his 1970 "Intellectual Autobiography."[36] Although it is not uncommon to find scholars claiming in passing that Nygren was influenced by Kierkegaard,[37] I am aware of no historical corroboration for this claim if it is interpreted in anything but the weakest possible sense. Robert T. Sandin reports that Nygren once told him in conversation that Kierkegaard's theory of the stages "could be regarded as at least a distant cousin of his own doctrine of the *a priori* forms of experience."[38] But this is hardly a full-throated profession of indebtedness.

As a professional theologian, a bishop in the State Church, and an international leader in ecclesial politics and ecumenicism, Nygren was what used to be called a "churchman." As such, he moved in circles very different from those that Kierkegaard inhabited or endorsed. Indeed, over the course of his career, Nygren took on many of the academic and churchly roles that Kierkegaard never tired of mocking. Perhaps Nygren most evidences his familiarity with Kierkegaard's thought by *not* rushing to assume that it naturally aligns with his own.

IV. Kierkegaard after Nygren

Nygren's lack of historical dependence on Kierkegaard does not, of course, imply that they cannot be fruitfully compared. Nygren offers one of the twentieth century's most influential theologies of love, and, as such, his paradigm is a readily available

---

[34]   Nygren, *Meaning and Method*, p. 131; p. 133; p. 304; p. 344. (*Mening och metod*, pp. 163–4; p. 166; p. 367; p. 411; p. 416.)
[35]   Anders Nygren, *Det religionsfilosofiska grundproblemet*, Lund: Gleerupska Universitetsbokhandeln 1921.
[36]   Nygren, "Intellectual Autobiography," trans. by Peter W. Russell in *The Philosophy and Theology of Anders Nygren*, ed. by Charles W. Kegley, Carbondale and Edwardsville: Southern Illinois University Press 1970.
[37]   Victor Warnach, "Agape in the New Testament," in *The Philosophy and Theology of Anders Nygren*, p. 153. Sharon Krishek, *Kierkegaard on Faith and Love*, Cambridge: Cambridge University Press 2009, p. 154, note 26.
[38]   Sandin goes on to show how Kierkegaard's theory of the stages is different (and, in his view superior to) Nygren's philosophy of the religious *a priori*. Robert T. Sandin, "Theology without Metaphysic," *Journal of Religion*, vol. 52, no. 4, 1972, pp. 455–6.

heuristic for approaching Kierkegaard's thought. Still, the differences between the two thinkers are more fundamental than their overlap. Even if some of their specific claims about love are analogous, they do not approach the topic from within similar overarching frameworks; recognizing these fundamental differences is vital to reading Kierkegaard well today. I will conclude this article by highlighting a few crucial differences between the two authors in the hope of sparking further analysis.

The first of these differences is lexical in nature. As we have seen, Nygren's distinction between *eros* and *agape* has frequently been compared to Kierkegaard's use of the two Danish words for love, *Elskov* and *Kjærlighed*. Nygren's distinction has guided the Hong translations of Kierkegaard's works in both obvious and subtle ways. But the analogy is deeply misleading. Although *Elskov* and *Kjærlighed* do connote different emphases in Danish, they by no means imply the polar opposition that Nygren constructs. *Kjærlighed* is the more common and the more general term for love—employed everywhere from pulp literature to the New Testament. *Elskov* has more specific connotations with passion, desire, romance, and poetry; it is especially prevalent in Danish Romantic literature, such as the plays of Adam Oehlenschläger.[39] Consider the following passage from *Either/Or*, in which Judge William presents *Elskov* as a specific determination of *Kjærlighed*, not its antithesis:

> The first thing I have to do is orient myself and especially you in the defining characteristics of what marriage is. Obviously the real constituting element is *Kjærligheden*—or, if you want to give it more specific emphasis, *Elskoven*. Once this [presumably *Kjærligheden* or *Elskoven*] is taken away, married life is either merely a satisfaction of sensuous appetite or it is an association, a partnership, with one or another object in mind; but *Kjærligheden*, whether it is the superstitious, romantic, chivalrous *Kjærlighed* or the deeper moral, religious *Kjærlighed* filled with a vigorous and vital conviction, has precisely the qualification of eternity in it.[40]

Judge William here uses *Elskov* and *Kjærlighed* in a complementary, even synonymous, fashion that Nygren would emphatically refuse. Throughout their translations, the Hongs generally render *Elskov* as "erotic love" and *Kjærlighed* simply as love (although some contexts force them to render both interchangeably as "love"[41]). The most problematic consequence of importing Nygren's binary opposition into Kierkegaard's writing in this way is that it implies that *Kjærlighed*—Christian *Kjærlighed* above all—cannot be erotic in nature.[42] But Kierkegaard

---

[39]   See the entries *"Elskov"* and *"Kærlighed"* in *Ordbog over det danske Sprog*, vols. 1–28, Copenhagen: Gyldendal 1918–56, respectively vol. 4, columns 310–11 and vol. 11, columns 1156–62. I am grateful to Niels Jørgen Cappelørn for his insight into the history and usage of these terms.

[40]   *SKS* 3, 40 / *EO2*, 32.

[41]   For an example in the same book of this unacknowledged inconsistency in the Hong translations, see *EO2*, 192–3 / *SKS* 2, 186–7.

[42]   Note also that Kierkegaard can simply use the words *Eros* and *Erotik* when he wishes to refer to this theme specifically. For example, *SKS* 1, 102ff. / *CI*, 41ff. *SKS* 2, 405 / *EO1*, 417–18.

routinely uses *Kjærlighed* to name romantic and sexual love,[43] and he almost always uses it in his discussions of love in Plato.[44] Moreover, he frequently uses *Elskov* in a laudatory rather than condemnatory sense. For example, in the fairy tale told by Johannes Climacus in Part Two of *Philosophical Fragments*, the king's *Elskov* for the maiden serves as the best available analogy to illustrate God's motivation for becoming incarnate.[45]

Though I am aware of no perfect solution for rendering *Elskov* and *Kjærlighed* in English, I believe it is vital to cease translating *Elskov* as "erotic love," since it is over-specific and suggests a foreign dichotomy that is not present in Kierkegaard's writing. In their translation of *Works of Love*, the Swensons generally translate *Elskov* as "earthly love"—or simply as "love."[46] Another solution would be to translate *Elskov* as "romantic love," since this would capture its associations with passion and desire, as well as with Romantic literature, without implying that it alone is "erotic."

These lexical quibbles aside, however, might the basic argument of *Works of Love* still be analogous to Nygren's *eros/agape* paradigm? Does Kierkegaard's distinction between Christian love for the neighbor and pagan preferential love not amount to virtually the same thing? Tempting as this comparison can be, it obscures some of *Works of Love*'s most important features. For example, from the beginning of the book, Kierkegaard insists that all love, however imperfect, emerges from a single source in God. Unlike Nygren, who claims that *eros* and *agape* are "two conceptions which have originally nothing whatsoever to do with one another," Kierkegaard characterizes love's varied expressions as being like water flowing from a single source "along many paths."[47] Rick Anthony Furtak analyzes this passage well when he writes: "It is one of Kierkegaard's most important points that diverse forms of love can be traced to a common origin, such that the 'truest' kind of love does not need to abolish drives and inclinations but only to refine these crude expressions of the one 'fundamental universal love' into a more unselfish kind."[48] For Kierkegaard, Christian love is not a rejection of preferential love or *eros* but their purification; it infinitizes them through the mediation of love for God. He does speak of Christian neighbor love as the highest and truest love, but this statement calls for a proper ordering of loves, not for excluding any one of love's particular expressions.

---

[43]   In addition to Judge William's use of *Kjærlighed* in the displayed quotation above, consider that Aesthete A provides a rapturous review of a play titled *Den første Kjærlighed*—even though it depicts little but what Nygren would describe as "vulgar eros." *SKS* 2, 225ff. / *EO1*, 231ff.

[44]   For example, *SKS* 1, 106ff. / *CI*, 45ff. Furtak provides other illuminative examples in *Wisdom in Love*, p. 102, notes 78–80.

[45]   *SKS* 4, 234 / *PF*, 27–8.

[46]   For example, *Works of Love*, trans. by David F. Swenson and Lillian Marvin Swenson, Princeton: Princeton University Press 1949, pp. 37–8; p. 25. This translation is to be faulted, of course, for not at least placing the two different Danish words in parentheses.

[47]   *SKS* 9, 17 / *WL*, 9.

[48]   Furtak, *Wisdom in Love*, p. 102. Sylvia Walsh makes a similar point in "Kierkegaard's Philosophy of Love," in *The Nature and Pursuit of Love: The Philosophy of Irving Singer*, ed. by David Goicoechea, Amherst, New York: Prometheus Books 1995, p. 173.

Kierkegaard also differs significantly from Nygren on the question of whether Christian love can truly be represented. One of the most recurring themes of *Works of Love* is that love resists direct representation—both in language, and in a finite individual's existence. Kierkegaard's twice-repeated preface flags this theme from the start. As he explains there, the book is "not about *love* but about *works of love*,"[49] because love itself "*essentially* cannot be described."[50] The book's first meditation is titled "Love's Hidden Life and Its Recognizability by Its Fruits." Kierkegaard insists that there is not a single word or work in all of human language and existence that definitively makes love manifest; all depends on the inward source from which these outward fruits spring.[51] Love's nature, he argues, is that "when you think you see it, you are deceived by a reflected image, as if that which only hides the deeper ground were the ground."[52] Kierkegaard returns to these themes of love's foreignness to representation in the first discourse of the book's second series. There, he maintains that to write about love at all requires using language that is "carried over" or "transferred" [*overført*] from a realm to which it is not native, the realm of the "sensate-psychical."[53] Since love is intrinsically spiritual for Kierkegaard, all language about it is necessarily marked by a "quiet, whispering secret."[54]

Nygren's difference from Kierkegaard on the theme of love's amenability to representation could not be starker. Nygren takes pains in *Agape and Eros* to argue that *agape* is eminently accessible to language and thought. He condemns portrayals of *agape* as anything other than "simple," "clear," and "easily comprehensible." He permits himself to apply the words "paradoxical" and "irrational" to *agape*, but he immediately specifies that he means these terms only in the most contingent, limited, and relative sense. In a passage that seems as though it could be targeting Kierkegaard directly, Nygren writes:

> Putting it in terms that are often used—and misused—we might say that Agape gives expression to the paradoxical and irrational nature of Christianity. In saying this, however, it is important that we should make it clear that the idea of Agape is *not* paradoxical or irrational in the sense in which those terms are commonly used. There is in many quarters today an unhealthy cult of the paradoxical and irrational, almost as if the lack of clarity and consistency were sufficient evidence of religious or Christian truth. When we describe the idea of Agape as paradoxical and irrational, we do not for a moment suggest that it contains any logical contradiction or implies a *credo quia absurdum*. The idea of Agape is by no means self-contradictory. On the contrary, it is a quite simple and clear and easily comprehensible idea. It is paradoxical and irrational only inasmuch as it means a transvaluation of all previously accepted values.[55]

---

[49]   *SKS* 9, 11 / *WL*, 3.
[50]   *SKS* 9, 211 / *WL*, 207.
[51]   *SKS* 9, 20–1 / *WL*, 13.
[52]   *SKS* 9, 18 / *WL*, 10.
[53]   *SKS* 9, 212 / *WL*, 209. The Hongs translate *overført* as "metaphorical," but I resist this both because Kierkegaard has *metaforisk* available to him and because *overført*'s concrete sense is what is most significant here.
[54]   *SKS* 9, 213 / *WL*, 210.
[55]   Nygren, *Den kristna kärlekstanken*, vol. 1, p. 166. (*Agape and Eros*, pp. 204–5).

Nygren's point here is that however "paradoxical and irrational" Christianity may *seem* to the uninitiated, this is not due to any intrinsic contradiction or inaccessibility, but to the historically contingent fact that it was unknown in paganism. He means nothing more by his use of the Nietzschean language of "a transvaluation of all previously accepted values" than a historical accident of ignorance. Christ helps Christians discover *agape*, he is saying, and, once they do, it becomes directly communicable as Christian doctrine.

These differences between Kierkegaard's *Works of Love* and Nygren's *Agape and Eros* are significant, but it is important to ask whether *Works of Love* is even the most appropriate Kierkegaardian text to be compared to Nygren's book. As we have seen, ethical issues are secondary in *Agape and Eros*, which is focused on the proper basis of fellowship between human beings and God. Achieving fellowship with God—that is, the process of "becoming a Christian"—is the central preoccupation of Kierkegaard's authorship in its entirety. Like Nygren, Kierkegaard always trusts that the ultimate basis of this fellowship is divine grace, but much of the originality of his account of becoming a Christian is that he never construes grace as antithetical to human longing. Indeed, he consistently depicts longing for the eternal and for Christ as essential components of the life of faith. As he writes in an early journal entry that would doubtless provoke Nygren's ire, "Longing is the umbilical cord of the higher life."[56] Eliciting such longing is central to Kierkegaard's understanding of his authorial purpose. At the close of his retrospective account of his authorship in *The Point of View for My Work as an Author*, he imagines a poet eulogizing him as having "historically died of a mortal disease," but having "poetically died of a longing for eternity."[57] In an early edifying discourse, he describes sacred scripture itself as fundamentally oriented toward the elicitation of desire. He writes:

> Just as apostolic speech is essentially different in content from all human speech, so it is also in many ways different in form. For example, in order to draw an individual forward, it does not halt the listener and invite him to rest; it does not halt the speaker and allow that he himself forgets to work. Apostolic speech is concerned, ardent, burning, inflamed, everywhere and always stirred by the forces of the new life, calling shouting, beckoning, explosive in its outbursts, brief, disjointed, harrowing, itself violently shaken as much by fear and trembling as by longing and blessed expectancy, everywhere witnessing to the powerful unrest and the profound impatience of the heart.[58]

When Kierkegaard describes biblical language as "beckoning," "burning," and "inflamed," "stirred by the forces of new life" and marked by a "powerful unrest," he is not simply inverting Nygren's binary—choosing what Nygren would call *eros* at the expense of what he would call *agape*. Rather, Kierkegaard is refusing the straightjacket that Nygren will impose. Contrary to much modern Protestant thought, Kierkegaard figures grace as so transcendent and abundant that faith's appropriation of it is an ever-intensifying movement of desire, not an objectively available satisfaction.

---

56   *SKS* 18, 8, EE:3 / *KJN* 2, 4.
57   *SV1*, XIII, 582 / *PV*, 97.
58   *SKS* 5, 78 / *EUD*, 69.

216 Carl S. Hughes

Nowhere is longing's integral relationship to grace more apparent than in Kierkegaard's Communion Discourses.[59] These texts are quite literally concerned with Nygren's central theme—what Kierkegaard calls "fellowship with our Savior and Redeemer."[60] In them, Kierkegaard never strays from affirming that God in Christ is the source of such fellowship—that salvation is due to grace alone. But, contrary to Nygren's entire logic, this affirmation does not exclude but incite human longing. Consider the prayer with which the first of Kierkegaard's Communion Discourses begins:

> Father in heaven! We know very well that you are the one who gives both to will and to accomplish, and that longing, when it draws us to renew fellowship with our Savior and redeemer, is also from you. But when longing grasps hold of us, oh, that we may also grasp hold of the longing; when it wants to carry us away, that we may also surrender ourselves; when you are close to us in the call, that we might also keep close to you in our calling to you; when in longing you offer us the highest, that we may purchase its opportune moment, hold it fast, sanctify it in the quiet hours by earnest thoughts, by devout resolves, so that it might become the strong but also the well-tested, heartfelt longing that is required of those who worthily want to partake of the holy meal of Communion! Father in heaven, longing is your gift; no one can give it to himself; if it is not given, no one can purchase it, even if he were to sell everything—but when you give it, he can still sell everything in order to purchase it. We pray that those who are gathered here today may come to the Lord's table with heartfelt longing, and that when they leave it they may go with intensified longing for him, our Savior and Redeemer.[61]

Kierkegaard presents longing here, not as a misguided attempt at self-justification, but as a veritable "gift" from God, which "no one can purchase." This longing is a matter of "self-surrender," rather than a selfish desire to possess. Although Nygren always conceives of desire as obeying a finite economy of lack, need, and satisfaction, the longing that Kierkegaard describes here grows only more intense the closer it draws to Christ, as the concluding lines of this prayer make clear.

Nygren has left us no evidence signaling how he would interpret this passage (or any other) in Kierkegaard's works, but there is little reason to expect that he would view it favorably. Whatever Nygren's view of Kierkegaard may have been, reading Kierkegaard well today means learning to read him apart from Nygren's influence—or allowing Kierkegaard to overtake and upset it from behind.

---

[59] Niels Jørgen Cappelørn provides an extensive study of this topic in "Longing for Reconciliation with God: A Fundamental Theme in 'Friday Communion Discourses,' Fourth Part of *Christian Discourses*," *Kierkegaard Studies Yearbook*, 2007, pp. 318–36.
[60] *SKS* 10, 265 / *CD*, 251.
[61] *SKS* 10, 265 / *CD*, 251; translation modified.

Bibliography

I. References to or Uses of Kierkegaard in Nygren's Corpus

Meaning and Method: Prolegomena to a Scientific Philosophy of Religion and a Scientific Theology, trans. by Philip S. Watson, Philadelphia: Fortress Press 1972, p. 131; p. 133; p. 304; p. 344.

II. Sources of Nygren's Knowledge of Kierkegaard

Undetermined.

III. Secondary Literature on Nygren's Relation to Kierkegaard

Casey, T.G., "Kierkegaard and Levinas on More Perfect Human Love," *Irish Theological Quarterly*, vol. 75, no. 1, 2010, p. 20.

Furtak, Rick, *Wisdom in Love: Kierkegaard and the Ancient Quest for Emotional Integrity*, Notre Dame, Indiana: University of Notre Dame Press 2005, p. 102; p. 178, note 77.

Hampson, Daphne, *Christian Contradictions: The Structures of Lutheran and Catholic Thought*, Cambridge: Cambridge University Press 2001, p. 5; pp. 258–63; p. 276.

Krishek, Sharon, *Kierkegaard on Faith and Love*, Cambridge: Cambridge University Press 2009, pp. 154–8.

McDonald, William, "Love in Kierkegaard's *Symposia*," *Minerva—An Internet Journal of Philosophy*, vol. 7, 2003, p. 64; p. 85.

Obayashi, Hiroshi, "Agape and the Dynamics of History," *Studia Theologica*, vol. 35, 1981, pp. 22–4.

Olesen, Simon, "En analyse og vurdering af selvkærligheden i Anders Nygrens 'Den kristne kærlighedstanke' og Søren Kierkegaards 'Kærlighedens Gerninger,'" *Nordisk Teologi*, vol. 3, 2008, pp. 1–12.

Outka, Gene, *Agape: An Ethical Analysis*, New Haven and London: Yale University Press 1972, p. 2, note 1; pp. 13–24; p. 255.

Sandin, Robert T., "Theology without Metaphysic," *Journal of Religion*, vol. 52, no. 4, 1972, pp. 455–6.

Walsh, Sylvia, "Kierkegaard's Philosophy of Love," in *The Nature and Pursuit of Love: The Philosophy of Irving Singer,* ed. by David Goicoechea, Amherst, New York, Prometheus Books 1995, p. 173.

Warnach, Victor, "Agape in the New Testament," in *The Philosophy and Theology of Anders Nygren*, ed. by Charles W. Kegley, Carbondale and Edwardsville: Southern Illinois University Press 1970, p. 153.

Williams, Daniel Day, *God's Grace and Man's Hope*, New York: Harper 1949, p. 70.

Index of Persons

Abraham, 37, 38, 48, 49, 70, 77, 116, 119, 120, 126, 137, 163–7, 176, 181.

Adam and Eve, 148, 149.

Allen, E.L. (1893–1961), 95.

Altizer, Thomas J.J., (b. 1927), American theologian, 54.

Anselm of Canterbury (1033–1109), Scholastic philosopher, 94.

Aquinas, Thomas (ca. 1225–74), Scholastic philosopher and theologian, 205.

Augustine of Hippo (354–430), church father, 51, 90, 144, 149, 205, 209.

Aulén, Gustav (1879–1977), Swedish theologian, 207.

Baillie, Donald, 133, 134.

Barth, Karl (1886–1968), Swiss Protestant theologian, 31, 50–58 passim, 63, 65, 67, 68, 72, 85, 86, 89–93, 96–9, 107, 108, 127, 134, 135, 144, 152, 157, 179, 206.

Berdyaev, Nicholas (1874–1948), Russian philosopher, 116, 118.

Berry, Wanda, 150, 151.

Bonhoeffer, Dietrich (1906–45), German Lutheran theologian, 26–8, 31, 41, 42.

Brightman, Edgar S. (1884–1953), American Christian theologian, 4.

Brunner, Emil (1889–1966), Swiss Protestant theologian, 50, 52, 53, 56, 59, 65, 85–92 passim, 96–8, 147.

Buber, Martin (1878–1965), Austrian-born Jewish philosopher, 40, 56, 115, 116.

Bultmann, Rudolf (1884–1976), German Protestant theologian, 50, 52, 56, 65, 105, 106, 108, 179.

Calvin, John (1509–64), French Protestant theologian, 88, 149.

Camus, Albert (1913–60), French author, 74, 179.

Carnell, Edward John (1919–67), American Christian theologian, 3–23.

Caspari, Carl Paul (1814–92), Norwegian theologian, 192.

Christ, 7–17 passim, 30, 31, 40, 71, 72, 76–8, 86, 89, 91, 93, 94, 98, 107, 118, 126, 128, 132, 134–7, 146, 161, 163, 184, 185, 201, 215, 216.

Clark, Gordon (1902–85), American Evangelical thinker, 4.

Clausen, Henrik Nicolai (1793–1877), Danish theologian and politician, 194.

Cobb, John B. Jr., 54.

Collin, James, 47.

Cox, Harvey Gallagher. Jr. (b. 1929), American Protestant theologian, 25–44.

Croxall, Thomas, 47.

Denney, James (1856–1917), Scottish theologian, 86.

Dennis, Lane T., 176.

DeWolf, Harold, 175.

Descartes, René (1596–1650), French philosopher, 76.

Don Quixote, 112.

Dostoevsky, Fyodor Mikhailovich (1821–81), Russian author, 67, 72.

Eckhart or Meister Eckhart (ca. 1260–ca. 1328), German mystic, 128.

Eklund, Peter, 207.

Origen (ca. 185–ca. 254), church father, 209.

Otto, Rudolf (1869–1937), German Lutheran theologian, 122, 205, 207.

Outka, Gene (b. 1937), American theologian, 157–71, 206, 210.

Ousland, Godvin, 196–9.

Pannenberg, Wolfhart (b. 1928), German Christian theologian, 49, 50, 54, 59.

Pascal, Blaise (1623–1662), French mathematician, physicist and philosopher, 52, 53, 77, 95, 127, 211.

Paton, H.J., 114.

Paul, 88, 209, 210.

Peter, 71.

Petersen, Fredrik (1839–1903), Norwegian theologian, 191.

Phillips, D.Z. (1934–2006), British philosopher, 161.

Plato, 208, 210, 213.

Pojman, Louis, 112.

Poole, Roger, 40, 42.

Price, George, 119–21.

Pseudo-Dionysius the Areopagite (5th-6th century), anonymous theologian and philosopher, 209.

Radford Reuther, Rosemary (b. 1936), American feminist scholar and theologian, 54.

Rahner, Karl (1904–84), German Jesuit and theologian, 106.

Ramm, Bernard (1916–92), American Evangelical theologian, 53.

Ramsey, Paul (1913–88), American Christian ethicist, 59, 157.

Reeder, John P., Jr., 157.

Ritschl, Albrecht (1822–89), German Protestant theologian, 51, 85, 86, 91, 96, 98, 207.

Robinson, Edward, 105.

Roll, Karl, 199.

Rousseau, Jean-Jacques (1712–78), French philosopher, 178.

Sandin, Robert T., 211.

Santurri, Edmund, 165–7.

Sartre, Jean-Paul (1905–80), French philosopher, 48, 74, 115, 179, 211.

Schaeffer, Francis (1912–84), American Evangelical theologian, 173–87.

Scheler, Max (1874–1928), German philosopher, 106.

Schleiermacher, Friedrich D.E. (1768–1834), German Protestant theologian, 51, 86, 88, 89, 96, 122, 135, 137, 200, 201, 205.

Schopenhauer, Arthur (1788–1860), German philosopher, 95.

Schweitzer, Albert (1875–1965), German-born French philosopher and physician, 67.

Socrates, ix, 136, 208.

Speer, Robert E. (1867–1947), American religious leader, 64.

Swenson, David F. (1876–1940), American translator, 80, 147, 213.

Swenson, Lillian M., 213.

Tertullian (ca. 160–235), church father, 52, 131.

Thistedahl, Christian (1813–1876), Norwegian translator of the Bible, 200, 201.

Thue, Henning Junghans (1815–51), Norwegian classical philologian, 196.

Tillich, Paul (1886–1965), German-American Protestant theologian, 39, 50, 53, 56, 179, 211.

Torrance, Thomas F. (1913–2007), Scottish Protestant theologian, 91, 98, 99.

Troeltsch, Ernst (1865–1923), German Protestant theologian, 207.

Unamuno, Miguel de (1864–1936), Spanish philosopher and author, 63–5, 68, 72, 112, 113.

Index of Subjects

subjectivity, 3, 10, 12, 16–20, 30–2, 36, 40,
		42, 55, 65, 89, 92, 97, 117–19, 144,
		146–8, 151, 153, 159, 182–5, 193,
		200.
suffering, 19, 31, 73, 76, 77, 128, 164, 198.
suspension, see "teleological suspension."
synthesis, 10, 13, 121, 123, 127, 145, 152,
		153, 175.
system, the, 48, 111, 145.

teleological suspension of the ethical, 48,
		49, 119, 122, 162–4, 166, 167.
temporality, see "time."
theology,
	dialectical, 86, 88, 90.
	evangelical, 51.
	feminist, 151.
	liberation, 26, 27, 39.
	Lundensian, 207.
	natural, 106.
	postmodern, 39.
	Princeton, 173, 177, 185.
	radical, 27.

Thomism, 130.
time and eternity, 10, 11, 15–17, 20, 31, 90,
		92, 95, 96, 107, 127.
transcendence and immanence, 11, 51, 53,
		90, 91, 96, 107, 127, 130, 139, 146.
Trinity, 58, 96.
truth, 3–20 passim, 31, 32, 35, 39, 42, 52,
		55, 64, 69, 70, 73–7, 80, 81, 89,
		117–19, 122–4, 127, 129, 131, 133,
		145, 147, 151–3, 175–9, 181, 183–5,
		200, 214.
	as subjectivity, 3, 10, 12, 16, 17, 20, 31,
		42, 55, 119, 122, 200.

urbanization, 25, 27–9, 33, 39.

vertigo, 39, 121.

witness, 37, 81.